ARTHURIAN STUDIES XXI

CAMELOT REGAINED

ARTHURIAN STUDIES

I ASPECTS OF MALORY, *edited by Toshiyuki Takamiya and Derek Brewer*

II THE ALLITERATIVE *MORTE ARTHURE*: A Reassessment of the Poem, *edited by Karl Heinz Göller*

III THE ARTHURIAN BIBLIOGRAPHY, I: Author Listing, *edited by C. E. Pickford and R. W. Last*

IV THE CHARACTER OF KING ARTHUR IN MEDIEVAL LITERATURE, *Rosemary Morris*

V PERCEVAL: The Story of the Grail, by Chrétien de Troyes, *translated by Nigel Bryant*

VI THE ARTHURIAN BIBLIOGRAPHY, II: Subject Index, *edited by C. E. Pickford and R. W. Last*

VII THE LEGEND OF ARTHUR IN THE MIDDLE AGES, *edited by P. B. Grout, R. A. Lodge, C. E. Pickford and K. C. Varty*

VIII THE ROMANCE OF YDER, *edited and translated by Alison Adams*

IX THE RETURN OF KING ARTHUR, *Beverly Taylor and Elisabeth Brewer*

X ARTHUR'S KINGDOM OF ADVENTURE, The World of Malory's *Morte Darthur*, *Muriel Whitaker*

XI KNIGHTHOOD IN THE *MORTE DARTHUR*, *Beverly Kennedy*

XII LE ROMAN DE TRISTAN EN PROSE, tome I, *edited by Renée L. Curtis*

XIII LE ROMAN DE TRISTAN EN PROSE, tome II, *edited by Renée L. Curtis*

XIV LE ROMAN DE TRISTAN EN PROSE, tome III, *edited by Renée L. Curtis*

XV LOVE'S MASKS, Identity, Intertextuality, and Meaning in the Old French Tristan Poems, *Merritt R. Blakeslee*

XVI THE CHANGING FACE OF ARTHURIAN ROMANCE: Essays on Arthurian Prose Romances in memory of Cedric E. Pickford, *edited by Alison Adams, Armel H. Diverres, Karen Stern and Kenneth Varty*

XVII REWARDS AND PUNISHMENTS IN THE ARTHURIAN ROMANCES AND LYRIC POETRY OF MEDIEVAL FRANCE: Essays presented to Kenneth Varty on the occasion of his sixtieth birthday, *edited by Peter V. Davies and Angus J. Kennedy*

XVIII CEI AND THE ARTHURIAN LEGEND, *Linda Gowans*

XIX LA3AMON'S *BRUT*: The Poem and its Sources, *Françoise H. M. Le Saux*

XX READING THE *MORTE DARTHUR*, *Terence McCarthy*

ISSN 0261-9814

CAMELOT REGAINED

THE ARTHURIAN REVIVAL AND TENNYSON
1800 – 1849

Roger Simpson

'now, from the ruins of time, we carefully rescue
Ev'ry precious fragment, and thence imagine, when perfect,
How the sublime structure once rose in splendor among men.'

John Parker, 'The Celtic Annals'

D. S. BREWER

First published 1990 by D. S. Brewer, Cambridge

D. S. Brewer is an imprint of Boydell & Brewer Ltd
PO Box 9, Woodbridge, Suffolk IP12 3DF
and of Boydell & Brewer Inc.
Wolfeboro, New Hampshire 03894-2069, USA

ISBN 0 85991 300 7

British Library Cataloguing in Publication Data
Simpson, Roger *1938*
    Camelot regained: the Arthurian revival and Tennyson, 1800-1849.
    1. English literature, 1800-1900. Special subjects. Arthur, King.
    Critical studies
    I. Title   II. Series
    820.9′351
    ISBN 0-85991-300-7

Library of Congress Cataloging-in-Publication Data
Simpson, Roger, 1938-
    Camelot regained : the Arthurian revival and Tennyson, 1800-
1849 / Roger Simpson.
        p.   cm. — (Arthurian studies; 21)
    Includes bibliographical references.
    ISBN 0-85991-300-7 (alk. paper)
        1. Tennyson, Alfred Tennyson, Baron, 1809-1892. Idylls of the
king. 2. Arthurian romances—Adaptations—History and criticism.
3. Medievalism—Great Britain—History—19th century.
4. Medievalism in literature. 5. Arthurian romances in art.
6. English literature—19th century—History and criticism.
I. Title.   II. Series.
PR5560.S45   1990
821′.8—dc20   89-22304
                                                              CIP

∞ The paper used in this publication meets the minimum requirements of American National Standard for Information Sciences — Permanence of Paper for Printed Library Materials, ANSI Z39.48-1984.

Printed in Great Britain by St Edmundsbury Press, Bury St Edmunds, Suffolk

Contents

Acknowledgments

List of Illustrations

Introduction   1

1.   The Historical Arthur   5

2.   The Topographical Arthur   55

3.   The Comic   114

4.   Fairyland Allegory   148

5.   Tennyson and the Arthurian Revival   190

     Appendices: Catalogues of Arthuriana 1800-1849

     A.   Poetry, Drama and Prose Fiction   255

     B.   Minor Allusions   262

     C.   Chronological Table   267

     D.   Paintings   271

     E.   Graphics   274

     Index   276

Acknowledgments

It is a pleasant task to acknowledge my many debts of gratitude.

Information was very kindly sent to me by H. Allan, County Library, Nottingham; Dr Iain Brown, National Library of Scotland; Amanda Fielding and Anna Jackson, Theatre Museum, London; Paul Goldman, Department of Prints and Drawings, British Museum; Wayne G. Hammond, Chapin Library, Williamstown, Massachusetts; Lionel Lambourne, Victoria and Albert Museum; Richard H. Lewis, National Library of Wales; Sarah Richardson, Laing Art Gallery, Newcastle; Peter Walne, Hertford County Record Office; and Alan Welton, Carlisle Library.

For other information, I wish to express my thanks to Sue Gill, Brian Long, S. M. Mischler and Janet Scott.

For permission to quote from Charles Hoyle's unpublished poem 'Cambria', I would like to thank the Master and Fellows of Trinity College, Cambridge. The memoranda on Lytton's *King Arthur* are quoted by permission of Lord Cobbold and the Hertfordshire County Record Office.

I am obliged to the Editors of *Folklore* and *Tennyson Research Bulletin* for giving me permission to make use of material which originally appeared, in somewhat different form, in their journals.

I am very appreciative of the care taken of my studies by Jon Cook and Jennifer Searle, my supervisors when this present work began its life as a doctoral thesis at the University of East Anglia. I should also like to record my gratitude to Peter Field of the University College of North Wales for his continuing interest in the later fortunes of this thesis.

My extreme good fortune has been to have had a family, and in particular a wife and son, who have maintained over the years their sympathetic interest in, and encouragement of, my increasing absorption in the Matter of Britain. To them my final, and warmest, thanks are tendered.

Illustrations

The illustrations are placed between pp. 120 and 121.

1a   Bewick: Sir Lanval
1b   Bewick: Sir Gawaine
2a   Thompson: King Arthur and the Queen of Beauty
2b   Anon: King Arthur and Merlin
3a   Stothard: King Arthur and Guendolen
3b   Stothard: The Knights of the Round Table
4a   Uwins: The Lady of the Lake and Excalibur
4b   Uwins: King Arthur and the Questing Beast
5a   Uwins: The Vision of Sir Percivale
5b   Uwins: Sir Launcelot fights a Dragon
6a   Craig: The Death of Sir Launcelot
6b   Craig: The Damsel of the Lake and Excalibur
7a   Craig: The Parting of Sir Tristram and La Beale Isond
7b   Craig: The Battle of Sir Launcelot and Sir Tristram
8a   Craig: Prince Arthur obtains the Sword from the Stone
8b   Craig: Sir Percival fights a Serpent
9a   Williams: King Arthur at Tintagel
9b   Leech: King Arthur knights Jack the Giant Killer
10a King Arthur and the Syrens
10b Anderson in the role of King Arthur
11a Crowquill: Harlequin King Arthur
11b Hine: King Arthur's Court
12   Corbould: Sir Lancelot
13   Franklin: Sir Lukyn throws Excalibur into the river
14   Pickersgill: *Amoret, Aemylia and Prince Arthur in the cottage of Sclaunder*
15   Selous: Merlin casts a spell on Gyneth
16   Scott: *King Arthur carried to the land of enchantment*

Photographic acknowledgments
British Library: 6a-8b, 9b.
Trustees of the British Museum: 3a, 3b.
Syndics of Cambridge University Library: 2a, 4a-5b.
Chapin Library of Rare Books, Williams College, Massachusetts: 2b.
Tate Gallery: 14.
University of East Anglia Library: 1a, 1b, 10a-11b, 16.

Introduction

The nineteenth century revival of interest in the Arthurian legends has attracted widespread critical attention, which has chiefly been focused upon Tennyson's *Idylls of the King*, and the Pre-Raphaelite influence in poetry and art. In contrast, there has been little scholarly investigation, in depth, of the precise course followed by the Arthurian Revival during the first half of the nineteenth century.

In so far as Tennyson's Arthurian poetry has been related to that of his contemporaries, the most influential critical viewpoint has claimed that

> one of Tennyson's difficulties, as modern readers are not always aware, was that his matter was new. In 1842, Arthurian story was still strange to the ordinary reader, and even felt to be unacceptable as a subject for poetry.[1]

This view has since been so widely adopted that it has become axiomatic for Tennyson to be treated as 'father of the Arthurian renaissance'.[2] A re-examination of this claim is, however, overdue, and will provide my primary focus.

That the matter was held to be 'new', with the inference that Tennyson pioneered the subject, was due, in large measure, to the lack of a satisfactory bibliography of Arthurian literature that appeared within the period. Too great a reliance has been placed upon Northup and Parry's list: one which is generally accurate in the details it gives, but which is grossly incomplete for

On first reference, line and stanza numbers are normally included in the notes. Thereafter, references are normally incorporated, within brackets, in the main text: Arabic numerals are used to indicate line numbers, and roman numerals for stanza numbers. Instead of attempting to impose standardised spelling upon the varying forms of Lancelot/Launcelot or Guinevere/Guenevere/Gwenyver etc., when I discuss a particular work I use the spelling adopted by its writer. Unless otherwise stated, the place of publication is London.

[1] Kathleen Tillotson, 'Tennyson's Serial Poem'; in Geoffrey and Kathleen Tillotson, *Mid-Victorian Studies* (1965), 82.

[2] David Staines, 'Tennyson'; in *The Arthurian Encyclopedia*; edited by Norris J. Lacy (New York, 1986), 543.

the first half of the nineteenth century.[3] Reference to my own bibliography (Appendix A) will reveal that the sum total of Arthurian works was, in fact, much greater than has previously been allowed. In all, I have added another fifty items to the previously known twenty-seven in the list from 1800 to 1849, and have provided a previously unsuspected pre-1850 dating for three other items, besides noting an additional eleven for the eighteenth century.[4] To supply an ampler documentation of the high incidence of Arthurian allusion, I also make frequent reference to, and have catalogued in Appendix B, those works which, although not solely nor even mainly Arthurian, nevertheless made mention of the Arthurian legends.

My research has been specifically directed towards the early nineteenth century's annuals, periodicals and literary magazines. The object has not only been to rediscover neglected poems and short stories, but also to ascertain how contemporary critics reacted to Arthurian works produced by Tennyson's predecessors and coevals. Such an investigation has also served to redress the critical balance that has recently been heavily weighted in favour of the 'antiquarian' nature of the assumed audience for Arthurian poetry. Moreover, as Merriman correctly observes, literary history 'cannot be a mere record of the work of heroes': the lesser figures provide an indispensable context of continuity, and may often prove a trustier indication of the distinctive qualities of an era.[5]

A symptom of the failure hitherto of literary scholarship to have located and described much of early nineteenth century Arthurian literature is an over-preoccupation with the influence of Malory. Recognising the importance of Malory to the Pre-Raphaelite Brotherhood and to Tennyson, modern critics have assumed too readily that a similar concern must have expressed itself in the earlier part of the century, and this quest for a core Malorian tradition has resulted in other major influences, such as Geoffrey of Monmouth, being ignored or belittled. One such result of this outlook has been to limit the total field of search unnecessarily, on the assumption that where no Malorian

---

[3] Clark S. Northup and John J. Parry, 'The Arthurian Legends: Modern Retelling of the Old Stories: An Annotated Bibliography', *Journal of English and Germanic Philology*, 43 (1944), 173 – 221; and Paul A. Brown, 'The Arthurian Legends: Supplement to Northup and Parry's Annotated Biobliography', *JEGP*, 49 (1950), 208 – 16. See also James Douglas Merriman, *The Flower of Kings: A Study of the Arthurian Legend in England between 1485 and 1835* (Lawrence, Kansas, 1973); J. Phillip Eggers, *King Arthur's Laureate: A Study of Tennyson's 'Idylls of the King'* (New York, 1971); Beverly Taylor and Elizabeth Brewer, *The Return of King Arthur: British and American Arthurian Literature since 1800* (Cambridge, 1983).

[4] I have excluded from this list Alaric Watts's poem 'The Lady and Merlin', *Gentleman's Magazine*, 96 (February 1826), 67. Although Northup and Parry, Taylor and Brewer, and Eggers claim this as Arthurian, the poem's 'Merlin' is, in fact, a hawk, and not the Arthurian enchanter. See my notes 'Merlin: Wizard or Bird?', *Notes and Queries*, 229 (December 1984), 479 – 80; and 'Newton's Merlin Located', *N&Q*, 233 (September 1988), 313. As Appendix A denotes those items which I have added to the list between 1800 and 1849, my footnotes do not normally draw attention to the novelty of my material. However, my notes will indicate where I refer to an eighteenth century work not previously mentioned by Merriman.

[5] Merriman, *Flower of Kings*, ix.

connection may be detected no Arthurian literature could have been created. Secondly, it fails to take into account the rich diversity of alternative sources that were, in fact, available. Even more seriously, it does not accord sufficiently close attention to the important non-romance sources, in particular the pseudo-historical and the topographical traditions. These latter fields have, of course, been made the subject of innumerable separate studies, but little or no attempt has hitherto been made to ascertain how early nineteenth century historians and topographers treated the Arthurian subject, or to relate these findings to the early nineteenth century Arthurian Revival in poetry and fiction. Finally, because overmuch attention has been given to one literary strand, other manifestations of Arthurian interest (namely by Peacock and Lytton) tend to be treated as isolated and original sports, eccentrically unrelated to the main development of a Malorian orthodoxy. A notable instance of this manner of critical oversight — the failure to locate individual works or to see their relatedness — has been the neglect of the very powerful burlesque tradition that flourished in the nineteenth century.

In presenting, therefore, a general survey of the field and in focusing attention on the larger literary movements, I have chosen to avoid an analysis which concentrates on only a few main figures and proceeds chronologically author-by-author, in favour of one which allows a greater synthesis and which provides a series of broad frameworks that afford the opportunity for emphatic contrast between Tennyson and other writers on Arthurian themes. The classification that has been adopted is unorthodox but has been selected because it reflects not only the major sources which stimulated and diffused Arthurian materials, but also indicates some of the critical concerns of the early nineteenth century. It is not assumed that my categories are exhaustive; neither is it claimed that there will be no overlapping of works (notably Peacock's) from one category to another, but these broad classifications will enable me to examine the literary conventions that shaped, and were shaped by, the individual works that made up the Arthurian Revival.

Within these wider terms of reference, I have felt free to support my argument with pertinent evidence from painting and graphic arts, for Arthurian work in this period has received scant attention to date.[6] As for the initial and terminal limits which have been chosen for my study, the year 1800 was adopted as a conveniently conventional point to begin because, although many of the springs of the Arthurian Revival are to be found in the previous half-century, specifically in the work of Thomas Percy and Thomas Warton, and, more generally within the context of the Medieval Revival (a phenomenon ably delineated by Alice Chandler), it is only after 1800 that a

---

[6] Debra N. Mancoff, *The Arthurian Revival in Victorian Painting* (doctoral dissertation, North-western University, 1982), 2 vols, University Microfilms International, Ann Arbor, Michigan.

widespread interest in Arthurian literature becomes apparent.[7] Since one
purpose of my survey is to describe a pre-Pre-Raphaelite literary scene, 1849
has been selected as a final date in order to avoid material spilling over into the
PRB's sphere of influence, as the year 1850 also marks a new direction on
account of Holman Hunt's preliminary designs for his *The Lady of Shalott*.
Neither date, however, will totally preclude my occasional reference across
these necessarily artificial demarcations.

---

[7] Alice Chandler, *A Dream of Order: The Medieval Ideal in Nineteenth Century Literature* (Lincoln,
Nebraska, 1970). For Percy and Warton, see Arthur Johnston's excellent *Enchanted Ground: The
Study of Medieval Romance in the Eighteenth Century* (1964).

1

The Historical Arthur

An account of the Arthurian Revival, and the role which Tennyson played within it, needs to begin not with Malorian romance but with an acknowledgment of the importance of the historical perspectives which influenced much early nineteenth century treatment of the subject. As these literary treatments were often closely related to the findings of those historians who presented and evaluated the evidence for Arthur's historical significance, a summary of these historical concerns should first be considered.

The major medieval source of King Arthur's fame was a work which purported to be a history: Geoffrey of Monmouth's *Historia Regum Britanniae* (c. 1136).[1] Extravagant in its valuation of Arthur as a great European conqueror, the book marks the apogee of his historical reputation. More critical histories, notably William of Newbury's *Historia Rerum Anglicarum* (c. 1198) and Polydore Vergil's *Anglica Historia* (1534), would treat Geoffrey's claims with scepticism, but the attrition of these claims proved to be an extremely slow and extended process, lasting until the nineteenth century, for the extent of Geoffrey's influence had been vast. In addition to the huge cycles of Arthurian romance which developed, however indirectly, from Geoffrey's influence, his work had also provided the basis for the chronicles written by the medieval historians, such as John Hardyng and Robert of Gloucester. With the Renaissance, more scholarly historical approaches tended to search for authentic primary sources but, as is evident in Holinshed's *Chronicles* (1577), a pronounced reservation as to the fables surrounding the Arthurian era is accompanied by lengthy recapitulations of Arthur's campaigns against the Saxons, his marriage to Guenevere, Mordred's usurpation of the realm, the consequent battle at Camlan, and Arthur's burial in a grave at

---

[1] For information on medieval Arthurian literature, I am indebted primarily to *Arthurian Literature in the Middle Ages: A Collaborative History*, edited by Roger Sherman Loomis (Oxford, 1961).

Glastonbury that was rediscovered in 'the daies of King Henrie the second'.[2]
Additionally, Holinshed cites the Welsh tradition of there being two, or three
Gueneveres, and mentions the incident whereby one of these ladies was
kidnapped in the marshes near Glastonbury (chap. 14).

An important contributory factor in the retention of a residual Galfridean
core was that, with the exception of sparse materials from Gildas, Nennius and
the Welsh triads, there was no rival written account of the interregnum
between Roman and Anglo-Saxon dominance: in the absence of archaeological research, Geoffrey's tale was retained to fill a vacuum. Thus, whereas
the lack of any further edition of Malory after 1634 until 1816 signifies a
neglect of a major romance source component of Arthur's fame, Geoffrey's
Historia was translated into English by Aaron Thompson in 1718, and
Geoffrey's concept of the historical Arthur displayed a corresponding
resilience. His medieval reputation as one of the Nine Worthies persisted, and
such popular works as Nathaniel Crouch's *History of the Nine Worthies*, which
was first published in 1687 and had reached a fifth edition by 1759, provided a
copious account of Arthur's claim to valour through a military and civil
career. He was awarded further renown and authenticity by being claimed as
progenitor of the Tudor and Stuart royal lines, and although he suffered a
parallel neglect or disparagement from those seventeenth century historians
researching the Anglo-Saxon period as the source for the growth of British
common law and constitutional liberty, he remained potent as a symbol for
royalists. Drawing on the shreds of the historical tradition, and relating
Arthur to the new monarch of the House of Orange, Dryden's *King Arthur*
(1691) and Blackmore's *Prince Arthur* (1695) and *King Arthur* (1697) testify to
Arthur's surviving fame in this respect.[3]

Most eighteenth century historians in attempting to distinguish sharply
between 'Truth' and the 'fabulous History of pretended Victories' which have
'prov'd an inexhaustible Fountain of absurd and ridiculous Things', further
eroded faith in Arthur's historicity.[4] Nevertheless, a considerable corpus of
Arthurian history remained widely available.[5] Even the standard Whig *History
of England* (1726 – 1731) by Paul de Rapin-Thoyras may dispel claims for
Arthur's European conquests or the discovery of his tomb at Glastonbury, but
it still retains from earlier medieval chronicle sources a very detailed

---

[2] Raphael Holinshed, *Chronicles: England, Scotland and Ireland*, 6 vols (New York, 1965), I, Chapter
13.
[3] See Roberta Florence Brinkley, *Arthurian Legend in the Seventeenth Century* (Baltimore, 1932).
[4] Paul de Rapin-Thoyras, *The History of England*, translated by N. Tindal, second edition, 2 vols
(1732), I, 39.
[5] See Ernest Jones, *Geoffrey of Monmouth 1640 – 1800* (Berkeley, 1944). By tending, however, to
accept at face value later historians' judgements of Geoffrey, Jones continually underrates the
actual use of Galfridean-derived material.

description of the battles fought in Arthur's campaigns against Cerdic or against the Goths in Armorica. Arthur is said to have been born at Tintagel, crowned at Caerleon and buried at Glastonbury, after being slain by the usurping Mordred in the last battle. The three Gueneveres again make a brief appearance. A comparable treatment is given in Thomas Carte's *A General History of England* which decries the 'senseless fictions' of later bards and other romantic writers who have provided a 'fabulous' account of Arthur's birth and descent.[6] Wholly rejecting the historicity of Uther, Carte maintains, however, an exalted role for Arthur himself. On the authority of Llewarch Hen, it is accepted that Arthur was a monarch, and Carte accumulates a list of the virtues displayed by the king, including his generosity of mind and 'ardour of courage', military skill and experience, piety and zeal for religion. Besides this account of Arthur's achievements, Carte also includes the story of Melwas and Guenevere, which had been derived from Caradoc of Llancarfan's *Vita Gildae* (c.1140).

As the eighteenth century progressed, Arthur was steadily reduced in importance, and he declined to the status of a minor sixth century chieftain as historians concurred in rejecting the 'fables' of Geoffrey. But whilst George Lyttelton, for example, was highly sceptical as to the very existence of 'the supposed British prince', many others found firmer evidence for an historical Arthur.[7] Even David Hume, who may be considered to represent an exemplary Enlightenment approach, and to have 'had no interest in, or sympathy with, the Middle Ages', nevertheless found 'some foundation' for Arthur's 'heroic valour' which 'sustained the declining fate of his country'.[8] Later, John Whitaker's *History of Manchester* advanced a vindication of Arthur on 'historical principles' and, by means of a lengthy analysis of Nennius, attempted to locate the modern sites of Arthur's twelve battles.[9] To Gibbon, a belief in Arthur was based on 'the simple and circumstantial' testimony of Nennius, and he considered that Whitaker had 'framed an interesting, and even probable, narrative of the wars of Arthur'.[10] Robert Henry's *History of Great Britain* (1771) cautiously noted 'sufficient evidence' for Arthur being 'a brave and virtuous prince . . . who had the chief command among the Britons, and at their head obtained several victories' over the Saxons,

[6] Thomas Carte, *A General History of England*, 4 vols (1747 – 1755), I, 201 – 05.
[7] George Lyttelton, *The History of the Life of King Henry the Second*, 4 vols (1771), IV, 359 – 60.
[8] John Philipps Kenyon, *The History Men* (1983), 50. David Hume, *The History of England*, 3 vols (1880), I, 22: this was first published in 1754 – 1761.
[9] John Whitaker, *The History of Manchester*, 2 vols (1771 – 1775), II, 32 – 42.
[10] Edward Gibbon, *The Decline and Fall of the Roman Empire*, edited by Oliphant Smeaton, 6 vols (1910), IV, 94 and n. This volume was first published in 1788.

including that at Mount Badon in A.D. 520.[11] Neither was the chronicle
tradition quite defunct, for the account of Arthur's reign in William
Warrington's *The History of Wales* and in John Milner's *The History of
Winchester* is substantially that of Holinshed.[12]

Paradoxically, the developing interest in the Middle Ages often
accomplished little for Arthur's historical position. A greater desire to study
the origins of British social and political structure led to a stringent
reassessment of all available historical records. As a result, Arthur tends to
fade into insignificance ('a fable') in Henry Hallam's *View of the State of Europe
during the Middle Ages* (1818) and in Algernon Herbert's *Britannia after the
Romans* which treats him as a mythological figure, equivalent to Hercules ('if
Arthur lived and fought, he did so with a preponderance of ill-success').[13] For
Macaulay's *History of England* (1848) likewise, 'Arthur and Mordred are
mythical persons'.[14] But if Francis Palgrave's *The Rise and Progress of the English
Commonwealth* could 'neither doubt the existence of this Chieftain, nor believe
in the achievements which have been ascribed to him', other historians
betrayed less scepticism.[15] Whilst John Lingard's *The History of England* (1819)
admitted that 'we know neither the period when he lived, nor the district over
which he reigned', it was still concluded that Arthur was a British chieftain
who 'fought many battles', was murdered by his nephew, and buried at
Glastonbury.[16] With greater confidence, John Daniel's *Ecclesiastical History of
the Britons and Saxons* (1815) asserted that Arthur had made a 'noble stand' by
fighting 'many battles . . . and at last obtained a glorious victory over the
Saxons' at Mount Badon in 520.[17] J. M. Lappenberg's *History of England under
the Anglo-Saxon Kings* rejected what was 'fabulous' but accepted the account of
Arthur's defeat in a battle against Mordred on the river Camel, his burial at
Glastonbury, and the rediscovery of the grave by King Henry II.[18] For
Thomas Miller, too, in his *History of the Anglo-Saxons* (1848), 'there cannot be a

[11] Robert Henry, *The History of Great Britain*, second edition, 12 vols (1788), III, 9.
[12] William Warrington, *The History of Wales* (1786), Book II. 69 – 79. John Milner, *The History,
Civil and Ecclesiastical and Survey of the Antiquities of Winchester*, 2 vols (Winchester, 1798 – 1801), I,
73 – 80.
[13] Henry Hallam, *A View of the State of Europe during the Middle Ages*, 3 vols (1878), III, 439.
Algernon Herbert, *Britannia after the Romans*, 2 vols (1836 – 1841), I, 89.
[14] Thomas Babington Macaulay, *The History of England*, edited by Charles Harding Firth, 6 vols
(1913), I, 5.
[15] Francis Palgrave, *The Rise and Progress of the English Commonwealth*, 2 vols (1831 – 1832), I, 401.
[16] John Lingard, *The History of England*, sixth edition, 10 vols (1851), I, 51.
[17] John Daniels, *Ecclesiastical History of Britons and Saxons*, second edition (1823), 63.
[18] J. M. Lappenberg, *History of England under the Anglo-Saxon Kings*, translated by Benjamin
Thorpe, 2 vols (1845), I, xxxi, 103.

doubt about the existence of King Arthur'.[19] The antiquarian concern for medieval history, which had long been promulgated by *Gentleman's Magazine*, allowed an anonymous contributor to this journal in 1842 a series of five articles in order to pursue his researches into Arthurian history.[20] Following Nennius, but rejecting Whitaker's views as 'void of any solid foundation', he traces with great assurance Arthur's campaigns between 488 and 520, and has no doubt as to the 'splendour of Arthur's achievements'.

Besides these defences of an historical Arthur, there were other histories which in attempting a judicious analysis of all early sources had quoted extensively from Arthurian materials, which latter may have been condemned as history but were thereby given continued currency as legend. In this manner, Sharon Turner's *A History of the Anglo-Saxons* (1799) concedes only 'a moderate greatness' to Arthur, but in the process of reaching this evaluation Turner encapsulates much of the traditional Arthurian biography, including the rape of Guenevere by Melwas, and Giraldus Cambrensis' account of the discovery of the Glastonbury tomb.[21] Similarly, the Melwas incident recurs in Joseph Ritson's *The Life of King Arthur*, as does the Welsh tradition of the three Gueneveres.[22]

The central historical concern was summarised by J. A. Giles, who sought the middle ground in his *History of the Ancient Britons*:

> Whilst we set aside fables as unworthy of serious attention, we are not justified in asserting with some incredulous historians, that no such person as Arthur ever lived and fought; still less may we compromise the claims which history justly makes . . . by considering Arthur as a personification of the sun, and viewing his round table with the twelve Paladins, as a poetical description of the Zodiac with its twelve signs.[23]

This great debate among the historians had already been epitomised in verse by J. H. Merivale's 'A Chronicle of England', which allots Arthur to his historical post-Roman era:

---

[19] Thomas Miller, *History of the Anglo-Saxons*, second edition (1850), 82.

[20] 'An Inquiry into the True History of King Arthur. I: The Aera of Arthur', *Gentleman's Magazine*, NS 17 (April 1842), 385 – 87; 'II: The Locality of Arthur's Kingdom' (May 1842), 485 – 88; 'III: Arthur's Battles with the Saxons of Lothian' (June 1842), 596 – 99; 'IV: The Later Battles of Arthur', NS 18 (July 1842), 28 – 32; 'V: Conclusion' (August 1842), 135 – 37. See also J. G. N[icholl]'s letter (September 1842), 253 – 55; and Plantagenet's letter, NS 19 (March 1843), 267. For *GM*'s readership, see Alvin Sullivan ed. *British Literary Magazines: The Augustan Age and the Age of Johnson, 1698 – 1788* (Westport, Conn., 1983).

[21] Sharon Turner, *History of the Anglo-Saxons*, fourth edition, 3 vols (1823), I, 268 – 82.

[22] Joseph Ritson, *The Life of King Arthur* (1825), 69.

[23] J. A. Giles, *History of the Ancient Britons*, 2 vols (1847), I, 393. Giles is here attacking the attempted mythologising of Arthur by Algernon Herbert's *Britannia after the Romans*. See also Chapter 4.

Then lived renowned Arthur, who, as old stories tell,
Was begotten of a dragon, with aid of Merlin's spell.
But of him, or his queen Guiniver, or the 'fifty good and able
Knights, that resorted unto him, and were of his round table,'
I need no more relate, nor of 'Lancelot du Lake,
Nor Tristram de Leonnois, who fought for ladies' sake,'
Nor how the hero sleeping lies in the vale of Avalon;
Dreams once received as true in lordly hall and bower;
The solace since of youth and age in many a vacant hour;
But now no longer prized, while all they seem to show
Is, that there lived in Britain, thirteen hundred years ago,
A valiant native price, who his country's cause upheld,
And Cerdic, with his ravagers at Badon's mount repell'd.[24]

This long quest for the historical Arthur would have, as will be shown, a significant effect on poetry and fiction in the period of the Arthurian Revival. Since many historians had continued either to accept an historical role for Arthur or to transmit a considerable body of lore about him, an Arthurian subject matter had been preserved, which could be used as the basis for literary creation. Arising from this historical concern sprang a host of literary allusions to Arthur, which have largely gone unregarded by later literary historians. But before proceeding with an account of the major works within this tradition, a preliminary analysis is required of this abundant material which focuses on Arthur's minor roles.

A Minor Role

Of the many minor roles assigned to Arthur, a number of typical patterns emerge, which are chiefly determined by the temporal relationship which the work established between Arthur and other historical heroes, or by whether Arthur's role was perceived within the context of a particular national development.

The Arthur of fable was often given a vicarious historical verisimilitude by being incorporated within a poetic framework of widely accepted historical truth, and which thereby lent the latter the glamour of romantic chivalry. An early and notable prototype of such an approach was provided by Gilbert West's *Institution of the Order of the Garter* (1742), the footnotes to which

---

[24] Lines 85 – 98; in John Herman Merivale, *Poems Original and Translated*, 2 vols (1838), II. In ll. 87 – 88, Merivale quotes from the traditional ballad of 'Sir Lancelot du Lake', ll. 6 – 8; and in ll. 89 – 90 from the burlesque poem 'St. George for England', ll. 3 – 4. Both of these were included in Thomas Percy's *Reliques of Ancient English Poetry* (1765).

acknowledge the author's indebtedness to Elias Ashmole's *History of the Order of the Garter* (1672) and to Rapin-Thoyras's *History of England*.[25] Towards the conclusion of this 'Dramatic Poem' which portrays King Edward III's founding of his royal Order, there is introduced a chorus of Bards. These then praise Edward for restoring at Windsor the Round Table which had originally been inaugurated by King Arthur, who had repaired thither after winning 'Badon's long-contended plain'. The inevitable accretion of 'fable' and 'Superstition's magic veil' which later obscured Arthur's 'great story' would not, however, prevent Edward's discerning 'the genuine lustre' of the earlier hero's prowess. Accordingly, Edward withdraws Arthur from 'the cloud of fiction', and reasserts his 'ancient praise'. But such tributes are, of course, mutual, for Edward is also endowed with the aura of heroic tradition, and receives an appropriate encomium. The Bards thus sing:

> But see in heav'nly panoply array'd,
> Whose streaming radiants skirts the clouds with gold,
> I view Pendragon burst the veiling shade,
> And all his blazing magnitude unfold!
> O'er yon broad tow'r he takes his airy stand,
>   And pointing, Edward, towards the royal throne,
>   To his fam'd knights around, a laurell'd band,
> Shows on thy knee the bright sky-tinctur'd zone.
>   Virtue, he cries, (th'ethereal sound
> Thy gross material organ cannot hear)
> Virtue on earth by British Edward crown'd.
>   Her rev'rend throne once more shall rear.   (1076 – 87)

West's introduction of Arthurian material within a later and royal medieval context was adopted and greatly developed by a key figure in the Arthurian revival: Thomas Warton. As a pioneer of literary historical scholarship, Warton has received fitting recognition; not only for his rediscovery of medieval Arthurian romances and his analysis of the Malorian sources of Spenser's *The Faerie Queene*, but also for his perception that medieval or Renaissance romance literature could not adequately be judged by later neo-classical criteria.[26] However, although his major Arthurian poem, 'The Grave of King Arthur' (1777), displays a like historical concern and has been widely anthologized, it has not been awarded due emphasis, in the present century, for its important role in the development of historically-oriented poetry on Arthurian themes.

---

[25] Gilbert West, *Institution of the Order of the Garter*; in *Works of the British Poets*, edited by Robert Anderson (1795), IX. This important poem is not mentioned by Merriman.
[26] See René Wellek, *The Rise of English Literary History* (New York, 1966); and Johnston, *Enchanted Ground*.

Citing 'the Chronicle of Glastonbury' as a source from which he has on occasion departed, Warton deepens the historical context of the Arthurian material by placing it within a framework of King Henry II's military expedition against the Irish. Whilst halting on his outward journey across Wales in 1170, he is told that Arthur's Glastonbury tomb lies desecrated by Time and the 'ruthless Dane'; but, if he is to locate and honour this tomb, his reward will be a victory in Ireland.[27]

Warton's interest in the exhumation of Arthur was echoed in a number of other instances. The subject had already been painted by John Hamilton Mortimer, in about 1767, who had shown the inscribed leaden cross being raised from the tomb.[28] As for source, since he owned a copy of John Speed's *History of Great Britain* (1611), which contains an account of the exhumation, it is most probable that Mortimer found the story and the drawing of the cross there. A minor poet, Caesar Morgan, in 'The Shrine of King Arthur' acknowledged his debt to Warton, also setting the opening of his poem at Cilgerran Castle, the stopping place where Henry II heard the bards sing of Arthur's fame.[29] Both Warton's poem and an historical source (Charles Eyston's 'Little Monument') which was prefixed to Richard Warner's *History of the Abbey of Glaston* (1826) were drawn on by a later poem, Christopher Cookson's *Glastonbury Abbey*, which relates how King Henry on his return journey from Ireland hears the harpers lauding the 'valourous deeds of Arthur's time', and

> How many a hoarse and Boreal flood
> Ran purpled with unchristian blood,
> Or flash'd his cross-embellish'd shield
> In triumph on Badonis' field.[30]

Henry, who is 'ravish'd' by these 'tones', speeds to Glastonbury:

> And to the grave imparts the word
> Which lifts from earth the giant lord . . .
> Perchance his sad repentant heart
> Quail'd at the rod's remember'd smart,
> Reverting ever with self hate

---

[27] 'The Grave of King Arthur', in *The Three Wartons: A Choice of their Verse*, edited by Eric Partridge (New York, 1970).

[28] See John Sunderland, 'Mortimer, Pine and Some Political Aspects of English History Painting', *Burlington Magazine*, 116 (June 1974), 317 – 26.

[29] Caesar Morgan, *Poems* (Cambridge, 1783). These are not mentioned by Merriman.

[30] *Glastonbury Abbey* (Taunton, 1828), ll. 1247 – 50. This poem was published anonymously, but the author is named as C. Cookson by R. A. Aubin, *Topographical Poetry in Eighteenth Century England* (New York, 1936), 363. Internal evidence within the poem points to an identification with the Christopher Cookson who contributed verse to *Forget Me Not* and *Bijou* in the early 1830s, and who was a cousin of William Wordsworth.

To Becket's sacrilegious fate,
And gave to Avalon's control
The requiem of his harrow'd soul.   (1261 – 72)

The more orthodox historical account, stemming from Giraldus Cambrensis, had not represented Henry as being present at the actual exhumation in 1190 – 1191, for the good reason that he had died in 1189. It would appear that Warton's poem, which concludes with Henry's plan to rebury Arthur 'with arching sculpture crown'd, / . . . The daily dirge and rites divine' (175, 177), had later been interpreted as implying that Henry would effect these deeds in person, particularly as a Warton gloss testifies that 'Henry visited the abbey'. Besides Cookson's version of this, there was George Cattermole's Royal Academy painting of 1826, entitled *King Henry II discovering the relics of King Arthur in Glastonbury Abbey*, and in 1842 Aubrey de Vere followed this heterodox account by publishing a poem on 'King Henry at the Tomb of King Arthur'.[31] De Vere's footnote states that the 'incident will be found recorded in Speed's *History*' although, in fact, Speed's version says merely that 'King Henry caused the ground to be digged', and does not indicate that he was present at the actual disinterment.[32] Unlike Mortimer, who had remained more faithful to Speed's account, De Vere's treatment had included Henry II, and thereby allowed a dramatic confrontation between two widely separated historical epochs as epitomised by their respective monarchs, one living and one dead. Thus, whereas the elegiac tone of Mortimer's painting is governed by the tender wistfulness of the seated female figure who watches the exhumation, De Vere's concentration upon the brash participation of Henry endows the poem's *sic transit* theme with a more severely realised sense of moral reproof.

A complementary revival of pseudo-historical legend from medieval chronicles *via* eighteenth century antiquarianism connects this exhumation of Arthur with the later military and chivalrous achievement of King Richard I. The medieval chronicler Benedict of Peterborough had recorded in his *Gesta Regis Ricardi* (c. 1192) Richard's gift of Caliburnus ('gladium optimum

---

[31] Algernon Graves, *Royal Academy Exhibitors 1769 – 1904*, 8 vols (1905 – 1906). Although Cattermole's exhibit is now untraced, it is possible that his undated watercolour *Interior of Glastonbury Abbey* (Laing Art Gallery, L. 35 – 45) may be a related design. This latter shows two men, and an opened grave in the floor of the abbey: a tonsured monk(?) who is standing within the grave is showing a skull to the other (cowled) figure. Aubrey de Vere, *The Waldenses, or the Fall of Rora: a Lyrical Sketch with other Poems* (Oxford, 1842). De Vere may have been attracted to this subject by an article on 'King Arthur' in *Saturday Magazine*, 17 (31 October 1840). 163 – 65. Besides quoting from Warton's poem, this article cites Speed, and provides a detailed account of the exhumation.

[32] John Speed, *The History of Great Britaine*, second edition (1627), 334.

Arcturi') to Tancred, King of Sicily.[33] Rapin-Thoyras's *History* had referred to
this incident, as had Warton's *History of English Poetry* (1778 – 1781).[34] In his
notes to Way's *Fabliaux* (1800), George Ellis provided a wealth of scholarly
illustrative detail and cited Walter Coventry and Roger Hoveden as
authorities for reporting this gift and stating that the sword had been found in
Arthur's coffin.[35] Most importantly, Warton provided a poetic context for this
allusion in his 'The Crusade', which relates how

> Richard leads his faithful host!
> Aloft in his heroic hand,
> Blazing, like the beacon's brand,
> O'er the far-affrighted fields,
> Resistless Kaliburn he wields.   (60 – 64)

Warton's reference was to prove the first of a cluster of others. There was, for
example, the epic poem of *Richard the First* by Sir James Bland Burges, wherein
the Abbot of Glastonbury narrates his part in Arthur's exhumation:

> As gazing we contemplated his strength,
> In his right hand this massy Sword we view'd:
> Its weight surpassing, its unusual length,
> And blade high-temper'd, led us to conclude
> This was the fam'd EXCALIBOR, endued
> By potent MERLIN with endowments high.[36]

The sword was not, however, reburied with the monarch: retained by the
Abbot, it is later effusively proffered to Richard. In taking it, Coeur de Lion
symbolically assumes the role of a second Arthur, particularly in contemplat-
ing an invasion of Normandy:

> As a propitious omen I receive
> This sacred pledge . . .
> May ARTHUR'S spirit in my bosom flame,
> Teach me deeds worthy of himself t'atchieve.   (XIII. xxxiv)

For sources, Burges had drawn not on Warton but on the medieval chronicler
Matthew Paris (c. 1253), and the later chronicles by Knighton and Brompton.
Another epic on the same theme, Eleanor Ann Porden's *Coeur de Lion*, relates a
comparable scene, with the difference that she denotes that Richard himself
was responsible for the opening of the grave: he

---

[33] Quoted in E. K. Chambers, *Arthur of Britain* (Cambridge, 1964), 274.
[34] Rapin-Thoyras, *History of England*, I, 39. Thomas Warton, *History of English Poetry* (1871), 89.
[35] *Fabliaux or Tales: Abridged from French Manuscripts of the XIIth and XIIIth centuries by M. Le Grand*,
selected and translated into English verse by G. L. Way, new edition, 3 vols (1815), I, 196.
[36] Sir James Bland Burges, *Richard the First*, 2 vols (1801), II, Book XIII. stanza xxxi.

> raised the stone beneath her altar's shade,
> Where by Geneura's side the Monarch laid;
> Time had not changed his form, august though pale,
> Nor loos'd one rivet from his iron mail.
> Kneeling, the King evoked the mighty dead,
> Whose hand relaxing loos'd the gifted blade,
> Then vow'd that sword, by favouring powers bestow'd
> Should fight the battles of his injur'd God.[37]

Porden's footnote on the passage discloses her source to have been Warton's 'The Grave of King Arthur', and draws attention to her deliberate adaptation of it by transferring to King Richard the traditional role of Henry II. A further allusion occurs in John F. Pennie's 'Richard Coeur de Lion's Arrival on the Coast of Palestine' where the eponymous hero's 'fierce sword' is said to be the blade which 'still gave victory to the British prince, / Arthur renown'd in the happy isles of the West.'[38] Revealing another slight modification of tradition, this 'celebrated Calebvino' (sic!) according to Pennie's footnote, had been given *to* Richard by the King of Sicily. But it is to a Wartonian precedent, however, that Joseph Anstice appeals in his Oxford prize poem on 'Richard Coeur de Lion' (1820), whose

> healthful hand
> Wielded the terrors of the magic brand,
> By Arthur borne, beneath whose charmed spell
> Each shadowy knight and phantom warrior fell,
> Nor less shall Mecca's paynim heroes turn
> Still from thy edge, 'resistless Kaliburn'.[39]

Warton's *History of English Poetry* was then cited as authority in John Conybeare's Cambridge prize poem *Richard the First in Palestine* (1840), whose hero seems to 'wave in fight his magic brand'.[40] Far more substantial is John Sterling's treatment in the 'Coeur de Lion' which he composed in 1842 – 1843.[41] Once again, the main protagonist is equipped with

> the Caliburn of wondrous ages,
> Worn by King Arthur when our misty North
> All flamed with deeds of knights and songs of sages,

---

[37] Eleanor Anne Porden, *Coeur de Lion: or the Third Crusade*, 2 vols (1822), I, Book VI. ll. 273 – 80.
[38] John F. Pennie, 'Richard Coeur de Lion's Arrival on the Coast of Palestine', ll. 22 – 24; in *Literary Magnet*, NS2 (1826), 356 – 60.
[39] Lines 59 – 64; reprinted in *Oxford Prize Poems* (Oxford, 1839).
[40] Line 43.
[41] See Thomas Carlyle, *The Life of John Sterling*, second edition (1852), 285, 299, 320, 322, 326. John Sterling, 'Coeur de Lion': Canto I in *Fraser's Magazine*, 39 (February 1849), 170 – 78; and (March 1849), 277 – 82; Canto II (April 1849), 405 – 16.

> And, as a lighted minster, sparkled forth
> Into the dark a shrine for pilgrimages.   (I.xxxii)

Moreover, this sword, besides being a superficially attractive accessory, is of great importance in the development of Sterling's plot: the weapon is lost down the crater of Mount Etna, recovered by a fisherman, and is then acknowledged by Richard as the 'call divine to noble deed' (I.lxxix).

As noble exemplars of an heroic age, Arthur's knights could be lauded even at the French court in Robert Southey's early epic poem *Joan of Arc* (1796), where the trouvere sings:

> Of Lancelot du Lake, the truest knight
> That ever loved fair lady; and the youth
> Of Cornwall, underneath whose maiden sword
> The strength of Ireland fell; and he who struck
> The dolorous stroke, the blameless and the brave,
> Who died beneath a brother's erring arm.[42]

Southey then proceeds to point a dramatic contrast between such a 'lofty lay', beloved by 'Virtue and Genius', and the effete ambience of King Charles's entourage. Two other occasions on which Arthur is evoked in close and suggestive propinquity to later historically authentic leaders reveal how even the Arthur of 'romance' could be fully admitted into the pantheon of British heroes, who are then endowed with a glory reflected from, and sanctioned by, his numinous role. The first of these instances occurs in a poem on *Wallace* (1802) by John Finlay, when the hero's mother inspires his childhood with her songs of chivalry:

> And now of Charlemagne's proud peers she sings,
> Their courage, truth, and loyalty, renown'd,
> And Arthur and the courtly knights and kings
> Who throng'd at Caerleon his table round;
> Their pomp, their tournaments, and merry sound
> Of minstrels, harping strains of antique lore,
> Of Launcelot's valour — of the fairy ground,
> That lies enchanted on th'Armoric shore,
> of Avalon's blest isle, and Snowden's summits hoar.[43]

The second instance concerns Alfred the Great, the hero of an epic poem by G. L. Newnham Collingwood. In distress, Alfred seeks refuge at Glastonbury, which he finds deserted:

---

[42] Book IV. ll. 175 – 82: in Robert Southey, *Joan of Arc, Ballads, Lyrics and Minor Poems* (1865). In his consideration of Southey, Merriman does not mention this poem.
[43] John Finlay, *Wallace; or the Vale of Everslie, with other poems*, second edition (Glasgow, 1806), Book I. st. xx.

> In the midst
> Gay flower'd the wintry thorn, sprung from the staff
> Upon the sacred soil by Joseph left,
> When he arriving from that distant land
> Arimathea, found his final rest.
> About its shrine were hostile monarchs laid,
> And chiefest he, Arthur, the theme of bards,
> Who with his peerage circling round his board,
> Long against fate upheld the British name;
> Now deep beneath those sculptured pyramids
> Sleeps in his hollow'd oak.[44]

Once again, an exact historical source may be ascertained, for Collingwood's annotation discloses that he had derived the incident from a passage in Sharon Turner's *History of the Anglo-Saxons*.

In all these instances, a precise historical setting is provided for the detailed, later medieval world in which Arthur is remembered, whereas the earlier more properly Arthurian era itself remains distant, shadowy and largely undefined, like a remote and mysterious background glimpsed beyond the hard-edged precision of the medieval foreground. Conversely, a more finely delineated chronology for Arthur's reign is given in those poems which, like medieval chronicles, narrate the history of England by grouping events under a succession of monarchs. These re-creations of medieval genre, which were sometimes intended as pedagogic guides to English history, could often totally avoid the so-called Dark Ages by beginning their survey with the reign of William the Conqueror, but in many of them King Arthur takes his place as an historical ruler. Of J. H. Merivale's version mention has already been made above, but there were also several earlier instances than his. W. R. Johnson, for example, stated on the title page that his *History of England, in easy verse* was 'written for the purpose of being committed to memory by young persons of both sexes'. In this chronicle, Arthur makes his appearance within a historical context:

> The Saxons now, possessors of the soil,
> Invite their countrymen to share the spoil.
> Succeeding chiefs with hostile numbers land,
> 'Gainst whom the Britons make a valiant stand,
> By royal Arthur led, alas! in vain,
> Such crowds of foreign tribes usurp the plain.[45]

This is a brief appearance but is supported by a note claiming that, although 'this prince's history is involved in much obscurity, . . . all agree that he was a

---

44 George Lewes Newnham Collingwood, *Alfred the Great* (1836), Book II, ll. 1080 – 90.
45 W. R. Johnson, *The History of England, in easy verse* (1806), Book IV. ll. 1 – 6.

most heroic prince, and he is said to have defeated the Saxons in twelve
successive battles'. A comparable schoolbook chronology formed the basis,
too, of Thomas Love Peacock's *The Round Table* (1817), albeit there is greater
prominence given in this to Arthur and Merlin, both of whom occupy central
pivotal roles, for the poem postulates that, after the battle of Camlan, Arthur
was taken to a solitary island to which Merlin later summons for
commendation or reproof all the monarchs who have succeeded to the throne
of Britain. The author ('R') of 'English Chronicles' in *Juvenile Forget Me Not*
manages only a passing reference to Arthur, sandwiched between alien
invaders:

> first the Roman emperors sought our shore,
> And brought us luxuries all unknown before;
> When, tempted by our wealth, a barbarous band
> Of Saxons and of Danes invade the land.
> King Arthur and his knights their power maintain,
> The Saxons struggling, next dominion gain.[46]

Of more substance is Henry Sewell Stokes's determinedly melioristic *The Song
of Albion* which provides an historical resumé from the Ancient Britons up to
the year of writing, when Stokes looks forward to the passing of the
Parliamentary Reform Bill: 'Oh beautiful will be the historic page / Of
William, Brougham, Grey, Russell, Althorp, telling!'[47] Earlier British heroes
are projected as heroic antecedents of Albion's rise to greatness:

> Yet was there many a Briton brave:—
> Through the dark pages of romance
> Truth glimmers like a starry glance.
> The tomb on marge of azure wave
> Of Vortimer memorial gave,
> Who did the Saxons thrice repel:
> Of Arthur and the Armoric knights
> The marvellous story Fame delights
>   Through many an age to tell.   (I.222 – 30)

The most ambitious of all such poems, however, was John Walker Ord's
England: A Historical Poem. Not only is it massive — it runs into two volumes —
and not only does it replace the simple rhyming couplet form with a variety of
other metres, but Ord's poem (like Stokes's) is not addressed to children:
instead, (as a later section will reveal) it is offered as serious comment on the
political development of England. Ord had abandoned medical studies at
Edinburgh where he was acquainted with James Hogg and John Wilson, and

---

[46] R., 'English Chronicles', ll. 5 – 10; in *Juvenile Forget me Not* (1830), 156 – 58.
[47] Henry Sewell Stokes, *The Song of Albion, a poem commemorative of the crisis; Lines on the fall of
Warsaw, and other poems* (1831), III. ll. 626 – 27.

would later enjoy a minor literary reputation in London, where he started the *Metropolitan Literary Journal* in 1836. Despite his own disclaimer against the poem having any merit 'as a history', the *Monthly Review*, with an insight which significantly draws attention to the poem's historical concern, considered that Ord had opened up a new branch of literature by combining poetry with history.[48] Probably on account of Ord's vitriolic attack on the Scots, the poem received a fair amount of critical publicity, which was mainly adverse.[49] Despite, or because of, this the work went into a third edition within five years. In attempting a poetical history of England, Ord avoided the commonplace method of relating the events of all reigns, but chose instead to select key dramatic scenes such as 'the Roman invasion' or 'Lady Jane Grey', and amongst these tableaux he included 'King Arthur. A.D. 516'. A footnote curtly states that 'King Arthur ruled over Cornwall in the sixth century', but the poetic text itself endows Arthur with the ambience and prestige of Geoffrey of Monmouth's hero, or that of the old French romances. Ord narrates with gusto the prodigious and bellicose exploits of the King:

> He slew the Saxons — made the Scots be gone —
> Made Ireland, Denmark, Norway homage bring,
> And over Gallya wav'd the conquering wing.
> Five Paynim kings he took; and, what is more,
> He won them, Jesu Christ, his praise to sing;
> And, when again, he sought his native shore,
> A hundred thousand men were buried in their gore.[50]

In the fifteen Spenserian stanzas of this section, the Arthurian court is celebrated as an emblem of patriotism, chivalry and 'old heroic times' (83), times which have since passed into eternity, as Arthur's court has been transferred to those 'fairy halls beyond the morn' to continue its life where all 'is beauty, youth and harmony' (131). Admitting that this was a 'noble and fruitful subject' which could have been more extensively treated (as 'a highly talented friend' had suggested), Ord's decision not to do so was due to his being unwilling to disturb the overall balance of the poem ('to intrude on other portions' of his work). Nevertheless, his footnote (p. 94) lingers admiringly over the attractiveness of the theme to English poets.

Accompanying this primarily secular concern with the past, a minor variant on the nineteenth century English verse chronicle took the form of tracing the development of the Anglican Church in Britain. The Venerable Bede's *Historia Ecclesiastica Gentis Anglorum* (731), the major early source for this subject, had contained no reference to Arthur, but he had been allotted a

---

[48] *MR*, 2 June 1834, 273 – 74. The question of genre will be treated more fully in Chapter 5.
[49] See *Athenaeum*, 20 June 1835, 472; *Fraser's*, 10 (September 1834), 344 – 48; *Gentleman's Magazine*, NS 4 (August 1835), 163 – 64; and *Literary Gazette*, 2 February 1839, 71.
[50] John Walker Ord, *England: A Historical Poem*, 2 vols (1834 – 1835), I, ll. 102 – 08.

minor role within, for example, Thomas Fuller's *Church History of Britain* (1655). This work mocks the extravagant traditional claims made for Merlin ('Let Merlin be left in a twilight as we found him'), and derides 'the Monkish Fictions' whose hyperbole had discredited Arthur's later historical reputation.[51] Yet Arthur is admitted to the chronicle, as the son of Uter, and 'on the best evidence' that the Glastonbury exhumation 'undeniably' afforded.

In composing his *Ecclesiastical Sketches* (1822), William Wordsworth made use of a wide range of ecclesiastical historians, Bede and Fuller among them, but he also read the more modern Sharon Turner's *History of the Anglo-Saxons*, where he could have met Nennius's description of 'the image of the cross and of Mary' on Arthur's shoulders at the battle of Castle Gunnion.[52] Wordsworth's approach to the development of the English Church is, in fact, historical rather than theological. Constructed on an analogy with a river flowing in time, from St Paul's conjectured English visit (I.ii) to the building of nineteenth century churches, the sequence describes each stage of growth, both civil and religious. The river image suggests that the course of the church is a natural and inevitable evolution that may be temporarily obstructed but which cannot eventually be prevented. Within this view of social progress, Arthur has derived from the Christianised Druid tradition, and is, like his predecessor Aneurin, or his successor Urien, representative of the struggle of the Britons against pagan barbarians. But the momentarily victorious pagans will rapidly be converted to Christianity, with the result that the Anglo-Saxon Church becomes heir to the original native tradition. Within this sequence, special significance is assigned to Arthur as a warrior patriot and as a Christian:

> Amazement runs before the towering casque
> Of Arthur, bearing through the stormy field
> The virgin sculptured on his Christian shield.[53]

In contrast with Wordsworth's sparing, though vivid, evocation of Arthur, Henry Alford's 'The Ballad of Glastonbury' (1832) restricts the scope of its survey of the English Church to a view of Glastonbury from the Quantock Hills, and from this narrowed angle Arthur rises in importance.[54] In the development of the Abbey, he is one of the three great heroes (the others being Joseph of Arimathea and Alfred the Great) whereas King Henry VIII is the villain. Sleeping 'in a charm' (xvi), Arthur is carried to burial in a spot 'hallowed' by ages, past the mystically blooming thorn (xvii) whilst the Christian connotations of 'angel-bell . . . chapel . . . requiem . . . holy sleep' (xviii) endow him with a sanctified role in ecclesiastical hagiography. As in

[51] Thomas Fuller, *The Church History of Britain*, new edition, 3 vols (1837), I, 64 – 67.
[52] Turner, *Anglo-Saxons*, I, 273n.
[53] *Ecclesiastical Sketches*, I. x. ll. 5 – 7. Unless otherwise stated, all Wordsworth quotations are from *Poetical Works*, edited by Ernest de Selincourt and Helen Darbishire, 5 vols (Oxford, 1946).
[54] Henry Alford, 'The Ballad of Glastonbury'; in *The School of the Heart*, 2 vols (1835), I.

Wordsworth, the 'pagan blazonry' (xxi) of the victorious Saxon is succeeded by 'better days' (xxii). However, from his position as a firm and mainstream Anglican, Alford condemns the Catholic Church's decline into 'a glitter of pomp'. Such 'pride of the earth' is, he believes, fittingly punished by the inevitable spoliation of the monasteries 'by a wicked king's behest'. The Abbey is now reduced to 'a ruin rough and gray' (xxx) which, Alford hopes, may by 'some pious hand' (xxxii) possibly be restored to its former religious 'glory'. Written only three years after the passing of the Act of Catholic Emancipation, Alford's poem may thus be seen as a topically relevant portrayal of the evolution of an English National Church which yet remained deeply suspicious of Roman Catholicism. In both poems, Arthur is an integral part of a far-reaching historical process that has shaped the English Church and, consequently, contemporary English society. Neither poet suggests that finality has been achieved in this process: the modern world looks into a problematic and unknown future which 'sleeps as a snake enrolled / Coil within coil'.[55]

As Warton's 'The Grave of King Arthur' had intimated, the Welsh had long maintained a strong claim to be the chief authorities on Arthurian fact, the earliest recorded references to Arthur having, of course, derived from Welsh sources. A number of later Welsh chronicles, or *Bruts*, were, like their English counterparts, based on Geoffrey, and were assumed to narrate a grand historical tradition, which did not immediately dissolve after the Renaissance, for Welsh historians, too, continued to devote considerable attention to Arthur. It is to Sir John Price's account that Holinshed turns for his allusion to the three wives of Arthur, 'each of them bearing the name of Guenever'.[56] An identical indebtedness is recorded by Percy Enderbie in his history of Wales, *Cambria Triumphans*, which celebrates Stuart kingship, and traces Charles II's descent from Welsh forebears, and Arthur's own lineage to Joseph of Arimathea.[57] As late as 1786, Warrington's *The History of Wales*, while aiming to discard 'those illusions, that fancy or affection has raised', still preserves a considerable residue from Holinshed.[58] Besides relating the usual biographical details of Arthur, Warrington claims him as 'a great warrior' whose death decided 'the fate of Britain': thereafter, Britain's 'aera' of 'splendour' was clouded (pp. 78 – 79).

In the meantime, a revival of interest in Welsh studies had been fostered by literary antiquarians. Welsh medieval manuscripts, which had been rescued from destruction after the dissolution of the monasteries, were collected, catalogued and published. Amongst this salvage was Evan Evans's edition of *Some Specimens of the Poetry of the Antient Welsh Bards*, which brought back into circulation medieval Welsh poems that contained incidental allusions to the

---

55 *Ecclesiastical Sketches*, II. xlvii. ll. 1 – 2.
56 Sir John Price, *The historie of Cambria* (1584); cited in Holinshed, I, 580.
57 Percie Enderbie, *Cambria Triumphans* (1661), 185 – 98.
58 Warrington, *Wales*, 69.

Arthurian world. For example, in 'Myfanwy Vechan' the hero is 'pensive like Trystan', and in 'To Llewelyn ap Iorwerth' foemen 'were destroyed, as the adversaries of Arthur in the battle of Camlann'.[59] Apparent in much Anglo-Welsh verse of the period is a determinedly patriotic focus on the vanished heroic past of Celtic civilisation. Thus, a later, and original, poem by Evan Evans, entitled *The Love of Our Country* (1772), defends the achievements of 'Cambrian science' and the military prowess of the Britons in their fight against invaders:

> When Heaven offended sent the Saxon o'er,
> And weak Gwrtheyrn Britain's sceptre bore,
> The brave Ambrosius for his country stood
> And made his sword drink deep of hostile blood.
> Anon great Arthur, Britain's glory, rose,
> For valour formed, the terror of his foes:
> Immortal bards his virtue still rehearse
> And each true patriot kindles at the verse.[60]

A richly extended treatment of a distinctively Welsh concern for Arthur is revealed in a poem which has been briefly noticed above: Caesar Morgan's 'The Shrine of King Arthur'. Although Morgan, a Pembroke-born Anglican clergyman who became a Canon of Ely, has been wholly ignored as a poet by modern critics, his *Poems* have great relevance for a study of the Arthurian Revival in the eighteenth century's final phase. 'The Shrine of King Arthur' is explicitly derived from Warton's 'Grave', but whereas Warton rejects the account given by Welsh bards in favour of a Cornish story of Arthur's burial at Glastonbury, Morgan reshapes the respective values accorded to the English and to the Welsh. In his poem, the scene opens on King Henry II at Cilgerran Castle, but the monarch is described as a Saxon (sic!), and thus as a later representative of the original enemies of Arthur. And although Morgan follows Warton in rejecting the claim for Arthur's removal by 'fairy troops' (68) to an 'enchanted island' (72), and accepts that Arthur was interred in 'Avalonia's vale' near 'Joseph's fane' (84 – 85), Morgan does not suggest that the correct version was derived from an English source: the speaker is 'an ancient Bard' (78) and as 'Cambrian' as the others. Accepting for truth the account of a Glastonbury burial, Henry immediately orders his chiefs to locate the site. On piercing the ground, they find the 'letter'd cross' (96) and then rebury the bones in 'a hallow'd shrine' (100). Yet, for Morgan, the focus of attention is not directed at Henry but at a Welsh bard called Modred, his name most probably deriving from Gray's Modred whose 'magic song / Made

---

[59] Evan Evans, *Some Specimens of the Poetry of the Antient Welsh Bards* (1764), 15, 32.
[60] Quoted in *Anglo-Welsh Poetry 1480 – 1980*, edited by Raymond Garlick and Roland Mathias (Bridgend, 1984), 99 – 100.

huge Plinlimmon bow his cloud-topt head'.[61] Morgan's patriot had listened
with indignation to the 'degenerate Bards' (39) who had soothed 'the cruel
ear' (46) of the King, and he had then secretly and scornfully observed the 'set
forms of hireling monks' (102) who had carried out the rites of re-interment.
After their departure, he prays to Pendragon's 'sainted' son (150) to inspire a
Welsh rebellion against their Saxon rulers. In answer to this prayer, Arthur
rises from the shrine, accompanied by Taliessin and a hundred bards. Modred
is urged to teach 'Cambria's sons' (177) to 'brave the hostile spear' (184) in
their struggle for freedom. Ultimately, it is promised, 'British kings' will
regain the throne, and spread the benefits of freedom throughout the world. A
similar promise had, of course, been frequently made in contemporary
literature (e.g. in Gray's 'Bard' and Cowper's 'Boudicca') but whereas Gray
had represented the Tudors as 'genuine Kings' whose splendour would
obliterate any desire to 'bewail' a 'long-lost Arthur', the latter is not thus
eclipsed in Morgan's poem. Arthur, as the 'sainted chief' who returns to the
'seats of bliss' remains a quintessentially British hero of immense reputation
and influence which extends from a Dark Age past, through a medieval
present, and onward into a prefigured late eighteenth century.

Besides admitting that the subject had been 'exquisitely adorned with all the
graces of Poetry by Mr. T. Warton', Morgan acknowledges other scholarly
sources for his poem (67n). Thus, in alluding to Arthur's victory 'At Douglas
conscious flood', Morgan adds a footnote citing Whitaker as authority for
giving this modern place-name to Nennius's 'Dubglas' (107n). For details of
Arthur's exhumation, recourse is again had to Whitaker's relation of the
original account by Giraldus (81n); and, on Taliessin, a further note, drawn
from Whitaker and Evan Evans (163n). Such a scholarly apparatus, as had
previously been displayed in poems by Gray and Warton, provided further
historical underpinning to the poetic text by enclosing the main historical
subject within a framework of later historical scholarship. It marked, also, a
close association within this period between poetry and history. In part, this is
a reflection of a commonly-held culture — before the rise of modern
specialisations — when an educated and enlightened mind could venture upon
a wide variety of disciplines, as the range of topics in Gentleman's Magazine
(established 1731) makes apparent. Moreover, in literature which was seeking
out fresh subject matter, the quest could extend not only into foreign lands
(the Orient, in particular) but into that other foreign country, the medieval
past, which was increasingly seen as providing terrain for literary attention.
Both Gray and Warton were historians, and were historians of literature, and
by deriving poetic inspiration from antiquarian researches they strengthened
the affinities between the two, which thereby encouraged a romantic history
and a historical romance.

---

[61] Thomas Gray, 'The Bard', ll. 33 – 34; in Poems, Letters and Essays (1912).

That a romantic and antiquarian patriotism encouraged grandiose claims, especially on behalf of the historical Arthur's sphere of influence, was deplored by Edward Williams ('Iolo Morgannwg'). His own poem 'To Ivor the Liberal' (a translation from the medieval Welsh poet Dafydd ap Gwilym) expresses a hope that 'Great Ivor's friendship shall inspire / His Bard with ARTHUR'S martial fire', but the long footnote which he appends reduces Arthur to 'no more than the son of MEIRYG, the King of Glamorgan, elected to the chief command of the British armies against the Saxons'.[62] Rejecting Geoffrey of Monmouth's 'fables', he bases his own account on 'the ancient register of the cathedral church of Landaff' (on which he cites Carte's *History*) and 'many old books of pedigrees', 'some genuine fragments of history that are to be met with in Wales', and the triads, wherein, he claims, no fiction was ever incorporated. His moderate 'opinion' would, he believed, 'have no great weight with some Welshmen, who love their own nation and country better than truth'. However, in spite of Williams's misgivings, the constant Welsh preoccupation with Arthur did not usually adopt outlandishly extravagant claims. Indeed the more aberrant interpretations by Edward Davies, for example, were concerned with mythological parallels rather than with history (see Chapter 4). The leading Welsh scholar, William Owen-Pughe, attempted a careful distinction in his *Cambrian Biography* between this 'Arthur of history' and that of 'mythology'.[63] For the historical figure, Owen-Pughe provides an ample biographical entry for Arthur, which remains, though, as similarly restrained as was the viewpoint of his associate Williams.

On one particular aspect of Arthurian legend, the Welsh scholars are significantly silent or sceptical: Henry II's discovery of the grave. Very probably, they were influenced by the traditional Welsh belief that Arthur's burial place remains unknown. Again, although Caesar Morgan's poem had asserted a Glastonbury burial, his reduction of Henry's role is symptomatic of a Welsh orientation later seen in the work of Peter Roberts. A translator of the Welsh *Brut* attributed to Tysilio (1811), Roberts had previously published his *Sketch of the Early History of the Cymry*, which remained silent on the Glastonbury findings but, otherwise, reported Arthur as 'a warrior and chief . . . worthy of celebration'.[64] Another history, John Hughes's *Horae Britannicae*, displays considerable reservations about the exhumation, and, following Usher, Carte and Turner, admits that Arthur 'had no real authority but in Cornwall and Wales', although some 'transactions in the North' are attributed to him, on

---

[62] Edward Williams, *Poems, Lyric and Pastoral*, 2 vols (1794).

[63] William Owen[-Pughe], *The Cambrian Biography, or Historical Notices of Celebrated Men among the Ancient Britons* (1803), 13 – 18.

[64] Peter Roberts, *Sketch of the Early History of the Cymry* (1803), 142 – 47.

account of an alliance with 'Modred, a prince of Cumberland'.[65] More importantly for the Arthurian Revival, Hughes signals the interrelatedness of poetry and history, for he refers in his 'Appendix on the Sepulture of King Arthur' to Morgan's 'fine poem' (p. 398n); and he also adopts the practice of quoting legendary material in detail, such as the story deriving from Caradoc of how Melwas captured Guenevere (p. 239). The dispute as to where Arthur was buried had been dramatically rendered in Joseph Cottle's *The Fall of Cambria* (1808), an epic poem on King Edward I's military campaign against Llewelyn ap Griffith. Here, a prophetess threatens revenge, in the manner of Gray's 'Bard', on the English King for his defeat of the Welsh. This revenge will be accomplished by the return of Arthur. Edward's response is to say that her prophecy is probably false because:

> Arthur is dead! Neath Glastonbury's pile,
> Once he was laid, and ages now have waned,
> Since he, with earth, hath blended his last dust.[66]

Cottle here adds a lengthy footnote on the historically-testified re-opening of the tomb by Edward I in 1278; besides including a long quotation from Geoffrey of Monmouth on Arthur's combat with the Giant of Mont St Michel. In contrast with this English outlook, the Sibyl maintains that 'Arthur still doth being share': even thought he remains invisible, he communicates 'solemn truths' to her; and his sword will shortly drive 'proud' Edward from 'Cambria's land' (II.396 – 406).

Paradoxically, the theme of Arthur's second coming, an apt symbol for a Celtic literary renaissance, attracted scant mention by Welsh poets of this period. In accordance with the caution expressed by Edward Williams, few extraordinarily ahistorical claims were made for Arthur, whose role was regarded less as a purely Messianic culmination of Welsh patriotism than as an important forerunner of the great Welsh princes of the twelfth and thirteenth centuries. But, as these heroes were the protagonists of the many epics and metrical romances that were carefully based on the available historical records, Arthur's minor precursory role is frequently sketched in. For example, Richard Llwyd's poem on 'The Castle of Harlech' associates with 'Arthur's days' the era in which the castle was built, and, after describing Arthur as 'Dragon-crested', Llwyd supplies a note explaining that 'our historians agree' in assigning this device to Arthur's helm.[67] Southey's epic *Madoc* (1805) is exemplary: its dense annotation indicating an extremely thorough background research into sources which include Giraldus, Holinshed, Powel, Warrington, Sharon Turner and Owen-Pughe. The action of

[65] John Hughes, *Horae Britannicae; or, Studies in Ancient British History*, 2 vols (1818 – 1819), II, 194 – 204.
[66] Joseph Cottle, *The Fall of Cambria*, second edition (1811), Book XI. ll. 384 – 86.
[67] Richard Llwyd, *Poems, Tales, Odes, Sonnets, Translations from the British* (Chester, 1804).

the poem, set in the twelfth century, treats of the fortunes of the sons of Owen
Gwyneth, one of whom (Madoc) sails for America, an occasion which mirrors
a previous westward voyage undertaken by Merlin 'with his band of Bards'.[68]
Arthur is similarly portrayed as a predecessor of medieval Welsh grandeur.
Having been taught to 'lisp the fame of Arthur' (XI.142) and made aware of
his descent from 'old Cassibelan / Great Caratach, immortal Arthur's line'
(III.206 – 07), Madoc is represented as a patriot worthy of inclusion in our
'old illustrious annals' (XI.141), when setting out on his Atlantic voyage in
search of liberty. As Madoc departs, his nephew announces his own intention
of mounting the Welsh throne so that he, too, may join this pantheon of
heroes:

> and the Bard of years to come,
> Who harps of Arthur's and of Owen's deeds,
> Shall with the Worthies of his country rank
> Llewelyn's name.   (XVIII. 67 – 70)

M. E. Jeffreys's *Hoel the Hostage*, a long poem set in Henry II's reign, was
another work which was studiously researched from medieval and modern
authorities, and which again employs the distinctive allusion to Arthur and
Owen as those 'whose fame / Stands chronicled in tale and song'.[69] The
Llewellyn who was styled 'the Great' was to figure as eponymous hero of
W. E. Meredith's epic *Llewelyn ap Iorwerth*, where he is described as
descending 'from great Arthur's glorious line'.[70] And this Arthurian aura is
pervasive for, in the final stanza of the poem, a mourner over 'noble
Caradoc's bier' is reminded of 'how mighty Arthur fell / By traitor's hands at
Camlan's willowy flood' (V. xl).

These tragic resonances were most powerful in the work of Elizabeth Smith
(1776 – 1806), whose poems were published posthumously in 1808, together
with a biography of her by Henry Bowdler, the father of one of her particular
friends. A devotee of 'Ossian', ('I support him against all other poets'), she
adopts from Macpherson her scenes of heightened emotional anguish set
against a backdrop of lightning and torrents, and then places her poetic action
within an averred historical authenticity.[71] From her reading of Warrington,
whose Arthurian references she quotes in a letter to another friend in 1792, she
derives the incident of Llewellyn ap Gryffyd (the grandson of the 'Great')
being slain near Buillt on the river Wye. Her ensuing composition is then
entitled 'A supposed Translation from a Welsh poem, lately dug up at

---

[68] *Madoc*, Book XI. l. 105; in *Poems of Robert Southey*, edited by Maurice H. Fitzgerald (1909).
[69] M. E. Jeffreys, *Hoel the Hostage* (1842), Canto IV. ll. 15 – 16.
[70] W. E. Meredith, *Llewelyn ap Iorwerth* (1818), Canto I. st. iv.
[71] Elizabeth Smith, *Fragments of Prose and Verse*, new edition (1810). A claim that his prose poem
was 'a fragment from the original British' was also made by the anonymous author of 'Bwrdd
Arthur: or the Institution of Arthur's Round Table', in *Cambro-Briton*, 2 (1821), 181 – 82. As with
Elizabeth Smith's poem, an Ossianic inspiration is evident.

Piercefield, in the same spot where Llewellyn ap Gryffyd was slain, Dec. 10th, 1281'. The poem describes the author's visit to Merlin's Cave in Snowdonia during an 'elemental' storm. When Merlin appears, he mournfully prophesies that Llewellyn's imminent death will signal the fall of Cambria; an event which will occasion his own retirement to 'some deep and rocky cell / Amidst the thick entangled wood to dwell' (91 – 92). These lugubrious forebodings are matched by later poems which paraphrase Taliesin's prophecy of Welsh doom. For example, *Cambro-Briton* published an anonymous poem entitled 'The Prophecy of Taliesin' which foretold at great length the downfall destined for Cambria when 'valorous Arthur's old domain / Must crouch beneath a Saxon's reign'.[72] Felicia Hemans voiced a like concern in her poem of the same year, in which Taliesin again testifies to 'the sceptre' passing away 'from Uthyr's kingdom'.[73] Another poem that also makes use of ancient Welsh material from a triad source is *Cardiff Castle* by Taliesin Williams, the son of Iolo Morgannwg. This metrical romance on the storming of the Norman-held castle by the heroic Ivor Bach celebrates Ivor's lineage, which had an Arthurian connection:

> His ancient sire, with Arthur brave,
> On Camlan field found gory grave:
> Th'ensanguined field, whence no one came,
> Save warriors three, of awful fame.[74]

More frequently, Arthur's role as a generic hero is cited not only as reason for lament but as a symbol of past Welsh endeavours which have proved to be the basis for later British prowess. As early as 1789, *Gentleman's Magazine* had printed a birthday ode addressed to the Prince of Wales which had named Arthur as one of the most illustrious of Welsh chivalric heroes.[75] As a defender of Britain's right to self-determination, he is acknowledged, too, in David Lloyd's 'British Valour; or, Saint David's Day. A Patriotic Ode' (1812), which declares:

> Of brave King Arthur and a train
> Of heroes, bold and strong,
> Who dar'd their Country's rights maintain,
> Old Fame has loudly sung.[76]

---

[72] 'The Prophecy of Taliesin', ll. 59 – 60; in *Cambro-Briton*, 2 (1821), 185 – 88.
[73] Taliesin's Prophecy', l.11; *The Poetical Works of Felicia Dorothea Hemans* (1914). For date of composition, see Peter W. Trinder, *Mrs Hemans* (Cardiff, 1984), 30 – 31.
[74] Taliesin Williams, *Cardiff Castle* (Merthyr Tydfil, 1827), ll. 221 – 24.
[75] A., 'An Ode, on the Birthday of His Royal Highness, the Prince of Wales, August 12 1789', *GM*, 59 (August 1789), 743 – 44.
[76] Stanza ii; in David Lloyd, *Characteristics of Men, Manners and Sentiments: or, The Voyage of Life*, second edition, revised (1812).

Celebrating the accession of the Tudors in 1485, Richard Llwyd's 'To his Countrymen' sees therein a return to his country's 'ancient days', including those of Arthur.[77] J. H. Parry, whose *Cambrian Plutarch* had included a twenty page account of the historical Arthur, also wrote a poem on 'the Heroes of Cymru' (1821).[78] Prominent among these, 'brave Arthur' may indeed live 'no more', but his spirit, like that of Llewelyn's, 'glows . . . as of yore / In Cymri's noble race' (13 – 14). As a result, a modern Welsh soldier such as Sir Watkin Williams Wynn is regarded as a later embodiment of a comparable gallantry. T. J. Llewelyn Prichard's 'The Worthies of Wales' salutes an extensive parade of Welsh heroes, and even reiterates the ancient hope:

> Hail Arthur, the father of Chivalry's fights,
> His heroes and bards, and his round-table knights;
> Not wrong were the legends, or prophecy's strain,
> Which told that King Arthur should yet rise again.[79]

A 'Welsh War Song', which was addressed to Llewellyn's warriors, invokes the 'spirit of Merlin' to inspire them.[80] Again, an obscurely adumbrated promise that Arthur will return to 'his father's mountain land' concludes Ellylles's 'The Grave of King Arthur', which is squarely founded on Taliesin's allusion to the unlocated grave as a 'mystery of the world'.[81]

The visit of the thirteen year old Princess Victoria to Wales in 1832 was the occasion for further reference. At the eisteddfod which she attended at Beaumaris Castle, an ode was recited 'with proper action and pathos' by Henry Davies of Cheltenham.[82] This welcome to the future Queen consists of the customary tribute to Cambria's past struggles, and ends upon an optimistic and climactic note by acknowledging the presence of 'the princely heir to British Arthur's crown' (96). The same occasion was treated by George Haslehurst's *Penmaen-Mawr*, which presents a bard before Victoria at the eisteddfod, invoking in song the 'days of old' when the Saxon quailed before Arthur's army; lamenting the death at Camlan caused by a traitor 'knave'; and rejoicing in the fitting revenge taken by the dying king:

> brave Arthur's brand
> In his princely hand
> Pour'd forth the dastard's soul,

[77] Llwyd, *Poems, Tales, Odes, Sonnets*.
[78] John Humphreys Parry, *The Cambrian Plutarch* (1824), 1 – 20. 'The Heroes of Cymru' in *Cambro-Briton*, 2 (1821), 89; reprinted as 'The Heroes of Cambria' in *The Cambrian Wreath; a Selection of English Poems on Welsh Subjects*, edited by Thomas Jeffery Llewelyn Prichard (Aberystwyth, 1828).
[79] Lines 9 – 12; in Prichard ed. *Cambrian Wreath*.
[80] In *Carmarthen Journal*, 9 March 1827, 4.
[81] Line 40; in *Cambrian Quarterly Magazine*, 2 (July 1830), 276 – 77.
[82] See *CQM*, 4 (1832), 526 – 52.

> Which to Erebus sunk
> While the ghastly trunk
> Writhing, — was seen to roll
> On the gore-stained ground.[33]

Although John Lloyd's 'Ode to Princess Victoria', which was written for the Cardiff eisteddfod in 1834, makes no such Arthurian reference, it does provide evidence that much of Victoria's appeal to the Welsh on these occasions arose from the claim that she was descended from the Tudors, with the result that she was, according to Lloyd, who paraphrases Gray, regarded as 'The genuine issue of Britannia's kings'.[84]

A yet ampler treatment of Arthur's role occurs in John Parker's 'The Celtic Annals', which traces early British history up to the Norman period. Unlike many of the chronicles discussed above, Parker's work is loftily conceived: his choice of blank verse hexameters aims at the dignity of a Homeric style, and the eclecticism of endowing a British subject with a classical form is paralleled by Parker's fusion of Celtic and Saxon cultures.[85] Drawing his information primarily from Welsh triad sources, Parker attempts a close archaeological reconstruction of the Arthurian era:

> He celebrates Easter, where Cornish fortifications
> Of primitive structure hail their victorious owner, . . .
> But when pale winter, proclaimed in stormy December . . .
> Then with glad merriment his royal feast is attended
> By his lordly barons, in halls where some classic artist
> With Roman workmanship adorn'd their sumptuous arches;
> Where the chequer'd pavements are fraught with musical emblems,
> Mosaic enrichment: they called these fair habitations
> Caerlleon of South Wales; upon Usk; hard by the Severn Sea:
> But the foreign Romans nam'd it Silurian Isca.[86]

Although his handling owes much to Welsh sources, as shown by the spelling of 'Medrawd' and 'Gwenhwyvar', or the details of the three men who survived the battle of Camlan, Parker infuses an additional chivalrous element by endowing these ages with responsibility for the emancipation of woman from 'contempt or slavery' to a position of 'Christian privilege', as epitomised by the universal reverence for Mary, the 'Mother and Virgin'. The Arthurian age of the Round Table, 'where all were counted as equals' and where glory

---

[83] 'Song', ll. 18 – 24; in George Haslehurst, *Penmaen-Mawr, and Daybreak* (1849).
[84] John Lloyd, 'Ode to the Princess Victoria', l. 14; in *Poems* (1847).
[85] A comparable eclecticism was frequently practised. See, for example, Heber's introduction of Titania into a Loathly Lady story in *The Masque of Gwendolen* (1816); Peacock's amalgamation of Arthurian and Roman mythology in *Calidore* (1816); and Lytton's incorporation of an Etruscan heroine within his *King Arthur* (1848).
[86] John Parker, *The Passengers: containing 'The Celtic Annals'* (1831), 217.

was won by 'virtue', is represented as surpassing the era of 'classical heroes, or sons of Rome' on account of the greater 'magnificence of soul' which, in turn, taught Europe 'higher actions'. Furthermore, Parker unites his soberly delineated study of an 'elected Pendragon', who requires no robe 'of needless adornment', with the traditional English version of his burial at Glastonbury, recounted with a detailed accuracy derived from Giraldus:

> In fertile Avalon's green isle, in a gloomy sepulchre,
> Lay the renown'd Arthur: his bones enclos'd in a vast oak;
> O'er him two pointed pyramids of deeply-figur'd stone.   (p. 219)

Parker follows Giraldus, again, in his record of the exhumation of the 'majestic / Hero's mortal ashes'. This recovery of the buried truth after centuries of neglect may also fittingly symbolise the nineteenth century historian's arduous task of sifting through evidence to reconstruct a past culture:

> now, from the ruins of time, we carefully rescue
> Ev'ry precious fragment, and thence imagine, when perfect,
> How the sublime structure once rose in splendor among men.
>
> (p. 220)

Moreover, Parker's historical vision points forward, after the ensuing conflicts between Celt, Dane and Saxon, to the nobility of the Saxon Alfred: for 'wheresoever worth is, we honour, we praise, we adorn it: / And our own England has rivall'd Arthur in Alfred. / Lawgiver and hero!' (p. 221). Transcending a purely Welsh outlook, this thematic concern with the ultimate unity of Celt and Saxon, which was to play a dominant part in nineteenth century versions of the Arthurian legend, will be treated more fully in the following section.

Milman, Peacock, Pennie and Lytton

Besides the many minor references to Arthur that occurred in the works briefly outlined above, there were also four works that dealt extensively with the historical background of their Arthurian subject: two were epics, one a novel, and one a poetic drama. The importance of these works demands, therefore, a much fuller analysis of the historical setting which they provided for Arthur.

These four major works differ in many important respects but they share a common dependence upon a generally conceived historical basis by being set in the sixth century, and by being heavily concerned with the contending British and Saxon dynasties within that period. Milman's *Samor, Lord of the*

Bright City (1818) is a 'heroic poem' in twelve books, with the declared aim of celebrating Britain's renown. The action covers the era of Vortigern's marriage to Rowena, the slaughter of the Britons on Salisbury Plain, and the successful combination of Aurelius, Uther and Gorlois to defeat the Saxon invaders. Samor is a 'historical character', known to the medieval chroniclers as Eldol, or Edol, the Lord of Gloucester. He is the pivot for initial resistance to Hengist and Vortigern; and, by persuading Gorlois to cede Igerna to Uther, creates the triple alliance essential for British success. Arthur appears as a young child, to be hailed by Merlin as a 'bright arrow from the bow of Destiny' and a 'Strong reaper in the harvest of renown' who shall 'o'erbear the vaunting Saxon'.[87] When the contending armies have assembled, Arthur spontaneously leads the onset; an action which impels the British chiefs to charge into battle to his rescue. The Saxons are consequently defeated, Hengist taken prisoner, and then executed.

Peacock's *The Misfortunes of Elphin* (1829) focuses on Taliesin's rescue of the imprisoned Elphin, the King of Caredigion. To effect this, Taliesin enlists the help of Arthur by first securing the release of Gwenyvar from her captivity by Melvas, whose kingdom lies 'on the eastern shores of the Severn'. This latter quasi-historical event had already been recounted, it will be recalled, in the histories by Carte, Hughes and Ritson. There is, of course, considerable authorial irony in the telling of what Peacock describes as 'the present authentic history' and 'veridicous narrative', but this action is nevertheless set naturalistically at the beginning of the sixth century, with Arthur returning victorious to Caerleon from the battle of Badon, and holding, like Uther, 'nominal sovereignty' over a number of 'petty kings'.[88]

Pennie's *The Dragon-King* is the third in an ambitious series of six plays entitled *Britain's Historical Drama; a series of National Tragedies, intended to illustrate the manners, customs and religious institutions of different early eras in Britain*. These eras range from Ancient British to Norman. In the play under discussion, the Saxon Cerdic invades Britain, establishes a camp at Winchester, and routs Arthur outside the city of Sorbiodunum (= Old Sarum). Arthur's kinsman, Mouric Medrawd (= Mordred), elopes with the willing Gwenyfar. Both are caught but Mouric escapes to join the Saxon forces, whereas Gwenyfar is banished by an enraged Arthur to the Saxon camp. There she becomes the tenth wife of Cissa, King of the South Saxons. Since he is killed in the final battle, she is forced into a ritual suttee on the funeral pyre. The dying Arthur is carried to Glastonbury, having given instructions that, in the event of his

---

[87] *Samor*, Book X. ll. 199 – 209; in *The Poetical Works of the Rev. H. H. Milman*, 3 vols (1839).
[88] *The Misfortunes of Elphin*, chapters 1, 6, 11, 16; in *The Works of Thomas Love Peacock*, edited by H. F. Brett-Smith and C. E. Jones (New York, 1967), IV.

death, 'the veil / Of dim uncertainty' should be flung over his fate.[89] As a
result, his

> warlike name will keep the patriot fire
> That burns in Celtic hearts, for ever bright;
> And when in after years shall other chiefs
> For Britain draw the sword, the wild harp's song
> Will be of [his] return from fairy-land.   (IV. iv. 111 – 15)

The outline of Pennie's main action rests squarely on historical tradition in so
far as the play is primarily concerned with the clash between Saxon and
Briton; and Pennie's main characters (Cerdic, Arthur, Kenrick, Gwenyfar,
Cissa and Porta) are all taken from historical sources, chiefly the Welsh triads,
the *Anglo-Saxon Chronicle*, and Sharon Turner's *Anglo-Saxons*. But within this
broad historical schema, Pennie severely reshapes his material. The historical
time-scale is, for example, readjusted so that Cerdic (who died in 534) may be
present at Arthur's final defeat (assumed to take place in 542 by Turner), a
battle which is equated with Kenrick's victory at Old Sarum (552 in the
Chronicle). The considerable amount of amatory incident is largely the product
of Pennie's free invention but, in general, Pennie's drama accommodates
itself to the framework of historical probability or likelihood. Thus, Mouric
Medrawd's portrayal as an 'amiable, enchanting, gallant youth' (I. iii. 37)
was an interpretation which Pennie justified by citing the Welsh triadic
description of Medrawd as a 'most engaging person, to whom it was almost
impossible to deny any request' (p. 533). As his marriage to Gwenyfar had
also been recorded by Geoffrey of Monmouth and Holinshed, Pennie's
attribution to Medrawd of a quasi-Lancelot role is historically justifiable, and
economical in its ban on French importations. It also made good historical
sense to adopt the literary romance tradition of Gwenyfar's being sentenced to
death at the stake, but to recast the event as a human sacrifice conducted by
pagan Saxons.

Lytton's poem in twelve books, *King Arthur* (1848), while admitting much
fanciful allegory, assigns to Arthur 'his place in history'.[90] Even though
Lytton's preface acknowledges that he has not adopted the 'Manners' which
'the rigid Antiquary would appropriate to the date of that historical Arthur, of
whom we know so little', Lytton casts Arthur, nevertheless, in the strictly
historical role of 'the brave Prince of the Silures', whose function it is to
preserve his country against the attacks of pagan Saxons by prosecuting the
successful defence of Carduel against siege.

---

[89] John Fitzgerald Pennie, *Britain's Historical Drama . . . First Series: The Dragon King* (1832), Act
IV. scene iv. ll. 109 – 110.
[90] Lord Lytton, *King Arthur*, revised edition (1870), xii. The nature of Lytton's allegory will be
examined in Chapter 4.

Stemming from the new historicist awareness of the cultural differences between epochs, there is a fascinated close observation of the minutiae of period detail.[91] Comparable to those contemporary theatrical productions that sought to present historically authentic costumes for plays set in the Middle Ages, or to artists who endeavoured to portray such subjects with archaeological exactness, there was among these writers a determined rejection of the 'unhistorical'; Pennie, for example, dismissing 'the dream-ings' of Geoffrey of Monmouth, and, with an antiquarian zeal, drawing his reader's attention to the fact that the drama employs 'the exact coronation oath of the Saxon war-kings' (pp. 523, 537). Critical support for such accuracy was found in William Taylor of Norwich's praise of Christopher Wieland's German Arthurian poem, *Geron der Adelige*. Nowhere, wrote Taylor, do we find 'an anachronism of costume or idea: the device on every shield is allotted aright with the accuracy of an antiquary'.[92] In the tradition of Scott and Southey, each work is equipped with scholarly footnotes pointing to an impressive array of historical sources. These include the recognised modern authorities, such as Sharon Turner, Whitaker, Palgrave, Milner, Percy's translation of Mallet's *Northern Antiquities*, and Strutt's *Sports and Pastimes*. In line, however, with developing nineteenth century scholarship, there is a marked adherence to original or early sources, namely Tacitus, Caesar, Nennius, Gildas, Bede, and the Welsh bards and triads. Such reading, whilst not suffusing the poems with the density of descriptive and anecdotal detail that occurs in the historical novels of Scott and Lytton, is deliberately used to provide authentic period colour. There is, for example, the description of Hengist 'with his wreath of amber beads' (*Samor*, II. 360), a detail which Milman obtained from Peter Roberts's translation of Tysilio's *Brut*; or the account of the idol Flint, which was derived from Verstegen's *Restitution of Decayed Intelligence*:

91 See Thomas Preston Peardon, *The Transition in English Historical Writing 1760 – 1830* (New York, 1933).
92 William Taylor, *Historic Survey of German Literature*, 3 vols (1828 – 1830), I, 323. Cf. the lack of historical concern in Thomas Stothard's *Theatrical Portrait of Miss Farren as Emmeline in 'Arthur and Emmeline'* (one of a series published by Lowndes in 1785 – 1786) which endows Arthur with a fancifully plumed helmet but represents Emmeline in fashionable dress of the 1780s. For the advance in historically accurate costume designs which the antiquarian J. R. Planché had supervised for Charles Kemble's revival of *King John* in 1824, see Roy Strong, *And when did you last see your father?* (1978), 53. Strong also provides much information on artists who used early portraits as sources for armour, costume, furniture and physiognomy (61 – 63). When William Dyce was awarded the commission to paint Arthurian frescoes in the Palace of Westminster, he painstakingly researched details of appropriate armour and costume. In particular, he sought for a print representing 'a chalice which professed to be the original St. Grail or a rival one . . . now in Spain': letter from Dyce, quoted in Marcia Pointon, *William Dyce 1806 – 1864* (Oxford, 1979), 104. Art critics could display a like zeal for archaeological accuracy: see the *Art Union* critique of F. R. Pickersgill's RA painting *Amoret, Aemylia and Prince Arthur in the Cottage of Sclaunder*:
    although, in subject matter of this kind, licences of all sorts are overlooked, it had been wiser to have painted Prince Arthur equipped entirely in mail, without any improper mixture of plate armour.
AU (1845), 180.

On his flint pedestal, his skeleton shape
Garmented scantly in a winding sheet,
And in his hand a torchblaze   (XI. 381 – 83)

Similarly with Pennie's Arthur's address to his troops:

Lift our blest banner
Wide on the morning winds, and fling abroad
The battle-summons from the brazen throat
Of the deep-thundering dudag.   (IV. ii. 5 – 8)

A footnote then directs attention to the fact that Pennie has obtained the archaic term 'dudag' from 'General Vallancy'.[93] Lytton, too makes occasional forays into specified period detail: 'In Cymrian lands — where still the torque of gold / Or decks the highborn or rewards the bold.[94] And Peacock shows a kindred delight in getting the technical description correct, as in his very precise delineation of the manner in which Elphin constructed his salmon weir (chapter 5).

Consonant with a soberly historical framework is the conscious reduction of supernatural elements which had accompanied the original legends or chronicles. Thus, the birth of Arthur in *Samor* is the product of a conventional bridal couch (X. 58) unvisited by a magically disguised Uther. Caliburn does not arrive in a magic stone, nor is it brandished above the mere by the Lady of the Lake. It has instead been more prosaically 'Blest by the midnight vision of St. Joseph, / At his high shrine' (*Dragon King*, II. i. 180 – 81). Just as Pennie has drawn nothing 'from the wild and mythological fables of the *Mabinogion*, but only from those resources which are authentic' (p. 538), so Peacock treats sceptically the *Mabinogion's* accounts of Taliesin's magic birth and reincarnations. Even in Lytton's *King Arthur*, which designedly admits much of the 'Marvellous', the main setting is credibly located at the siege of Carduel, and on journeys to the Great North: danger in both areas has to be circumvented naturalistically — a dog bites through Gawaine's bonds, and a spear saves Genevra from being sacrificed. The supernatural is limited to the private quest by Arthur and, even then, is usually internalised by being presented through the mode of vision or swoon.

Despite this evidence of sociological accuracy, and a naturalistic approach to the construction of the main narrative, each writer faced the major difficulty that neither early sources nor contemporary authorities could provide more than the sparest factual outline for Arthur's questionable military and political achievement. Aware of the dilemma, Southey had written to Wynn in 1804 to

[93] i.e. Charles Vallancey, the historian and philologist: author of such titles as *An Essay on the Primitive Inhabitants of Great Britain and Ireland. Proving that they were Persians or Indoscythae* (Dublin, 1807).
[94] *King Arthur*, Book IV. xl; in *The Poetical and Dramatic Works of Sir Edward Bulwer Lytton*, 5 vols (1852 – 1854).

say that although he had 'great drawings of mind' towards an Arthurian subject, he did not proceed because Arthur's history was 'such a chaos', and 'his actions are of no consequential importance'.[95] Milman's solution to this problem was to limit the totally Arthurian material and instead to derive the main plot from the chronicles, a conception dating back to his 'fancy' at Eton 'for searching our old Chronicles for subjects for poetry'. The result is that Samor is a 'historical character, as far as such legends can be called history': and these thus endow him with the modicum of historical basis necessary for the creation of a national epic hero:

> The fullest account of his exploits is in Dugdale's *Baronage* under his title of Earl of Gloucester. William Harrison, however, in the 'Description of Britain' prefixed to Holinshed, calls him Eldulph de Samor. But all concur in ascribing to him the Acts which make the chief subject of the fifth and last books of this poem.[96]

These 'acts' are his single-handed resistance to Hengist's treacherous attack on the Britons at Stonehenge, and Samor's eventual judicial revenge by obtaining punitive decapitation of the offender. As authority for Uther's siege of Tintagel, Milman cites 'the romantic histories' or 'historical romances'. These, in turn, he modifies to suit his own moral viewpoint: Gorlois is made 'a crafty kite' (X. 44) who snatches Igerna, on 'some cold and antiquated plea' (X. 62), from her lawful husband, Uther. With a mysterious eloquence, undisclosed by Milman, Samor later manages to persuade Gorlois to right the position. What was certainly inspired by chivalric romance was the foreshadowing of the Arthurian world:

> From a round table, knights in sunlike arms,
> Shields bossy with rich impress quaint, and fair
> Their coursers, as the fire-hoof'd steeds of Morn.
> To white-arm'd Ladies in a stately court
> Bards hymn'd the deeds of that fam'd chivalry (VIII. 304 – 08)

Even more evocative of the romance tradition is the foretelling of

> knights and ladies, glorious in old song,
> White-handed Iseult, Launcelot of the Lake,
> Chaste Perceval, that won the Sangreal quest. (XI. 393 – 95)

On other occasions, into Milman's Dark Ages slip the unintentional solecisms of 'morion' (VI. 355), 'vizor'd helmet' (VI. 436) and 'bright-scutcheon'd

---

[95] *Selected Letters of Robert Southey*, edited by John Ward Warter, 4 vols (1856), I, 295.
[96] Milman, *Works*, I, xi.

biers' (XII. 249), all being appurtenances derived from a later age. More importantly, the very arrangement of his historical material was questioned in a *Quarterly Review* article by John Coleridge:

> Mr Milman's choice of a subject would have been in many respects a happy one, if all our impressions from history did not run counter to the truth of its catastrophe. He celebrates the defeat and expulsion of the Saxon invaders from this country with the re-establishment of the British monarchy . . . but unfortunately we have been familiar from our earliest years with Saxon victories and British defeats . . . It is impossible therefore not to feel something unsatisfactory and imperfect in the close of the story . . . we [know] that [the British] joys are delusive, and their calamities respited only a moment.[97]

Such a criticism could not, however, be made against Pennie's drama, because it is coherently organised around the Saxon invasion, with the first scene opening on the pavilion of Cerdic to the sound of 'shouts, cymbals, trumpets and clashing of spears', followed by the entry of Cerdic in a 'Triumphal Car of Shields'. Enclosed in the centre are the tragic events of Arthur's marital and military defeats, whilst the finale includes the ritual sacrifice by the Saxons of Arthur's sister, imagined here to be Imogenia. Evidently, the Saxons are victorious and possess the future. Critically, the work aroused conflicting reactions: *Monthly Magazine*, for example, being scornful of the play's failure to achieve historical verisimilitude, and finding it full of anachronisms; whereas *Athenaeum* grudgingly conceded its 'antiquarian accuracy'.[98]

The historical accuracy of Peacock's novel impressed the *Cambrian Quarterly Magazine*; and, as Lytton claimed to have invented 'an entirely original story', no reviewer judged him in strictly historical terms.[99] Even so, the *New Monthly Magazine* compared him to Macaulay, the only other man who 'could alike recal the love of the past and unfold the secrets of the present'.[100] The reviewer, however, conceded that King Arthur was 'as Macaulay says, one of those "mythical persons whose very existence may be questioned" '. Such a critique made two major assumptions: that the present was bound up with the past, and that mythical material might yet contain a contemporary relevance.

Macaulay's narrative recreation of the past by means of a series of vivid tableaux is related to a demand, which was frequently expressed in the nineteenth century, for modern men 'to enter into the spirit of the middle

---

[97] *QR*, 19 (1818), 328 – 47. The article is attributed to John Coleridge by Arthur Milman's *Henry Hart Milman* (1900), 38.
[98] *MM*, 13 (February 1832), 240 – 41. *Ath*, 4 February 1832, 73.
[99] *CQM*, 1 (1829), 231 – 40.
[100] *NMM*, 85 (March 1849), 307 – 14.

ages'.[101] The pioneers of such a historical empathy were, according to John Stuart Mill's account of Thierry, the literary works of Scott and Chateaubriand since the task of understanding the life of 'former ages' required not the eye that was solely modern, but that which could see with imagination and 'some of the qualities of a poet'.

Mill's prescription for this imaginative historicism had been predated by Pennie, who gave on his title page a relevant quotation from Horace Walpole:

> Belief in every kind of prodigy was so established in those dark ages, that an author would not be faithful to the *manners* of the times, who should omit all mention of them. He is not bound to believe them himself, but he *must* represent his actors as believing them.

Pennie's ensuing action, therefore, presents what appears a convincingly brutal account of Dark Age barbarism: Gwenyvar is thrown helpless to the Saxon camp, then is eventually burnt at the stake; and men fight to the death amid blazing huts. Pennie also attempts to portray dramatically the mental aberrations of heathen prophetesses who laid claim to supernatural visions in which, for example, 'Sognor, the king of elves, with meteors crowned' rushed by (III. ii. 71). Again, Milman's pagan Caswallon, when fighting berserk after the death of his son, is rendered with a romantic poet's chameleon delight in the energy displayed. More frequently, a nineteenth century narrator presents an inimical archaic outlook but distances himself from it by means of irony, as for example in Taliesin's account of how he had been born from the cauldron of Ceridwen:

> Where Taliesin picked up the story which he told of himself, why he told it, and what he meant by it, are questions not easily answered. Certain it is, that he told this story to his contemporaries, and that none of them contradicted it. It may, therefore, be presumed that they believed it; as anyone who pleases is most heartily welcome to do now.   (chap. 15)

Pervasive in Milman's work is the careful qualification of pagan belief by his suggesting a rational explanation for it: as when the British kings meet clandestinely in an ancient grove, and where Milman's rhetorical device invites the reader to distance himself from an ignorant and superstitious viewpoint:

> On every brow
> Indignant sorrow and sad vengeance lower.
> Them had the Pagan peasant deemed his Gods,
> In cloudy wrath down stooping from the heavens   (II. 15 – 18)

Similarly, when the Saxons range the forest for prey:

---

[101] John Stuart Mill, 'Recent French Historians', *Edinburgh Review*, 79 (January 1844), 1 – 39.

That night were seen along the dusky wood . . .
Pale faces circled with black iron helms;
. . . the peasants thought
Demons of evil that sad night had power   (II. 517 – 22)

This desire to explain rationally the causes of primitive religion is also closely linked to the early nineteenth century concept of partial illumination (as seen in Lytton's Druids who had glimpses of 'angel tracks', X. cv), and to Milman's later theory of the necessary accommodation of religion to its own historical period.[102]

On the other hand, in spite of the fact that individual character, scene or narrative may be re-created through a sympathetic imaginative power, it remains extremely uncommon, whatever the claims made for itself by historical science, for literature not to reflect, in some measure, its own age. Milman, Peacock, Pennie and Lytton regarded the past through their own early nineteenth century eyes, and shaped and judged it, albeit unconsciously, from their own viewpoints. Each viewpoint is, of course, idiosyncratic to some extent, but there is a nexus of attitudes to the past, shared by all four writers; and even when Peacock seems incongruent, it is merely to present a different profile of the others' beliefs.

Implicit in these poets was a passion for the past as past. Milman's Etonian reading has already been mentioned; Lytton, too, recalls how in his first vacation from Cambridge:

I resolved to make a desperate attempt to obtain for my listless mind some object of intellectual interest. I chose the History of England. . . . I took Rapin's dry, grand work for the main road of my researches, and diverged by the way into chronicles and memoirs . . . I filled commonplace books with comments and abridgments. This was the first subject to which I had ever grappled with the earnest spirit of the scholar.[103]

There was, besides, an especial interest in the importance of early history. This interest was largely fuelled by a Rousseau-like confidence in the nobility of the savage; a Wordsworthian insight into the elemental bonds between man and nature; a horror of contemporary industrial development; a growing antiquarianism; a wish to extend the bounds of scientific and imaginative knowledge and experience; and the attempt to locate a precedent for religious and political usage. Since history was increasingly regarded in terms of a growth and a political development, the present was consequently the outcome

[102] 'Religion is one great system of accommodation to the wants, to the moral and spiritual advancement of mankind', wrote Milman in *History of Christianity* (1840); quoted by Duncan Forbes, *The Liberal Anglican Idea of History* (Cambridge, 1952), 75.
[103] *The Life of Edward Bulwer, first Lord Lytton*, by his grandson, the Earl of Lytton, 2 vols (1913), I, 73.

of past events, and thus the present could be studied and comprehended by means of an examination of its sources in the past.

In contrast with a late eighteenth century drama which ostensibly shares the same historical setting, the nineteenth century works under discussion approach the past in a radically altered way. The point of comparison is William Henry Ireland's *Vortigern* (1799).[104] This latter has references to Britons and Saxons, yet the work is essentially ahistorical as the focus is upon the hero's moral character *sub specie aeternitatis*. But the nineteenth century works are heir to such historians as Gibbon and Volney, whose long temporal perspectives had narrated the previous rises and falls of the world's great empires. The grandeur and the immensity of the past had thus given rise to a new category of the Burkean sublime, but one linked with Time rather than with Landscape or Size. Thus, the reader is here aware not only of one past but of many, for behind the narrative time is perceived a long prior perspective. Arthur, in each work, is seen against a background of Roman remains which, in turn, recall the struggle of the British against Caesar; Stonehenge implies a Druid connection; beyond the enemy Saxons lie the Gothic invaders of Rome. The densely organised classical and biblical allusion in both Milman and Lytton is used effectively to evoke further temporal corridors, distantly echoing with the fall of the empires of Medes and Hittites. There is an apprehension of historical crisis as states collapse:

> The frame
> And fabric of our world is breaking up . . .
> Leaving confusion lord of this wide ball   (*Samor*, I. 307 – 12)

Further back in prehistory lie 'the green barrows of the ancient dead' (VI. 9). At the uttermost limit, Arthur (the 'Conqueror in the Halls of Time', *KA*, X. xiii) is compelled to undertake a metaphysical quest among the fossil relics of the earth's first ages. There, in the more distant vistas of geological time revealed by Charles Lyell's *Principles of Geology* (1830 – 1833) and by Lytton's immediate source, Gideon Mantell's *Wonders of Geology* (1838), Arthur is shown how

> the foul, earliest reptile spectra lay,
> Distinct as when the chaos was their home;
> Half plant, half serpent, some subside away
> Into gnarl'd roots (now stone)   (*KA*, X. xxxviii)

Endemic to this concern with origins was a consciousness of race and nationhood. With Peacock, his preference for the Welsh results in little dramatic conflict because his Saxons are invariably off-stage villains: and, in

---

[104] William Henry Ireland, *Vortigern, an Historical Tragedy*, Eighteenth Century Shakespeare Series, 21 (1971).

The Round Table's catalogue of kings, Alfred was scarcely the only Saxon 'worth naming'.[105] In the three other writers, each race has its distinctive cultural pride in ancestry, worship and homeland. Pennie's Cerdic, for instance, on hearing that his son is in love with Arthur's sister, declaims that the son of Odin must never 'wed with one whose veins / Are tainted with the hateful blood of Romans' (*DK*, I. i. 202 – 03). Lytton may soften the distinction between Cymri and Saxon (although preserving a clearer separation from the more southerly Etruscans) but his generalised typology frequently names individual characters as 'the Saxon' or 'the Vandal' or 'this Cymrian'. Rowena's pleading, in Milman's *Samor*, for the life of her father — a Saxon — is resisted thus by British Samor: 'Rowena, when a Nation speaks, / The irrevocable sentence cannot change' (XII. 368 – 69). And in this context the emphasis on natural scenery, which may otherwise have appeared as a distinctly late-Romantic decorative effect, helps to underpin the physical reality of characters' emotional ties with their native land.[106]

That 'early history is the most important in our annals', and that 'the great achievements of the Britons and the Anglo-Saxons' formed the basis for the gradually evolving modern British state, implied that this body politic was ancient and organically intricate, founded on historical precedent and adaptation rather than on rationalist and revolutionary prescription.[107] An essential stage in the growth of such a state was the eventual fusion — not conquest — of the previously distinct races of Saxon and Briton. The celebration of this melding is one of the most distinctive themes of Arthurian literature in the early nineteenth century. Two poetic conventions are herein employed. There is, firstly, the device of a panorama of British monarchs. Thus, in *Samor*, Merlin is granted by the Archangel a vision of Britain's future greatness:

> Moments were years; and lo, the Island's sons
> Nor Briton they, nor Saxon, nor the stock
> Of those new comers [= Normans], but from each had flow'd
> All qualities of honour and renown,
> The foul dishonest dregs had drain'd away,
> And the rich quintessence, unmix'd, unsoil'd,
> An harmony of energies sublime,
> Knit in that high-brow'd people.   (VIII. 367 – 74)

Similarly, in Lytton's *King Arthur*, the Halls of Time portray under the aegis of Queen Victoria:

---

[105] Line 36; in *Works*, VI.
[106] This topographical concern will be treated at greater length in Chapter 2.
[107] Pennie, v – xvi.

the Cymrian's changeless race
Blent with the Saxon, brother-like; and both
Saxon and Cymrian from that sovereign trace
Their hero line; — sweet flower of age-long growth (VII. lxxx)

This neo-Burkean theme was recognised and applauded by John Forster in his review of Lytton's poem:

Civilization is the theme. But it is the civilization which does not destroy, but incorporates, develops, and advances; in which every period of time has its type and meaning; and where the manhood of the rude ages, the chivalry of those which succeeded, the knowledge of the later, and the poetry in all, are seen in harmonious unison and progress, and developing themselves to a sure and beneficent end.[108]

A second, and local, agency for embodying this promised fusion of the separate and warring races is realised through the effect of romantic love within the poems. Milman's epic includes sub-plots in which the Saxon Abisa has an affair with a British girl, Myfanwy; whilst in Pennie there is an attachment between the Saxon Kenrick and the British Imogenia. Most dramatically, Lytton's Arthur obtains in marriage the Saxon Genevieve, and Lancelot her friend, Genevra. The 'love knots' (XII. cciii) are, of course, conventionally romantic but they are also dynastic in import because:

From Cymri's Dragon England's power shall date,
And peace be born to Cymri from the Dove.
Eternal links let nuptial garlands weave,
And Cymri's queen be Saxon Genevieve! (XII. cxcix)

In line with these dynastic concerns, Arthur's historical setting as partisan fighter is transmuted into that of nationalist leader, in which he subsumes three distinct but interlocked roles. The first is that of monarch, but this is a carefully qualified position. The European conquests vaunted by Geoffrey of Monmouth having been discarded, Arthur remains, legitimately, on the defensive against the invading Saxon imperium. Absolute monarchy, or usurpation, tyranny and despotism, is condemned in the person of Huel (*Dragon King*) or Vortigern and Caswallon (*Samor*), for they overstep their kingly rights by demanding an utter submission to their will from their subjects. Moreover, yielding like Vortigern to an invading usurper is to forfeit popular goodwill; and on this latter is founded a true kingship, since the king should be, and Arthur is, a dutiful guardian leader and protector of the weak: 'We right the balance, if the sword we draw!' (*KA*, VII. xviii). Left to themselves, the plebeians in *Dragon King* would offer a craven surrender to

[108] *Examiner*, 27 January 1849, 52–54.

Cerdic: it is the arrival of Arthur, the 'deliverer of his country' (II. ii. 114), that stiffens their resolve. In the last resort, the king should be prepared to be a 'martyr' for his 'country' (IV. ii. 53 – 54).

The second aspect of this heroic role is that it should defend 'Liberty', for the defence of the native land implies the preservation of 'the noble rights / Of manly freedom' (*DK*, II. i. 87 – 88), 'the steps of freemen' (*S*, VIII. 138), or 'freedom' dearer 'than life' (*KA*, III. iiv). Arthur's association with Liberty seems to have been largely of eighteenth century provenance, and takes two related forms. On the one hand, as military defender of the realm he is a preserver of Liberty in the sense of national independence and self-determination; whilst on the other hand, there are frequent indications that Freedom also represented some measure of safeguarded 'ancient liberties' through a traditional framework of judicial and parliamentary institutions. Accordingly, James Thomson's confident assertion that Britons never will be slaves was given an Arthurian resonance by William Hilton's verse drama *Arthur, Monarch of the Britons* (1759) and by Caesar Morgan's 'The Shrine of King Arthur', both of which made use of an Arthurian past to forecast a future era of patriotic virtue and freedom.[109] In the early nineteenth century works, it is evident from their presented visions of Britain's future monarchs that the keystone of civil development is seen to be a constitutional settlement such as that of 1688, and not a violent revolution, fears of which were widespread in the years after 1815. Merivale, Peacock (in *The Round Table*) and Milman concur in regarding the accession of William and Mary as a necessary culmination in the struggle for British political liberty; whilst Lytton postpones the achievement of 'Crowned Liberty' until the reign of Queen Victoria. For Lytton, also, there are extra dimensions of 'freedom': intellectual, in that the Reformation freed man's mind (VII. lxv), and deeply personal in that an individual is ultimately responsible for freeing himself (X. lxxxix). In political terms, there is significance in that, whereas the villainous Ludovick and Astutio plot and scheme in court chambers, the leaders of the Cymri debate matters in the Council Hall at Carduel. The conference of the British chiefs in *Samor* is termed a 'proud Senate' (II. 80), and the apostrophe to Freedom at the start of Book XII operates upon an extended metaphor whereby Freedom is compared to the sun which lights our 'starlike commonwealth' that is ranged hierarchically downwards from 'golden royalty' to 'plenar and patrician orbs', then to those 'mean lamps / Modestly glimmering in their sphere retir'd' (XII. 1 – 7).

The third tine in the Arthurian trident is Religion: the battle lines being clearly drawn up between Christianity and paganism. Any potential conflict that might have arisen between religious and libertarian goals is circumvented by presenting a liberal and secularised theology. In Milman's *Samor*, as one

---

[109] James Thomson, 'Rule Britannia', in *The Masque of Alfred* (1740); in *The Poetical Works of James Thomson* (1878). *The Poetical Works of William Hilton*, 2 vols (Newcastle, 1775 – 1776).

would expect in a work by the future Victorian Dean of St Paul's, the religious
ambience is dominant, particularly with regard to the refinement of individual
moral sensibility (such as Rowena's pleading for mercy on behalf of Hengist,
or Samor's pity for the dead Abisa), but in spite of the descriptions of
Westminster Abbey, saintly chapels and church altars, advocacy of the
ecclesiastical power is faint-hearted. One extremely telling incident is St
Germain's presence at the Alleluia victory over the Saxons, an event which
represented for Milman the power of faith and prayer. Although his quoted
source is Holinshed, Milman omits all reference (so also does Lytton, who
cites Bede) to the fact that Germain visited Britain in order to eradicate the
Pelagian heresy. Christianity is thus represented by Lytton and Milman as a
non-doctrinal Broad Church. There are good nuns (see Lytton) but priests
tend to be associated rather with paganism, where their influence is immense
and malign: they attempt human sacrifices in all three poems; and Lytton's
ossified Alpine kingdom, 'moulded in antique forms' by 'antique law' and
'religion's . . . awe' (III. cx) is controlled by priestcraft. Into this vacuum left
by the church militant, steps Arthur with numinous power, 'God's elected
Man' (*KA*, XII. cxlii), whom 'the everlasting Lord of Fate / Hath summon'd'
(*S*, X. 210 – 11). Although Pennie pictures him fighting beneath 'St. Mary's
banner' (II. i. 257), wearing a 'holy badge of meekness on his robes' (II. ii.
98), and with a 'Mother of God' oath frequently upon his lips, he is typified
less in explicitly Catholic terms than as a moral exemplar, a prince of chivalry,
with a later avatar in Richard Coeur de Lion. As religion is linked with
freedom and the struggle for national independence (a 'just God . . . sanctions
Freedom's steel', *KA*, XI. clxxiii), the undenominationally secular figure of
Arthur, as agent of a Providential direction of history, becomes an effective
symbol of the harmoniously unified British state of 'A Throne, an Altar and a
Senate House'.

Peacock's interpretation of the past often appears to be in sharp contrast
with that of Milman, Pennie and Lytton: for, feeding off the main tradition,
he offers an antithetical variant. While conscious of the great cultural
differences between historical periods, the view he posits in *The Four Ages of
Poetry* (1820) is cyclic but not progressive: a civilization may follow a typical
pattern of development, but the end yields no necessary improvement, and the
cyclic process may then be repeated. Accordingly, though Peacock seems to
display a distinct favour to Britons over Saxons, the British defeat is not
mitigated or sublimated by an eventual Hegelian synthesis. The 'March of
Mind' is treated ironically throughout: succeeding ages may have brought
their advantages of better 'building, apparel, cookery . . . and wine' (*ME*,
chap. 6), but these advantages have been outweighed by the introduction of
atmospheric pollution, paper credit and an over-complicated legal system. For
Peacock, despite the variations of states, peoples and times, the world had
remained basically very much the same: kings and priests have hypocritically
cloaked their self-interest and called it 'sacred and glorious'; and liberty, in so

far as it has exceeded 'words, words, words', has generally been com-
promised, repressed or abnegated.

As a result of his assumption that the past is roughly commensurate with the
present, Peacock is empowered, like Milman and Lytton, to describe the past
in a later idiom, but his own critique is couched in terms of an alternative early
nineteenth century viewpoint: a philosophical utilitarianism, albeit one
humanely modulated by Peacock. The world of Elphin is thus portrayed in
terms of use: in the novel this is the key concept for evaluation of character,
action and motive.[110] Gwythno and Seithenyn are adjudged failures as they
cannot ensure the stability of the embankment (itself a typical project for
nineteenth century engineering); but Seithenyn achieves some redemption by
his part in the persuasion of Melvas to release Gwenyvar. In this world,
Merlin's magic is reduced to the sending of a relief food hamper to the flood
victims of Gwaelod. Elphin with his Salmon weir is, surely, the most practical
of princes. Moreover, Taliesin's conduct is consistently adroit, and his bardic
powers are put to practical effect in gaining release for Elphin. Maelgon's
punishment (to defray Taliesin's wedding expenses) has, too, an explicitly
fiscal practicality. Arthur's position in this society never achieves the heroic or
semi-divine status conferred by Lytton or Milman, as both religion and
military glory have pejorative connotations for Peacock. But Arthur appears
to much better effect than do the other kings in the novel. As he has often
defeated the Saxons, who are always held in disrepute, he cannot be accused,
like Gwythno, of devoting too much time to harping, singing, feasting and
hunting. Nor can he be tasked, like Melvas, with pursuing purely selfish aims,
for his victories bring a general protection to the British state against the
invader. And, in one important respect, Peacock has deliberately chastened
Arthur's character, by departing from Welsh tradition. Arthur's penchant for
the company of the ladies Indeg and Garwen may suggest a flirtatious
disposition, but the original Welsh triads, which were certainly known to
Peacock, spoke of Indeg, Garwen and Gwyl as 'the three Chief Mistresses of
Arthur'.[111] Peacock may thus be thought to have palliated the amorous
connection. In all, Arthur as preserver of the civilized Roman city of
Caerleon, the organiser of a felicitous Bardic Congress, and the judicious
apportioner of rewards and punishments, appears a remarkably liberal
protector of intellectual and material prosperity; and thus to have pronounced
affinities with the sovereign lauded by Pennie, Milman and Lytton. Peacock's
apparently antithetical approach therefore results in the portrayal of a
complementary heroic figure.

[110] See Marilyn Butler, *Peacock Displayed: A Satirist in his Context* (1979).
[111] See 'Triads of the Isle of Britain: Relating to Arthur', *Cambro-Briton*, 3 (1822), 388. Peacock's
library sale included this work: see A. N. L. Munby ed. *Sale Catalogues of Libraries of Eminent
Persons. Volume I: Poets and Men of Letters* (1971), 163.

Contemporary Relevance

If the past was viewed through nineteenth century eyes and seen as the foundation of modern society or, as in Peacock, a directly comparable image of modernity, then the corollary was that a literary work could, though set in the past, have considerable and intentional reference to the contemporary age.

A deeply felt concern with the present was widely and variously expressed. For Milman, it was Merlin's vision of Britain's future that provided the connection which bound past to present; and his underlying image, as in Wordsworth's *Ecclesiastical Sketches*, is of a river (VIII. 409), implying a natural, crescent and progressive flow, augmented by tributaries. The 'river's name was Freedom' (415); a 'gallant Prince' (418, meaning Charles I) had tried to check the 'powerful stream' (420) but had been opposed by a rebel tide (= Commonwealth) which destroyed 'that fair throne' (423). 'Foamy menace' is again aroused by the dissolute court of Charles II and the Roman Catholicism of James II, but the 'fleet' (449) of William and Mary brought religious sanction to the reformed monarchy. Beside the stream, a Burkean 'Tree' (459) sprang out, 'deep in earth its gnarled roots / Struck down' (461 – 62), and its 'broad branches spread so wide, its shade / Lay upon distant realms' (465 – 66). This growth of the British State and Empire, with 'twin eagles' of 'Victory and Renown' resting in the boughs (478 – 79), shelters a 'Throne, an Altar, and a Senate-house' (488). As the poem was being composed from 1810 to 1818, there is an evident analogy with continental politics: the Bourbons representing 'the slow decay within' (502) which could threaten a state's growth; tyranny as representative of Napoleon; and 'the foreign axe' (502) the French Revolutionary guillotine or the Napoleonic wars.

Many differing emphases may be discerned in the application of Arthurian themes to early nineteenth century politics. The more pessimistic imagined, like Burke, that the age of chivalry was gone for ever, having been replaced by a world of 'sophisters, oeconomists, and calculators'.[112] Looking back on the Middle Ages as golden and lost, David Moir's 'The Decay of Chivalry' (1825) laments that 'The poetry of life hath passed away, / And men become mere citizens'.[113] Neither is any indication given of the viability of a revival when Thomas Hood punningly mourns in his 'Lament for the Decline of Chivalry' that litigants are the only people who now engage 'at tourneys'. As a result

---

[112] *Reflections on the French Revolution*; in *Burke. Select Works*, edited by E. J. Payne, 2 vols (Oxford), II, 89.
[113] Lines 1 – 2; in *Poetical Works of David Moir*, 2 vols (1852).

The bold King Arthur sleepeth sound.
So sleep his knights who gave that Round
Old Table such eclat.[114]

A particularly gloomy outlook is presented in Ord's preface, which reveals his
motives in writing *England*, acknowledging that he 'was first introduced to the
task' by seeing the 'terrible state of insubordination and dissatisfaction' into
which England had 'fallen by a long continuance of seditious and
revolutionary measures, on the part of ministers bred in the school of French
and anti-national politics.'[115] His picture of Arthur's court is correspondingly
idealised: its denizens all handsome, valiant, loyal, artistic and cheerful; their
radiance still enduring in fairy 'halls beyond the morn' where they enjoy a
serene eternity. This is in determinedly stark contrast to the everyday world of
the 1830s, where the 'old heroic times' are dead, tradition uprooted, and
royalty and religion shaken:

> The rascal rebel lingers in our halls;
> The soot-brow'd traitor tramps each pleasant way;
> They seek for other flowers upon the walls
> Than clothe the abbey seams, with gold and purple palls.
>
> Like vipers, they are twined in the grass,
> And hiss at every royal thing of state; . . .
> The air is rank with death: they lie in wait
> Among our palaces, and yell with hate   (87 – 95)

As this poem was issued in 1834, it would appear probable that Ord was
delivering, from an ultra-Tory position, a vigorous polemic against the
passage of the Parliamentary Reform Bill in 1832, and the spread of what he
regarded as radical and populist policies.

Peacock, too, used the Arthurian age as a stalking horse for an onslaught on
certain aspects of his own society. His attacks on contemporary industrialisa-
tion, hard-edge Benthamism, *realpolitik* (see Maelgon's 'Might is Right') and
Tory resistance to a reformed suffrage, as in Seithenyn's defence of his
embankment ('Decay . . . is one thing, and danger is another'), have always
been readily acknowledged, and were apparent to the earliest reviewers:
Literary Gazette remarking with approval that the 'story is of the beginning of
the sixth century; but its application is to the nineteenth'; but *Westminster
Review* objecting to his 'caustic jibe' which insinuated 'the superiority of half-
barbarous states of existence' by 'partially adverting to the evils consequent
upon higher stages of civilisation'.[116] That this radical journal reacted so
sensitively to Peacock's witticisms at the expense of 'political economy' should

---

[114] Lines 13 – 15; in *Bijou* (1828), 81 – 85.
[115] Ord, *England*, I, vii.
[116] *Lit Gaz*, 7 March 1829, 153 – 55. *WR*, 10 (April 1829), 428 – 35.

indicate the manysidedness of Peacockian irony, which cannot be confined too straitly into an anti-conservative mould, despite the attempt by later radicals to confine Peacock in this way. Marilyn Butler, for example, has indicated the close relationship between Peacock's novel and Macaulay's article in *Edinburgh Review* (1827) on the administration of Canning, in which Macaulay describes the French Revolution as a devastating flood.[117] In Peacock's use of the analogy, Teithryn could perhaps stand for the reforming Turgot, the dispossessed Gwythno for the French nobility in exile after the Revolution, and the Tower that succumbed would represent the Bastille. Butler, nevertheless, goes much too far in promoting the *Misfortunes* as a *roman-à-clef*, by suggesting that Gwenyvar represents the 'helpless populace' when she is kidnapped by Melvas, for Peacock's queen ill becomes the role of persecuted Third Estate. Her marital infidelity is indicated by Seithenyn's equivocal oath that the released queen had 'returned as pure as on the day King Melvas had carried her off' (chap. 16). Nor does Gwenyvar appear 'helpless', for she reacts to Gwenvach's sarcasm by slapping the latter in the face, a public humiliation that prompts Modred's enmity, and thus leads to the battle of Camlan.

Contemporary allusions were immediately spotted in Lytton's *King Arthur*. His description of the bravery of Arthur's men in the polar seas, and his consequent homage to 'our England's sons, in the later day' (IX. xvii), was seen by *Literary Gazette* as alluding to 'our present cares about Franklin and Crozier, and the noble daring of Ross (his name should be Arthur) and his gallant companion, Bird'.[118] For *Athenaeum* there could be no doubt that the verses which 'will be most admired and quoted' are those which, in the shapes of the Vandal King Ludovick and his crafty adviser Astutio, represented King Louis Philippe and his minister Guizot.[119] Lytton's confirmation that the latter identifications are correct was given in a letter of 1847 to Forster, noting that the writer was 'particularly anxious' to publish the poem 'as soon as possible', largely because 'if any accident should happen to Louis Philippe . . . one main chance of success would be gone.'[120] In the event, the publication date coinciding with the 1848 Revolution, Lytton wrote to Forster asking him to

> either say something that may claim attention (as a matter still of interest) to the L. Philippe and Guizot passages, or else pass those passages over altogether.[121]

Accommodating himself to this request, Forster's review made no specific reference to French events, but instead stated ambiguously: 'We meet at every

[117] Butler, *Peacock Displayed*, 156.
[118] *Lit Gaz*, 3 February 1849, 76.
[119] *Ath*, 11 March 1848, 262–63.
[120] Letter of 7 November 1847; in *Life of Edward Bulwer*, I, 97.
[121] Letter of 1 March 1848; in *Life of Edward Bulwer*, I, 98.

turn with figures of a modern day, which we laugh to recognise in antique garb.'[122] The *New Monthly Magazine* identified 'the portraits of several living' statesmen: Cymon was a 'sketch' of Lord John Russell; in Geraint was seen the Duke of Wellington ('bending with a world's renown', V. xiv), and the 'ribald scoffer' stood for Cobden.[123] It was, however, the *Sun* which provided the amplest series of decodings.[124] Of these, Palmerston was represented by Aron, the chivalrous Counselling Knight with 'the warm instincts of the knightly heart, / That rose at once if insult touch'd the realm' (vii). The late Lord Durham was identified with Elidir, 'who with eastern hues and haughty brow, / Stern with dark beauty, sits apart' (viii).[125] Anglesey, who lost a leg at Waterloo, was denoted by the Warrior Knight Owaine, the chieftain from Mona who 'survives' though 'scathed by the storm' (xii). An accompanying warrior role is filled by another Waterloo veteran, Hardinge of Lahore (who was also MP for Launceston), who was represented by Cadwr, 'Cornwall's chief' who gave 'Northern standards to the Indian sun' (xiii). Among the Chiefs of Eloquence are found Macaulay (= Drudwas, with his 'pomp of period', xvi), Stanley (= Eliwlod, famed for his aristocratic 'rush of manly sense', xvii) and finally, and most interestingly, Disraeli as Gawaine, with 'careless Cupid's face' and 'arch Mercury's wit', who 'with bland parlance prefaced doughtiest blows, / And mildly arguing — arguing brain'd his foes' (xviii). Significantly, Lytton's heroes are drawn from the ranks of both Whigs and Tories: in effect, by equating the British chieftains with members of the Houses of Parliament, and the Vandals with the French court, Lytton's cyphered representations give further depth to his historico-political allegory, particularly as the vision in the Halls of Time had forecast that the culmination of British history would be achieved in Victoria's 'Crowned Liberty' and Empire 'far outstretch'd along the unmeasured sea' under the shadow of 'that guardian throne' (VII. lxxix). On one of the rare occasions on which Lytton lifts the curtain on the 'People', they are revealed as gloomy, pauperised and famished creatures of the hungry 1840s: 'over fireless hearths cower'd shivering Age . . . / And Youth all labour-bow'd, with wither'd look' (xlii – xliii). Clearly Lytton regards them as the victims of a Benthamite laissez-faire economic system:

> This is the state that sages most approve;
> This is Man civilised! — the perfect sway
> Of Merchant Kings; — the ripeness of the Art
> Which cheapens men — the Elysium of the Mart.   (xlvii)

---

[122] *Examiner*, 27 January 1849, 52 – 54.

[123] *NMM*, 85 (March 1849), 307 – 14.

[124] *Sun*, 22 January 1849, 3. Further confirmation that these personal references were intended by Lytton is provided by a private memorandum at Hertford Courty Record Office (ref. D/EK W21). This collection also includes the manuscript for most of *King Arthur*.

[125] The perfidious 'friend' of Elidir is identified as Brougham by Michael Sadleir, *Bulwer and his Wife: a Panorama, 1803 – 1836*, new edition (1933), 379.

Utilitarianism is satirically ascribed as a suitable philosophy for the heathen Danes, who justify their intended sacrifice of Gawaine on the grounds of

> 'The greatest pleasure of the greatest number.'
> No pleasure like a Christian roasted slowly,
> To Odin's greatest number can be given;
> The will of freemen to the gods is holy;
> The People's voice must be the voice of Heaven.   (VIII. lxx – lxxi)

Rejecting also populist theories, Lytton would, then, advocate a modern Carlylean hero, 'Nature's masterpiece, perfected Man' (XII. clxxvii), as occupant of a guardian throne.

A Second Coming

Contemporary military successes against the French had been celebrated in a number of epic poems, which had thereby raised their British protagonists to the rank of classical epic heroes.[126] Moreover, a tendency developed, in other works, to compare British heroes not only with Achilles and Hector but with the chief figures of medieval romance. These comparisons develop beyond the metaphoric compliment into a gratified awareness of a literal rebirth of a heroic age. In an early instance of this, Horace Walpole's verses (now lost) commemorating Admiral Hawke's destruction of the French invasion fleet in 1759 at the Battle of Quiberon Bay had recalled the days of Arthur and Merlin. On being shown the poem, Lord Beauchamp had then suggested an intensification of Merlin's role as prophet of British grandeur under Queen Elizabeth and her successors.[127] Shortly afterwards appeared Joseph Warton's 'To His Royal Highness the Duke of York' (1761), a patriotic and royalist address which purports to have been written at Winchester where the militia were encamped during the Seven Years War.[128] At night the form of Arthur is seen ('in iron mail / Of ancient guise', 57 – 58) on the towers of what was once his castle. Expressing joy that the modern volunteers should have left their 'pleasant villas, for the din of arms, / And midnight watches in the chilling dew' (67 – 68), he forecasts that the Hanoverian royal brothers will prove

---

[126] See A. D. Harvey, 'The English Epic in the Romantic Period', *Philological Quarterly*, 55 (Winter 1976), 241 – 59; and my 'Epics in the Romantic Period', *Notes and Queries*, 231 (June 1986), 160 – 61.

[127] *Yale Edition of Horace Walpole's Correspondence*, edited by W. S. Lewis, 46 vols (1973 – 1983), XXXVIII, 50 – 51. This poem is not mentioned by Merriman.

[128] On first publication of this poem, the author had been named as Richard Phelps. For attribution to Joseph Warton, see Hugh Reid, 'A Probable Addition to the Poetical Works of Joseph Warton', *Review of English Studies*, 38 (November 1987), 526 – 29. The poem is not mentioned by Merriman.

victorious on land and sea, and give to Albion 'Peace, plenty, power, wealth, liberty and fame' (77). Again, E. Thomas, who was a member of the Society of Ancient Britons, paid tribute in 1782 to Admiral Rodney's victories by claiming that 'Like noble Arthur in the days of yore, / His name [would] be echo'd from each grateful tongue'.[129] During the Peninsular War, such allusions became much more frequent. Felicia Hemans, two of whose brothers were fighting in the Peninsula, records in her poem *England and Spain* (1808) her perception of a progressive tradition of 'Britannia's heroes' living 'from age to age', from the 'painted natives' of the 'ancient days' to the 'manly hearts' of 'these Augustan' times whose recent trophies have surpassed those won by 'doubtful Arthur, hero of romance' (129). Later poets did not, however, downgrade Arthur to the level of doubtfulness, but tended instead to portray Wellington (the former Sir Arthur Wellesley) as the embodiment of a second King Arthur. Thus, an anonymous poem on 'The Battle of Vittoria' apostrophises Wellington: 'In thee, Arthur's chivalry returns; / In thee, her Marlborough's kindred spirit burns'.[130] An epic poem by J. H. Merivale on the romance subject of *Orlando in Roncesvalles* adverted, in a similar manner, to this Wellingtonian renewal of heroic achievement:

> Sleeps Arthur in his isle of Avalon?
> High-favour'd Erin sends him forth once more
> To realize the dream of days far gone,
> The wizard strains of old Caer-merddhyn's lore.[131]

The allusion was detected and quoted by the reviewer in *British Critic*; and to the same year belongs Milman's 'Judicium Regale', an ode 'written after the fall of Buonaparte' and previous to the Oxford visit by the Allied Sovereigns.[132] In this celebration of the French defeat, Wellington's Peninsular campaign is described as shaking 'the base slavery' (260) from Spain: 'And that new British Arthur's virgin shield / Won its rich blazon on Vimeira's field' 261 – 62. Of two poems, also written in 1814, by Sir Hardinge Giffard, the first, titled 'Roncesvalles', draws the parallel, as did Merivale, between the paladin Roland and the modern Sir Rowland Picton, and between

---

[129] 'Briddyn Jubilee, 1782. An Ode', ll. 7 – 8: in *European Magazine*, 2 (August 1782), 153 – 54. The Most Honourable and Loyal Society of Ancient Britons, founded in 1715, aimed to demonstrate the loyalty of the London Welsh to the House of Hanover, and to provide charity to boys of poor Welsh parents: see Meic Stephens ed. *The Oxford Companion to the Literature of Wales* (Oxford, 1986).
[130] 'The Battle of Vittoria', ll. 53 – 54; In *European Magazine*, 64 (August 1813), 146 – 47.
[131] John Herman Merivale, *Orlando in Roncesvalles* (1814), Canto IV. ll. 329 – 32.
[132] *British Critic*, 2 (1814), 264. *Judicium Regale*; in Milman, *Poetical Works*, II.

Wellington and the earlier 'Arthur's glory'.[133] The second poem, 'St Michael's Mount', imagines the guardian angel of the Mount, still 'our long-lost Arthur's guide and shield', looking across to Spain, where the modern British troops display a traditional Christian symbol:

> Thy ruby Cross aloft they raise,
> Thine ancient star of victory;
> They emulate our Arthur's days,
> And Arthur's self again they see.   (25 – 28)

A further example occurs in M. J. Sullivan's 'St Patrick's Day' which enthuses over the awakening of the 'harp of Old Erin' now that Britain can 'boast / Her conquering host / Has vanquish'd what France call'd invincible pow'rs'.[134] Within this context, a reference to 'ARTHUR the Hero that leads them' (10) certainly indicates both Wellington and Pendragon, as does the 'Arthur' chorused by 'all Wales' in Leigh Hunt's 'The Dogs' (1822).[135] In John Hookham Frere's *The Monks and the Giants* (1817), Sir Launcelot replaces Arthur as the ironic point of comparison:

> Sir Launcelot was chief of all the train . . .
> Britain will never see his like again.
> Of all the Knights she ever had the best,
> Except, perhaps, Lord Wellington in Spain.[136]

Eleanor Porden resumes the heroic tone with her 'Ode to the King's Most Excellent Majesty' (1822), which elevates Nelson and Wellington to the British pantheon:

> For he that late her Trident bore,
> And he to whom thy hand her Sword consigns,
> Shall mate with Arthur's peers, and Richard's knights of yore.[137]

More humorously, Percival Leigh's poem *Jack the Giant Killer* makes an emphatic connection between King Arthur and 'Arthur the Second, / As

---

[133] Ambrose Hardinge Giffard, *Verses* (Colombo, 1824).

[134] M. J. Sullivan, 'St Patrick's Day', ll. 5 – 7; in *The Prince of the Lake, or O'Donaghue of Rosse* (1815).

[135] 'The Dogs', ll. 293 – 94; in *The Poetical Works of Leigh Hunt*, edited by H. S. Milford (1923).

[136] Canto I. st. xiii; in John Hookham Frere, *The Monks and the Giants*, edited by R. D. Waller (Manchester, 1926).

[137] Lines 48 – 50; in Porden, *Coeur de Lion*, I.

Arthur of Wellington may be reckoned!'[138] Even as late as 1846, the theme
found very full expression in Rowland Williams's 'The Hall of the Nations'.
Merlin herein reveals that the Hall shelters an international host of former
heroes, and since none has 'surpassed our long-lost Arthur's fame' he sits
above the rest, whilst 'all the wondrous triumphs of his name' are 'high
displayed.'[139] After a lengthy account of European heroes and history,
Williams highlights the Napoleonic wars, when 'as of old, Britannia's Genius
woke, / And sent our second Arthur to the plain' (335 – 36). But, from the
1830s onwards, even though Wellington remained a potent source for literary
inspiration (see Charlotte Bronte's Glasstown hero), it was becoming rarer for
him to be commended for being a second Arthur. Ord, it is true, had
dedicated his second volume of *England* to him as the 'commander, whose
deeds have / tended so much to ennoble the chivalry of modern times; to excite
the old heroic spirit of England'.[140] Nevertheless, and especially in Whig
circles, Wellington's Arthurian connotation was more often the target of
ridicule — a subject which Chapter 3 will resume.

The accession of Queen Victoria in 1837 occasioned a poem by George
Darley which intimated that the new monarch might prove a focus for
Arthurian interest.[141] In this work, King Arthur does not return to earth but
signifies that he is alive and actively benevolent. The harbingers of peace and
'gentle tidings' (15) to the new sovereign are 'wise Merlin's potent Daughters'
(7), the handmaidens of Morgain-le-Fay, who have sailed from the far isle of
Avalon with coronation gifts from their mistress and from 'Pendragon's Son'
(39). Morgain's present is a 'magic Trident, virtue-stored', whilst Arthur
sends 'Caliburn, his enchanted sword' (40). With these bequests is retailed
Merlin's prophecy announcing that they will enable Victoria, 'with grace of
God and her good Cause' (48) to rule the sea and defend the land, for '''tis no
common sword and sceptre / Shall sway futurity' (51 – 52). In retrospect, the
accession had also been hailed by Lytton, whose national prophecy had ended
contemporaneously with the union of the Saxon and British races exemplified
in Victoria: 'Cymri's Daughter on the Saxon's throne'. In the heavens is set a
'rainbow cloud' which 'shall not pass, until, the cycle o'er, / The soul of
Arthur comes to earth once more' (*KA*, VII. lxxxiv).

Paradoxically, as belief in the historical Arthur waned, it became
increasingly possible to predict metaphorically an Arthurian second coming.
Just as a legendary Arthurian age had been employed by Ord as a critical
touchstone by which to evaluate and censure the degeneration of modern

---

[138] *Jack the Giant Killer*, with illustrations by Leech (1843), 53.
[139] Lines 74 – 76; in Goronva Camlan (= Rowland Williams), *Lays from the Cimbric Lyre, with various verses* (1846).
[140] Ord, *England*, II, iii – iv.
[141] G.D., 'Merlin's Last Prophecy', *Athenaeum*, 14 July 1838, 495 – 96.

society, the legend of the Messianic return could be used as a symbol of the need for a radical readjustment of social values. The theme of the Rex Futurus who would relieve Britain in her hour of need was to recur in many poems, particularly in the 1840s. The stock theme that the Arthurian world had entirely disappeared was, for example, to be challenged in an important, but recently ignored, sonnet by a Cambridge poet, Thomas Whytehead. This poem is prefaced by a note acknowledging its source as the Arthurian legend of Ysaie le Triste, which Whytehead had most probably encountered in John Dunlop's *History of Prose Fiction* (1814).[142] In the traditional tale Ysaie, who is the son of Tristan and La Belle Yseult, is instructed by Merlin to proceed to the hermitage of Lancelot so as to be knighted by the great hero. But, on arriving, Ysaie finds that Lancelot is dead and entombed. Nonetheless, an accompanying hermit then raises the lid of the tomb, and dubs Ysaie a knight by using the right arm of the skeleton. Whytehead reshapes this original narrative to his own very different application. In brief, the octet states that one should not assume that chivalry has departed merely because a 'lance and waving crest' are no longer visible, for the chivalrous ideal has been transmuted: the 'skirt of steel' may have been exchanged for a 'studious vest', but the 'old heart' still lives, as does the type of 'knightly vow' which endowed the world with 'lofty deeds', and conferred dignity on 'meanest things'. The sestet then avers that the dead are still 'around' us, and that the past is ours 'as an inheritance to stir / High memories'. Furthermore, from 'truth's romantic shrine' of such fictions, 'Arthur's self' may yet be 'unsepulchred', and knighthood again be derived from 'his skeleton arm'.

The notion that Arthurian chivalry may re-emerge in contemporary guise with a present, rather than merely historical, function recurs in A. J. Beresford-Hope's *Poems*. Ex-Trinity College, Cambridge, and a member of the Young England Group, Beresford-Hope's wish for an Arthurian Revival illustrates a reaction against what was held to be an increasingly mercantile and rationalist culture:

> O for an hour of Arthur to awaken
> High feelings chivalrous, and turn men's minds
> From pelf and politics' engrossing strife,
> To quiet contemplation of old times.[143]

Another poem in this medieval revival, 'A Dream', quotes the final three lines of Whytehead's poem as epigraph, then states that 'Pendragon's son' still 'sleeps in Avalon', with a burnished Excalibur at his side, and that his values are certain to return:

---

[142] 'Deem not the lack of lance and waving crest'; in Thomas Whytehead, *Poems* (1842). See John Colin Dunlop, *History of Prose Fiction*, new edition, revised by Henry Wilson, 2 vols (New York, 1969), I, 214.
[143] 'A Vision of Babylon', ll. 1 – 4; in Alexander James Beresford Hope, *Poems* (1843).

> Again shall chivalry,
>   In rivalry
> Of its old glorious days,
>   O'er Albion blaze
> Its holy banner bright,
> Displayed again in might,
> To cheer our aching sight.

Beresford-Hope proved a true prophet: the matter of what his footnote described as a 'beautiful old belief' would be translated into fact, with the revival of chivalrous values in the nineteenth century.[144]

---

[144] For the revival of chivalry, see Mark Girouard, *The Return to Camelot: Chivalry and the English Gentleman* (1981). Girouard does not, however, include reference to these Arthurian poems by Whytehead and Beresford-Hope.

2

The Topographical Arthur

A corollary of the traditional quest for the historical Arthur was a strong topographical concern, as a chronological placing of the Arthurian era also usually implied a physical location. This topographical perspective represents a second and powerful shaping influence on the ways in which early nineteenth century literature derived and expressed its Arthurian subject.

The attempt to determine the actual Arthurian topography was manifested as early as the ninth century *Historia* of Nennius, which provided a named setting for Arthur's battles, from the first at the mouth of the river Glein to the twelfth at Mount Badon. In contrast to the difficulty encountered by later writers who attempt to relate Nennius's details to later placenames, an instantly identifiable setting is provided in Geoffrey of Monmouth's *Historia*, for Arthur here rules over a conventional medieval Britain, with its well-known towns of London, Southampton, Lincoln and York, or — across the Channel — Paris, Barfleur and Chinon. But besides adopting this orthodox geo-political framework, Geoffrey also provides a distinctive basis for most later Arthurian topography by means of his emphasis on certain key areas. Thus, Merlin's childhood was spent at Carmarthen but he prophesied to Vortigern in Snowdonia, and removed Stonehenge from Ireland: Arthur was born at Tintagel, fought a giant on St Michael's Mount, held a high court at Caerleon, combated Mordred at the river Camel, and was carried from there to the Isle of Avalon. Similarly, all later accounts of the exhumation of Arthur at Glastonbury in about 1190 are ultimately based on Giraldus Cambrensis' two descriptions of the event, in *De Principis Instructione* (c. 1193) and *Speculum Ecclesiae* (c. 1215).

A special interest in visiting, and recording observations on, Arthurian sites is evident as early as the *Itineraries* kept by William Worcester from 1477 to 1480.[1] Noting the ruined state of Castle-an-Dinas and Tintagel, he records

---

[1] *William Worcestre: Itineraries*, edited by John H. Harvey (Oxford, 1969).

that Cador was slain at the former, Arthur born at the latter; near Cirencester he passes 'Grismond's Castle . . . where King Arthur was crowned'; and at Glastonbury he tries to obtain from a monk the 'chronicles and the acts of King Arthur'. Further north, he recalls that King Arthur kept the Round Table in Stirling Castle.

Whereas Worcester's reflections had been made privately in a record not intended for publication, the travels and discoveries of British antiquities which were noted by John Leland were deliberate attempts to preserve the medieval records that were being rapidly dispersed and lost because of the dissolution of the monasteries. Besides being the first 'known modern commentator' to identify Camelot with the Somersetshire village of South Cadbury, he also saw the leaden cross from Arthur's tomb at Glastonbury, and recorded the inscription that he had read on it.[2] Such local detail, which was employed by Leland to provide authenticity in his defence of the historicity of Arthur against the scepticism of Polydore Vergil, was given widespread circulation by being included in Leland's *Assertio Inclytissimi Arturii Regis Britanniae* (1544), a work which was translated into English by Richard Robinson as *A Learned and True Assertion of . . . Prince Arthure* (1582). Glastonbury figures prominently, too, in another first-hand account, William Camden's topographical survey, *Britannia* (enlarged 1607). In addition to quoting Joseph of Exeter's panegyric of Arthur, in Latin and in an English translation, and summarising Giraldus' report of the exhumation, he thinks 'it proper to subjoyn a draught' of the 'Inscription', the only written memorial, he laments, made by the 'barbarity' of the Middle Ages.[3]

The Cornish claim for a major association with Arthur had already been pressed by Richard Carew's *Survey* of the county in 1602. Carew follows the historical tradition by claiming Tintagel as the place of Arthur's conception, and the river Camel as the site of the 'last dismal battle', an assertion which Carew substantiates by reference to local lore and relics: 'For testimony whereof, the old folk thereabouts will shew you a stone bearing Arthur's name though now depraved to Atry'.[4] Carew had already freely alluded to the Arthurian associations of Tintagel in his poem *A Herring's Tale* (1598),[5] and his first-hand knowledge of the site is revealed in the detailed descriptive poem he includes in his *Survey*:

> A bridge these buildings join'd, whom now
>   The fallen cliffs divorce,
>   Yet strengthen'd so, the more it scorns

---

[2] Lacy ed. *Arthurian Encyclopedia*, 335.
[3] William Camden, *Britannia*, translated into English, revised by Edmund Gibson (1722), 80 – 81.
[4] *Carew's Survey of Cornwall, to which are added notes . . . by Thomas Tonkin*, edited by Francis, Lord de Dunsterville (1811), 284 – 88.
[5] Included in Richard Carew of Antony, *The Survey of Cornwall*, edited by F. E. Halliday (1953).

Foes' vain attempting force.
There, cave above, entry admits,
    But thoroughfare denies,
Where that beneath alloweth both,
    In safe, but ghastly wise.   (5 – 12)

Of import too, is Carew's theory, and one which was supported by John Norden's *Description of Cornwall* (1610, published 1728), that the 'submerged' land of Lyonesse lies off the south Cornish coast.[6] Such a location provides, also, the cue for Carew to note that Tristram of Lyonesse appears in Spenser's *Faerie Queene*, from which a footnote then quotes.

It was entirely appropriate for antiquarian topography to adduce so fluently a poetic reference, for poetry in that period would produce two works which had been influenced by, and were to be vastly influential upon, Arthurian topography: Spenser's *Faerie Queene* and Michael Drayton's *Polyolbion* (1612). Spenser's poem makes only a glancing reference to the Welsh locale for Arthur's tutelage:

Under the foot of Rauran mossy hore,
From whence the river Dee as silver cleene
His tombling billowes rolls with gentle rore.[7]

But, for Merlin's cave near Maridunum (the later Carmarthen), Spenser provides an amplified account. Although no cave may now be traced, and the neighbouring river is the Towey not the Barry, Spenser adopts a topographical mode by providing from hearsay an imaginatively detailed itinerary for a supposed intending traveller:

And if thou ever happen that same way
To travell, goe to see that dreadful place:
It is an hideous hollow cave (they say)
Under a rocke that lyes a little space
From the swift Barry, tombling down apace,
Emongst the woodie hills of Dynevowre   (III. iii. 8)

Drayton's topography is, however, immeasurably more inclusive since the *Polyolbion* is a celebration of every British region, wherein a description of natural scenery — and rivers and mountains in particular — evokes a kaleidoscopic series of historical associations. In the opening books, which deal with the western counties, Arthurian allusions are profuse, and take three main forms. There is the material which stems from Geoffrey of Monmouth: Arthur's arms, overseas conquests and the battle at the river Camel; the courts

[6] Carew, *Cornwall* (1811), 6 – 7.
[7] Book I. ix. 4; *The Poetical Works of Edmund Spenser*, edited by J. C. Smith and E. de Selincourt (1912).

at Caerleon and Winchester; Merlin's birth at Carmarthen and his prophecies
at Dinas Emrys. Then, there is the account deriving from Giraldus of how
Henry II heard the Welsh bards harping of Arthur, and the consequent
discovery of the Glastonbury grave. Finally, Drayton records those sites which
preserve their legendary aura. For instance, in Cumberland he observes that
there is 'a little piece of ground, / A little rising bank, which of the table round,
/ Men in remembrance keep, and Arthur's table name.'[8] Accompanying
Drayton's poem in 1612 were 'illustrations' (i.e. notes) by John Selden.
Although their author distances himself from the 'too hyperbolique' stories of
Arthur, the annotations are continually directed towards placing Arthur
within a topographical setting marked with some precision. Thus, 'Neere
Camel about Camblan, was Arthur slain by Mordred, and on the same shore,
east from the river's mouth, borne in Tintagel Castle'.[9] Regarding the site for
Badon, Selden remarks, on the evidence of a manuscript of Gildas which
Camden had noted, that this location is 'Baunsedowne in Somerset (not
Blackmore in Yorkshire, as Polydore mistakes', IV, p.87). He cites John
Stow's description of the reputed Arthur's Round Table at Lansannan,
Denbighshire (a spot previously visited by Leland) 'on the side of a stonie hill
. . . with some xxiv. seats unequal' (IV, p. 89); and, whilst following Leland's
and Stow's reports, recounts in his most celebrated passage, with memorably
sober delineation:

> By South Cadbury is that Camelot; a hill of a mile compasse at the top,
> foure trenches circling it, and twixt every of them an earthen wall; the
> content of it, within, about xx. acres full of ruines and reliques of old
> buildings. (IV, p. 68)

The Antiquarians

Provided with such a firm basis, Arthurian topography continued to maintain
its attraction for the later seventeenth, and eighteenth, century, and
powerfully interacted with the continuing concern for a historical Arthur. In
the wake of an additional impetus from the Medieval Revival in the mid-
eighteenth century, the antiquarian zeal for describing extant relics from the
Middle Ages found a fit subject in two matters that were of great relevance to
Arthurian studies: the Round Table at Winchester, and Arthur's Glastonbury
grave. In both instances the influence of Thomas Warton is apparent.

---

[8] Song 30. ll. 331 – 33; in *The Works of Michael Drayton*, edited by J. William Hebel, 5 vols
(Oxford, 1961), IV.
[9] Drayton, *Works*, IV, 19.

Warton's *Description of the City, College and Cathedral of Winchester* was an account of a city with which he had close personal ties. He may have attended the College there: his brother Joseph did, and went back later as Headmaster. The *Description* surveys the 'Ruins of a strong and stately Castle which according to Tradition was built by King Arthur Ann. Dom. 523'.[10] Inside this structure is found 'what is commonly called King Arthur's Round Table', an attribution which extends back to Caxton's edition of Malory, and to John Hardyng's *Chronicle* (c. 1464). Acknowledging that the table could not be as old as was claimed, Warton, however, presses the case for a moderate antiquity, and he notes that the names inscribed on the frame are those of Malory's knights (p. 9). In a sonnet published in 1777, Warton returns to the subject but has either modified his opinion as to the table's provenance, or has suspended his incredulity for the course of the poem, for this treats of the table as definitely 'Old Arthur's Board', with its 'Druid frame' and fading 'British characters'.[11] Even though later historical scholarship, in the form of Milner's *History of Winchester*, would date the table as being no older than King Stephen's reign, the Arthurian associations proved extremely resilient and steadily recurred throughout the early nineteenth century, on account of the strength of local and literary tradition.[12] The *New Monthly Magazine*, for example, in an article on 'Winchester' chooses as epigraph Drayton's lines: 'Great Arthur's seat ould Winchester prefers, / Whose ould Round Table yet she vaunteth to be hers.'[13] A William Hone *Yearbook* carried a comparable account, quoting from Drayton and the Percy ballad of 'Sir Lancelot', and providing the complete sonnet by Thomas Warton.[14] A very similar article, using identical quotations, appeared in *Saturday Magazine* the following year.[15] The more exacting scholarship of Alfred John Kempe, in *Gentleman's Magazine*, appears to accept the dating proposed by Milner, and offers an alternative suggestion that it might have belonged to one of those processions of archers popularly termed 'Arthur's show' (as in Shakespeare's *Henry IV, Part 2*).[16] Kempe repeated the contents of this essay in the paper which he wrote for the Second Congress of the British Archaeological Association, which met at Winchester in August of that year.[17] In the following month, the same city

---

[10] Thomas Warton, *A Description of the City, College, and Cathedral of Winchester* (1750), 7.
[11] 'On King Arthur's Round Table at Winchester'; in *The Three Wartons*.
[12] Milner, *Winchester*, II, 171 – 72.
[13] *NMM*, 8 (May 1823), 225 – 26.
[14] 'King Arthur's Round Table', *Yearbook* (1832), 81 – 82.
[15] 'King Arthur's Round Table at Winchester', *Saturday Magazine*, 2 (18 May 1833), 188 – 89.
[16] 'Notes on the Table called Arthur's Round Table, preserved at Winchester', *GM*, NS 24 (September 1845), 236 – 40.
[17] See *Transactions of the British Archaeological Association* (1846), 473 – 76; and W. Harrison Ainsworth, 'The British Historical Society at Winchester', *New Monthly Magazine*, 2nd Series, 75 (September 1845), 110 – 16.

hosted the Annual Meeting of the Royal Archaeological Institute, at which another leading antiquary, Edward Smirke, delivered a lecture on the Round Table, an object which, he suggested, may have been derived from the medieval symbol of mutability, the Wheel of Fortune.[18]

The second main subject of topographical enquiry was the search for Arthur's grave at Glastonbury. Complementary to the topographical concern of Warton's poem 'The Grave of King Arthur' was the scholarly appreciation, investigation and recording of Gothic buildings. Such interests were advanced by Francis Grose's series of *Antiquities*, and since Glastonbury Abbey featured therein as a notable ruin, Grose's historical account of the building inevitably touched upon the question of Arthur's tomb, and thereby included a summary of Giraldus' testimony.[19] Other works revealed a similar tendency. John Collinson's county history had included in its Glastonbury section a summary of Arthur's interment, quoted Latin and Middle English elegies on the hero, and *à propos* of South Cadbury cited Drayton on Arthur's Camelot.[20] Grose's account was, in turn, taken up and expanded by the Reverend Nightingale, who follows Leland and Selden on the Arthurian connections of South Cadbury, and eulogises Arthur as 'one of the greatest and most accomplished monarchs that ever governed any kingdom'.[21] A further massive survey of architectural antiquities was undertaken by John Britton, and in his section on Glastonbury (1814) the usual account is drawn from medieval sources.[22] In about the same year, George Cattermole had been placed as an artist with Britton, and he later executed drawings for the series.[23] This training would, therefore, seem to have heavily influenced Cattermole's later stylistic treatment and his choice of an antiquarian subject in such a painting as his *King Henry II discovering the relics of King Arthur* (see Chapter 1). The same year saw the publication of the work richest in Arthurian associations, the Reverend Richard Warner's *An History of the Abbey of Glaston*. Warner's interest in the historical Arthur had already been evinced in his *History of Bath* which contains a generous tribute to Arthur as victor of Badon, a location

---

[18] 'On the Hall and Round Table at Winchester', *Proceedings of the Annual Meeting of the Archaeological Institute* (1846), 44 – 67. His lecture formed the subject of 'The True History of the Round Table at Winchester', in *Sharpe's London Magazine*, 5 December 1846, 90 – 92.

[19] Francis Grose, *The Antiquities of England and Wales* (1777 – 1787), V, 31.

[20] John Collinson, *The History and Antiquities of the County of Somersetshire*, 3 vols (Bath, 1791), II, 72, 240 – 42. Collinson's Middle English excerpt ('But for he skaped ye batell ye wys . . .') is taken from *Arthur*, Longleat MS 55. A. Crocker had recently produced an edited form of this early fifteenth century verse chronicle: see 'King Arthur, A Poem', *Gentleman's Magazine*, 68 (September 1788), 820 – 21; (November), 1012; Supplement, 1172 – 75.

[21] Joseph Nightingale, *A Topographical and Historical Description of the County of Somerset* (1801), 367, 278, 503 – 04.

[22] John Britton, *The Architectural Antiquities of Great Britain*, 5 vols (1807 – 1826), IV, 189 – 91.

[23] See *DNB* entry for Cattermole.

equated with Bath by Warner.[24] In his history of Glastonbury, Warner acknowledges that there are 'few credible facts' in 'an almost impenetrable cloud of fiction', and he offers his opinion that 'there were more Arthurs than one'. Nevertheless, the tenor of his work is far from sceptical: on the contrary, it is pregnantly evocative of many facets of Arthurian legend. He commends highly, and quotes in full, Warton's poem on the grave; he supplies from the Latin text of John of Glastonbury a narrative of Arthur's seeing the infant Jesus transformed into the Real Presence at Mass in the oratory of St Mary Magdalene at neighbouring Beckery; and, however sceptical Warner may have been of this legend, it is nonetheless recorded.[25] Continuing this topographical interest in the Abbey, William Phelps acknowledges Warner's work, summarises Giraldus, provides a biography of Arthur, quotes from Enderbie the laws of the Round Table, and reproduces a vignette illustration of the Winchester Round Table.[26]

The continuation and dissemination of such material was thus effected by those county historians whose work formed a bridge between the national historians and more local topographers. Not only did they continue to provide resumés of the Galfridean core (as in Borlase 1769, Whitaker 1771, Collinson 1791), but a provincial partisanship appears to have encouraged a strong readiness to stress the local setting, to present events from a regional angle, and to bear witness to local legend even though remaining sceptical as to its veracity. Moreover, the erudite allusiveness of the works invariably entails quotation from medieval, or later, Arthurian texts, or translations from the Welsh, besides the introduction of much important detail. John Whitaker's *The History of Manchester* is a notable example which, in addition to reproducing the Camden drawing of the Glastonbury cross, supplies an ample historical account drawn from the usual authorities, and attempts to provide modern sites for Nennius's twelve battles. Frequent reference is made to Malory's *Le Morte Darthur*, and an intensely North-Western interpretation is provided for much of the Arthurian narrative: the encounter between Sir Lancelot and Sir Turquin is placed within Lancashire, and Whitaker adduces his awareness of the Tamworth Castle wall-painting of this episode.[27] A similar incident is

---

[24] Richard Warner, *The History of Bath* (Bath, 1801), 41.

[25] Richard Warner, *An History of the Abbey of Glaston* (Bath, 1826), 160 – 71.

[26] William Phelps, *The History and Antiquities of Somersetshire*, 2 vols (1836 – 1839), I, 402, 535 – 36; II. 46 – 47.

[27] Whitaker, *Manchester*, II, 31 – 72. Warton had related that:

in the hall of the castle of Tamworth, in Warwickshire, there is an old rude painting on the wall, of Sir Launcelot du Lake, and Sir Turquin, drawn in a gigantic size, and tilting together . . .

Observations on the Fairy Queen of Spenser, second edition, 2 vols (1762), I, 43. As this painting was whitewashed over in 1783, it is no longer visible: see Roger Sherman Loomis and Laura Hibbard Loomis, *Arthurian Legends in Medieval Art* (1938), 5. Sir Turquin's local fame persisted in

narrated by William Hutchinson, who alludes to a local tradition that the cave of Tarquin was situated on the bank of the river Eden: a reference that occasions Hutchinson's quotation of the entire Percy ballad of 'Sir Lancelot du Lake'. He also records that the 'circular entrenchments' at Penrith are called 'Arthur's Round Table', and that in Carlisle there used to stand 'an antient building, called Arthur's chamber, taken to be part of the mansion house of King Arthur'.[28] This Penrith earthwork had previously been noted by Joseph Nicolson and Richard Burn, who state that 'the country people call it king Arthur's round table'.[29] A comparable feature would be recorded by John Hodgson when visiting the Kielder region of Northumberland in August 1814, as in Kennel Park there was a 'circular ditch' with 'seats cut out of the earth', which was also 'called Arthur's Round Table'.[30] As David Williams's *The History of Monmouthshire* made clear, archaeological finds at Caerleon had already revealed that what was locally known as King Arthur's Round Table had, in fact, been a Roman amphitheatre. Conceding, too, that the story of Uther Pendragon and Igraine had been copied 'from the amour of Jupiter with the wife of Amphitryon', Williams nevertheless follows Carte in accepting the historicity of Arthur, and would locate the ancient British court at Caerleon. Williams then lists the twelve 'Articles of the Round Table', and summarises the Melwas affair, the perpetrator of which he makes a 'Northern Prince' who disguised himself as 'a satyr' to frighten the female attendants of the Queen, before carrying off the latter.[31] Similarly, the stories of Elphin and Taliesin are amply recounted, with a wealth of related modern translations from Welsh poetry, in Samuel Rush Meyrick's history of Cardigan, whilst Robert Williams supplies a slender account of the same events in his history of

---

Lancashire into the nineteenth century: the 'remains of his castle being shown to this day', according to J. Roby, *Traditions of Lancashire*, 4 vols (1829 – 1831), I, 18. Roby devotes fifteen pages to the retelling of the Turquin and Lancelot story.
[28] William Hutchinson, *The History of the County of Cumberland*, 2 vols (Carlisle, 1794 – 1797), I, 292 – 93, 329; II, 606. Details of the Penrith earthwork ('which the country people term Arthur's round Table'), and of Pendragon Castle ('Prince Euter Pendragon is of doubtful existence, but is said to have died by treachery . . .') are also given in Hutchinson's earlier work, *An Excursion to the Lakes, in Westmorland and Cumberland* (1774), 83 – 85, 191 – 93. His description of the earthwork is quoted verbatim in John Housman, *A Descriptive Tour, and Guide to the Lakes* . . . (Carlisle, 1802), 68 – 70.
[29] Joseph Nicholson and Richard Burn, *The History and Antiquities of the Counties of Westmorland and Cumberland*, 2 vols (1777), I, 414.
[30] James Raine, *A Memoir of the Rev. John Hodgson*, 2 vols (1857 – 1858), I, 147. Although this site is not mentioned by Snell, Chambers, Ashe or Fairburn, I am informed privately by Brian Long (of the Kennels, Kielder) that the Arthurian associations of the earthwork are still sustained by some local inhabitants.
[31] David Williams, *The History of Monmouthshire* (1796), 47, 82, 93 – 95.

Aberconwy.[32] The most profuse treatment of the Welsh Arthurian locale is given by Peter Roberts, who devotes fifty pages to the biographies of Merlin and Arthur.[33] Here, Caerleon is selected as the seat of Arthur's court, the neighbouring village of Bassaleg as the birthplace of Merlin, and Bardsey as the island to which Merlin conveyed in a ship of glass the Thirteen Treasures of Britain.

The pervasive Cornish associations with Arthur are maintained by the scholarly Richard Polwhele. As early as 1786, Polwhele had, in his 'Ode written in a Picture Gallery', lamented the departure of the chivalrous 'worthies of old time', and those

> Tales of KALIBURN that mow'd
> A million down, where slaughtering ARTHUR strode;
> Who, though strong by magic steel'd,
> Fell a gigantic corse, and shook all Camlan's field.[34]

In *The History of Cornwall*, Polwhele judiciously distinguishes the attractions that Arthur has had for different groups of readers.[35] 'For such memoirs of the British hero as deserve the notice of the antiquary, the historian and the philosopher', the reader is referred to Whitaker's *History of Manchester*, a version that Polwhele evidently regards as authoritative; but he also supplies a 'curious legend of Arthur such as will, doubtless, amuse the common reader'. There follows a seven page footnote based on Hals, which provides an extended account of Uter's love for Gothlois's wife, Igerna. Intensely aware of the 'legendary personages crowding' around him, Polwhele also relates the Cornish reputation of Merlin as a prophet; and frequently incorporates the traditional literary allusions, quoting a Joseph of Exeter couplet on 'Dundagell', giving Walter Scott's summary of the Tristrem and Isonde story, and, because of Geraint ap Erbin's connections with the South-West, including the complete translation by William Owen of the Welsh elegy on Geraint, a figure whom Polwhele treats as probably synonymous with the 'knight so celebrated in the romances of Brittany by the name of Geron the Courteous'. Moreover, Polwhele reveals himself as an early investigator of Malory's *Le Morte Darthur*, on account of which activity the antiquary Carlyon had referred Walter Scott to him when Scott was preparing his edition of *Sir*

[32] Samuel Rush Meyrick, *The History and Antiquities of the County of Cardigan* (1810), 52, 54, 58 – 62, 65 – 66, 70 – 72. Robert Williams, *The History and Antiquities of the Town of Aberconwy* (Denbigh, 1835), 5 – 6.

[33] Peter Roberts, *The Cambrian Popular Antiquities* (1815), 57 – 80, 81 – 109.

[34] Lines 45 – 48; in Richard Polwhele, *Poems, chiefly by Gentlemen of Devon and Cornwall*, 2 vols (Bath, 1792), II.

[35] Richard Polwhele, *The History of Cornwall*, 3 vols (Falmouth, 1803), II, 2 – 10; III, 40 – 42, 91 – 96; and *passim*.

Tristrem (1804).[36] In his own investigations, Polwhele is evidently concerned with Cornish links with the Tristrem legend, but his principal aim is to defend his native county's knights from the insinuations of cowardice that Gibbon had derived from his earlier reading of Malory. Polwhele's verdict is forthright:

> Gibbon was a mere coxcomb in history . . . Can a sarcasm in a mere romance be admitted as sufficient evidence in the case before us?
>
> (I, p. 94)

Carew's *Survey* was reprinted in 1723 and 1769, and was republished in 1811, with the inclusion of Thomas Tonkin's notes edited by Francis, Lord de Dunstanville. It was succeeded by Fortescue Hitchins's *The History of Cornwall*, which follows Whitaker's evaluation of the admixture of the fabulous in Arthurian history, but assumes an essential core of truth in the story: indeed, he claims to 'prove' the great antiquity of Tintagel by noting that it was the birthplace of the 'renowned hero, Prince Arthur' about the year 500.[37] A ten page summary of Arthur's achievements is incorporated, derived largely from Giraldus, Selden and Leland, and eight lines are quoted from Drayton on Arthur's death at Camelford. Nonetheless, Hitchins contrasts Malkin's Welsh findings with English scepticism on the subject of Merlin:

> With us indeed, the predictions of Merlin have ceased to gain credit, and his magical power has lost all its influence. But in Wales, the 'enchantements of Merlin' suffer no diminution from the lapse of time, or the defects of probability. (I, p. 396)

Davies Gilbert's *The Parochial History of Cornwall* was founded on 'the manuscript histories of Mr Hals and Mr Tonkin', but Gilbert's own glosses are extremely sceptical as to the historicity of Arthur: he retained, he claimed, 'the fabulous history . . . with feelings similar to those which induced the Greeks to dwell on the twelve labours of their Hercules, or the Scandinavians to recount the exploits of Odin'.[38] Nevertheless, despite regarding Arthur as a mainly mythological hero, Gilbert records in great detail the legends narrated by earlier chroniclers. Thus, there is a birth at Tintagel (I, p. 323); an Arthurian court at 'East or West Camelot near Cadbury, Wilts' (I, p. 337); a final battle near Camelford (Carew's account of the Atry stone is cited, II,

---

[36] See Edgar Johnson, *Sir Walter Scott: The Great Unknown*, 2 vols (1970), I, 211.
[37] Fortescue Hitchins, *The History of Cornwall*, edited by Samuel Drew, 2 vols (Helston, 1824), I, 205, 389 – 99.
[38] Davies Gilbert, *The Parochial History of Cornwall*, 4 vols (1838), I, 341 – 42.

p. 403); and a grave at Glastonbury. In the presentation of Hals's account, which in turn is drawn from Upton, there is particular concern with the exact heraldric blazon of Arthur's shield, which is given as: 'A field Vert, a plain cross Argent; in the dexter quarter the image of the blessed Virgin Mary, holding the image of her blessed Son in her right hand . . .'(I, p. 326).

In general, then, although their role has been largely ignored by modern literary critics, the county historians played a significant role in preserving the traditional accounts of the historical Arthur, and their local patriotism tended to highlight, wherever possible, the bonds with a regional topography.[39]

The Guides

Complementary to the local historians' work as maintainers and transmitters of an Arthurian tradition was the role played by travel writers in the early nineteenth century. A greatly increased propensity for travel, particularly in Wales, was nurtured by the romantic taste for picturesque mountain scenery, and facilitated by the improved standards of the newly macadamised roads. An increasing affluence among the middle classes, endowed with ample funds and leisure for travel, provided a buoyant market for travel literature, especially when handsomely illustrated. That this movement was directed towards Wales and not to the Alps was partly due to the Continent's being virtually closed to British tourists during the Revolutionary and Napoleonic era, but the taste for Wales was also the outcome of the eighteenth century revival in Celticism, which had drawn attention to the non-classical cultural heritage of northern Europe. These travel writers were not, of course, primarily pilgrims to Arthurian sites, not all writers made even a perfunctory allusion, the Arthurian references are frequently merely incidental and their significance for the Arthurian Revival has been largely ignored by modern critics; but there was, in general, a marked interest in antiquities, as evinced by monuments or by local legend, and in the course of discovering and relating these the Arthurian story makes very regular appearance. Thus, tours in Wales often include descriptions of Caerleon, Carmarthen and Dinas Emrys; and in Cornwall, of Tintagel and Camelford.[40]

---

[39] The only just acknowledgment of their role is by Annette B. Hopkins, 'Ritson's *Life of King Arthur*', *Publications of the Modern Language Association*, 43 (1928), 251–87.
[40] Numerous landscape painters had toured Wales and made visual records of their itineraries; and the dramatically precipitous location of Tintagel, uniting as it did ruined castle, desolate headland and heroic legend, provided a powerful attraction for a succession of artists (including

The high level of antiquarian scholarship noted in the work of county historians was often matched in these guidebooks. Thomas Pennant, for example, whose tours set a high standard as early model, was a leading scholar of his day. Though disparaged by Bishop Percy, Pennant's *A Tour in Scotland* (1772) was defended by Dr Johnson, who had first-hand experience of the route taken: 'He's a Whig, sir; a sad dog. But he's the best traveller I ever read; he observes more things than anyone else does.'[41] On passing Wigan in Lancashire, Pennant notes that the neighbouring 'little river Douglas' was 'immortalised by the victories of our Arthur over the Saxons on its banks', an attribution for which he cites Henry of Huntingdon as authority.[42] In the Lake District he sees the 'circle called Arthur's round table' (I, p. 256) and, over the Scottish border, he narrates the philistine destruction of 'Arthur's Oven' by a local landowner who wished to construct a mill-dam with the materials (I, p. 242).[43] Born in Flintshire, and later resident in Holywell, Pennant shows himself deeply read in the literature of the Welsh Revival during his *Tour in Wales* (1784). For example, at the ruins of Dinas Emrys he retells (from Nennius, Drayton and Powel's notes on Giraldus) the story of Merlin (the son of a 'noble Roman' and a 'Vestal') and his prophecy to Vortigern.[44] Quoting Richard Williams's translation of a medieval Welsh poem on Myfanwy

---

Turner) and formed the subject of illustrations by Farington, Harding and Creswick for topographical studies of Cornwall. Occasionally, a painting would demonstrate by its title the Arthurian associations of the scene. Samuel Howitt's watercolour *King Arthur's Castle, Tintagel, Cornwall* (in the V & A) was executed in c. 1785 – 1790; Samuel Prout exhibited at the RA in 1808 his *Arthur's Castle at Tintagel*; and in 1821 T. H. Williams produced his lithograph of *King Arthur's Castle, Tintagel*. In 1843 William Collingwood's *Tintagel, the Birthplace of Arthur* was exhibited at the RA; whilst in July 1848 Samuel Palmer, then travelling through Cornwall, sketched 'the ruins of the castle in which King Arthur was born'. This sketch was later worked up into his watercolour *King Arthur's Castle, Tintagel, Cornwall*, and exhibited at the Royal Society of Painters in Watercolours in 1849.

[41] James Boswell, *The Life of Samuel Johnson*, 2 vols (1906), I, 197.

[42] Thomas Pennant, *A Tour in Scotland*, fourth edition, 2 vols (Dublin, 1776), II, 14.

[43] The antiquarian Richard Colt Hoare also noted during his 1800 tour the 'circular entrenchment, vulgarly called Arthur's Round Table': see M. W. Thompson, *The Journeys of Richard Colt Hoare through Wales and England 1793 – 1810* (Gloucester, 1983), 136. The rotunda near Falkirk, named Arthur's Oven (or O'on), had long been known to antiquaries, and Stukeley had published an engraving of it in 1720: see Kenneth A. Steer, 'Arthur's O'on: A Lost Shrine of Roman Britain', *Archaeological Journal*, 115 (1958), 99 – 110; and Iain G. Brown, ' "Gothicism, ignorance and a bad taste": the destruction of Arthur's O'on', *Antiquity*, 48 (1974), 283 – 87.

[44] Thomas Pennant, *A Tour in Wales*, edited by John Rhys, 3 vols (Caernarvon, 1883), II, 342 – 43).

Vechan, he traces in his footnotes the relationship between the Welsh forms of 'Garwy' and 'Trystan' and their Malorian counterparts, Gareth and Tristram (I, p. 362).

Possessed of comparable learning, and devoting much greater attention to Arthur, was Richard Warner, to whose histories of Bath and Glastonbury reference has already been made. He was, besides, a considerable traveller. *A Tour through the Northern Counties* led him to Penrith where he saw Arthur's Round Table, an ancient curiosity which he considered to be 'of Druidical antiquity'.[45] *A Walk through Wales* (1798) took him to Dinas Emrys where he referred to the story of Merlin and Vortigern, and to Conway, where he quoted twenty lines from Warton's 'Grave'.[46] There is in *A Second Walk through Wales* an especially detailed description of an Arthurian Caerleon, which draws on Drayton, and quotes in full Percy's ballad 'The Boy and the Mantle'.[47] *A Walk through some of the Western Counties* takes him to Glastonbury, and this provides him with the occasion for further quotation from Warton's 'Grave'.[48] In his *Tour through Cornwall* he includes Tintagel, where he quotes a dozen lines from the same Warton poem, and Camelford where he notes the tradition of the battle against Mordred.[49] Nor was Warner an isolated figure. Seven pages of John Evans's *Letters written during a tour through South Wales* are devoted to a summary of Arthur's biography, which admits Milton's and Lyttelton's doubts, but generally supports Arthur's historicity, on the evidence of the Welsh bards.[50] Similarly, Edward Donovan's *Descriptive Excursions through South Wales and Monmouthshire*, despite finding many fables 'inexplicable', nevertheless accepts a basically historical Arthur, and devotes ten of its Caerleon pages to a summary of the Arthurian dicta of Coxe, Whitaker and Turner.[51]

In addition to the influence exerted by the historians, there was another, and more powerful, background stimulus exerted by the topographical poetry

[45] Richard Warner, *A Tour through the Northern Counties of England, and the Borders of Scotland*, 2 vols (Bath, 1802), I, 86.
[46] Richard Warner, *A Walk through Wales*, second edition (Bath, 1798), 124 – 25, 154.
[47] Richard Warner, *A Second Walk through Wales* (Bath, 1799), 21 – 22.
[48] Richard Warner, *A Walk through some of the Western Counties of England* (Bath, 1800), 28 – 30.
[49] Richard Warner, *A Tour through Cornwall* (Bath, 1809), 335 – 36, 342. Twelve lines from Warton's 'Grave' are quoted, too, by F. W. Stockdale on his visit to Tintagel: see his *Excursions in the County of Cornwall* (1824), 111.
[50] John Evans, *Letters written during a tour through South Wales* (1804), 45 – 52.
[51] Edward Donovan, *Descriptive Excursions through South Wales and Monmouthshire*, 2 vols (1805), I, 113 – 23; II, 205.

of Drayton and Spenser. Travel writers who visited Carmarthen or the springs
of the river Dee commonly quoted the Spenserian stanzas on Merlin's Cave in
'Dynevowre' (see Manners, Donovan, Howells, Roscoe, and Beale) or the
account of Arthur's being reared by Timon at the foot of Mt Aran, or
'Rauran', (see Thomas Evans and George Nicholson).[52] Complementarily, a
visit to Dinas Emrys almost invariably adduced Drayton as source for this
being the place where 'Prophetic Merlin sate, when to the British king / The
changes long to come auspiciously he told' (Song 10. 14 – 15) — see Pennant,
Bingley, Gastineau, Wright, Roscoe and Parry.[53] Travellers further afield
could cite foreign authorities. As Anna Eliza Bray (the sister of Alfred Kempe)
remarked in her letters writter during a French tour, the Castle of Auray was
said by Froissart to have been originally erected by King Arthur; and she
observed, too, that 'many buildings in Brittany . . . bore the name of that
hero for their founder'.[54]

One distinctive trait of Celtic landscapes was the widespread occurrence of
Arthurian placenames: only the Devil, in fact, has more sites named after
him. Not only was the traditional Galfridean etymological derivation of
Carmarthen from Caer Merddin (= Merlin) generally heeded, but a
succession of prehistoric monuments and natural features attracted the
attention of the tourist. One such site was Arthur's Stone in the Gower area,
which was visited in 1811 by the antiquary Alfred Kempe. He believed it was
a Druid altar, and later reported his observations in *Archaeologia* and again in
Gentleman's Magazine.[55] Thomas Evans in his *Walks through Wales* remarks that
near Cader Idris is 'the supposed chair of Arthur'; in Carmarthenshire he
comes across the 'Bwrdd Arthur, or Arthur's Tables . . . circular stone
monuments'; and in Glamorgan he sees 'Arthur's stone' said to be 'fixed

[52] John Henry Manners, *Journal of Three Years Travels through Different Parts of Great Britain in 1795,*
1796, 1797 (1805), 115. Donovan, *Descriptive Excursions*, II, 205. William Howells, *Cambrian*
Superstitions (Tipton, 1831), 78 – 83. Thomas Roscoe, *Wanderings in South Wales* (1837), 189. Anne
Beale, *The Vale of the Towey* (1844), 39 – 40. Thomas Evans, *Walks through Wales*, second edition
(?1815), 100. George Nicholson, *The Cambrian Traveller's Guide* (Stourport, 1808), 26.
[53] Rev. W. Bingley, *North Wales*, 2 vols (1804), I, 377. Henry Gastineau, *North Wales Illustrated*
(1830). G. N. Wright, *Scenes in North Wales* (1833), 67. Thomas Roscoe, *Wanderings and Excursions*
in North Wales (1838), 148. Edward Parry, *Cambrian Mirror*, second edition (1846), 226.
[54] Anna Eliza Bray, *Letters written during a Tour through Normandy, Brittany and other parts of France, in*
1818 (1820), 240.
[55] Alfred John Kempe, 'Arthur's Stone', *Archaeologia*, 23 (1831), 420 – 25. 'On the Cromlechs
and British Monuments of Cornwall', *GM*, 103 (January 1833), 13 – 14.

there by that hero'.[56] The same stone was visited by the author of the *Cambrian Directory* (1801), and by Benjamin Heath Malkin whose *The Scenery, Antiquities and Biography of South Wales* also describes Merlin's Bridge near Milford Haven, another Arthur's Stone (Maen Arthur) in Cardiganshire, and an account of Sir Gawaine's Chapel in Pembrokeshire, a legendary site that can be traced back to William of Malmesbury.[57] That these Arthurian associations were widely known is suggested by the fact that Edwin Pugh deliberately departed from his main route through North Wales in order to see Arthur's Round Table in 1816.[58] The blasé admission by the Reverend Newell that he did not 'toil up the mountain Cwm Bryn' to see King Arthur's Stone indicates that such efforts had, in fact, become regular tourist attractions.[59] In like manner, William Howells claims to eschew a hackneyed theme: 'The traditions of Beth Celert, Arthur's Chair, and a few others, as they are generally known, I have thought proper to withhold.'[60] Even when pursued, such expeditions could turn out disappointingly. John Henry Manners observes that, because 'somewhere in the woods' about Carmarthen there was 'supposed to be the famous cave of Merlin, the Enchanter', many had searched for it 'but as yet it has not been found'.[61] On ascending Dinas Emrys, Richard Fenton complained that he had been unable to locate much evidence of earlier encampments:

> The area at top, which Pennant talks of to have appeared to him, must have been the effects of Merlin's wand, or to have been concealed from me.[62]

Nevertheless, this fascination with seeking out Arthurian localities betokens a widespread acquaintanceship with the legend. That claims for Arthurian loci were so frequently and variously made is implied, too, by Pedestres' ironic comment on the early history of Sidmouth:

> When this remarkable place was founded, or by whom, it is somewhat difficult to determine. It was not a Roman station. King Arthur never took refuge in it in the days of his troubles.[63]

[56] Evans, *Walks through Wales*, Part I. 202; Part II. 99, 125, 129.
[57] *The Cambrian Directory*, second edition (Salisbury, 1801), 31. Benjamin Heath Malkin, *The Scenery, Antiquities and Biography of South Wales* (1804), 364, 489, 528, 552–58, 589.
[58] Edwin Pugh, *Cambria Depicta: A Tour through North Wales* (1816), 37.
[59] Robert Hazell Newell, *Letters on the Scenery of Wales* (1821), 48.
[60] Howells, *Cambrian Superstitions*, 154n.
[61] Manners, *Journals*, 114.
[62] Richard Fenton, *Tours in Wales 1804–1813*, edited by John Fisher (1917), 221.
[63] 'Pedestres', *A Pedestrian Tour of thirteen hundred and forty seven miles through England and Wales*, 2 vols (1836), I, 46.

Besides memorialising the extant monuments of Celtic culture, these travel writers were conscientiously intent on furnishing evidence of local legendary beliefs. Being at Camelford in 1801, Adam Clarke, the Wesleyan preacher and antiquarian, inquired of the local population as to where tradition said the battle had been fought. He was conducted by an 'intelligent friend' to see 'what is still called Arthur's Tomb-stone'.[64] Having narrated the conventional accounts by Geoffrey of Monmouth and Giraldus, Clarke proceeds to decipher the inscription, which he reads as 'Latin hic jacet filius magni arturi', and which he translates as 'Here lies Latin, the son of Arthur the Great' (p. 76). During his visit to Carmarthen in 1798, Warner recorded that one of Merlin's predictions was still 'floating in a traditional form amongst the inhabitants'.[65] This relic of ancient wisdom vouched that Carmarthen would be 'destroyed by an earthquake, and the place it stands on be converted into a vast lake' when a bull should 'walk to the top of the church.' At Caerleon, Warner observed that a 'tradition' of Arthurian 'revels' still existed in the town; and one public house displayed a sign portraying a 'military figure, intended to represent King Arthur, and subscribed with the following lines:

> 1200 years and more are pass'd
>   Since Arthur ruled here:
> And that to me once more he's come
>   Think it not strange or queere.
> Though o'er my door, yet take my word,
>   To honour you he's able;
> And make you welcome with good Ale,
>   And Knights of the Round Table.   (p. 22)

To indicate the existence of a legend did not, of course, bind the narrator to a belief in its authenticity: indeed, the narrative tone is generally one of ironic amusement at the credulity of the local denizens. For instance, William Coxe grants that 'the natives of Caerleon . . . point out the remains of the Roman amphitheatre, under the name of Arthur's Round Table', but he declines to accept any historical foundation for this 'legend'.[66] Parochial pride, probably allied to the hope of fiscal return, was also displayed at Tintagel. As Polwhele comments, in spite of the 'more rigid' historians who have 'actually doubted' the existence of Arthur,

> the village historian, conducting us to the castle, points out with confidence the bed on which he slept, the hall in which he feasted, and the pathway to his church.[67]

---

[64] *The Miscellaneous Works of Adam Clarke*, 12 vols (1837), XI, 69.
[65] Warner, *Second Walk through Wales*, 255.
[66] William Coxe, *A Historical Tour in Monmouthshire* (1801), 92–94.
[67] Polwhele, *History of Cornwall*, II, 2.

In contrast, the guide adopted by John Evans attempted to distance himself from such credulity:

> Down Temple-street our Ciceroni shewed what is vulgarly called Arthur's round table. But with a sneer, that intimated he was not the dupe of such idle stories, and in an authoritative tone of voice that demanded submission to all he was going to say, he observed, 'Gentlemen, this is the spot where once stood a beautiful temple of Diana'.[68]

A year later, Edward Donovan heard the 'current tradition' that Arthur and his two thousand knights 'sunk into the abyss of the earth, in the midst of . . . jovial feastings.' Arthur was then 'conveyed unhurt to fairyland'.[69] At Carmarthen, a local shepherd boy pointed out to the same writer 'Merlin's grove', and a nearby cavity, representing in 'general belief' Merlin's Cave (II, p. 205). Nor were these legends confined to the British mainland, for Anne Plumptre found evidence in Brittany of a belief that Merlin had been born in 'the isle of Sein, a little islet off the western coast', and 'according to some traditions' he was still alive, 'enclosed in a tree somewhere thereabouts by the power of a greater enchanter than himself'.[70]

The persistence of local legends was attested by a correspondent in *Gentleman's Magazine* who complained of a specific instance of 'popular ignorance' he had encountered at Newport.[71] Enticed by a board inscribed 'Here is to be seen the tomb of King Arthur', he entered a 'humble cottage' where he was shown a skeleton in a stone coffin, and the handle of a large vessel with the letters L.A.S. stamped upon it. The custodian, 'an old dame', informed him that these meant 'Lord Arthur Sovereign', and that she had bought the coffin in Gloucester for £16! Local knowledge could also prove very superficial, as William Howitt discovered on his visit to Tintagel, for although a 'troop of lads' readily volunteered the information that it was 'Prince Arthur's castle' they were unable to supply any further details of the hero.[72] Nevertheless, at this surface level the traditions appear to be endemic. Thus, Thomas Roscoe remarks of Merlin's Hill that 'near the brow is an opening in the rocks, which the country people still credulously show as the place in which

[68] Evans, *South Wales*, 39 – 40.
[69] Donovan, *Descriptive Excursions*, I, 114.
[70] Anne Plumptre, *A Narrative of a Three Years' Residence in France*, 3 vols (1810), III, 187.
[71] D., 'Tomb of King Arthur', *GM*, NS 1, (February 1834), 176.
[72] William Howitt, 'A Day-Dream at Tintagel', *Athenaeum*, 18 July 1835, 545 – 47; and 25 July 1835, 569 – 70. Reprinted in William Howitt, *Visits to Remarkable places*, 2 vols (1840), I.

the seer practised his incantations'.[73] And for Cornwall, as Cyrus Redding records, 'in the traditions of the country, King Arthur is fresh in renown'.[74] So it was, too, in parts of Brittany. T. Adolphus Trollope reports that a 'tradition of the peasants' spoke of an Arthur's Camp, and these same people 'firmly believed' that Arthur would return 'at some future period to rule again over his faithful Celts on either side the Channel'.[75]

Indicative of a split between intellect and fantasy, which paradoxically leads to a symbiotic relationship between fascination and disbelief, an interest in the currency of traditional legend is accompanied by a belief in the power and value of the human faculties variously denoted as 'imagination' and/or 'fancy'. In this manner, even though the case for an historical Arthur may be forfeited, he is evoked instead as a symbol of man's poetic imagination which can, through association with certain scenery or buildings, establish a connection with the past, and then re-create that past anew. At Caerleon, for instance, John Evans thinks that 'it would be impossible for a mind alive to recollection to pass Caerleon, without recurring to the days, when lived that celebrated subject of British prowess and valour, King Arthur'.[76] With greater intensity, Edward Donovan perceived at the same site that

> sportive fancy, unrestrained by authority, and priding in her own delusions, would fain arouse the slumbering spirits of romance: — would conjure us the shades of an immortal Arthur, and his splendid train of heroes, to revel in the place once celebrated for their presence.[77]

Whilst Donovan exerts some restraints on this 'fancy' and the 'idle notion and fable' of an Arthurian translation to fairyland, he still provides a 'factual' study of his hero's career. The antiquarian Warner, who ironically detected that Camelford 'exhibits no heroes or patriots now', nevertheless saw that 'every feature' connected with Tintagel Castle 'is formed to foster the flights of fancy'; and in his introduction to the castle's history he deliberately suspends any latent power of disbelief, in favour of a mood of imaginative reverie.[78] He thus addresses his supposed reader:

> You, I presume, together with all our heretic antiquarians of the present day, are sceptical as to the existence of this hero; but we, not to miss the magical effect that imagination might throw over such a celebrated scene, determined to 'hold each strange tale devoutly true', which monkish writers or poets had handed down of this ancient assertor of

---

[73] Roscoe, *South Wales*, 189. Roscoe's *Wanderings and Excursions in North Wales* contained a ten page summary of Arthur's history.
[74] Cyrus Redding, *An Illustrated Itinerary of the County of Cornwall* (1842), 36.
[75] T. Adolphus Trollope, *A Summer in Brittany*, edited by Frances Trollope, 2 vols (1840), II, 83 – 86, 172 – 75.
[76] Evans, *South Wales*, 45.
[77] Donovan, *Descriptive Excursions*, 114.
[78] Warner, *Tour through Cornwall*, 335.

British liberty. As we approached its venerable ruins, we conjured up all the visions of its ancient magnificence, its martial splendour, and festal gaiety; its round table begirt with many a hero bold.

The Miltonic phrase is apposite, and the frequency with which quotation is made from the poetry of Spenser, Drayton or Warton is significant, for the literary tradition is thus adduced as co-inspirer of the Arthurian myth. A tendency to see landscape largely in terms of a literary Arthurian world is demonstrated by Thomas Price's 'A Tour through Brittany' in a considerably heightened state of literary awareness:

> The wood of Brocéliande, it is true, though still in existence, no longer displays those waving honours which distinguished it in the days of Merlin, and the voice of that magician is now but seldom heard within its precincts: the mouldering turrets of the Joyeuse Garde no longer echo the acclamations of the tournament: the *Dame du Lac* has drawn closer round her the veil of secrecy which envelopes her abode; and the fountain of Baranton has ceased to obey the accustomed spell.[79]

Against Price's elegiac sense of loss is, however, offset the lasting influence which the age of chivalry has achieved: for its 'style of thought and tone of sentiment' has encouraged a modern literature from Shakespeare to Scott that has awakened 'playful fantasies', 'mysterious gloom' and a 'due estimation of the female sex'. Even more literary than Price's is the popularising belle-lettrist pilgrimage which William Howitt undertook in his 'A Day-Dream at Tintagel' and which achieved a wide circulation by being printed in the rapidly expanding *Athenaeum*.[80] Howitt quotes from Milton, Warton, *Sir Launfal* and Percy, and evidently knows the plot of Chrétien's *Yvain*. As is suggested by his use of literary rather than historical citation, Howitt's intention is to evoke an atmosphere of wild landscape and the court of the 'morning star of chivalry', as the visitor passes with imaginative re-creation into the 'very land and times of old Romance'. This poetic world, with its architecture, pageantry, minstrelsy, feasting and enchantment, has been the stimulus for all later human nobility and altruism; and it represents values which Howitt compares favourably with the 'bald-spirited' utilitarianism of his own age. Another, and very detailed, account of 'A Trip to Tintagel' appeared in *Cambridge University Magazine*. Freely adducing historical authorities from Nennius to Sharon Turner, and employing the customary quotation on Tintagel from Warton's 'Grave', the article provides a description of the 'wreck of ages' and 'nature in her grandest and most awful form', then develops its main theme which is to contrast the richness of the past with an

---

[79] Thomas Price, 'A Tour through Brittany', *Cambrian Quarterly Magazine*, 3 (1831), 9–10.
[80] For *Athenaeum*, see Alvin Sullivan ed. *British Literary Magazines: The Romantic Age, 1789–1836* (Greenwood, Conn., 1983), 21.

ultimate human transience.[81] Parallel to this account, which makes use of
Tintagel as an introductory frame for a homilectic meditation, is Coventry
Patmore's article on Malory, which initially presents a pictorial image of the
promontory of Tintagel 'hard by the dirty town of Trevena'.[82] A description
that is evidently drawn from personal experience ('we grew giddy and sick to
see the precipices on either side of us, and were glad to crawl, on all-fours,
back to safer footing') leads into an extensive survey — scenic, geological and
economic — which provides Patmore with an initial topographical focus with
which to begin his sympathetic critical study of *Le Morte Darthur*: a romance
work is thereby lent the sanction of authenticity:

> This is the site, these are the ruins of the Castle of Tintagil, wherein the
> chaste Igraine, who had been conjured by Merlin into the arms of Uther
> Pendragon, bore unto him the renowned Prince Arthur.[83]

Imaginations that had been reared on Arthurian romance found an
unexpected pleasure in discovering, like T. Adolphus Trollope in his *A Summer
in Brittany*, that fiction could have a local habitation and a name:

> Here places and names surround us, with which the romances of the
> round table have made us familiar, but to which Fancy has assigned a
> locality in fairy-land rather than in any veritable portion of the earth's
> surface.   (II, p. 83)

A comparable sensibility pervades Cyrus Redding's *Illustrated Itinerary*, where
'Imagination' recalls the 'potent hero of the west' (p. 37). Less concerned with
'truth' than with the 'pleasure of fiction', Redding's account is evocatively
atmospheric in tone. Like Francis Bacon, he accepts the reasonableness of the
claim for Arthur's historicity, but Redding's Arthur is the hero less of the
historians than of the troubadours, the 'bards of Italy', and the minstrels of
the North. Consequently, Redding conveys the elegiac ambience of a Tintagel
where sunken musical bells may be heard offshore, the same 'which some said
had tolled for King Arthur as he was borne a corpse from the field of blood
near Camelford'. This is a conjectured scene over which Redding lingers:

[81] T. V. W., 'A Trip to Tintagel', *Cambridge University Magazine*, 2 (1843), 365 – 73.
[82] Coventry Patmore, 'Arthur and his Knights of the Round Table', *Lowe's Edinburgh Magazine*, I
(May 1846), 417.
[83] Other travellers whose visits to Tintagel had explicit Arthurian connotations included Robert
Southey (December 1836), Barclay Fox (August 1841) and Charles Dickens (October-November
1842). See *Selected Letters of Robert Southey*, IV, 483; *Barclay Fox's Journal*, edited by R. L. Brett
(Totowa, New Jersey, 1979), 242 – 43; and *Letters of Charles Dickens*, edited by Madeline House,
Graham Storey and Kathleen Tillotson: *Volume III, 1842 – 1843* (Oxford, 1974), 358n, 414n,
416. This visit to Tintagel is reflected in Dickens, *A Child's History of England* (1852), which
regards the history of King Arthur with a non-committal cautiousness, but refers to the Cornish
claim for Tintagel: 'there are very ancient ruins, which the people call the ruins of King Arthur's
Castle' (chap. 2).

Here fancy nurses her day dreams of what has been in story, and further depicts the British hero borne back from Slaughter Bridge, mortally wounded, the tears of beauty unavailingly shed for him, the mournful countenances of his warriors, and the last moment when he rendered up his soul to God.   (p. 38)

Insistently literary, too, is Louisa Costello's *The Falls, Lakes and Mountains of North Wales*. Reporting 'Welsh traditions' that there was to be found in Snowdonia the 'famous Grotto' which Merlin constructed for love of the 'fairy Viviana, or the White Serpent', Costello whimsically suggests that:

The voice of the mighty master may . . . be frequently heard here amongst the hollow rocks, reverberating along the mountains in thunder, and bewailing his weakness in yielding to the force of beauty.[84]

Moreover, she playfully indulges the spirit of fancy by advising her readers on the benefits accruing from intrepidity:

Whoever has courage to enter a black cavern nearly on the top of Snowdon, may, by searching far enough, discover the golden chair which Merlin concealed there from the Saxons, and the jewels and money which still lie scattered in heaps around.

Thus, although a strictly historical authenticity was more rarely vouchsafed to Arthur, local topography continued to provide a focus for Arthurian legend, whether stemming from folklore or literary creation. The various interactions between these forces were to have a profound effect on the development of the Arthurian Revival.

Topographical Poetry

In the second half of the eighteenth century, there had developed an increasing inter-relatedness between poetry and topography. A number of factors were contributory. Besides a Rousseau-ist yearning to return to a pure primitivism which was to be found on the wilder edges of civilised society, there was also the new-found attraction of exploration and discovery of territory, particularly the untamed. Again, the relics of Gothic architecture so frequently sought out provided not only a spatial novelty but also added a fourth dimension, the entry to a vista of the past, especially of the Dark and Middle Ages. Additionally, a concern with particularity, with the idiosyncratic quality of

---

84 Louisa Stuart Costello, *The Falls, Lakes and Mountains of North Wales* (1845), 123.

loci, and with the immediacy of inspiration, encouraged the naming of places, with the result that a great number of poems take their titles, and their themes, from a visited location. Within this context of named areas, not only do Arthurian allusions abound, but major treatments of the material also tend to be given a determinedly topographical orientation.

In the course of describing a landscape, writers occasionally drew attention to the special features of Arthurian interest. An early example had occurred in Edward Davies's poem *Chepstow* (1784), which had alluded to the Brecknock Hills where 'the Cambrian swain' could quaff his ale and breathe 'untainted air', high on the 'summit of King Arthur's Chair'.[85] A formidably antiquarian work with more footnotes than poetic text, Richard Llwyd's *Beaumaris Bay* annotates a mention of the nearby Din Sylwy as 'one of the several places still called by the name of Arthur's Round Table, Bwrdd Arthur'.[86] In a later verse narrative, 'The Cambrian Legend of St. Keyna and Cadoc', the heroine flees from an arranged marriage with a Welsh prince, by escaping to 'Cader Arthur's awful height', the same locality as in Davies's poem but given its Welsh name.[87] Its English appellation was restored in John Lloyd's 'Drugarn, or the Druid's Cairn', which claimed that it was not 'strange' that 'fond superstition' had sought to endow 'Arthur's beacon chair' with the qualities of the 'loved lost chiefs of old'.[88] Attention to such local features was prominent, too, in Walter Scott's early work, where they are used to endow landscape with a richly historical, and human, depth. Of the city of Stirling in *The Lady of the Lake* (1810) a footnote refers to the 'romantic legend which connected Stirling with King Arthur', and avers that 'the ring within which jousts were formerly practised, in the castle park, is still called the Round Table'.[89] In *The Bridal of Triermain* (1813), Henry the page rides past 'red Penrith's Table Round, / For feats of chivalry renown'd' (I, vii), an event which is of dramatic moment in the narrative, because it prefigures the major Arthurian action that is to unfold, for Henry is shortly to hear from Lyulph a 'mystic tale', handed down from 'Merlin's age'. In the novel *Waverley* (1814) there is introduced a like antiquity. Echoing the chivalric resonances of Edward Waverley's adolescent imagination is the description of the Baron of Bradwardine's courtyards wherein stood 'a tun-bellied pigeon-house, of great size and rotundity, resembling in figure and proportion the curious edifice called

---

[85] Quoted in Garlick and Mathias eds, *Anglo-Welsh Poetry*, 96.
[86] Richard Llwyd, *Beaumaris Bay, a Poem with Notes, Descriptive and Explanatory* (Chester, 1800), 6n, 7n.
[87] M., 'The Cambrian Legend of St. Keyna and Cadoc', *European Magazine*, 62 (September 1812), 201.
[88] John Lloyd, *Poems*.
[89] Canto VI. st. xxviii. n; in *The Poetical Works of Sir Walter Scott*, edited by J. Logie Robertson (1904).

Arthur's Oven', the Roman building near Falkirk, to which Pennant and other guides had called attention.[90]

Stonehenge was also to feature within an Arthurian aura, for widespread popular legends, which generally stem from Geoffrey of Monmouth, attributed to Merlin its transportation from Ireland.[91] Once again, a Warton poem provided a later focus, as his sonnet on 'Stonehenge' had considered the possibility of Merlin's aid in the erection. A conjecture that 'Merlin's self' had been responsible recurs in an anonymous *Stonehenge. A Poem.*[92] Moreover, the choice of Stonehenge as subject for the Oxford University Poetry Prize in 1823 provided occasion for a spate of such allusion. In February of that year, *Gentleman's Magazine* devoted a few pages, 'at the request of an Oxford Correspondent', to the consideration of the 'probable origin and purposes of this extraordinary monument'.[93] After employing Warton's sonnet as epigraph, *GM* supplies a summary of all contending theories, and incidentally alludes to Merlin's participation. The prize was won by Thomas Salmon, whose poem evoked the 'mystic horrors' of the spot: 'Here wizard Merlin, where the mighty fell, / Waves the dark wand, and chaunts the thrilling spell.'[94] This poem was accorded considerable publicity, as *GM* printed it in full in June 1823, Llewellyn Prichard included it in *The Cambrian Wreath*, and it was also reprinted in the 1839 edition of *Oxford Prize Poems*. Nor was attention confined to Salmon. *GM* printed at the end of 1823 an anonymous poem on the same subject, which again alluded to the speculation 'that at Merlin's voice, by sorcery made, / Uprose the vast stupendous Colonnade'.[95] The Reverend Cornwall, too, included a 'Stonehenge' among his *Miscellaneous Poems*, a work also in heroic couplets, and containing a similar acknowledgment of the role that 'legends tell of Merlin's magic pow'r' since the 'stupendous fabric' was obviously the product of 'a mightier hand' than the averagely human.[96] And although Charles Hoyle does not include a Merlin reference in his 1828 sonnet upon 'Stonehenge', his companion sonnet on the comparable megaliths at Avebury declares that the antiquity of these lies much further back than the times of 'Uther'.[97]

---

[90] Walter Scott, *Waverley*, chap. 8; in *Waverley Novels*, 47 vols (Edinburgh, 1901 – 1903). All quotations from Scott's novels are taken from this edition.
[91] See, for example, the mid-eighteenth century story that Merlin employed the Devil to take the stones from Ireland where they stood in an old woman's back garden: John Wood, *Choir Gaure* (1747), 73 – 75; quoted in Christopher Chippindale, *Stonehenge Complete* (1983), 40.
[92] *Stonehenge. A Poem, Inscribed to Edward Jerningham* (1792), 3.
[93] *GM*, 93 (February 1823), 127 – 30.
[94] Thomas Stokes Salmon, *Stonehenge; A Prize Poem* (Oxford, 1823), ll. 29 – 30.
[95] 'Stonehenge', *GM*, 93 (1823), ii.
[96] Ebenezer Cornwall, *Miscellaneous Poems*, second edition (Havant, 1828).
[97] 'Avebury', *GM*, 102 (May 1832), 452. This poem was signed 'C.H.'. I assign it to Hoyle on account of its subject, style, and the fact that it is addressed 'Overton, Wilts', Hoyle's home at the time.

From the 1790s there was a steady pattern of allusion to Arthurian legend in
the work of many poets who toured the western counties and made poetry out
of their travel experiences. An eminent forerunner of this type is William
Sotheby, whose poetical tour refers at Caernarvon to 'Merlin's mystic verse',
and, whilst at Llangollen, apostrophises the river as: 'Pure Dee! swift-swelling
forth from Raran hoar / Where Arthur listened to the wizard's lore.'[98] To this,
he adds a note on his allusion to Spenser's *Faerie Queene* (I. ix). Edward
Hamley, who had been born at St Columb, narrated how on revisiting
Cornwall he felt the attraction exerted by 'Tintaggel's ruin'd seat' which

> Might stay the curious pilgrim's feet,
> Scatter'd on the jutting mound,
> For mighty Arthur's birth renowned.[99]

In his landscape poem 'Ode to Plynlymmon Hill' Joseph Sterling, too,
represents himself 'stretch'd by the spring, beneath a spreading beech', a
vantage point from which he can see and hear the former British heroes who
haunt the mountain's upper slopes. Here, 'illustrious Arthur, with his
diamond shield,' (a footnote acknowledges a Spenserian echo) laments over
later Cambrian defeats but takes pride in the enduring fame of his knights
(Launcelot, Tristram, Gawain and 'chaste Galahad' are named), for, as
another note indicates, there is 'a tradition among the Welch that Arthur is
still alive.'[100] Merlin's Hill in Carmarthenshire was climbed by John Penn,
and he composed a sonnet to record the event, in which he describes the vista
that Merlin would have seen, alludes to Merlin's seduction by the Lady of the
Lake (a footnote quotes Spenser), reflects on Merlin's 'godlike gifts' of
prophecy, and commends to a later sceptical age the moral value of the
perennial truths that Merlin uttered.[101]

Robert Bloomfield, who spent ten days visiting the Wye in 1807,
memorialised the occasion in *The Banks of the Wye*. Although his footnotes
indicate that he consulted acknowledged antiquarian and travel books such as
Coxe's *Monmouthshire*, Heath's *Excursion down the Wye*, and Jones's *History of
Brecknockshire*, he did not draw any explicitly Arthurian material from them;
but his poem reveals that the Wye region was suggestive to him of Arthurian
legend, and he lauds, in the area about Monmouth, the fame that Arthur had
derived from Geoffrey's work:

---

[98] 'Llangollen', ll. 137 – 38; in *Tour through Part of Wales* (1794).
[99] 'On Revisiting Cornwall'; in Edward Hamley, *Poems of Various Kinds* (1795); reprinted in
Poetical Register, 5 (1807), 350 – 54.
[100] Joseph Sterling, *Odes* (1794). This poem is not mentioned by Merriman.
[101] 'Sonnet Written on Mount Merlin in Wales, 1796'; in John Penn, *Critical, Poetical and
Dramatic Works*, 2 vols (1796 – 1798), I. The poem is not mentioned by Merriman.

Soon round us spread the hills and dales
Where Geoffrey spun his magic tales,
And called them history. The land
Whence Arthur sprung, and all his band
Of gallant knights. Sire of romance,
Who led the fancy's mazy dance,
Thy tales shall please, thy name still be,
When Time forgets my verse and me.[102]

A stronger candidate than Bloomfield for oblivion was a minor Sheffield poet, Marmaduke Middleton, whose travels had taken him through Glastonbury, where the traditional allusions are woven into his verse:

Four Christian centuries scarce their course had run,
Ere from the earth to rise yon pile begun,
In which, if legendary tales we trust,
Some mighty ashes mingle 'dust with dust',
Where sainted Joseph rests, and Arthur there,
'Tis said, was carried on funereal bier.[103]

This glancing account of 'legendary tales' received fuller treatment by two other poets who knew the area extremely well. The first of these was William Lisle Bowles, who was born of Wiltshire stock, and had been educated at Winchester when Joseph Warton was Headmaster (Bowles later wrote an elegy on him), and at Trinity College, Oxford, when Thomas Warton was in residence as a Senior Fellow. Bowles then returned as a clergyman to Wiltshire, completing a topographical study of Lacock Abbey (which also alludes to Merlin's connection with Stonehenge), whilst his poetry would include both long poems on a particular local site (*Banwell Hill*, 1829) and shorter occasional pieces such as his *Sonnets written chiefly during various journeys* (1797).[104] A much later poem, 'Glastonbury Abbey and Wells Cathedral', points a moralistic opposition between the true religion practised at Wells, which has not abandoned the 'word' of God, and the physical ruin that has befallen Glastonbury as a result of its former ecclesiastical corruption.[105] A sign of temporal decay is that 'even the mouldering shrine is rent away, / Where in his warrior weeds the British Arthur lay' (17 – 18). A footnote indicates that 'part of a sculptured lion remains'. As its subtitle indicates, the poem was 'written after viewing the ruins of the one, and hearing the church service in the other'. After personally inspecting the spot, Bowles makes

---

102 Robert Bloomfield, *The Banks of the Wye* (1811), ll. 441 – 48.
103 Marmaduke Middleton, *Poetical Sketches of a Tour in the West of England* (Sheffield, 1822), Part III. p. 66.
104 William Lisle Bowles, *Annals and Antiquities of Lacock Abbey* (1835), 61n.
105 William Lisle Bowles, 'Glastonbury Abbey and Wells Cathedral', *Gentleman's Magazine*, 95 (July 1825), 70; reprinted in *Friendship's Offering* (1826), 64.

apparent that his finding of the foot of a sculptured lion corroborates Leland's account of there having been 'Duo leones sub pedibus Arthuri'. It is also pointed out that 'the masonry over the sacred well, discovered by Mr Warner, is eminently beautiful'.

Bowles's allusions are further developed in the Arthurian section of Christopher Cookson's long poem *Glastonbury Abbey* (see Chapter 1), which testifies to a Wartonian influence by being written in octosyllabic couplets, by echoing Warton's descriptive style, and by offering a footnote testimony to 'Warton's beautiful lines on the exhumation'. In comparison with the religious purity of Wells (372n), Glastonbury's 'pomp' and 'Popery' are again admonished; and the date of the poem suggests that it should be read as a warning against an incipient Catholic Emancipation. Nevertheless, Cookson derives from Warner's *History of the Abbey of Glaston* an account that Warner himself had summarised, from John of Glastonbury's *Chronicle*, of a vision that King Arthur had at the neighbouring hermitage of St Mary Magdalene at Beckery. In this first modern poetic version of the tale, an angel bids Arthur to worship at dawn in the Magdalene's oratory. On doing so, he is overcome by repentance, and is granted a vision of the Virgin and Child, but then he sees the Child sacrificed upon the altar:

> No *emblematic* Host he lies,
> Of *real* flesh the sacrifice —
> There they partook of carnal food,
> And drank *indeed* the Saviour's blood   (477 – 80)

Immediately after this, the Child springs back unharmed into the Virgin's embrace. Apparently embarrassed at repeating a legend concerning the Real Presence in the Mass, Cookson moves rapidly on to deplore 'superstition' ('each vain unhallow'd charm, / The nurse's tale, the babe's alarm') and he adverts to the ruined tomb of Arthur with its mutilated lion (a footnote mentions Leland) as appropriate conclusion for worldly pride (488n).

The Abbey of Glastonbury also provided the sole stimulus for the Arthurian allusions in the poetry of Henry Alford. His links with the region were close: he was descended from a Somersetshire family of clergymen, of whom many had lived at Curry Rivell, a dozen miles from Glastonbury. Although born in London and receiving his early education at Charmouth in Devon, he had transferred at fourteen to Ilminster Grammar School (about twenty miles south of Glastonbury) and at sixteen had written a poem on the neighbouring great house, Burton Pynsent. A Wartonian influence may also be detected, for he learnt in November 1826 'a piece of Warton's "Pleasure of Melancholy" ', and in the previous August he had been at work upon a 'poem of the Crusades', a subject already treated by Warton.[106] During the Easter vacation

---

[106] *Life, Journals and Letters of Henry Alford*, edited by his Widow [Fanny Alford] (1873), 21, 26.

of his third year at Cambridge (i.e. 1831), he spent a few days' holiday in the West Country, when his journal records a view from Cheddar 'all over Sedgmoor, Glastonbury, and Bridgewater' (p. 69). On a Long Vacation tour in Somerset the following year, he composed a number of poems which, very probably, included his sonnet on Glastonbury, his 'Ballad of Glastonbury', and a relevant section of his long reflective poem, *The School of the Heart* (1835). All three are concerned, to varying extents, with the Arthurian legend, and it is noteworthy that Alford's poetry nowhere else treats this subject: his Arthur is thus totally confined within a Glastonbury context. Not only is he so circumscribed, the importance of his role is, in each instance, similarly delimited. In the 'Sonnet XIV. Glastonbury', Alford esteems Arthur for being 'the flower of knightly chivalry'. Nevertheless, neither his 'holy relics' nor the architectural splendour of the Abbey building, with its 'ancient towers / And shafts and clustered pillars', can obscure what is for Alford the chief attraction of the place: that Christianity first took root here in England. A comparable evaluation and subordination of Arthur is rehearsed in *The School of the Heart*, wherein the pacific sleep of the 'righteous souls' after death is held to surpass the legendary slumbers in Lemnos's cave of sleep, or that of Sarpedon's 'ambrosial trance', or

> the charmed slumber of that British king
> Resting beneath the crumbled abbey-walls
> In the westward-sloping vale of Avalon   (Lesson Sixth. 340 – 42)

There is, though, an ampler and more sympathetic treatment of Arthur in 'The Ballad of Glastonbury' (see Chapter 1), where the description is explicit: the introductory note describes Arthur as 'glorious', and quotes the Latin inscription from the Glastonbury cross. Sleeping in a 'charm' as he is carried on his funereal bier, he is deemed 'the flower of knights and lords', and the liturgical diction of Alford's eulogy accords him the veneration due to a saint. However sanctified though, he epitomises only one aspect of Glastonbury's history as, for Alford, the prime event remains the missionary arrival of St Joseph of Arimathea. Alford's later career as a churchman would account for his subsequent neglect of an Arthur whom he had tended to regard as inferior to the more orthodox exponents of Christian piety, but it is possible that Alford's lifelong removal from Somerset thereafter would also have contributed to this neglect, for his Arthurian reference seems to have been stimulated chiefly by these local and specific impulses.[107] His own affection for the Abbey is marked as he reveals a determined concern with authenticity of description: his introductory note explains, for example, his own accuracy in terming the autumnal colours of 'the mingled blossoms of heath and furze' as

---

107 A much later visit to Cornwall again furnished him with the occasion for Arthurian allusion. A letter written in 1868 at Tintagel notes that he is 'far from all railways', and in 'the enchanting abode of King Arthur and Sir Galahad and the rest':.*Life*, 415.

'purple and gold'; and a footnote adopts a precise circumstantiality as to the poem's having been written in the Quantock Hills above Nether Stowey. As an evocative local legend, Arthurian reference would thus arise quite unconstrainedly within this milieu.

A like association of Arthurian legend with specific place was epitomised by the work of Robert Stephen Hawker, who spent his honeymoon at Tintagel in 1823. A letter written forty years later recalled how he and his bride had stayed

> close to the Castle of King Arthur and amid the legends of his life and deeds. There we used to roam about and read all that could be found about those Old-World Histories, and often was [the] legend of the Sangraal talked of as a fine subject for verse.[108]

Hawker was later to settle on the north Cornish coast at Morwenstow, and although his major Arthurian poem, *The Quest of the Sangraal* (1864), lies beyond the limits of my present book, a number of minor Arthurian allusions occur in Hawker's poetry during the 1830s. He speculates in 'Trebarrow' (1834) on whether the 'race of Pendragon' had died there; and in 'The Silent Tower of Bottreau' (1831) mention of a 'chough' prompts a footnote explaining that 'the common people believe that the soul of King Arthur inhabits one of these birds', and that Hawker had failed with 'entreaty or bribe' to 'induce an old Tintadgel quarry-man to kill' him one.[109] This folklore belief is given ampler treatment in 'The Wreck', which describes 'Arthur's stern and rugged keep' (30), and notes the presence there of this distinctive bird. Claiming that the spirit of 'the long-lost King / Pass'd in that shape from Camlan's flood' (35 – 36), Hawker declares that the King's 'fierce soul' still inhabits this storm-tossed form.[110]

Whereas Hawker stresses the continuity of local legend among ordinary people, a locale of more purely literary association could also inspire Arthurian reverie. John Mitford, a close Oxford friend of Reginald Heber and later himself the editor of *Gentleman's Magazine* from 1834 to 1850, provides an instance of such literary topographical association in his 'Dedicatory Epistle to the Rev. Alexander Dyce' which prefaced Mitford's edition of *The Poetical Works of Thomas Parnell* (1832). On referring to Milton's verse, Mitford then associates Milton's early interest in the Arthurian legend with the seventeenth century poet's sojourn in landscape traditionally associated with Arthur:

---

[108] C. E. Byles, *The Life and Letters of R. S. Hawker* (1905), 412.
[109] *The Poetical Works of Robert Stephen Hawker*, edited by J. G. Godwin (1879).
[110] Robert Stephen Hawker, *Poems: containing the Second Series of Records of the Western Shore* (Stratton, 1836). The fact that this poem was not included among the collected poems edited by J. G. Godwin (1879) and Alfred Wallis (1899) may account for its being overlooked by later Arthurian scholars.

Him by far Deva's banks the Muses found
(Their favourite haunt) or Severn's sweetest bound,
Musing on Merlin's art (his earliest theme),
Or Uther's son.[111]

In more extensive manner, David Macbeth Moir illustrates this phenomenon on his visit to the Tower of Erceldoune, since the place was reputed to have once been the home of Thomas the Rhymer, the putative author of the medieval *Sir Tristrem*, a poem known to Moir through Scott's edition and George Ellis's account in *Specimens of Early English Metrical Romances*. By means of a retrospective vision of the medieval writer's illuminated manuscript page, Moir achieves a fluent transition into a summary of the Tristrem story:

Backward my spirit to the sway
Of shadowy Eld is led away,
When underneath thine ample dome,
Thomas the Rhymer made his home, . . .
And fresh as yesterday appears.
Secluded here in chamber lone,
Often the light of genius shone
Upon his pictured page, which told
Of Tristrem brave, and fair Isolde,
And how their faith was sorely tried,
And how they would not move, but died
Together, and the fatal stroke,
Which still'd one heart, the other broke.[112]

Three long excursions into Celtic countries were made by the scholarly Charles Hoyle who, after winning the Cambridge Seatonian Prize for sacred poetry in 1804 and 1806, and acting as Librarian of Trinity College Cambridge from 1803 to 1809, had remained Vicar of Overton, Wiltshire from 1813 until his death in 1848. A close friend of Bowles, Hoyle is remembered in Bowles's *Banwell Hill* as 'a scholar, unobtrusive, yet profound' who had sounded his 'summer-wand'ring reed' on visits to 'Killarney's Lake, and Scotia's hills'.[113] Whilst the first of these trips resulted in only a few Arthurian references derived from his modernisation of Chaucer's *The Squire's Tale*, but none of which are topographically based, the second visit gave rise to *The Pilgrim of the Hebrides*. Like a later Childe Harold, Hoyle records in Spenserian stanzas his poetic reaction to the impact of wild, mountainous romantic scenery. His meditations often range widely afield from their

---

[111] 'Dedicatory Epistle', ll. 693 – 96.
[112] 'Delta' (= David Macbeth Moir), 'The Tower of Erceldoune', ll. 29 – 32, 36 – 44; in *Blackwood's*, 28 (October 1830), 695 – 97.
[113] *Banwell Hill*, Part Second. ll. 657 – 61; in *The Poetical Works of William Lisle Bowles*, 2 vols (Edinburgh, 1855), II.

initial impetus: a passage through the Grampians near Aviemore, for
example, prompts his comparison between this precipitous landscape and the
wildness of a 'necromantic realm' raised by the power of imagination: under
the spell of local atmosphere he is 'beguiled' by a 'thousand idle dreams'
which recall the medieval world to life. The imagined scene he then portrays is
richly Arthurian, for it narrates in ten stanzas the brief appearance of the Grail
to Titurel, his consequent quest for it, the building of a sacred temple near
Salvatierra to receive it, and the Grail's eventual removal to the East.[114] It is
then suggested that the Grail reappeared to new heroes in Arthur's court, that
this cyclic pattern will be repeated, and that Arthur will revive 'the age of
gold'. Although it is possible that Hoyle intended an iconic parallel between
the Grampians of his own journey and the Pyrenees of Titurel's quest,
Hoyle's acquisition of Arthurian material was not derived from Scottish
legend but resulted instead from his reading of Albrecht von Scharfenberg's
Der jüngere Titurel, and from his study of the Helio-Arkite theories of George
Stanley Faber's The Origin of Pagan Idolatry. Since Hoyle dedicated a poem to
Faber ('Friend of my heart'), it may be assumed that Faber's theory of
recurrence was the source for Hoyle's concept of a recurring Grail; and Faber
was, doubtless, Hoyle's authority for naming the Severn ('Sabrina's wave') as
the aquatic destination of Arthur's sword.[115] Despite the fact that another long
topographical poem, 'Cambria', was completed by Hoyle, it was never
published in its entirety, only excerpts appearing in Gentleman's Magazine and
Literary Souvenir between 1828 and 1833. The manuscript poem, which is
deposited in Trinity College Library, consists of four cantos, each of which
describes a specific Welsh route: from Beachley to Brecon, thence to
Aberystwyth; Shrewsbury to Meifod, and thence to Llangollen.[116] The main
narrative is in Spenserian stanzas but this is interspersed with tales, odes and
hymns, in a variety of metrical and stanzaic forms. There is no Arthurian tale,
but, on account of its orientation towards Welsh scenery and legend, the poem
contains three separate references to Merlin. On Snowdon, it is recalled, he
led Milman's Samor 'to commune with the fates'; in the Nant Francon
section, he is named as the summoner of Gwydion from the cave where the
champions of the Cymry slumber; and, at Llanbadarn-Fawr, Hoyle indicates
the intimate relationship that existed between Cornish and Welsh legend:

> A thousand echoes over mead and fell
> Bear voice and tidings from the days of yore,
> And passages of strife or union tell
> Between Cornubia and the Cambrian shore,

[114] Charles Hoyle, The Pilgrim of the Hebrides: a Lay of the North Countrie (1830), Canto II. Part 3. st.
xiv – xxiii.
[115] George Stanley Faber, The Origin of Pagan Idolatry, 3 vols (1816), III, 319.
[116] 'Cambria', Trinity College Cambridge, MS R. 17. 18.

How from the guarded mount Tregagel fled
Chased by the archangel sword, and how by lore
Of sorcery and fraud the enchantress drew
Sage Merlin to his monumental bed
Far from the living world, in caverns of the dead.[117]

This novel artistic device of employing tours of Wales in order to provide a framework for interspersed local histories and legends is given another and original interpretation by John Parker. Born at Sweeney Hall, Shropshire, educated at Eton and Oxford before taking orders in the Church of England, he served as Vicar of Llanmarewic, Montgomeryshire, from 1827 to 1844. During his early years in this living, he wrote an idiosyncratic work entitled *The Passengers* which consists largely of a prose account of a purported tour of North Wales, undertaken by three gentlemen travellers whose reflections on the incidents and scenery they encounter are presented in the form of conversation. One of these travellers, named Clanvoy, having previously discoursed on various verse forms, threatens to repeat a whole chapter of hexameters. Thus is prefigured the poem of 'The Celtic Annals', a work intended to exemplify the land's history from the time of the Ancient Britons to that of the Normans. As the historical aspects of the Arthurian content of this work have been related in the previous chapter, it suffices here to note the significant use of a contemporary topographical framework for an historical narrative, and to observe the typical and fluent inter-relationship, which Parker exemplifies, between landscape, history and poetry.

An intricate web of connections between joint friends, personal visits and published poetry is apparent in two works by Walter Savage Landor and Leigh Hunt. In the summer of 1832, Landor set out on a tour to the Lakes with Joseph Ablett, from the latter's country house, Llanbedr Hall near Ruthin. Landor's resulting poem, 'To Joseph Ablett', was first printed in Leigh Hunt's *London Journal* on 3 December 1834. In this form, the poem makes no Arthurian allusion, but when it was reprinted in the same journal on 15 April 1835 Landor had included a passage which addressed Ablett in the opening lines as:

Lord of the Celtic dells,
Where Clwyd listens as his minstrel tells
Of Arthur, or Pendragon.[118]

This wording is then retained in a further printing of the poem which Ablett included in his privately printed *Literary Hours, by various Friends* (1837). Meanwhile, in the summer of 1835 Leigh Hunt had visited Wales and called

---

[117] 'South Wales', Canto II. st. xlvi; in 'Cambria'.
[118] Lines 1 – 3; in *The Works of Walter Savage Landor*, edited by Stephen Wheeler, 3 vols (1935), III.

on Ablett at Llanbedr, an incident commemorated in Hunt's complimentary poem, 'Llanbedr. — 1835', which was first printed in Ablett's *Literary Hours*. Prior to meeting Ablett, Hunt had visited Bodryddan, Flintshire, as the guest of Anna Maria Dashwood, whose younger sister, Amelia, had married Reginald Heber in 1809. The poem which Hunt later wrote, 'Bodryddan', was published in *Monthly Repository* (October 1837) and was also included in Ablett's *Literary Hours*. Hunt had known the Arthurian legend well for twenty years, from English literary sources, but this stay at Bodryddan afforded him the occasion for a fresher and more personal approach to the theme, set within its traditional location. Having spent ten years almost wholly in London, Hunt finds himself in a 'green domain', released from metropolitan harassment into the world of Welsh romance. He then sees Wales anew: not now 'as one of an old faded line', but as a 'land of Druid and of Bard, / Worthy of bearded Time's regard' (101 – 04). And within this context of crescent strength, the poet achieves a vicarious rebirth by association with the local and legendary hero of a land in which

> Was born a third of chivalry,
> (And is to come again, they say,
> Blowing its trumpets into day,
> With sudden earthquake from the ground,
> And in the midst, great Arthur crowned)   (106 – 10)

Such visits continued to stimulate Arthurian allusion. Not only were there minor references, for example to 'Merlin's city' in Mrs Bowen's long descriptive poem *Ystradffin*, or to 'Arthur's wassail cup' which the American Lydia Sigourney saw at Carlisle Castle, and refers to in her ensuing collection, but there was, in addition, a guidebook by Louisa Costello which contained a rich Arthurian vein.[119] Among her many talents, she was a poet: her *Songs of a Stranger*, too, had included 'Lines written . . . at Bremhill, the Residence of the Rev. W. L. Bowles'.[120] She was also a scholar who had corresponded with Francisque Michel and Sir Frederick Madden, both of whom were leading Arthurian experts; and she was also a travel writer whose books were very favourably received.[121] A combination of all three talents is found in her *Summer amongst the Bocages and the Vines*. Set in north-western France, this incorporates a visit to 'Tumbe Helene', and an explanatory account that this

---

[119] Melesina Bowen, *Ystradffin, a descriptive poem* (1839), Part IV. l. 36. 'Carlisle', l. 10; in Lydia Sigourney, *Pleasant Memories of Pleasant Lands* (1843).

[120] Louisa Stuart Costello, *Songs of a Stranger* (1825), 132.

[121] A letter from Michel is quoted in Costello, *Specimens of the Early Poetry of France* (1835), xxxix – xlix. For a MS letter from her to Madden, see British Library, Egerton MS 2840, fol. 275.

was held to be the tomb of King Hoel's niece, who had been slain by the giant of Mont St Michel, an act later revenged on the giant by King Arthur.[122] Costello's interest in including copious details of local history, which supplement the topographical descriptions, then gives rise to a retelling of the history of Heloise and Abelard, in the course of which she remarks that Heloise was 'like Merlin' in her knowledge of the power of simples (pp. 303 – 04). A footnote is then provided on Merlin, which, in order to support his claim as a herbalist, includes a twenty-two line poem entitled 'Merlin the Enchanter' which presents Merlin as an unchristian seeker after such 'fatal secrets' as 'the golden herb' and 'the red egg of the sea-snake'. Although Costello describes this 'lay' as one which is 'popular in Cornuaille', she appears not to acknowledge her source for it. In fact, she is translating from Villemarqué's French version, which he had derived from a Breton original; and Costello's notes on the golden herb are clearly based on his.[123] At Nantes she unwillingly recalls the horrors committed there during the Reign of Terror, and therefore she endeavours only to remember 'the poetical recollections of this beautiful place where each street teems with historical recollections'. The memory she chooses to revive is that 'on these quays was proclaimed by the sound of trumpets the death of Tristan de Leonois', and that the 'snowy sail' of the Irish Yseult had sailed up the Loire (I, pp. 297 – 301). A two page prose resumé is given of the original legend, which Costello derives from 'the bard who has recorded their love' in an episode which is, 'perhaps, the most pathetic in any language'. There follows a sixty-six line poem in English entitled 'The Legend', which draws upon Tristan material that Costello knew very well: she had included translations of the 'Laie de mort de Tristan' and Marie de France's *Chevrefeuil* in her *Specimens of the Early Poetry of France* and she would have known Michel's edition of all the then extant Tristan texts in his *Grand Receuil* (1835). Costello's poem is, probably, loosely based on this edition, which includes the Norman-French *Tristan* of Thomas. Her poem treats of the closing stages of the story. The first section is in dialogue form, and consists of a dramatic interchange between the dying Tristan and an attendant maiden. His enquiries as to whether she can descry a snow-white sail are met by her lie that the approaching sail is black. His immediate death from despair is followed by the poet's reproof of the 'trait'rous maid', and then a narration of 'Fair Yseult's' arrival, her subsequent discovery of Tristan's death and then her own expiry. Costello has

---

[122] Louisa Stuart Costello, *A Summer amongst the Bocages and the Vines*, 2 vols (1840), I, 62 – 63. Milman reviewed this favourably in *Quarterly*, 68 (June 1841), 57 – 87.
[123] Theodore Claude Henri Hersart de La Villemarqué, *Barzas-Breiz, Chants Populaires de la Bretagne*, 2 vols (Paris, 1839), I, 58 – 63.

thus provided a significantly early poetic handling of the Tristan legend in the nineteenth century.[124]

Cave Legends

The legend that King Arthur lay sleeping in a British cave, whence he could be awakened at an hour of national crisis, was the subject of much folklorist and poetic attention.[125] As early as 1744, George Waldron had recorded the 'ridiculous' legend that Merlin the Enchanter had bound the giants of Castletown, Isle of Man, in a cave under the castle, with a spell that would remain 'indissoluble to the end of the world'.[126] The inchoate form assumed here by the legend is given a much clearer Arthurian alignment in many early nineteenth century versions. Allusion to this had occurred in William Sotheby's poetic drama *The Cambrian Hero* in which an ancient sybil aids her 'magic art' by summoning up various spirits, such as

> Those holy druids — high Heaven's first-born priests —
> They — who are waiting in king Arthur's court —
> And for a thousand years have been confined
> In a dark cave — i'th' bowels of the earth.[127]

As Sotheby had toured Wales in the 1790s, he may have been drawing on local Welsh legend here that he had acquired at first hand.

Folk 'ballads and tunes' had been sedulously collected by Walter Scott on his many tours along Liddesdale in the 1790s, and thus a local source was probably the inspiration for his projection of a prose romance 'in the first year of the [nineteenth] century' on the subject of a Border horse-dealer, Canobie Dick, who regularly trades with a man of 'venerable appearance' — later to be revealed as Thomas the Rhymer.[128] Led into the Eildon Hills on one occasion, Dick sees a long range of horses, and knights in coal-black armour with drawn swords. The Rhymer tells him that whoever sounds the horn and draws the

---

[124] Cf. the claims made for Matthew Arnold's 'Tristram and Iseult' (1852): it 'is the first modern treatment of the Tristram legend in English': *The Poems of Matthew Arnold*, edited by Kenneth Allott, second edition, revised by Miriam Allott (1979), 207. Thomas Hogg had also included a lengthy account of the drug-induced love of Tristram and Isonde in his *Fabulous History* (1827).
[125] Some of the material in this section has previously appeared in my article 'King Arthur's Enchanted Sleep: Early Nineteenth Century Legends', *Folklore*, 97 (1986), 206 – 09.
[126] George Waldron, *The History and Description of the Isle of Man*, second edition (1744), 8 – 12.
[127] William Sotheby, *The Cambrian Hero, or Llewelyn the Great* (Egham, ?1800), V. i. 36 – 39.
[128] See Appendix to the General Preface, *Waverley Novels*, I, xxxix – xlvii.

sword lying there on an 'antique table' will become King of Britain. Afraid, however, to unsheathe the sword, Dick manages to blow the horn, but on attempting to seize the enchanted sword he hears a voice pronounce: 'Woe to the coward, that ever he was born, / Who did not draw the sword before he blew the horn!' Scott's original draft does not say who these sleeping knights are, but his later 'Appendix to the General Preface to Waverley' (1829) cites the comparable tradition in his friend John Leyden's autobiographical account of Teviotdale, *Scenes of Infancy* (1803). Leyden had collected much material for Scott's edition of *Ancient Minstrelsy of the Scottish Border* (1802 – 1803), and was sensitive to Arthurian topographical resonances: 'the grave of Merlin', he notes, 'is placed by tradition at Drummelzier, in Tweeddale, beneath an aged thorn-tree'.[129] His *Scenes* also reveals the identity of the subterranean king. According to Leyden's verse, an eventual awakener will 'bid the charmed sleep of ages fly', as he sounds the summons:

> While each dark warrior rouses at the blast,
> His horn, his falchion, grasps with mighty hand,
> And peals proud Arthur's march from Fairyland   (II. 518 – 20)

Leyden's interpretation is, moreover, richly suggestive, for in revealing that this awakening will be accomplished by a poet, and in naming Scott as the most suitable, an Arthurian return becomes a symbol of the recovery, through literature, of a lost world of chivalrous romance, because Scott's powerful verse

> Shall many a tale of elder time recall,
> The deeds of knights, the loves of dames proclaim,
> And give forgotten bards their former fame.   (526 – 28)

Discussion of the location of Thomas the Rhymer's hiding place was extended by Robert Southey. In his review of Scott's edition of *Sir Tristrem*, he suggests that a possible venue may be found in Glamorgan in

> the cavern under the roots of the hazel-tree, on Craig y Dinas, where King Arthur and all his knights are lying asleep in a circle; their heads outward.[130]

Southey had probably learnt of this variant through Edward Williams, for he had sought Williams's knowledge of medieval Welsh poetry, when researching

---

[129] *The Life and Poems of Dr. John Leyden, with Memoir by Thomas Brown* (1875), 280.
[130] *Annual Review*, 3 (1805), 555.

an authentic bardic background for his epic poem *Madoc*.[131] An extended prose account of the cave legend was drawn up by Williams himself at some time before his death in 1826, but it was not published until Elijah Waring included it in his *Recollections and Anecdotes of Edward Williams*.[132] According to this version, the cave is discovered under the root of a large hazel. Within the cave is a heap of gold, which the later Welsh visitor is allowed to remove. However, on accidentally touching a bell near the entrance, he fails to observe the stipulated condition of giving the correct formulaic reply to an awakening Arthurian warrior, and the visitor is therefore ejected empty-handed from an entrance which he can never afterwards discover.

Another notable variant of this cave legend was provided by Matthew Gregory ('Monk') Lewis, for whose ballad collection *Tales of Wonder* (1801) Scott had contributed five items. Lewis had already revealed in his novel *The Monk* (1796) his own acquaintanceship with the Tristan and Iseult stories in medieval romances, and, while staying at Howick, the Northumbrian seat of Earl Grey, he composed 'Sir Guy the Seeker', which he claimed was 'founded upon a tradition current in Northumberland'.[133] He sets his narrative at the neighbouring Dunstanburgh Castle where, in addition to the hundred sleeping knights, is discovered a beautiful captive maiden. There is a specifically Arthurian connotation in that the ritual test for an intruder lies in the choice between a jewelled sword and a 'horn of ivory fair' that was 'Merlin's horn of yore'.[134] When the seeker errs by blowing the horn, the guardian wizard shouts scornfully: 'Now shame on the coward who sounded a horn, / When he might have unsheatht a sword!' (271 – 72). The fullest Northumbrian version, however, was enacted at Sewingshields. In a collection of *Metrical Legends of Northumberland* there appeared an anonymous poem 'The Legend of Shewin' Shiels', a footnote to which states:

> popular tradition says that King Arthur and his court are enchanted near the ruins of Shewin' Shiels Castle, in 'the cavern of the enchanted warriors'.[135]

The poem itself describes how Sir Cuddy, a Northumbrian squire, is carried off wounded after a medieval Border skirmish, and awakes within a cave amongst sleeping knights. On taking up a sword, he hears a voice call 'Forbear', upon which he drops the sword and seizes a horn. The sound causes the knights and the chamber to vanish:

---

[131] See Arthur Johnston, 'William Owen-Pughe and *The Mabinogion*', *Journal of the National Library of Wales*, 10 (1957 – 1958), 323 – 28.

[132] Elijah Waring, *Recollections and Anecdotes of Edward Williams* (1850), 95 – 98.

[133] A romance entitled *The Loves of Tristan and the Queen Iseult* is read to Donna Rodolpha; in *The Monk*, edited by Howard Anderson (Oxford, 1980), 134.

[134] Matthew Gregory Lewis, *Romantic Tales*, 4 vols (1808), I, 291 – 307.

[135] *Metrical Legends of Northumberland*, edited by James Service (Alnwick, 1834). 129 – 33.

'Tis gone! he views the crags of Shewin' Shiels,
And recollects the tale of Arthur's knights,
And trembles as he thinks upon the sights
Just vanished in that fair and fairy hall,
The seven green sleepers and the magic call!
He crossed himself, and blessed the gracious hour
That snatched him timely from enchantment's power!   (83 – 89)

He then realises, however, that seven hundred years have elapsed while he
was in the cave, and thus in the world he re-enters the date is now 1826. The
choice of that particular date would seem to indicate that the poem had been
either composed or first published in that year: it also brings the poem into
vivid proximity with the nineteenth century, for the hero emerges into the
world of the Industrial Revolution a year after the opening of the Stockton –
Darlington goods railway. Paradoxically, the new industrial era with its
newly-created railway, and with its improved agriculture, housing, roads and
bridges, appears to him as another fairyland. And although the awakened
Cuddy expresses a preference for the men — though not the women — of
seven hundred years ago, the general burden of the poem is to extol with local
pride the benefits accruing from industrialism, and humorously to contrast
modern times very favourably with those 'days of yore' which 'all who know
them not so warmly praise' (1 – 2).

Further testimony to the prevalence of local Arthurian legends at
Sewingshields was provided by John Hodgson, the county historian, who
obtained the 'broad outline' of his story 'from the enquiries and graphic pen of
Miss Carlyle, of Carlisle', and had derived 'parts of its detail and colouring'
from 'old inhabitants of the neighbourhood'.[136] In this version, a farmer who
was knitting among the ruins of the castle lost his ball of wool, and on chasing
this he found a subterranean passage. Certain that it would lead to King
Arthur's hall, he entered, found the sleeping sovereign and his knights, and
attempted to perform the necessary rite. His failure to do so correctly is
admonished by Arthur:

O woe betide that evil day,
On which this witless wight was born,
Who drew the sword — the garter cut,
But never blew the bugle horn!

---

[136] John Hodgson, *History of Northumberland* (Newcastle, 1840); quoted in Moses Aaron
Richardson, *The Local Historian's Table Book. Legendary Division*, 3 vols (1843 – 1846), II, 43. A
private communication from Alan Welton suggests that Hodgson's informant may have been
Susanna Maria Carlyle (1752 – 1833): the sister of Joseph Dacre Carlyle (who became Professor
of Arabic at Cambridge University), she edited his *Poems* in 1805.

A very well-documented essay by J. Hardy on 'Legends of King Arthur and of Sewingshields' which appeared in Moses Aaron Richardson's *Local Historians' Table Book* quotes Hodgkin's account in full, and then adds a slightly modified version of the same legend that had fallen under his own notice.[137]

Lewis, too, had indicated his awareness of other contemporary manifestations of this legend, his introductory note having stated that 'adventures nearly similar' to Sir Guy's were to be found in various parts of Britain. He names the Pentland Hills in Scotland (by which he may refer to the Eildon Hills legend), and alludes to Sir John Stanley's passing through iron gates to enter an enchanted cavern near Chorley, Lancashire. This adventure seems to have been based on the letter that 'A Perambulator' had sent to the *Manchester Mail*, which described how a Mobberly farmer who was riding his milk-white horse to market was stopped by an old man who offered to buy the horse.[138] Eventually agreeing to sell, the farmer is led through a pair of iron gates into the hillside. The caverns within contain sleeping men, their horses, and piles of treasure, from which the farmer is paid. These sleepers will awake, he is told, in a moment of national crisis, when they will 'decide the fate of a great battle, and save their country'. After he leaves the caverns, the iron gates vanish, never to be found again. This form of the legend was also to generate metrical narratives. Of these, the first was a 285 line anonymous work in crisply ironic octosyllabic couplets, 'The Iron Gates. A Legend of Alderley', which adheres very closely to the tale as printed in the Manchester newspaper.[139] Both display an exact knowledge of the area about Alderley Edge, both emphasise the promised return of the knights in an hour of national need when 'George, the son of George' shall reign, and neither makes specific reference to Arthur or Merlin. In this guise, the legend is also repeated in the Hon. Miss Stanley's prose account of *Alderley Edge and its Neighbourhood*, and she also reprints 'The Iron Gates', with the comment that it 'has long been out of print'.[140] That there was, or had developed, an explicit Arthurian claim on the material may be seen in a letter to Mary Howitt from Elizabeth Gaskell on 18 August 1838. Included in a description of 'country customs' and vanishing 'poetical beliefs' around Knutsford, is her offer to show the local habitations of such beliefs:

[137] Richardson, *Table Book*, II, 37 – 46.
[138] *Manchester Mail*, 28 May 1805, 3: see William Axon, *Cheshire Gleanings* (Manchester, 1884), 56 – 68.
[139] Reprinted in *Ballads and Legends of Cheshire*, edited by Egerton Leigh (1887), 56 – 68.
[140] Hon. Miss Louisa Dorothea Stanley, *Alderley Edge and its Neighbourhood* (Macclesfield, 1843), 58 – 69. The volume was published anonymously, and is listed so in British Library and Cambridge University Library. The author is named as Hon Miss L. D. Stanley by J. P. Earwaker, *East Cheshire: Past and Present*, 2 vols (1880), I, 611; and by Axon *Cheshire Gleanings*. I have supplied her Christian names.

if you were on Alderley Edge, the hill between Cheshire and Derbyshire, could not I point out to you the very entrance to the cave where King Arthur and his knights lie sleeping in their golden armour till the day when England's peril shall summon them to her rescue.[141]

Mrs Gaskell knew the region well, having spent most of her childhood and youth there until her move to Manchester in 1838. A similar version of this legend was also recorded by another Knutsford resident, James Roscoe. An insurance agent who contributed three humorous prose articles to *Blackwood's Magazine* in 1838 to 1839, Roscoe also turned this local story into a poem, 'The Iron Gate: A Legend of Alderley', which appeared in *Blackwood's*.[142] The narrator of this 349 line poem, who loves 'those tales of ancientry', and claims to have learnt the story, when a child, from his 'grandame', tells how a miller sells his horse to an aged man, 'clad like to a monk', who then leads him into the hillside, and shows him the armed men, who are evidently Arthur and his knights:

> For good King Arthur did not die,
> As idle tales have said; . . .
> But Merlin from the battle bore
> His friend and king away:
> That he might lead his chivalry,
> In England's needful day.   (145 – 52)

Merlin exerts his power in order to preserve newly acquired horses, and he keeps the hillside gate from view until the moment of Arthur's promised return. As a result, the miller having departed laden with treasure is unable to find the iron gate a second time. Whereas the earlier poem had narrated the incident as 'a strange tale' with overtones of Gothick mystery, whilst its neatly-turned couplets had maintained an acerbic irony at the expense of the cupidity of 'Cestrian hind' and Parliamentary 'patriot', the later (1839) version more explicitly admits the fancifulness of the legend, but claims that these 'tales of ancientry' are yet 'true' to 'fancy' and contain inherently substantial matter. Enclosing the tale within admissions that it is a fiction, Roscoe gives the central narrative to the grandame, whose colloquial idiom is therefore accommodated within a ballad form.

There was, besides, a rival tradition which sought to locate the sleepers' cave beneath St Michael's Mount in Cornwall. A certain 'J. H.', for example, published in the *European Magazine* his 'Lines, supposed to have been written

---

[141] *Letters of Mrs Gaskell*, edited by J. A. V. Chapple and Arthur Pollard (Manchester, 1966), 28 – 33.
[142] 'The Iron-Gate — A Legend of Alderley', *Blackwood's*, 45 (February 1839), 271 – 74. The author is named as James Roscoe by Earwaker and Axon.

on St Michael's Mount, Cornwall'.[143] In the poem, the Mount is regarded as a
retreat, far 'from Bodmin's murky plain, / And every rude unsocial swain'
(3 – 4), where the poet may ponder on Chaucer, Gower or even the 'fairy
days, / When Arthur's knights provok'd the lays' (7 – 8). In the course of this
reverie, he considers that he will

> hold dark converse with the sprite
> That guards St Michael's holy height.
> Him will I call from his deep cell,
> Where Arthur's giant warriors dwell   (21 – 24)

The circumstances of the poem's creation are of relevance here. 'J. H.''s
previous submissions to the magazine had met with the following editorial
reply:

> J. H. will perceive that another Correspondent is furnishing us with
> translations from Anacreon: we would rather wish, therefore, that
> communications of J. H. may have some other object.[144]

This advice seems to have been promptly acted upon: the author's footnote to
'Lines' explains that 'a part of the poem' had been printed 'about a year back,
in one of the morning papers', but his reading of a description of St Michael's
Mount in *European Magazine* had given him the 'idea of finishing it in its
present form'. The original article had been a conventional account of the
Mount and had not referred to the Arthurian cave legend, so J. H. may have
perhaps made the fanciful connection himself, and, were there no corroborat-
ing accounts, one might dismiss the matter summarily.[145] However, there is a
similar reference in Sir Ambrose Hardinge Giffard's 'St Michael's Mount', a
poem dated April 1814. As epigraph, Giffard notes:

> The romantic Castle of St Michael . . . is the theme of many a Cornish
> legend; the most prevalent supposes that their 'long lost ARTHUR'
> resides there, under the immediate guardianship of the Archangel, until
> the time appointed for his return to earth.[146]

Giffard does not reveal a precise source for his knowledge of the legend. It is
possible that he knew of it from family tradition, for, although born in Dublin,
the son of the High Sheriff, he came of Devonshire stock.[147] Alternatively, he

---

[143] *EuM*, 62 (December 1812), 450.
[144] 'Acknowledgements to Correspondents', *EuM*, 62 (November 1812), 338.
[145] See M., 'Description of St. Michael's Mount', *EuM*, 62 (September 1812), 201.
[146] Giffard, *Verses*, 29.
[147] See Giffard entry in *DNB*.

may have learnt of it through correspondence with the eminent Cornish antiquary, Richard Polwhele. A copy of Giffard's poetry had been given to Polwhele by the *Quarterly* reviewer, John Wilson Croker, himself a Devonshire man.[148] Moreover, the British Library copy of *Verses* is an inscribed presentation copy of July 1824 'to Mrs Croker in grateful recollection of her kindness, from Hardinge Giffard'.[149]

This line of influence was continued as Giffard's epigraph was later employed, and with due acknowledgement of him, in 'C''s poem 'St Michael's Mount', which appeared in *Fisher's Drawing Room Scrapbook*.[150] Whilst a scholarly footnote points to the comparable legends of Owen of the Bloody Hand, Sebastian of Portugal, and Frederick Barbarossa, the poem itself proclaims that

> Entranced beneath St Michael's keep,
> Now Arthur and his warriors sleep
> Their charmed slumber, long and deep
> In magic thraldom bound.   (5 – 8)

The knights will remain so until a 'wizard horn' rouses them, but the contemporary political myth of Messianic return is here given an unorthodox interpretation, for the poet assumes that no Arthurian return will be required so long as 'Britain's flag' remains triumphantly 'unfurl'd / . . . throughout the world'. Such is the success of British arms that the poet commends Arthur and his knights to a protracted wait:

> So sleep ye on, ye ancient men!
> Entombed within your murky den,
> 'Tis dull enough; if not till then
> Ye quaff the circling toast.   (21 – 24)

Regional Setting

In addition to those poems which were firmly linked through local lore, or tourism, to a specific site, most other Arthurian poems tended also to be given a marked regional setting.

A remarkable instance of the creation of a physical locale for an Arthurian poem concerned Edward Atkyns Bray. Later an antiquarian Vicar of Tavistock who was to marry Alfred Kempe's sister Eliza, Bray was intent in

---

[148] See Richard Polwhele, *Traditions and Recollections: Domestic, Clerical and Literary* (1826), 782 – 85.
[149] British Library pressmark 11642. c. 9.
[150] C., 'St. Michael's Mount', *Fisher's Drawing Room Scrapbook* (1832), 11 – 12.

youth on devising poetic inscriptions for the granite rocks in his father's garden at Bairdown on Dartmoor. By 1806, he had written a four line poem 'To Merlin', and had planned to institute an appropriate setting for his 'druidical' work.[151] He wrote:

> It will add to the effect to call a recess, or kind of grotto, that is contiguous to [an] island, Merlin's Cave, and on a rock which may be considered as his tomb, to inscribe:-
>> These mystic letters would you know,
>> Take Merlin's wand that lies below.   (p. 286)

Other poets adhered to a more commonly accepted topography. As befits a national epic, in Milman's *Samor* the landscapes are, necessarily, widely varied, ranging from Cornwall to Snowdon, York and Derwent Water. Moreover, the often very detailed descriptions, such as that towards the close of the following account of Tintagel, appear to have been drawn from personal observation:

> Before him yawn'd the chasm, whose depth of gloom
> Sever'd the island Castle from the shore.
> The ocean waves, as though but newly rent
> That narrow channel, tumbled to and fro,
> Rush'd and recoil'd, and sullenly sent up
> An everlasting roar, deep echoed out
> From th'underworking caverns; the white gulls
> Were wandering in the dusk abyss; and shone
> Faint sunlight here and there on the moist slate.   (X. 92 – 100)

Such landscapes provide authenticity and an appropriate naturalism for the dramatic occasion: at Tintagel, for example, Gorlois fears an attack by Uther, and hence the Castle's strategic situation is crucial. On another level, the physical landscape is a distinctive feature of the country, and thus embodies an essential quality of nationalism. The note of personal belonging and commitment is sounded in the opening lines: 'Land of my birth, oh Britain! land beloved! / Whose tongue my song would speak' (I. 1 – 2). This involvement with Britain is expressed aesthetically through emphasis on the 'Beauteous Isle' (3), and lent grandeur by means of the spatial extension suggested, for instance, by the series of beacon fires lit from St Michael's Mount to Helvellyn in order to celebrate the coronation of Emrys (= Aurelius Ambrosius) (X. 343 – 422). An extra chronological dimension is achieved through Milman's viewing his topography from an historical angle, and by his constant awareness of Britain's long development: thus, the opening scene in

---

[151] *Poetical Remains of Edward Atkyns Bray, with a Memoir of the Author by Mrs Bray*, 2 vols (1859), II, 292.

Troynovant is immediately placed in comparison with the later city (London) on that site; and the 'jealous circuit' of the ancient walls is contrasted with the 'illimitable grandeur' of the 'mighty wilderness of streets' in the nineteenth century metropolis (I. 28 – 33). These features are not peculiar to Milman's verse, for they are general to the period. But what characterises him is his ambitious inclusiveness of theme since other writers tended to limit themselves to a single region. The region selected was often that to which the writer belonged. J. F. Pennie is a notable case in point. Born in Dorset, and spending much of his life there, he created a determinedly Wessex setting for *The Dragon King*. This background was also admirably suited to his avowed historical approach which, as has been shown in Chapter 1, rejected 'wild and mythological fables'. Pennie's drama is therefore organised coherently around the Romano-British centres of the fifth century, with the Saxon advance having reached Venta, 'the splendid city of Belgarium' (= Winchester), whilst the Britons attempt to maintain their hold on Arthur's capital at Sorbiodunum, (= Old Sarum). The drift of the action is consequently westwards: the dying Arthur is borne off to 'Avalonia's isle' (= Glastonbury); and Medrawd offers Gwenyfar a seductive escape to the Cornish castle of Restormel, among the 'groves of Fowey'. Particular local features are integrated: Porta, the Saxon chief, is named as the founder of Porchester Castle; a Saxon prophetess wanders 'where the wizard depths / Of Cheddar's chasms yawn like Hela's gulfs!' (III. ii. 53 – 54); and Pennie's antiquarian zeal is revealed by a textual reference to 'the demon cavern of stern Ochus' (III. ii. 80) followed by a footnote pointing out that 'we have his name and abode handed down to the present day in Somersetshire'; and he then quotes appositely on 'the famed grotto Ochihol' from Blackmore's *King Arthur*.

Most other writers did not, however, focus on Winchester. The dominant centres lay elsewhere: in the North-West, in Cornwall, and in Wales.

The attraction of the North-West was largely the result of the influence of two of Percy's ballads ('The Marriage of Sir Gawaine' and 'The Boy and the Mantle'), both of which had named Carlisle as the seat of Arthur's court. Supplementing this was the publication by John Pinkerton of medieval Arthurian texts which were of northern provenance, namely *Golagros and Gawain* and *Awntyrs of Arthur* (1792). There was, besides, the additional interest bestowed on such features as the Round Table at Penrith, a site mentioned in Scott's *The Bridal of Triermain* and by Alexander Macleod's *The Age of Chivalry*.[152] There was, too, an additional weighty reason which was not directly connected with Arthurian history: the fact that the scenery and the inhabitants of the Lake District exerted a powerful attraction over poets in this

---

[152] Alexander Macleod, *The Age of Chivalry* (Glasgow, 1839), st. xxxi.

period, as the residence there of Wordsworth, Coleridge and Southey illustrates.

Birth and residence in the area could also prove a strong determinant, and Reginald Heber's provision of a North-Western location for his *Morte d'Arthur* may have been partly attributable to the fact that, although he had been born in southern Cheshire, his family on both sides originated in Yorkshire, the Hebers being traced there back to 1461.[153] Heber's Arthurian capital is named Carduel, as in the *Fabliaux* translated by Way. Since Heber's source for his account of the *enfances* of Lancelot was George Ellis's *Specimens*, he would have been aware that Ellis had cited Froissart's identification of Carduel with Carlisle; and such an identification accords with the *Morte*'s frequent reference to a naturalistic topography.[154] When King Ryence of North Wales invades, he crosses the river Ribble; when repulsed, he quits the 'Lancastrian meadows' drenched with blood, before he is eventually drowned in the Mersey.[155] In the meantime, Ladugan has sent his daughter Ganore up into the Lake District for safety, to be brought up near 'Derwent's lonely mirror', where she may tend sheep on 'Skiddaw's summit lone', and live like Wordsworth's Lucy 'Unhonoured there, unknown, and undescried' (I. xi). From Arthur's court at Carduel, Modred is despatched 'for Scottish land' in quest of King Pellea's uncle, whilst Arthur's hunting trip takes him to 'drink in Cattraeth's woods the cooler breeze, / And rouse the dun deer from Terwathlin's side' (III. vi). By the latter would be meant Tarn Wadling, a Cumberland lake that had featured in Percy's 'The Marriage of Sir Gawaine'. As for Cattraeth, this had traditionally been linked with Catterick in Yorkshire, but in a footnote to his *The Vision of Don Roderick* (1811) Scott had followed Leyden in supposing the site of this famous battlefield to lie 'on the skirts of Ettrick Forest' in Selkirkshire, and this spot would not appear too far north for a hunt setting out from Carlisle.[156]

Two poems by Frere and Moultrie, both of which will be treated in greater depth in Chapter 3, share this North-Western orientation. The first of these is John Hookham Frere's *The Monks and the Giants* in which the main action begins at Carlisle when, as in ballad tradition, Arthur is celebrating Christmas. Over a day's journey away lie the mountains amongst which the giants have their castle. These 'huge mountains of immeasurable height', which suggest the English Lake District, provide an appropriate background for their gigantic denizens, and they also evoke the kind of battle terrain of the Peninsular campaign, with which Frere had been closely associated as Envoy and then Plenipotentiary to the Spanish Central Junta in 1808 to 1809. Moreover, in the description of these 'immeasurable' mountains there

---

[153] George Smith, *Bishop Heber* (1895), 6 – 10.
[154] George Ellis, *Specimens of Early English Metrical Romances*, second edition, 3 vols (1811), I, 309.
[155] Heber's *Morte d'Arthur; A Fragment* was first published in *The Life of Reginald Heber* by his Widow [Amelia Heber], 2 vols (1830), II, 529 – 83.
[156] *The Vision of Don Roderick*, Introduction. st. ivn; in *Poetical Works*.

appears a deliberate burlesque of the romantic awe of grandiose scenery. At the close of Canto III, Frere parodies the picturesque tour guidebook that offers 'Designs and etchings by an amateur', and he punningly alludes to the Welsh mountains under the comically irreverent names of 'Cader-Gibbrish' and 'Loblommon'. What is more, the rugged mountain country, the scene of heroic romance adventure, is dramatically juxtaposed with that of the humdrum outlook suggested by the ostensible authors, two harness-makers from Stowmarket in Suffolk, whose offer to the Muse is expressed in the tamely domesticated Cockney invitation to a 'nice airy lodging out of town, / At Croydon, Epsom, anywhere in Surrey' (III. i.).

Similar contrapuntally ironic effects are achieved in John Moultrie's *La Belle Tryamour*, wherein the narrator's frequent reminiscences hover over London theatres and Cambridge undergraduate life. In the Arthurian core of the poem, Moultrie introduces a Merlin from 'Caer-Mardin', whose demons' magic hammers still clink, as in Spenser, 'Under a rock that overhangs the vales / Of the "swift Barry" '.[157] Yet, that a northern lodestone strongly attracted Moultrie is evident in that he deliberately switches the location from that of his acknowledged source, Joseph Ritson's edition of Thomas Chestre's *Sir Launfal*.[158] Although the latter commences in Arthur's court at 'Kardeuyle', it rapidly moves to 'Karlyoun', with an incidental reference to 'Glastyngbery'. To meet Tryamour, Lanval is made to ride west from Karlyoun, i.e. into Wales. Moultrie's version does, however, follow Chestre's idiosyncratic version in making Guenevere the daughter of King Ryence, and in regarding him as the King of Ireland, instead of the more usual North Wales: a novel relocation which allows Moultrie to draw an ironic parallel between Arthur's pre-nuptial voyage, from Holyhead to Dublin, and King George IV's Dublin visit of 1821:

> The papers, which so loyally recorded
> King George's landing on the Irish coast,
> May serve for Arthur's, and are choicely worded,
> Especially the Times and Morning Post.   (I. cxviii)

This apart, Moultrie radically re-orients the poem's topography by locating Arthur's court solely at Carlisle, and arranging for Tryamour's birth to occur 'somewhere near / The classic margin of Winandermere' (III. xcix). A Wordsworthian impulse is present here: he had been quoted as epigraph to Canto I, and Moultrie had previously written an article on him for *The*

---

[157] 'Gerard Montgomery' [John Moultrie], *La Belle Tryamour*, I. xlv; in *Knight's Quarterly Magazine*, 1 (June 1823), 145 – 79. Canto II appeared in *KQM*, 1 (October 1823), 378 – 418; and Canto III in *KQM*, 2 (January 1824), 115 – 27.

[158] Moultrie, *Tryamour*, I, xlii. Thomas Chestre's *Sir Launfal* was included in Joseph Ritson, *Ancient Engleish Metrical Romanceës*, 3 vols (1802), I.

Etonian.[159] Appropriately then, the description of Westmorland acknowledges its genius loci:

> The ground is still enchanted — a magician,
> The mightiest of our times, hath fix'd his dwelling
> Among those haunts of ancient superstition
> O'ershadow'd by huge Skiddaw and Helvellyn   (III. c)

And although Tryamour's pavilion is pitched in a Fairyland 'surpassing all the beauty of North Wales' (III. cxl), its basic components of mountains, forests, rivers and 'giant lakes' point to a Cambrian or Cumbrian source of inspiration.

The persistent manner in which Arthurian personae were associated with the stimulus of a local Welsh tradition is indicated, for example, by the fact that when a provincial newspaper was founded at Newport in 1829 it adopted the title of *Monmouthshire Merlin*, and its first issue made clear the Arthurian allusion by printing 'Merlin Redivivus', a poem in which the Genius of Monmouthshire summons Merlin from the sleep of ages so that the awakened sage may wonder at, and applaud, the new prosperity created for Gwent by the Industrial Revolution.[160] Similarly, a predominantly Cambrian association with the Arthurian legend was often the outcome of residence in Wales for a substantial period. This Arthurian interest might often be manifested in a very general manner, without specific reference to any Welsh place. An early indication of this is Way's prefatory sonnet to his translation of Le Grand's *Fabliaux*. Addressed to his cousin the Reverend Henry Thomas Payne, who was then the vicar of Lanbedr and Patricio, two hamlets in Monmouthshire and Breconshire, Way's verse alludes to Payne's pastoral duties in 'Cambrian wilds by Usk's romantic side'.[161] Living there had 'impell'd' a 'love for the muse of Wales', which had prompted his research into the 'bards of yore'. Transcripts of their works having been sent to Way had allowed the latter to 'explore / Great Arthur's deeds embalm'd in Merlin's song' and thereby to 'save their rescued fame'.

Long residence in Wales had a comparable effect upon Felicia Hemans, who had moved there in 1800 at the age of seven, and had remained, with only a brief absence in 1812, until 1828. Many of her 'Juvenile Poems' reveal a concern with not only Welsh scenery ('happy regions of delight and joy') but also with the bardic tradition (traces of which were still extant according to 'The Harper of Conway'), and with Welsh history from Roman to medieval times. Greatly augmented by her reading of Owen-Pughe and Edward Jones, her knowledge of Welsh poetry of the medieval period dominates the series of

---

[159] 'On Wordsworth's Poetry', *Etonian*, 3 (December 1820), 217 – 29.

[160] *Monmouthshire Merlin*, 23 May 1829, 4.

[161] The 'Rev. H.T.P.' of Way's dedication is identified as Henry Thomas Payne by Phyllis G. Mann, 'Keats's Reading', *Keats-Shelley Memorial Bulletin*, 13 (1962), 39 – 47.

Welsh Melodies that she composed in about 1821, and some of which were performed at the London Eisteddfod in May 1822.[162] Within such a context, there consequently arises allusion to Merddin Emrys's western voyage, and Taliesin's dirge over the fate of 'Uthyr's kingdom'. A similar preoccupation informed the work of a later poet, Rowland Williams, who had been born and raised in Flintshire. This boyhood is recalled in 'The Hall of the Nations' when by 'Vyrniew's stream' he had yearned 'To wake once more the harp of Cambrian fame' (29 – 32). Because this early poetic dream had been noticed by Merlin, 'the wild diviner' later returned to bestow on Williams a vision of an international hall of heroes, which has a strong Welsh representation including an Arthur whom 'None have surpassed' (74).

Besides these limited references to Arthur, there were other works in which, as a result of personal experience, an ampler Welsh background was provided. Having spent two years trying to run a farm 'in the obscure and romantic village of Llys-Wen, in Brecknockshire' John Thelwall derived from his knowledge of this area an apt setting for *The Fairy of the Lake*.[163] A political radical, Thelwall was evidently sympathetic to a novel interpretation of the Lady of the Lake as an Egeria, a beautiful nymph held in mysterious seclusion for the indulgence of an illicit amour with King Arthur (a view which might claim Drayton as authority), but Thelwall restrains this speculative fancy, and confines his Lady to the role of 'benignant spirit', one that had been assigned by 'the ancient Cambrians' (p. 207). The lake in which she maintained 'her particular residence', Lynn Savadan, is retained by Thelwall as a distinctive symbol of her 'essential purity' because, as a 'tradition' still popular in the neighbourhood testified, the river Lunvey flowed through the middle 'without mingling any part of its waters with those of the Lake itself'. The strength of Thelwall's desire to localise is shown, too, in his footnote explaining that he has removed the situation of Gwrtheyrnion Castle (where Vortigern was burned in his palace) from 'the fastnesses of' Plinlimmon where Thelwall believed it stood 'in reality' to a nearby Brecon setting (p. 205). Since the Fairy manages a timely rescue of Guenever by quenching the flames with magically rising waters, Thelwall presents a dramatically mobile topography memorialising the Arthurian legend:

> A lake itself now spreads at my command,
> And long, an emblem of [Arthur's] Fame, shall stand,
> An alpine wonder in the Cambrian land.   (III. v. 179 – 81)

At the foot of the Brecon Beacons lie the thickets where Arthur spends so much time lost, and, given this orientation, there is inevitability in the choice of

---

[162] 'Written in North Wales', l. 1; in *Poetical Works*. For *Welsh Melodies*, see Trinder, *Hemans*, 31 – 32.
[163] John Thelwall, *Poems chiefly written in Retirement. The Fairy of the Lake, a dramatic romance* (Hereford, 1801), xxxv.

neighbouring Caerleon in 'all its fabled grandeur' as the final scene, where Arthur may be crowned, and Taliesin deliver his encomium.

In her notes to her printing of her husband's *Morte d'Arthur*, Mrs Heber had alluded to the 'traditionary traces' of Arthur which were 'still to be found in Wales and in parts of Shropshire'.[164] From his Cheshire boyhood, and the period of his residence in the vicarage at Hodnet, Shropshire, Heber had ample opportunity to familiarise himself with Welsh legend. He had friendly and familial connections, too, for his wife was the daughter of the Dean of St Asaph's, and had lived at Bodryddan. These Cambrian affinities would seem to have outweighed Heber's initial northern tendency, for in his later *The Masque of Gwendolen* (1816) he has, significantly, grafted a story from the Percy ballad of 'The Marriage of Sir Gawaine' on to a Welsh stock.[165] The eponymous heroine is 'Harlech's virgin'; a Llewellyn has been unjustly imprisoned by Arthur; and Merlin's rhetorically attempted seduction of Gwendolen offers her a throne loftier than 'Plinlimmon' or 'Idris's stony chair' (48).

Whereas both Thelwall and Heber admit into their poems figures from a Scandinavian or Classical mythology, Henry Davies's Welsh tale of 'The Enchanted Shield', is determinedly consistent at all levels.[166] Included in his volume of medievalist short stories, it matches Felicia Hemans in its concentrated Welshness. Arthur is presented as a Silurian prince whose court is held at Caerleon, and the dramatic action turns on an ideological conflict between Druidism and the Christian Church. Thus, whilst Geriant, a bard, pleads for Arthur to relieve the druids of Mona who are being slaughtered by Angle invaders ('Idda's raven'), Dubricius, who is Archbishop of Caerleon, suggests a rival mission in the shape of a quest for the Enchanted Shield that is held by the druids of the Isle of Bardsey. All key loci in this tale are founded upon a specifically Welsh domain. Geriant's adjuration, for example, is announced as a vision that he has been vouchsafed through sleeping in 'Great Idris's chair' (p. 169). The ambience is distinctly Welsh, and the traditional Welsh spellings are accorded to certain of Arthur's court: *viz* Geriant, Galath, Owen, and Gwalchmai the golden-tongued. Taken over from Geoffrey of Monmouth are the Welsh-sounding names of Arthur's spear and shield (Ron and Pridwen), whilst Arthur's faithful counsellor, Sir Aaron le Sage, appears to have been derived from the triads, where Aron ap Kynfarch was one of the Three Counselling Knights. In addition to the conventional properties, such as a hirlas blown by Lancelot, and a fallen cromlech, there is evidence of

[164] *The Poetical Works of Reginald Heber*, new edition (1861), 321.
[165] *Fragments of the Masque of Gwendolen*; in *Poetical Works*.
[166] 'The Enchanted Shield'; in *Stories of Chivalry* (1827). For identification of the author, see *Carmarthen Journal*, 31 August 1827, 4. It would appear probable that this author, a Librarian of the Royal Cambrian Institution, is identical with the Henry Davies 'of Cheltenham' who recited his 'Ode' at the Beaumaris Eisteddfod in 1832: see Chapter 1 and *Cambrian Quarterly Magazine*, 4 (1832), 544 – 45.

deeper background research in that Geriant's song 'Dream of a Bard' makes mention of 'Annwn', the ancient Welsh underworld or, as a footnote explains, 'the Hell of Druid mythology' (p. 172n). On account of its wholly Welsh Arthurian plot, 'The Enchanted Shield' is a notable precursor of Peacock's *The Misfortunes of Elphin*, particularly in view of the former tale's ironic anti-clerical tone, and its inclusion of songs at strategic points within the development of the plot. As the tale was reviewed and quoted at length in the *Cambrian Quarterly Magazine* in 1829, Peacock would probably have been made aware of it, but not before he had completed his own work.[167]

Although 'The Enchanted Shield' is clearly the product of an author well-acquainted with the literature of Welsh medievalism, scenic description is minimal and the tale does not evince a first-hand knowledge of the countryside. In massive contrast, the work of Peacock displays a close knowledge of Wales, in which he had spent a walking tour in 1810 – 1811, and revisited in 1812, 1813 and 1821.[168] As his letters reveal, he made occasional use in his novels of places he had visited: the 'dingle', for instance, in *Crotchet Castle* (1834) is borrowed from a 'real scene, on the river Velenrhyd, in Merionethshire'.[169] Certain descriptions in *The Misfortunes of Elphin*, too, have a specificity that probably associates them with a location that Peacock knew well: *vide* the account of Elphin's fishing on the river Mawddach, or that of the Craig Aderyn overlooking the river Dysyni. Moreover, the letters which survive from his initial journey show him to have read a topographical work on the area, Thomas Evans's *Cambrian Itinerary*, and, although Peacock mocks Evans's fearful descriptions of the precipitous scenery, he could also have noted in this guidebook the frequency with which Evans alludes to the Arthurian legends that cling to certain landscape features.[170] As he had married a Welsh lady in 1821, it may be presumed that Peacock either learnt some Welsh himself (his library contained two Welsh dictionaries) or that he made use of his spouse as a translator, for he draws on some source materials which were available only in Welsh: the germ of most of his lyrics, for example, may be traced back to the Welsh poems in *The Myvyrian Archaiology* (1801 – 1807). However, although creating a new unity out of formerly diverse materials, much of the relevant matter had already been translated and widely disseminated: Peacock's subject was not recondite. In spite of the

---

[167] *CQM*, 1 (1829), 368 – 78.
[168] Peacock's first Arthurian allusion (which is overlooked by Merriman *et al*) had also arisen from a topographical source: see his association of the river Severn with 'Merlin's spell' and 'Arthur's fate', in *The Genius of the Thames: A Lyrical Poem* (1810), Part I. ll. 108 – 11; in *Works*, VI.
[169] Letter of 11 July 1861; in *Works*, VIII, 253.
[170] *Works*, VIII, 182. Thomas Evans's *Cambrian Itinerary* (1801) was reissued as *Walks through Wales*, second edition (1815). The work's Arthurian allusions have been referred to above.

fact that the whole *Hanes Taliesin* had not been published — even in Welsh — yet scattered parts of the story had appeared quite frequently. In particular, Taliesin's song 'The Consolation of Elphin' had been partially translated by Evan Evans (1764), but an ampler version had been issued in 1770 by 'a fair countrywomen' of his, and her version had been given in full by Pennant's *A Tour in Wales*.[171] John Evans's *North Wales* (1802) had summarised the story of Taliesin, Gwyddno and Elphin, as had Bingley in 1804.[172] In 1806, Samuel Rush Meyrick's *History and Antiquities of Cardigan*, a work owned by Peacock, included a translation of Taliesin's autobiographical poem 'The History of Taliesin', and also 'The Consolation of Elphin'.[173] The 'fair countrywoman''s translation of the latter was again included in Thomas Evans's collection of *Old Ballads*.[174] Peacock's library also contained Edwin Pugh's *Cambria Depicta*, which quoted 'The Consolation', and summarised the Taliesin, Gwyddno and Elphin story.[175] As for the second main thread of Peacock's novel — the inundation of the Plain of Gwaelod — Meyrick included two translations by Anthony Todd Thomson: 'The Sorrow of Gwyddno', and 'The Inundation of Cantrev y Gwaelod, from the Welsh of Gwyddno Garanhir'. T. J. Llewelyn Prichard treated the whole story in his poem *The Land Beneath the Sea*, and the same writer's collection of Anglo-Welsh literature, *The Cambrian Wreath*, reprinted Thomson's translation of 'The Inundation', as well as the 'fair countrywoman''s 'Consolation'.[176] With regard to the third thread of Peacock's novel — the kidnapping of Gwenhwyvar by Melwas, and her later restoration to Arthur through the intercession of Gildas and the Abbot of Glastonbury — the story had been previously recounted (see Chapter 1) in, for example, Carte's *History*, John Evans's *South Wales*, John Hughes's *Horae Britannicae*, and in Joseph Ritson's *The Life of King Arthur*; and as the last-named was in Peacock's own library it would therefore seem to have been his most probable source.[177] For his description of ancient Caerleon, Peacock acknowledges his debt to Giraldus' account, which he read in Richard Colt Hoare's 1806 translation. Here he found details of the Roman remains (temples, aqueducts, theatres, gilded roofs, and central heating) which he

---

[171] Pennant, *Tour in Wales*, II, 308.

[172] John Evans, *A Tour through part of North Wales*, second edition (1802), 276 – 77. Bingley, *North Wales*, I, 125 – 28.

[173] Meyrick, *Cardigan*, 65 – 66, 70 – 72.

[174] Thomas Evans, *Old Ballads, Historical and Narrative*, new edition, revised by R. H. Evans, 4 vols (1810).

[175] Pugh, *Cambria Depicta*, 419 – 20.

[176] T. J. Llewelyn Prichard, *Welsh Minstrelsy: containing The Land beneath the Sea* (1824). *Cambrian Wreath*, 71, 73 – 75.

[177] Carte, *History*, I, 201 – 05. John Evans, *South Wales*, 56. Hughes, *Horae Britannicae*, II, 239. Ritson, *King Arthur*, 69.

integrated with the results of later archaeological discovery. In the eighteenth century 'a figure of Diana' had been unearthed, as is related by John Evans, Donovan and Willett: Peacock consequently introduces a disused Temple of Diana in which Bedwyr stores the court's wine.[178]

The portrait of the Arthurian world which Peacock draws is explicitly Cymric. Not only is there a quasi-*Mabinogion* quality in the 'beautiful huntresses, in scarlet and gold' (chap. 12), but the names of the court ladies are largely taken from those given in the triads (and translated in *Cambro-Briton*): Tegau, Dywir, Garwen, Enid and Indeg; whilst Trystan and Gwalchmai are awarded their traditional Welsh nomenclature.[179] Significantly, too, Peacock has given the whole novel an essentially Celtic orientation by highlighting the prowess and traditional social status of the bards. Not only is a poet (Taliesin) the novel's true hero, but the public role of poetry is constantly emphasised, and the finale of the Christmas entertainments is not a tournament or a quest, but a characteristically Welsh Bardic Congress attended by the recognised luminaries of early medieval verse: Taliesin, Merlin and Aneurin. Furthermore, this Welsh culture and scenery is not presented as a purely decorative backdrop, but is, instead, wholly integrated with the novel's structure, where it occupies an important function.[180] Within a convincing depiction of the pastoral framework of sixth century society, and the consequent importance of obtaining subsistence from farming and fishing, there is relevance in the precisely detailed description of Elphin's construction of the weir; and the artefact is functional in Peacock's narrative, for the coracle containing the infant Taliesin will be found inside this fish trap. Natural objects, and the restraints imposed by them, are employed dynamically within the novel, as when Taliesin immures Rhun inside the cave; or, at a level of great symbolic application, when the ocean engulfs the embankment that was intended to protect the Plain of Gwaelod. It is very probable that Peacock's interest in Gwythno's earthwork was influenced by the scheme of William Madocks, so warmly supported by Shelley, for reclaiming land at Tremadoc in 1812.[181] Certainly, Peacock adopts a high profile as narrator, and persistently reminds his reader of the contrast, or similarity, between his time past and the present, an effect which is often achieved by presenting the scene literally from the viewpoint of the modern observer. The tourists who abound in other Peacockian novels make their appearance here also, at the ruins of Glastonbury Abbey where

---

[178] John Evan, *South Wales*, 40. Donovan, *South Wales*, I, 120. Mark Willett, *A Stranger in Monmouthshire and South Wales* (Chepstow, ?1825), 154.
[179] 'Triads of the Island of Britain: Relating to Arthur', *Cambro-Briton*, 3 (May 1822), 387 – 94.
[180] See Butler, *Peacock Displayed*.
[181] See *The Letters of Percy Bysshe Shelley*, edited by Frederick L. Jones, 2 vols (Oxford, 1964), I, 326.

the musing moralist, . . . with folded arms, and his back against a wall, dreams of the days that are gone; or the sentimental Cockney, seating himself with much gravity on a fallen column, produces a flute from his pocket, and strikes up, 'I'd be a butterfly'. (chap. 13)

More frequently, the observing tones are those of the narrator himself who, besides noting that penillion-singing may still be found among the Welsh peasantry, says that a 'proverbial distich' about Gwythno Garanhir's sigh may yet be heard on 'the coast of Merioneth and Cardigan'. These echoes of the past may be accompanied by an actual physical exploration for which Peacock provides specific guidance:

the curious investigator may still land on a portion of the ancient stony rampart; which stretches, off the point of Mochres, far out into Cardigan Bay, nine miles of the summit being left dry, in calm weather, by the low water of the spring-tides (chap. 4)

Then, at modern Caerleon, Peacock surveys the view as historian and topographer of a 'little insignificant town', possessing nothing of its ancient glory but the unaltered name:

The rapid Usk flowed then, as now, under the walls: the high wooden bridge, with its slender piles, was then much the same as it is at this day . . . The same green and fertile meadows, the same gently-sloping wood-covered hills, that now meet the eye of the tourist, then met the eye of Taliesin; except that the woods on one side of the valley were then only the skirts of an extensive forest (chap. 12)

Although Peacock's achievement proved the apogee of Arthurian Celticism in the early nineteenth century, a minor afterglow may be discerned in Bulwer Lytton's work. This is indicated, at a very minor level, by his use of the Welsh form 'Gwynver' for the name of Arthur's Queen, in the 1842 edition of 'The Fairy Bride'.[182] More substantially, his *King Arthur* betrays the influence of Lady Charlotte Guest's translation of the *Mabinogion*. Arthur's capital is said to be at 'Carduel', a favourite designation in the *Fabliaux*, but whereas Ritson had argued cogently for the identification of Carduel with Carlisle, Lytton interprets it as Caerleon, 'the favourite residence of Arthur, according to the Welch poets'.[183] In stated intention, the poem promised to have had a very Welsh flavour as Arthur was to be treated as a 'patriot Prince of South Wales',

[182] In Edward Lytton Bulwer, *Eva, a True Story of Light and Darkness, The Ill-Omened Marriage, and Other Tales and Poems*, second edition (1842).
[183] Lytton, *Poetical and Dramatic Works*, II, 44.

with a claim to epic glory as the 'preserver of the Cymrian Nationality' (II, p.
5n). Moreover, the personae were to be treated in accordance with pure
Cymrian tradition. Gawaine, for example, who had been 'shamefully
calumniated' by Malory, would revert to his pristine character of Gwalchmei
(II, p. 47); Guenevere's 'fidelity' would be vindicated from that 'scandal
which the levity of French romance has most improperly cast upon it' (II, p.
145) whilst Lancelot's Gallic origin is disputed by the citing from Guest of a
Welsh etymology for his name: that 'Paladr-ddelt' had given rise to the term
'splintered spear' or lance (II, p. 159). Among the other knights are a Madoc,
an Elphin, and three sets of Welsh Counselling Knights, Knights of Battle,
and Ardent Lovers, adopted with only slight variation from Guest's
footnotes.[184] Most of the plot is enacted on the continent of Europe, but Lytton
sketches in a journey by Gawaine to Lake Bala in Merionethshire, where he is
tormented by the fairies of Gwyn ab Nudd under Nannau's legendary oak;
and the firing of the warning beacons provides Lytton, as it had Milman, with
the opportunity to portray a vista of Welsh mountains from Monmouthshire
to Snowdon. For minor local colour, the poem is endowed with torques,
coracles, an authentic war-cry, a druid throne for Merlin, and repeated
references to Carduel's 'domes of gold'. Nevertheless, despite Lytton's
sympathetic resolve to give 'something of the Cymrian characteristics or
colourings', his faculty of idealisation constantly reduces attention to visual or
emotional individuality (*vide* Book VI, where the minutely detailed Welsh
landscape of 'rock-born Caine' and 'prison'd' Mawddach's 'triple chain / Of
waters' soon fans out into comparison with 'Jura's roe' and 'Iran's shy
gazelle'); and by adopting 'Manners' from the age of 'the Arthur of
Romance', the poem consistently dilutes the Welsh admixture.[185]

Besides continuing to attract touring poets, Cornwall was also distinctive in
that a number of local writers, based mainly around Truro, adopted
Arthurian themes which showed a strong regional affiliation. Of this group,
George Woodley had been born in 1786 in Dartmouth, Devonshire, but, after
an early life at sea and then in Devonport and London, he settled in Truro in
1808 as editor of a Tory newspaper, *The Royal Cornwall Gazette*. For the next
twelve years he wrote poetry prolifically: in particular, a contemporary epic on
the Peninsular War, *Portugal Delivered* (1812), and two lengthy topographical
poems, *Cornubia* (1819) and *Devonia* (1820). The compendious subtitle of
Cornubia indicates that it is 'A Poem, in five cantos, descriptive of the most
interesting scenery, natural and artificial, in the County of Cornwall;
Interspersed with Historical Anecdotes, and Legendary Tales'. In the third of
these cantos, Woodley describes 'The Northern Coast', and in doing so he

---

[184] All of Lytton's borrowings from Guest appear to have been based on *The Lady of the Fountain*
(1838), the first volume of her translations from The *Mabinogion*.
[185] Lytton, *King Arthur* (1870), xii. *Works*, II, 5.

devotes a hundred lines to Tintagel. As is usual, the chasm is seen as a
romantic archetype of 'Terror's darkest guise', and as a fit subject for an *ubi
sunt* meditation on the 'wrecks of dreadful strength, that mark'd the dungeon-
keep' where now the 'lofty portals' are 'unpass'd, save by unconscious
sheep'.[186] Inevitably, the scene recalls 'tales of yore' and 'legendary lore'
(xviii), and after speculating on whether these 'ancient tales may be believ'd'
(xxvi) Woodley distances himself from 'monkish legends' that have 'dis-
figured' the history of Arthur; but he accepts the Francis Bacon proposition
that 'there was truth enough in his story to make him famous, besides that
which was fabulous'. 'Thought' then brings back 'long-vanish'd years' and
hears 'Arthur's fame in ev'ry sighing breeze' (xxviii). Woodley next provides
a summary of Arthur's birth there, his removal thence by the 'philosophic
Merlin', his upbringing as a page, his later victories over the Saxons, and his
battle against Modred at 'Cambula's stream (as old traditions tell)', a spot
denoted as 'the river Camel or Alan' (xxix). Woodley next draws together his
historical and philosophical themes by speculating that the occupants of
'yonder bark', which is passing 'Arthur's lofty turrets', have never surveyed
'the records of his acts', nor have heard of the 'eventful day' when Gorlois
('bold Cornubia's chieftain') tried to repel Uter Pendragon's 'lawless fires'.
Woodley then contrasts this neglect with the present fame enjoyed in Greece
by Achilles: the reason given is that Homer had immortalised the latter, and
hence Art is the surest preserver of heroic fame. As will be seen, a number of
Cornish poets attempted to remedy this deficiency, and to provide a poetic
immortality for Arthur.

For epigraph, Woodley had selected some lines on romantic scenery from a
poem entitled *The Influence of Genius* (1816) by James Brydges Willyams. This
latter had been born in 1771, the eldest son of a Truro banker, and after
taking a Cambridge degree had returned to Cornwall, to live in the family
mansion of Carnanton, and to serve as JP and Lieutenant Colonel of the
Royal Cornwall Light Infantry Militia. Woodley's *Royal Cornwall Gazette*
regularly reported throughout 1818 and 1819 the proceedings of the Cornwall
Literary and Philosophical Institution, of which Willyams was Honorary
Vice-President. In his introductory lecture to the 1818 series of meetings,
Willyams had lamented Cornwall's failure to produce a modern literature
worthy of the province, for no other county

> possesses a richer, a wilder, a more beautiful, a more sublime variety of
> rocks, waves and skies, a more abundant store of fairy legend and
> fabulous interest.[187]

Later in that year, the *Gazette* published an extract from a poem entitled *The
Fair Isabel*, which was prefaced by a note saying:

---

[186] George Woodley, *Cornubia* (1819), Canto III. st. xxii.
[187] *Royal Cornwall Gazette*, 17 October 1818, 2.

I doubt whether Col. W. can describe the days of Arthur (to which he seems so much attached) in stanzas superior to the following.[188]

There followed six Spenserian stanzas on the theme of chivalry and enchantment in 'Arthur's age', when Merlin 'proudly sail'd' about 'rough Tintagel's ramparts'. Moreover, Willyams himself also tackled such a theme, for at his death in 1820 he had, according to Henry Sewell Stokes, left an unfinished manuscript poem 'on the romantic theme of Arthur and his British and Armoric Knights, and their heroic adventures in their excursions from the impregnable sea-tower of Tintagel'.[189] Since Stokes was only twelve at the time of Willyams's death, and had not moved to Cornwall until about 1832, it is unlikely that he was shown the manuscript by the writer himself. His access to it was probably gained through James Brydges's brother Humphrey, the inheritor of Carnanton, to whom Stokes dedicated his own topographical poem *The Vale of Lanherne* in 1836.

Although Willyams's manuscript cannot now be located, his theme was successfully pursued by Thomas Hogg, a native of Kelso, Roxburghshire, who had settled in Truro from 1805 to 1829 as Master of the Grammar School, contributed verse to the *Gazette*, and was, besides, a member of the Institute.[190] In 1827 he published a very long poem, *The Fabulous History of Cornwall*, which sought to resurrect those 'histories having lain dormant in libraries for the last five hundred years' which are 'found to give an interest, hitherto unnoticed, to the early history of Cornwall'.[191] For the supply of such materials 'from many sources', he acknowledged his obligation by means of a dedication to Sir Christopher Hawkins of Trewithin, MP. An avowed aim of Hogg's work is to advance Cornish claims to historical importance through his revealing that 'Britain to the Duchy owes / The beam which first from History flows' (p. 24). Even though Hogg is vociferously aware of the fraudulence of 'monkish legend', he adopts from Geoffrey of Monmouth and Thomas Malory almost two hundred pages of verse about Arthur and his knights. Although Hogg does not cite the *Morte* by title, it is virtually certain that this would have been his source for several important sections, namely a detailed account of the *enfances* of Arthur, wherein Hogg, alone of early nineteenth century writers, recounts the incident of Arthur's drawing the Sword from the Stone; or that of Arthur's combat with the Giant of St Michael's Mount. On

---

[188] *RCG*, 21 November 1818, 4. The prefactory note is dated 27 October 1818. This poem was, in fact, by Richard Polwhele, and had previously been published in 1815.

[189] Henry Sewell Stokes, *The Vale of Lanherne, and other poems* (1836), 101.

[190] Hogg's verses 'On the Death of Her Majesty, the Queen' appeared in the *Gazette* on 28 November 1818, 2. In 1819 he delivered the introductory lecture for the season: see *RCG*, 4 December 1819, 4.

[191] Thomas Hogg, *The History of the Ancient Kingdom of Cornwall* (1827), xix. William Makepeace Thackeray owned a copy of Hogg's poem, with an 'autograph note by the author': see *Reprints of the Catalogues of the Libraries of Charles Dickens and W. M. Thackerary*, edited by J. H. Stonehouse (1935), 144.

other occasions, Hogg is obligingly candid in acknowledging his sources, not only by inserting these in footnotes but also weaving them into the poetic text: thus, Arthur's wars are related 'as Gaufride's page narrates' (p. 396), this appeal to authority lending the text the style of a medieval chronicle. Indeed, faithful here to the chronicle rather than the romance tradition, Hogg presents Arthur as an exemplar of moral virtue, and this aura pervades the idealised relationship of Launcelot and Guenever. All this collated material is viewed from a Cornish perspective in which Tintagel is the chief focus. This leads to a concentration on certain key elements of the Arthurian plot: in particular, Uther's role in wresting Igrene from Gorlois; the later use of the castle as residence by Isonde, the wife of King Marc; and the slain Arthur's being carried there after the final battle. Furthermore, Hogg places great emphasis on Arthur's cousin Cador, Duke of Cornwall, who becomes a leading counsellor, and who raises Guenever at his palace of Restormel. The scene of Arthur's own upbringing by Hector and Merlin is not specifically designated but it lies not beyond the distance of a hunting trip from Tintagel, as the widowed Igrene encounters her lost son one day whilst she is pursuing 'the bounding deer' (p. 220). The neighbouring Moray woods are the location, too, of Merlin's eventual confinement by Vivienne. Hogg also draws on the traditional topographical authorities, noting William Worcester's description of Tintagel, and Carew ('Cornwall's morning star') as evidence for the site of Arthur's demise:

> The slaughter-bridge, as proof, remains,
> Of blood that deluged Cornwall's plains:
> Old folk, a stone, through circling years,
> Show: — it King Arthur's name, still, bears.   (p. 399)

Through concentration of the action within a limited area so well known to him, Hogg exploits his intimate relationship with the landscape: as in the vignette of Launcelot crossing 'Camel's sedgy stream' before slowly ascending a 'furzy hill' (p. 244). As for Tintagel, Hogg is richly aware of its stones 'of azure blue and cinnabar'; its flora, from 'the spiky garlands' of autumnal thistles to 'the seapink' that crowns the peninsula; its prospect towards Lundy Island seven leagues to the north-east; and the local legend of a twice-yearly disappearance (pp. 203 – 07). Furthermore, as with Peacock, against a past landscape is occasionally juxtaposed a modern development: as when, on the frequent journeys that occur between Tintagel and Restormel, it is narrated of Launcelot and Tristrem that before crossing 'Fawy dale' they 'wend through copse, and flowery lands, / Where, now, Lanhydrock's mansion stands' (p. 335). As a schoolmaster, Hogg may be considered to have been well-placed to diffuse Arthurian influence. That there was some such contact is shown by the fact that a former pupil of his, the poet Francis Hingston, had contributed towards Hogg's poem a section entitled 'La Belle Isonde sings to the Harp',

which was an English version of an Isonde poem ('Ma Branguien, ma tant
fidelle amie') whose French text had appeared in the notes to Way's
Fabliaux.[192] Another pupil was, almost certainly, John Michell, who was born
in Truro, and whose younger brother, the prolific poet Nicholas Michell, had
definitely been at Truro Grammar School with two of Richard Polwhele's
sons, and had been made known to Thomas Campbell through an
introduction by Dr Hogg, the son of the Headmaster, the latter having retired
to London in 1829, and remaining there until his death in 1835.[193] What
seems to have been John Michell's sole published poem was addressed from
Calenick, a village two miles south of Truro, and contributed to *Forget Me Not*,
under the title of 'Tintagel Castle'. In reaction against the 'Eternal tumult of
the passing crowd' of city life, Michell finds release for 'Contemplation' and
'Fancy' only in 'rare-frequented solitudes'. One such is Tintagel, which
supplies him with the power to recapture in fancy the 'pristine glory' of the

> Birthplace of Arthur! scene of many a crime!
> Stupendous relics of a distant time!
> Oft the abode of Merlin — wondrous sage,
> Whose wand even ocean's fury could assuage![194]

Having continued to fancy for some time, he wakes and 'the vision fades
away' to leave the poet once more in the physical presence of 'the ruins' and
the 'giant rocks', with a recognition that since 'the days of chivalry are o'er',
only 'Tradition's tales' can prolong the fame of knighthood, for Arthur 'lives
but in romance or song!'

The manner in which a web of personal connections and local friendships
could help to spread a concern with the Arthurian legend may be seen in the
case of Henry Sewell Stokes, who had recommended Willyams's poem. Born
in Gibraltar in 1808, educated in Chatham and Southwark, he had
undertaken legal studies in Gibraltar, and had then been articled at Tavistock
in western Devon before settling in Truro in 1832, initially as a solicitor but
then he began a five year editorship of a Truro newspaper, the *Cornish
Guardian and Western Chronicle*, and entered upon a life of public office and
Liberal politics. In his poem advocating parliamentary reform, *The Song of
Albion* (see Chapter 1), he had cited Arthur as an early patriot; and the location
which is immediately described is Tintagel, 'grim and hoar'. This gives rise to
a snatch of autobiography:

> O, I have been in by-gone hours,
> With one (dear friend!) whose legend-lore

---

[192] Way, *Fabliaux*, III, 209 – 10.
[193] The probability of John Michell's attendance at Truro School is confirmed in a private
communication from Mr S. M. Mischler of Truro.
[194] John Michell, 'Tintagel Castle', ll. 19 – 22; in *Forget Me Not* (1829), 85 – 88.

That watching on that rock sublime,
So witch'd my soul to olden time,
Methought I saw the Island King,
Standing mid-air in bold relief.   (I. 237 – 42)

Probably by Stokes, too, is a poem in the *Cornish Guardian* on the subject of Dozmary Pool on Bodmin Moor. Looking into this pool, the poet's eye recreates an Arthurian scene at Tintagel, with

fair Guenevere's bowers,
And Merlin, with his prophet lyre,
And Arthur's knightly train,
The very flower of chivalry.[195]

Born in Penzance, the son of a Wesleyan minister, John Magor Boyle later produced his one known literary work, which is of great Cornish interest, *Gorlaye*. The land of his birth, which he apostrophises (III. i), has 'blue streams', 'rugged shores' and 'wild wastes, purpled by the heather bell'; and this Cornish alignment is evident in the poem's central plot. Although this plot is well-known and ultimately derives from Geoffrey of Monmouth in that it deals with the triangular amours of Uter, Igerne and Gorlois (here known as 'Gorlaye' to avoid any possible 'ambiguity in the pronunciation'), Boyle's main source was, nevertheless, almost certainly Hals's account which had been amply quoted in Polwhele's *History of Cornwall*, and which provides a detailed topography for the events, denoting in particular Uter's palace of 'Caer Segont' as Winchester, and 'Pendue' as Tintagel.[196] This verse tale in four cantos presents a vigorously partisan allegiance to the South-West, and to Dumnonian traditions and virtues: the main theme melodramatically portraying the noble and stoical Duke of Cornwall's unsuccessful struggle against the evilly lecherous Uter Pendragon, who 'Glared like a tiger on his prey, / Then gnashed his teeth in scorn' (I. xix). Despite opening at the latter's palace of Caer Segont, the narrative soon moves west to Isca (= Exeter) and thence into Cornwall, frequently stressing the local aspect, such as in the list of Gorlaye's knights:

---

[195] 'Cornubiana, No. 1. Dosmerry Pool', ll. 12 – 15; in *Cornish Guardian and Western Chronicle*, 3 October 1834, 7. The poem's author is given as 'HENRY'. It is probable that Stokes wrote all the verse that was signed 'HENRY', 'H.S.S.' and 'H.' in this newspaper. The newspaper also recorded a relic of Arthurian folklore in its review of Claude Hawker's *Lecture on the Bude Canal*, by noting

The ancient Cornishmen had a proverb whereby they intimated the stability of nature amid the changes of men:
Let Uther Pendragon do what he can
The Tamar River will run as it ran.

Cornish Guardian, 12 September 1834, 7.

[196] John Magor Boyle, *Gorlaye, or A Tale of the Olden Tyme* (1835), 129.

> Warriors of mettle true were they:
> Pendarves, Carminnow, and Bray,
> Bodrugan, with his dreadful spear (III. x)

Local allusion is sometimes very specific: whilst, for instance, night falls over 'Roughter's rocks', the knights take their rest in Dameliock's hall. Besides alluding to Carew on Dundagell (Boyle preserves the older spelling), the descriptive accuracy of the relationship between mainland, island, bay and cavern suggests a first-hand knowledge of the site, and Boyle is learnedly advanced in his incorporation of Ulette's cell within his topography. Leland had initially referred to the remains of a monastery that had been founded there by the missionary St Julian (or Juliot), who had crossed from South Wales in the fifth century. For his own purposes, Boyle adopts the hermit's chapel recorded by Polwhele, and fully integrates this site within his poem as the home of his imagined hermit, Ivor Dhu:[197] an innovation which enables Boyle to supply a final stanza in which the legend is verified and the past juxtaposed with the present:

> Beside a now neglected spring,
> 'Mid rocks and wild flowers murmuring,
> There is a stone on Ulette's isle,
>   Remaining yet, by moss o'ergrown,
> Where parting sunbeams longest smile,
>   A humble and neglected stone;
> Whose characters once rudely traced,
> Time's fingers have almost effaced:
> But once as olden legends say,
> It bore the name of Duke Gorlaye;
> With his, who faithful at his side,
> (And constant until death) had died:
> Yet all that now remains to view,
> Is this short record 'IVOR DHU'.   (IV. xxxiv)

---

[197] Polwhele, *Cornwall*, I, 104 – 05.

3

The Comic

The desire for an appropriate epic dignity had generally curtailed the inclusion of comic elements within those historical poems which had embodied a national theme. In the rival tradition of folklore and romance where, on the contrary, the claims for an historical Arthur were relaxed or abandoned, the material was frequently treated from a variety of comic viewpoints. A broad classification of some of the major comic modes then prevalent will therefore be made in order to concentrate attention upon the importance of comic treatments of the Arthurian legend in the early nineteenth century.

Broad Humour: The Ballads

The publication in 1765 of Thomas Percy's *Reliques of Ancient English Poetry* was, in Southey's phrase, 'the great poetical epoch of the present reign'.[1] Besides stimulating a ballad revival in contemporary literature, it became a major source for popular introduction to the Arthurian legends for, among the ballads thus restored to literary currency, six were Arthurian, and of these the two finest poems ('The Marriage of Sir Gawaine' and 'The Boy and the Mantle') display a humorous gusto for the grotesque, which Percy occasionally included in his collection (see 'The Witch of Wokey', 'Sir Aldingar' and 'The Dragon of Wantley' for non-Arthurian examples of the genre). 'The Marriage' describes the Loathly Lady, with a fascinated *schadenfreude*:

---

[1] Review of Joseph Ritson's *Metrical Romanceës; in Annual Review*, 2 (1804), 515 – 35.

> Her nose was crookt, and turnd outwarde;
>   Her chin stoode all awrye;
> And where as sholde have been her mouthe,
>   Lo! there was set her eye.[2]

The language has a racy forthrightness, as when revealing Guenever's instantly vituperative jealousy of Cradocke's lady:

> See you not yonder woman,
>   That maketh herself soe cleane?
> I have seen tane out of her bedd
>   Of men fiveteene;
> Priests, clarkes, and wedded men
>   From her bedeene   (135 – 40)

Moreover, the central situations are explicitly bawdy, in that humour resides in Gawaine's promise to go to bed with the crone, or in the spectacle of unfaithful wives being publicly humiliated through wearing a shrinking garment:

> When she had tane the mantle,
> Of cloth that was made,
> She had no more left on her,
> But a tassell and a threed   (89 – 92)

In complementary vein is another traditional ballad, 'The Cokwald's Dance', which David Laing transcribed from a fifteenth century manuscript in the Ashmolean Museum. This ballad was printed in a collection of *Ancient Metrical Tales* (1829) which was edited by Charles Hartshorne, an antiquarian country clergyman who had begun his research whilst at St John's College, Cambridge in 1821 to 1825. Hartshorne's work was owned by Peacock, and considered a 'curious volume' by Walter Scott in the 1830 introduction to *Ivanhoe*, but seems never to have obtained the vastly wider popularity enjoyed by the two Percy ballads. The appeal of their theme is attested by the appearance of John Seally's burlesque opera 'The Marriage of Sir Gawaine' in the *European Magazine*, which was 'humbly inscribed to those who love antiquity for its nonsense more than its sense'.[3] In this burlesque, Arthur's knights are treated as jovial tipplers: their novel justification is that:

---

[2] Lines 93 – 96; in Thomas Percy, *Reliques of Ancient English Poetry*, edited by Robert Aris Willmott, new edition (1867).
[3] John Seally, 'The Marriage of Sir Gawaine. An Opera'; in *European Magazine*, 1 (May 1782), 320 – 24; and 2 (July 1782), 18 – 21. This work is not mentioned by Merriman.

> when the word's to attack a dragon,
> We close should hug th'auxilial flaggon:
> For how can we his flame oppose,
> Better than with a fiery nose?   (scene ii. 29 – 32)

Arthur does not lack for personal bravery, and good-naturedly volunteers to help the captured princess, but he can also display a rakish cynicism when nominating Gawaine to be the hag's husband: 'Wed her he shall; nor need it much him distress, / For tho' she's ugly, he may keep a mistress (scene vi. 38 – 39). There was another treatment of the theme in Benedikte Naubert's German short story *Der kurze Mantel* (1789 – 1793), which was translated into English by George Soane for his *Specimens of German Romance*, and which features the traditional story of the shrinking mantle, with a particularly trenchant attack on the aristocratic ladies of the Arthurian court.[4] Not only was there a crop of contemporary allusions to 'The Boy and the Mantle' and to the Loathly Lady, but the latter — in the analogous form of Chaucer's *Wife of Bath's Tale* — provided the basis for a number of pictorial interpretations, such as a Thomas Stothard frontispiece (1782), and paintings by Richard Westall (1788), George Corbould (1802) and Henry Fuseli (c. 1812).[5] In the 1830s, however, there appears to have been a transfer of interest to two other Percy ballads, 'Sir Lancelot du Lake' and 'King Arthur's Death'. This change is perhaps due to the fact that Arthurian ballads were regarded as suitable for children's reading, and so their selection was increasingly controlled in terms of moral content. Moreover, the shift also reflects a wider literary and social reaction against what were coming to be regarded as 'immoral' Regency social values. Aptly illustrating the trend is the published work of Reginald Heber, whose *Masque of Gwendolen* is based on *The Wife of Bath's Tale* or the associated Percy ballad. Heber's poem is, as published, nowhere humorous in tone, and its fragmentary form obscures with a lacuna the potentially risqué scene of the bedroom debate. The poem may have been thus moralised, but it seems more probable that, since the poem was completed, and performed as a Christmas festivity in 1816, his widow exercised a censorial function by preparing a bowdlerised text for publication in 1830.[6] In this form, however, it attracted the approval of *Literary Gazette* and *Fraser's* for its 'romantic' qualities, and the temptation scene (which Heber

---

[4] *Specimens of German Romance*, 3 vols (1826), III, 95 – 259.

[5] Frontispiece illustration, engraved by Grignion, in *Poetical Works of Geoffrey Chaucer*, 14 vols (Edinburgh, 1782), III. Graves, *Royal Academy Exhibitors*. Gert Schiff and Paola Viotto, *L'opera completa di Füssli* (Milan, 1977), pl. 226.

[6] For the assumption that the work was never completed, see Merriman, 171; Taylor and Brewer, 63. Amelia Heber, however, states that: 'Heber commenced and subsequently completed a 'masque', taken from Chaucer's *Wife of Bath's Tale*. From the *'Masque'* . . . some excerpts [will] now be given': *Life of Heber*, I, 448.

models on that of Milton's *Comus*) earned special praise.[7] The 'Mantle' legend formed the subject of a six-hundred line poem contributed to *Democratic Review*.[8] Like Heber's masque, 'The Ylle Cutt Mantell' avoids bawdiness, and focuses instead on the virtuous qualities of the mantle winner, who is here idiosyncratically deemed to be 'sweet Coralie', a Normandy peasant-girl who had formerly been unjustly maligned by her courtly lover. Though considerably softened in tone, and reduced in significance, the comic aspect of the poem is nevertheless apparent, and revealed in a genial raillery directed against Queen Ginevra's public embarrassment before the smiles 'which the best courtiers could not hide, / Though they bit their lips till they almost cried' (281 – 82), and the acute discomfiture of her spouse:

> King Arthur wore an air
> Timid as that of startled rabbit;
> And fidgeted upon his chair,
> Which is a most disgraceful habit   (467 – 70)

Within a comic context, other traditional ballads featured Arthur as a predominantly humorous figure. Besides figuring in the nursery rhyme of the bag-pudding ('When good King Arthur ruled this land'), Arthur also appeared in 'The Life and Death of Tom Thumb', where the diminutive hero's birth is contrived by Merlin. Later, Tom visits the Arthurian court, jousts with Sir Lancelot and others, wears the King's signet ring as a 'girdle', dances 'a galliard brave / Upon his queen's left hand', and, on demise, is awarded by Arthur a marble tomb and forty days of official mourning.[9] This ballad, probably first printed in 1630, was widely available in eighteenth century chapbooks, which also supplied at least two continuations of the original.[10] It appeared, too, in such ballad collections as that of Thomas Evans (1810 edition), whilst the story was discussed by Joseph Ritson in *Pieces of Ancient Popular Poetry* and retold in works like Benjamin Tabart's *Popular Fairy Tales*, a collection which was accorded an extensive review by Francis Cohen in the *Quarterly*.[11]

The associated tradition of 'good King Arthur' bestows upon him the attributes found in the ballad of King Cole, thereby representing Arthur's reign as an epitome of jovial, festive Merrie England. Allusions to the virtues of this golden age are commonplace. Even Praed's light banter in 'Gog' conveys not derisive mockery but a warm celebration of cordial humour:

[7] *Lit Gaz*, 19 June 1830, 398 – 400. *Fr*, 11 (September 1830), 126 – 29.
[8] 'The Ylle Cutt Mantell; A Romaunt of the Tyme of Gud Kynge Arthur', *Democratic Review*, 14 (May 1844), 456 – 76. No author was named, but a female authorship may be presumed from the admission 'as a daughter of Eve / Myself' in ll. 118 – 19.
[9] Lines 187 – 88; in *The Legendary Ballads of England and Scotland*, edited by John S. Roberts (1868).
[10] See John Ashton, *Chap-books of the Eighteenth Century* (1882).
[11] *Pieces of Ancient Popular Poetry*, edited by Joseph Ritson (1791), 93 – 113. Benjamin Tabart, *Fairy Tales, or the Lilliputian Cabinet* (1819), 152 – 59. *QR*, 21 (January 1819), 91 – 112.

His ancient face, and ancient clothes,
His tables round and rounder oaths,
His crown and cup, his feasts and fights,
His pretty Queen and valiant knights,
Would make me up the raciest scene
That is, or will be, or has been.[12]

A comparable comic spirit appears, too, in George Colman's very popular melodrama *The Battle of Hexham*, which opened in 1789 and included a glee by John Wall Callcott which parodied the start of the traditional Percy ballad of 'Sir Lancelot du Lake':

When Arthur first, in Court, began
To wear long hanging-sleeves,
He entertain'd three serving-men,
And all of them were thieves![13]

The simple morality, practical joking, physical discomfiture, and stock butts of this broad humour (cuckolds, faithless wives and so on) recur in Bulwer Lytton's 'The Lady and the Dogs', a poem deriving from a *fabliau* source, which relates how a lady is rescued from an assailant, is then married to her rescuer Gawaine, but soon chooses to depart with the original assailant, whereas her dogs display greater gratitude by electing to remain with Gawaine: 'The happy bridegroom got the Dogs — that wretched man the Bride!'[14] Lytton later works the story into Book VI of *King Arthur*. Here, the expanded narrative is preceded, as in the medieval French *Le Chevalier à l'Epée*, by the episode of the enchanted sword and bed. Although Lytton knew Way's *Fabliaux*, which treats the same story under the title of 'The Knight and the Sword', Lytton's version replaces the delicate emotional sensibility of Way's tale with a reversion to a more vigorous and broader humour, as when Gawaine, in order to distance himself from the threatening sword, indignantly recoils from the attentions of his bride:

[12] 'Gog', ll. 5 – 10; in *Etonian*, 8 (1821), 222 – 34; and 9 (1821), 327 – 36; reprinted in *Poems*, 2 vols (1864).
[13] George Colman, the Younger, *The Battle of Hexham; or, Days of Old*, II. i. 1 – 4; in *The British Theatre*, edited by Mrs Inchbald, 25 vols (1808), XX.
[14] Line 51; in Lytton, *Eva*.

'But thou for Gawaine ne'er shalt be a mourner,
Thou keep the couch, and I — yon farthest corner!'
This said, the prudent knight on tiptoe stealing
Went from his bride as far as he could go,
Then laid him down, intent upon the ceiling;
Noses, once lost, no second crop will grow.   (VI. lxxiv – lxxv)

Burlesque, Pantomime and Spectacle: The Stage

The broad humour that was often displayed in Arthurian balladry was also
reflected upon the stage in the form of burlesque or pantomime, and
represents an unbroken, though little remarked, tradition of robust humour
which persisted throughout the first half of the nineteenth century.

A dominant Arthurian work in the eighteenth century theatre had been
Henry Fielding's burlesque of neo-classical heroic drama *The Tragedy of
Tragedies* (1730, 1731), which was based on the ballad story of Tom Thumb;
and Fielding's choice of the Tom Thumb legend was entirely appropriate to
his primary aim because the ballad provided an ironic analogy with Dryden's
selection of comparable material for his dramatic opera of *King Arthur* (1691), a
work which Fielding names as one of his targets for ridicule. Moreover, the
pygmy proportions of Tom Thumb reduce by association the heroic stature of
the neo-classical hero, as typified by King Arthur's being a 'passionate sort of
king, husband to Queen Dollalolla, of whom he stands a little in fear',
although on other occasions he struts and rhodomontades with an engaging
braggadocio:

> Petition me no petitions, Sir, today;
> Let other hours be set apart for business.
> Today it is our pleasure to be drunk,
> And this our queen shall be as drunk as we.[15]

The play was regularly performed in London theatres up to 1755 and in the
provinces for many years thereafter. With music by Thomas Arne, it was
remodelled as *The Opera of Operas* (1733); and, though robbing the original of
most of its allusive verbal subtlety, Kane O'Hara's adaptation *Tom Thumb*
(1780) continued to prosper as a simple broad farce with interspersed songs,

---

[15] Henry Fielding, *The Tragedy of Tragedies; or, The Life and Death of Tom Thumb the Great*, I, ii.
15 – 18; in *Eighteenth Century Plays* (New York, 1952).

and the augmentation of Merlin's role as enchanter. The popularity of the theme is shown, too, by the publication in 1785 of another version by an anonymous author.[16] O'Hara's complete text first appeared in 1805; J. H. Jameson issued drawings of Tom Thumb in his *Juvenile Drama Series* (1811); Thomas Rowlandson made a drawing of *The last scene of 'Tom Thumb'* at the Scarborough Theatre in 1813; Samuel de Wilde portrayed the contemporary actress Mrs Liston in the role of Arthur's Queen Dollalolla, a drawing which served as frontispiece to the British Stage edition of the play in 1817; and the same artist painted John Liston in the part of Lord Grizzle (RA, 1812); whilst George Cruikshank illustrated an edition of O'Hara's play.[17]

Other testimony suggests a widespread acquaintanceship with the Fielding or the O'Hara form of this burlesque. Henry Hart Milman, 'being of an elegant height', acted the part of the Queen of the Giants in an Eton College production in the first decade of the century; an 1813 letter from Tom Moore acknowledges his quotation from *Tom Thumb*; and in 1814 Walter Scott whimsically imagines himself exchanging quotations with Byron from Fielding's play.[18] Charles Dickens was later to recall the bathetic effect of the lines:

> I feel a sudden pain within my breast.
> Nor know I whether it arise from love
> Or only the wind-colic.[19]

And it was a song from the O'Hara version that Jingle quoted at the White Hart Inn as he went out to obtain the licence for his marriage to Miss Wardle: 'In hurry, post-haste for a licence, / In hurry, ding-dong I come back.'[20] Childhood visits in the early years of the century to Sadler's Wells and Astley's in order to see 'Beauty and the Beast, Tom Thumb and Cinderella' are remembered by John Moultrie in his autobiographical poem *The Dream of Life* (1843), whilst Praed's 'Private Theatricals' (1832) by including reference to Fielding's or O'Hara's version ('Huncamunca must have a huge sabre')

---

[16] *The Life, Death, and Renovation of Tom Thumb; a Legendary Burletta in one act, as it is performed at the Royal Circus* (1785): British Library pressmark 1175. c. 94.

[17] Rowlandson's drawing was used as an illustration in William Combe, J. B. Papworth and F. Wrangham, *Poetical Sketches of Scarborough* (1813). *Tom Thumb; a Burletta, altered from Henry Fielding*, by Kane O'Hara: With designs by George Gruikshank (1830).

[18] Arthur Milman, *Henry Hart Milman*, 18. *The Letters of Thomas Moore*, edited by Wilfred S. Dowden, 2 vols (Oxford, 1964), I, 275. John Gibson Lockhart, *The Life of Sir Walter Scott* (1906), 265.

[19] *Tragedy of Tragedies*, I. iii. 48 – 50. Letter of T. J. Cullingford, 24 January 1837; in *Letters of Charles Dickens*, I, 228.

[20] Charles Dickens, *The Pickwick Papers* (1948), chapter 10.

1a. Sir Lanval

1b. Sir Gawaine in The Mule without a Bridle

2a. *King Arthur and the Queen of Beauty.*
Thompson's illustration for Bannerman's 'The
Prophecy of Merlin' (1802)

2b. *King Arthur and Merlin. Illustration for Peacock's* The Round Table *(1817)*

Stothard's illustrations for Scott's The Bridal of Triermain, *in* The Royal Engagement Pocket Atlas *(1815)*

3a. King Arthur and Guendolen

3b. The Knights of the Round Table

Uwins's illustrations for Malory (Walker and Edwards, 1816)

4a. The Lady of the Lake and Excalibur

4b. King Arthur and the Questing Beast

Uwins's illustrations for Malory (Walker and Edwards, 1816)

5a. *The Vision of Sir Percivale*

5b. *Sir Launcelot fights a Dragon*

Craig's illustrations for Malory (Wilks, 1816)

6a. *The Death of Sir Launcelot*

6b. *The Damsel of the Lake and Excalibur*

Craig's illustrations for Malory (Wilks, 1816)

LA MORT D'ARTHUR.

The most ancient
and famous History of the renowned
Prince Arthur
and the
KNIGHTS of the ROUND TABLE.

by Sir Thos. Malory, Knt.

VOL. II

Battle of Sir Launcelot & Sir Tristram.

Sir Tristram that was wounded got out his sword and rushed
to Sir Launcelot, and gave him three great strokes on the
helmet that the fire sprang out.

LONDON

Printed & Published by R. Wilks, 89, Chancery Lane;
Sold also by Simpkin & Marshall, Stationers' Court, Ludgate Hill;
and all other Booksellers. 1816.

The parting of SIR TRISTRAM & LA BEALE ISOND
dramatic: and I, La Beale Isond, I promise you that I
shall not be married this seven years, but it be by your
assent. And then Sir Tristram gave her a ring, and
then she gave him another.

7b. *The Battle of Sir Launcelot and Sir Tristram*

7a. *The Parting of Sir Tristram and La Beale Isond*

Craig's illustrations for Malory (Wilks, 1816)

LA MORT D'ARTHUR.

The most ancient
and famous History of the renowned
Prince Arthur
and the
KNIGHTS of the ROUND TABLE.

by Sir The. Malory, Knt.

VOL. III.

Sir Percival gave the serpent such a buffet
that he had a deadly wound.
P. 101.

LONDON.

Printed & Published by R.Wilks, 89, Chancery Lane;
Sold also by Simpkin & Marshall, Stationers' Court, Ludgate Hill;
and all other Booksellers, 1816.

8b. Sir Percival fights a Serpent

PRINCE ARTHUR obtaining the SWORD.
then he pulled at the sword with all his might, but
it would not be. Now shall ye assay, said Sir Ector to Sir Arthur. With a good will, said Arthur.
And pulled it out easily.
Vol. I. Pa. 34.

8a. Prince Arthur obtains the Sword from the Stone

9a. King Arthur at Tintagel. Williams's illustration for Howitt's Visits to Remarkable Places *(1840)*

9b. King Arthur knights Jack. Leech's illustration for Leigh's Jack the Giant Killer *(1843)*

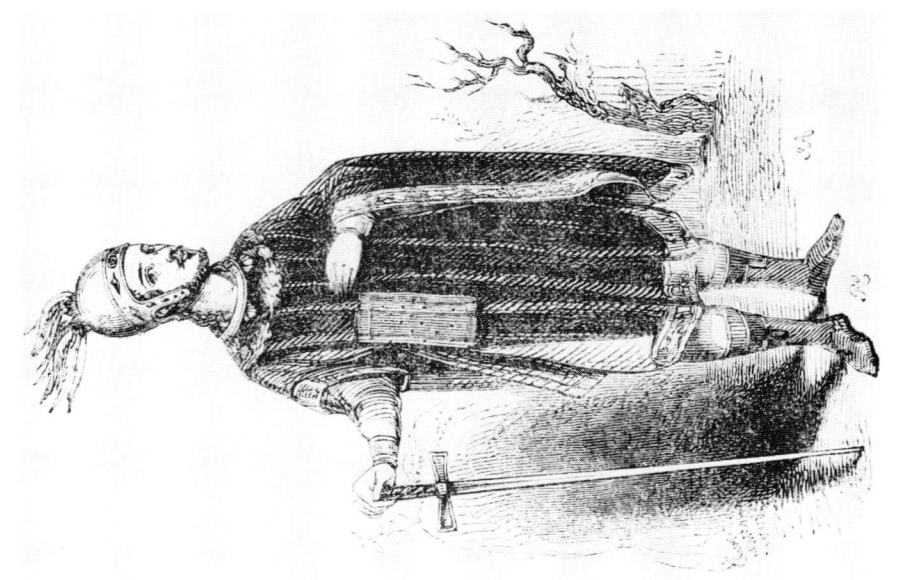

10b. Anderson in the role of King Arthur

Macready's production of Dryden and Purcell's King Arthur in 1842

10a. King Arthur and the Syrens

11b. Hine's Punch cartoon of 'King Arthur's Court' (1843)

11a. Harlequin King Arthur. Crowquill's cartoon of the Sadler's Wells production in 1842

HEN Arthur first in court began,
  And was approved king,
By force of armes great victorys won,
  And conquest home did bring.

Then into Britain straight hee came,
  Where fifty good and able
Knights, then repaired unto him,
  Which were of the Round Table :

12. Corbould's 'Sir Lancelot du Lake'

King Arthur's Death.

All sore astonied stood the duke ;
　　He stood as still as still mote be ;
Then hastend back to tell the king,
　　But he was gone from under the tree.

But to what place he cold not tell,
　　For never after he did him spy ;
But he saw a barge go from the land,
　　And he heard ladyes howl and cry.

And whether the king were there, or not,
　　He never knew, nor ever cold ;
But from that sad and direfull day,
　　He never more was seene on mold.

13. *In Franklin's 'King Arthur's Death', Sir Lukyn throws Excalibur into the river*

14. *Pickersgill*: Amoret, Aemylia and Prince Arthur in the cottage of Sclaunder *(1845)*

King Arthur.

And so lovely seem'd she there,
Spell-bound in her ivory chair,
That her angry sire, repenting,
Craves stern Merlin for relenting ;
And the champions, for her sake,
Would again the contest wake,
Till in necromantic night
Gyneth vanish'd from their sight.

15. *Merlin casts a spell on Gyneth. Selous's illustration for Scott's* The Bridal of Triermain, *in* Poems and Pictures *(1846)*

16. William Bell Scott: King Arthur carried to the land of enchantment, *engraved by Linton (1847)*

suggests that this burlesque was still in regular production by amateurs.[21] That this was indeed the case is revealed by the diaries of Princess Victoria, who watched a charade performed at Haddon Hall on 20 October 1832, the third act of which consisted of a scene taken from *Tom Thumb*.[22] Further evidence of the continuing popularity of the theme is provided by the appearance of a sequel at the English Opera House in 1840. In this work, entitled *The Second Part of the Tragycalle Historie of Thomas Thumbe*, Arthur is represented as a 'regal and recent widower, miserable accordingly', who later falls victim to a glass of rum poisoned by the courtier Doodle. When Noodle and Doodle eventually stab each other, Arthur's ghost arises to bewail their apparent deaths. His lament is representative of the play's burlesque of Shakespearean tragic declamation:

> What dead disturbing howl was that — what dismal holla?
> Oh! What a fall is here, my Dollalolla.
> All — our big and little ones in one fell swoop
> By fate sucked up like vermicelli soup.
> All flesh is soup — soup that is dished full soon.
> Death is the eater and dire fate the spoon.[23]

Besides these frequent humorous associations with the Tom Thumb legend, Arthurian personae had — as archetypally British symbols — long been linked with masques and spectacular royal entertainments, as in George Gascoigne's *Princely Pleasures* (1576), Ben Jonson's *Prince Henry's Barriers* (1610) and William Davenant's *Britannia Triumphans* (1637).[24] The adoption of such operatic and masque elements within Dryden and Purcell's *King Arthur* (1691) provided the eighteenth century audience with a widely performed precedent for the association of Arthur with spectacular theatrical effects. This work had also contained comic scenes, in the form of its merry-making Kentish countrymen. Given this congruence of the spectacular, the fairy, romantic love and the comic, the later appearance of a minor Arthurian pantomime tradition represents a natural development. Merlin, whose reputation as a wizard and prophet remained so great that he had achieved substantial autonomy as a character divorced from his earlier Arthurian setting, had long been associated with distinctively histrionic effects. This reputation, which was significantly perpetuated by Cervantes' portrayal of a purported Merlin's ghost delivering an admonitory speech aboard a triumphal chariot in a

---

[21] John Moultrie, *Poems*, 2 vols (1876), I, 376. 'Private Theatricals', l. 32; in *Selected Poems of Winthrop Mackworth Praed*, edited by Kenneth Allott (1953): first published in *Gem* (1832).
[22] *The Girlhood of Queen Victoria: a selection from Her Majesty's diaries between the years 1832 and 1840*, edited by Viscount Esher, 2 vols (1912), I, 55 – 56.
[23] British Library, Additional MS 42955, fols 940 – 974b.
[24] See Brinkley, *Arthurian Legend*.

masque-like procession, also formed the subject of a number of mid-eighteenth century stage entertainments.[25] Stemming in particular from Queen Caroline's installation of a neo-Gothic 'Merlin's Cave' at Richmond in 1735, there followed Edward Phillips's play *The Royal Chace, or, Merlin's Cave* (1736), one of the most popular works of the period, and which continued to be played until the end of the century, albeit often under the title of *Harlequin Skeleton*.[26] Complementary to this was Lewis Theobald's *Merlin, or the Enchanter of Stonehenge* (1734), which eclectically assigns Harlequin to the role of Merlin's aide, and makes Merlin himself a prime agent in the damnation of Faust. A further version of this was presented in 1767, whilst a similar eclecticism is evident in Aaron Hill's apparently unperformed play *Merlin in Love* (1760), which introduced Columbine as the object of the wizard's desires.[27]

A considerable influence in the revival of Arthurian fortunes, and hitherto a largely unrecognised one, was exerted by David Garrick, whose work shows the bonding that had developed between Arthurian legend and stage spectacle. In devising a play based on Dryden's verse tale *Cymon and Iphigenia*, Garrick restructured the material by introducing a major dramatic conflict between two rival enchanters: Urganda (who has been derived from the Peninsular romance *Amadis of Gaul*), and Merlin, her would-be lover. Repulsed, he vengefully and magically contrives to thwart Urganda's own passion for Cymon, but Merlin then assumes a dominant and largely benevolent role in pairing Cymon off with Sylvia. First produced on 2 January 1767, the piece was evidently intended as a Christmas entertainment. As Garrick's prologue had intimated, the audience was not to expect any 'Plot, Wit, or Humour', but in place of these there would be 'Dresses, Dances, Sinkings, Flyings and Scenes'.[28] What gives this play an additional interest for the Arthurian Revival is that into the grand finale marched 'a procession of knights of the different Orders of Chivalry'. Three years later, Garrick's interest in chivalric spectacle was again revealed by his revision of Dryden's *King Arthur* for a successful new production at Drury Lane, and in 1771 he staged his own *Institution of the Garter*, a masque which he had based on Gilbert West's poem (see Chapter 1). Although the extant sections of this masque contain none of West's Arthurian allusions, Garrick nevertheless maintains some of this

[25] Miguel de Cervantes, *The History of Don Quixote*, 2 vols (1905 – 1906), II, chap. 35.
[26] See *The London Stage: Part 2: 1700 – 1729*, edited by Emmett L. Avery, 2 vols (Carbondale, Illinois, 1960); *Part 3: 1729 – 1747*, edited by Arthur H. Souten, 2 vols (1961); *Part 4: 1747 – 1776*, edited by George Winchester Stone Jr, 2 vols (1962); *Part 5: 1776 – 1800*, edited by Charles Beecher Hogan, 2 vols (1968).
[27] Described by Hill as a 'Pantomime Opera': *Dramatic Works*, I, 319 – 42.
[28] David Garrick, *Cymon*; in *Bell's British Theatre*, 34 vols (1797), XXII. The play is not mentioned by Merriman.

connection by subtitling his work as *Arthur's Round Table Restored*.[29] The rival theatrical company of Covent Garden rapidly countered this production by staging another Garter play: George Colman's *The Fairy Prince*, a spectacular masque which, acknowledging its derivation from Ben Jonson's near-Arthurian *Masque of Oberon* and from 'a chorus of the late Gilbert West', included four references to Arthur's role as a pioneer of Windsor's royal fame.[30]

Pantomime thrived in the second half of the eighteenth century, deriving fresh impetus from the fact that minor London theatres such as Sadler's Wells were permitted by authority to present only musical and pantomimic shows.[31] Retaining only a marginal satirical content, these pantomimes, which were presented mainly — but not exclusively — at Christmas and Easter, developed in the direction of technical novelty and effect, indulged a genial and farcical humour, and, in their voracious search for new plot material, revealed a steadily increasing attention to historical, oriental and legendary themes, often fancifully combined into one mélange. The ostensible subject of the piece was generally used merely as an introductory framework, from which there ensued a series of transformations and startling ingenuities of stagecraft. The process may be seen at work in a letter which the actor John Philip Kemble wrote to Johnston, the machinist at Drury Lane, in 1789. Kemble's chief consideration was to stage a great historical procession, involving not only kings and dynasties but also such progressive concepts as 'Common Law, Trial by Jury and Oxford University'.[32] A further letter to his scene-painter, the elder Greenwood, indicated that an Arthurian frame could be used — as in Peacock's later poem *The Round Table* — for a panorama of English political history:

> Our fine procession, I am afraid, will do us very little good, if we have not some very pretty, short, laughable pantomime to introduce it. I have hit on nothing I can think of better than the story of King Arthur, and Merlin and the Saxon Wizards.

[29] David Garrick, *The Songs, Choruses, and Serious Dialogue of the Masque called 'The Institution of the Garter, or Arthur's Round Table restored'* (1771). Benjamin Vandergucht's RA painting *A Portrait in the character of Merlin* (1772) was probably stimulated by Garrick's revival of Dryden's *King Arthur*, which opened at Drury Lane on 13 December 1770 and was performed about twenty times that season. This play's heroine, Emmeline, also attracted artistic attention: see Thomas Stothard's *Theatrical Portrait of Miss Farren as Emmeline*, engraved by Heath for a series by Lowndes, 1785 – 1786; William Hamilton, *Emmeline* (RA 1792); and John Wood, *Emmeline* (BI 1832).

[30] *The Fairy Prince. A Masque, first acted at Covent Garden on 12 November 1771*; in *The Dramatic Works of George Colman*, 4 vols (1777), IV. The Arthurian references occur on pp. 237, 240 and 242. Merriman does not mention this play or Garrick's *Institution*.

[31] See Allardyce Nicoll, *A History of late eighteenth century drama, 1750 – 1800* (Cambridge, 1937), 208 – 10.

[32] *The Reminiscences of Thomas Dibdin*, 2 vols (1827), I, 197.

Kemble evidently refers to a prototype scene in Dryden's *King Arthur*, a play in which he had performed the lead role in a 1784 production that he had probably adapted himself from Dryden's original. Influenced by this handling, Kemble then evolves an elaborate fantasy:

> The pantomime might open with the Saxon witches lamenting Merlin's power over them, and forming an incantation by which they create a Harlequin, who is supposed to be able to counteract Merlin in all his designs for the good of King Arthur. If the Saxons came on in a dreadful storm, as they proceeded in their magical rites, the sky might brighten, and a rainbow sweep across the horizon, which, when the ceremonies are completed, should contract itself from either end, and form the figure of a Harlequin in the Heavens; the wizards may fetch him down how they will, and the sooner he is set to work the better.

Kemble then suggests that advice should be sought from 'Mr Lonsdale, the gentleman who makes the pantomimes for Sadler's Wells', since he is a man who seems 'to understand these entertainments very well':

> It must be very *short*, very LAUGHABLE, and very CHEAP; the procession to be introduced at the end, by way of amusing Arthur, after all his difficulties, with a prospect of the glories of his descendants.

This procession 'though prepared and nearly ready at great expense' was, however, for undisclosed reasons never staged.[33] On the other hand, a member of the great theatrical family of Dibdin, Charles Isaac Mungo Dibdin, did present at Sadler's Wells in 1802 a comic pantomime entitled *Wizard's Wake; or, Harlequin and Merlin*, wherein Merlin is portrayed as one of an international group of convivial wizards.[34] The play opens in 'Merlin's Cave', according to the announcement in *The Times*.[35] Since a combat is enacted between Sir John Bull and Citoyen Francoise (sic!), a pronouncedly anti-Revolutionary spirit may be presumed. The mage reappeared more prominently in an 1814 Astley's production called *Merlin's Cave; or, Harlequin's Masquerade*. Although this may have stemmed from Edward Phillips's 1736 play, the Astley's performance was, nonetheless, billed as 'an entire new Comic Pantomime', and though no text of it now survives, it may be deemed eclectic on the grounds of its including Harlequin, Columbine, Clown,

---

[33] *Ibid.*, I, 201.
[34] *Plots, Songs, Choruses, & Co. in the comic pantomime called 'Wizard's Wake: or Harlequin and Merlin'* (1803). Charles Isaac Mungo's father (i.e. Charles Dibdin b. 1745) had performed the role of Merlin in Edward Phillips's *The Royal Chace* at Covent Garden on 25, 28, and 30 October 1766: see *London Stage. Part 4*, Vol 2, 1191 – 92.
[35] *The Times*, 23 August 1802, 1.

Pantaloon and a 'grand Moorish Cymbal Pas de Quatre, by the Miss Adamses'.[36]

A more Arthurian ethos was achieved in Thomas Dibdin's 'entirely new' comic pantomime presented at Sadler's Wells, where he was director, in 1825.[37] As indicated by its title, *Merlin's Mount; or, Harlequin Cymraeg and the Living Leek*, this piece was influenced by the Cambrian Revival, and also by Dibdin's own acting tour in 1794 which took him to Swansea, Carmarthen and Haverfordwest: the visit to Carmarthen having been sufficiently felicitous to inspire his farce *St David's Day* (1800), which he dedicated to the memory of the liberality shown by the citizens of Carmarthen.[38] But Dibdin's play does not deal with the historical Arthur — indeed Dibdin makes no reference to him in his two-volume *A Metrical History of England* (1813). Instead, the plot is, according to *The Times* review, 'founded upon one of the numerous traditional legends current amongst the ancient Britons of their favourite enchanter Merlin'. Moreover, the 'fable', which was 'as usual in such cases, comic and romantic by turns', was made the 'vehicle of some pretty scenery, amongst which the prismatic palace of Merlin was favoured with immense applause'.

The concentration upon spectacle, both in terms of scenic effect and the introduction of equestrian novelties, reached a high point in Isaac Pocock's *King Arthur and the Knights of the Round Table* which ran at Drury Lane from Boxing Day 1834 to 6 February 1835. This was ostensibly a dramatisation of Scott's *The Bridal of Triermain*, but Pocock drastically reshapes Scott's narrative, gives the action a single time-scale, portrays Gyneth as Arthur's only child, who had been kept prisoner ('by means too horrible to name') by Morgana, Arthur's 'unnatural sister', who herself aims to wed Sir Roland; and to this young hero, Arthur lends Excalibur and his shield.[39] The incorporation of a Wicked Fairy role reveals the work's quasi-pantomimic nature; and although an extremely large cast of Arthurian knights is assembled, their task is chiefly confined to a participation in the physical storming of a castle, and to the equestrian jousting which this 'grand chivalric entertainment' provided in what was judged to be a performance 'in lieu of the usual Christmas pantomime'.[40] The spectacular nature of the event was augmented by the 'gorgeous' processions, by the 'magnificent' tableaux, and by Clarkson Stanfield's scene-painting. Henry Crabb Robinson recorded his pleasure in the 'glorious fighting' and in the 'most visionary' effect produced when the 'magical rocks' in the Vale of St John were, 'by means of a strong

36 *The Times*, 12 April 1814, 3.
37 Announced in *The Times* on 24 December 1825: reviewed on 27 December 1825, 3.
38 *Reminiscences*, I, 177 – 83.
39 *Songs, Choruses in 'King Arthur and the Knights of the Round Table'* (1834). For the complete text, see British Library, Additional MS 42928, fols 742 – 759b.
40 *The Times*, 27 December 1834, 2.

light' put behind them, 'made to become a castle with all its appurtenances'.[41]
What was intended as a humorous sub-plot was provided by the relationship
between Roland's armourer, John Galodin, and his betrothed, Dorothy
Stump, who sings in contrapuntal anti-heroic vein:

> I know, my dear Johnny, you love me so well,
> You think I shall die if we're parted;
> But I'll tell you the truth, and your sorrow dispel,
> I don't mean to die broken-hearted.

A revival was staged at Astley's in 1840, which ran from 14 September for at
least seven performances.

A pantomime plot could include extremely diverse elements, loosely
grouped around a few staple figures such as the ubiquitous Harlequin. An apt
example is provided by the prolific pantomime writer Richard Nelson Lee,
who presented his *Harlequin and Mother Red Cap; or, Merlin and Fairy Snowdrop* at
the Adelphi at Christmas 1839. In this, Mother Red Cap, who keeps a public
house, plans to wed her daughter to Squire Resolute. Merlin, who appears to
an introductory clap of thunder, is portrayed in his cave as 'the Astrologer of
the Olden Time', with a magic vial and wand.[42] The villainous role allotted
him, whereby he schemes to aid the Squire, is counteracted by the benevolent
intervention of Fairy Snowdrop and other flower fairies, who unite the
daughter with her loved Ploughboy: good fairies thus protect the poor,
especially those in love, against an unfeeling squirearchy. In addition to the
farcical and fairytale scenes of the introductory play, the ensuing 'entertainment' included a number of satirical topical allusions to the then imminent
royal wedding of Victoria and Albert: 'the bold pantomimist' venturing to
portray 'a little Prince Albert, a little Queen, and many little political
characters'.[43]

Minor topical references (to 'the China war and its termination', the tariff,
and the 'cold-water cure') recurred in a much more Arthurian pantomime,
Harlequin and Good King Arthur, presented at Sadler's Wells in December
1842.[44] In a climactic scene that followed the opening play, the Palace of
Allegory housed 'a splendid illustration of Great Britain, supported by
Wisdom and Valour, receiving homage from China and Hindostan'. Apart
from this celebration of such imperial events, the introductory play itself had
incorporated a burlesque on two recent theatrical performances. *The Times*
found the entry of the victorious Arthur 'an admirable burlesque of the march
of the knights in *King John*', a Shakespearean play which had been revived at

---

[41] *The London Theatre 1811 – 1866. Selections from the diary of Henry Crabb Robinson*, edited by Eluned
Brown (1966), 147. In this edition, Pocock's play is wrongly attributed to Dryden and Purcell.
[42] British Library, Additional MS 42953, fols 631 – 649.
[43] *Literary Gazette*, 28 December 1839, 831.
[44] No British Library MS exists of this play. I have therefore relied on the review in *The Times*, 27
December 1842, 5.

Drury Lane that season. Alfred Crowquill's cartoon of the pantomime, which appeared in *Illustrated London News*, was accompanied by a caption that also noted this burlesque of *King John*.[45] Moreover, the pantomime contained a 'diorama in burlesque imitation of the celebrated battle scene introduced in the opera of [Dryden's] *King Arthur*' at Drury Lane in the preceding month. This successful revival of Dryden had most probably given rise to the choice of an Arthurian subject for Christmas entertainment at Sadler's Wells that season. But despite incorporating the British-Saxon battle from Dryden, the pantomime included a more purely Malorian cast (such as Tristram and Ysonde), whilst burlesquing their Malorian attributes: Arthur's Queen thus becomes the 'fat and virtuous Guinever'. Once again, the introduction of a Fairy Queen lends a clearly polarized dramatic structure to the work: for in response to Merlin's contention that Arthur will never yield to a woman, the Fairy Queen here mischievously contrives that Arthur will become temporarily enamoured of Ysonde.

An additional distinct thread that led to Arthurian burlesque was derived from the story of Jack the Giant Killer. In early eighteenth century chapbook versions of this tale, there are three specific Arthurian allusions. Not only is the story set in 'King Arthur's time', but Jack meets and joins company with King Arthur's son; and after Jack rescues a duke's daughter from the giant Galligantus, Arthur prevails on the duke to reward Jack with his daughter's hand in marriage.[46] Of the later plays that adopted Jack as hero, few have survived, but the version that was played at the Royal Surrey Theatre in April 1846 (and which Allardyce Nicoll equates with that which was staged at the Lyceum on 18 August 1810) certainly had a strong Arthurian flavour.[47] Entitled *Jack the Giant Killer; or, the Knights of the Round Table*, the pantomime opens at the court of King Arthur, with a rousing choral variation on Callcott's glee:

> When Arthur first our King became
> He wore a coat with sleeves.
> He entertained all Knights of fame
> And none of them were thieves.[48]

These knights are given such unMalorian names as Sir John the Envious, Sir James the Generous and Sir Gregory Guffin the Valorous. As the 1810 version was announced in *The Times* as a 'Grand Mock Heroic Serio-Comic Ballet of Action', it is evident that these knightly protagonists are

[45] *ILN*, 31 December 1842, 539.
[46] See Ashton, *Chap-Books*, 188 – 91. Besides Percival Leigh's burlesque poem *Jack the Giant Killer* (1843), which has already been noted in Chapter 1, there was the version that Richard Doyle had written and illustrated in 1842, which had included the customary Arthurian references but which was not published until 1851 and 1888: see Rodney Engen, *Richard Doyle* (Stroud, 1983), 34.
[47] Allardyce Nicoll, *A History of English Drama 1660 – 1900*, 6 vols (Cambridge, 1959), VI, 249.
[48] British Library, Additional MS 42992, fols 679 – 710.

burlesqued.[49] An authorial prefatory note suggests that the part of Sir John
should be taken by a 'Low Comedian' and 'more effective' if by a 'Person of
short stature'. Their knightly prowess is, in fact, outshone by the giant-killing
feat of the peasant boy, Jack. Yet Jack had initially earned Arthur's
displeasure for winning the affections of Princess Elizabethina, King Arthur's
daughter, over whose loss her father indulges his grief:

> Oh how I grizzle
> That she should mizzle
> With such a villain
> Not worth the kil-ling
> To go so willing
> Without a shilling
> Oh I'm a wretched dad.

Jack is, of course, forgiven; and the plot is rounded out with the addition of a
Fairy Queen who lends him the necessary magical accessories of sword, cap
and cloak. There is, too, a spectacular palace fire extinguished by a fire engine
(which looks like a very topical allusion); a patriotic defence of English country
dances; and some extremely forthright condemnation of the French (those
'gallic dogs').

Our awareness of the existence of this considerable body of Arthurian stage
burlesque and pantomime may also enable us to perceive a larger framework
within which much other Arthurian literature of the period may be
accommodated; with the result that these other works appear less isolated and
idiosyncratic than they have hitherto seemed. Thus, John Thelwall's
unperformed poetic drama *The Fairy of the Lake* shares the same stage tradition
of spectacular transformations and of burning towers; and, besides a blank
verse central action, it contains complementary comic sections in prose,
featuring in particular the anti-heroic role of Tristram, here represented as a
garrulously jesting tippler who will

> never see dangers, but by reflection, on the outside of a goblet, or at the
> bottom of a well polished tankard; where the convexity of the medium
> diminishes their proportions and shrinks them into insignifi-
> cance. (III. i. 17 – 20)

Again, Reginald Heber's *Masque of Gwendolen*, an entertainment written for a
private Christmas party, is shorn of humour but displays an affinity with other

---

[49] *The Times*, 13 August 1810, 2.

Christmas shows because of its incorporation of Merlin in an important structural role, its eclectic mix of disparate personae (e.g. Arthur and Titania), and its dramatic use of magical transformations. A comparable adoption of the enchanter, transposed from his original setting, is also evident in Lambert Wilmer's unperformed poetic drama *Merlin* (1827), wherein Merlin controls a nineteenth century action on the banks of the Hudson River.

Remarkably, the figure known to Malory as Arthur's jester does not occupy that role in the early nineteenth century, with any frequency. Heber's *Morte* has an unnamed court jester but, significantly for Heber's anti-comic, emotional, moral tragedy, the clown is silent like others at the entry of the 'spectre damsel':

> Oh, they are silent all! the nimble tongue
> Of him, whose craft, by motley kirtle known,
> Had graver wits with seeming folly stung   (I. li)

Sir Dagonet, the Malorian court-fool, makes only two appearances in this period. As Gyles Dagonet he figures among the dramatis personae of Pocock's *King Arthur* but occupies an insignificant position in the drama. And, as *The Times* reviewer wrote, Webster, the actor who took this role, was 'as humorous' as the dullness of his part would suffer him to be.[50] Dagonet's second appearance occurs in Christopher Riethmuller's *Launcelot of the Lake*, which bestows on him a Shakespearean fool's role of shooting barbed truths from the security of his protective motley. Tricked by Mordred into betraying Gwenever to King Arthur, he makes some restitution by informing Launcelot of her danger but, whilst Launcelot and Bors rush off to rescue the Queen from the stake, he resumes his critical detachment from 'chivalry':

> Yes! there they go!
> As pretty a headstrong crew of martial mould
> As ever made monarch's throne too hot to hold!
> Ride, gallants, ride! and you shall see some sport:
> But after this, methinks, King Arthur's court
> Will be no place for me. What need I care?
> Light hearts grow lighter in a change of air.
> Is there not room enough beneath the sky
> For me to thrive, whilst others kill and die?

---

[50] *The Times*, 27 December 1834, 2.

> Let warriors bleed, let kingdoms rise and fall,
> The fool laughs on — and so outlives them all![51]

Though expressed with more pungency than was customary among the genial
burlesques of the early nineteenth century, Riethmuller's Dagonet neatly
epitomises, nevertheless, the comic anti-heroic treatment of Arthurian legend
that was of frequent occurrence in the theatre.

Irony: Literary Scholarship

Re-emerging after ages of neglect, medieval literature was often treated with
condescension as the product of a ruder, more barbarous and superstitious
age. Even Bishop Percy had remained on the defensive with regard to
publication of his *Reliques* in 1765:

> In a polished age, like the present, I am sensible that many of these
> reliques of antiquity will require great allowances to be made for them
> . . . To atone for the rudeness of the more obsolete poems, each volume
> concludes with a few modern attempts in the same kind of writing.[52]

If his apologia would rapidly prove needless on account of the public favour
shown to balladry, the longer medieval romances remained more intractable
matter for popular reading. Editions of these by Pinkerton (1792), Ritson
(1802) and even Scott (1804) were largely confined to readership within small
scholarly circles, and, despite the much wider dissemination of Warton's
History of English Poetry, George Ellis probably represented the views of many

---

[51] Christopher James Riethmuller, *Launcelot of the Lake, a Tragedy in five acts* (1843), III. ii.
102 – 12. According to Riethmuller, his play was offered to the management of the Drury Lane
Theatre, but Macready had retired (June 1843) before the play could be properly submitted to
him:
> Under these circumstances, with the gloomy prospects of the drama in general, any
> attempt to procure the representation of the play seemed for the present hopeless. The
> author was therefore advised to run the risk of publishing.
Launcelot, v. Macready's advice was delicately phrased:
> I am not prepared to say . . . I should have hazarded its representation on the stage, but I
> am sure I should have looked with interest and even eagerness to any future essay, that
> might have been forwarded to me with the recommendation of your name.
See Christopher James Riethmuller, *Early and Late Poems* (1893), 50n.
[52] Percy, *Reliques*, xxxviii.

contemporary readers in finding Warton's extract from Henry Lovelich's *Saint Graal* 'deplorably dull'.[53]

One strategy for accommodating medieval romance was to assume that it was a burlesque upon itself. The reception of Chaucer's *Tale of Sir Thopas* is a case in point. As Joseph A. Dane has shown, Chaucer's tale was not treated in the sixteenth and seventeenth centuries as a burlesque of medieval metrical romance.[54] It was only after the middle of the eighteenth century, with the introduction of a new critical idiom from France, that the advocates of a newly created literary genre of burlesque discovered in Chaucer's *Sir Thopas* an early example of the form. Thus, Hurd's novel assessment of *Sir Thopas* in 1762 is followed by that of Warton, Percy and Tyrwhitt, and then passes into general currency.

Where a medieval romance could not conveniently be deemed to be a burlesque upon itself, later eighteenth and early nineteenth century scholars themselves displayed an ironic attitude towards the work. George Ellis, for example, who had previously written much burlesque poetry for *The Anti-Jacobin*, enlivens his own *Specimens of Early English Metrical Romances* by bridging brief extracts of verse with lengthy prose summaries of the remainder. Like a later Augustan, his tone is urbane, his determinedly contemporary idiom portraying, with a mild irony that underlies a mock solemnity, the wilder flights or the differing morality of the medieval text:

> Merlin, though by now a minister of state, was always by taste a conjuror, and delighted in playing tricks upon the sovereigns whom he protected. He now met Arthur and his company in the disguise of an old 'charle' (peasant) with a bow and arrows, shot in their presence a couple of wild-ducks, and, on Arthur's proposing to cheapen them, took occasion to banter him pretty severely for his avarice. Having at length made himself known, he was received with due honours, and, finding it necessary to detain the court during some weeks at Breckenho, made Arthur amends by procuring for him an interview with the fair Lyanor, daughter of a certain Earl Sweyn, a damsel who had repaired to the king for the purpose of doing homage, and thus incidentally obtained the honour of giving birth to a son who was afterwards a knight of the round table. (I. p. 256)[55]

According to Scott, this tone resembled that of the Comte de Tressan who had edited the *Corps d'Extraits de Romans de Chivalerie* (1775 – 1780):

[53] Ellis, *Specimens of Early English Metrical Romances*, I, 193.
[54] Joseph A. Dane, 'Genre and Authority: The Eighteenth Century Creation of Chaucerian Burlesque', *Huntington Library Quarterly*, 48 (Autumn 1985), 345 – 62.
[55] Ellis's description of Merlin as a 'conjuror' may have derived from Fielding's *The Tragedy of Tragedies*:
    MERLIN: Thou hast no cause to fear, I am thy friend, Merlin by name, a conjuror by trade.
(III. viii. 9 – 10).

Both display an acute sense of the ludicrous, and can readily enliven, by a witty turn or lively expression, the dull or absurd details which they are occasionally obliged to narrate.[56]

All three contemporary reviews of the *Specimens* unite in commending its 'wit and elegance' (Scott), its selection of 'whatever is valuable' (Southey), and Ellis's 'taste and diligence' (Muirhead).[57] Nonetheless, they also concur in deprecating the editor's ubiquitous wit. As Muirhead comments:

> we wish that he had reserved his playful remarks and witticisms for the annotations, rather than have blended them with the narratives.

Scott questions whether this humour, in Ellis as in De Tressan, is not

> sometimes too much indulged . . ., since such licence, when frequently taken, is rather irreverent, and looks as if the jest were levelled at once against the reader, the editor, and the original minstrel.

Although Southey had 'heard' this 'levity' 'censured', and himself found it 'perhaps too frequently apparent', he partially defends Ellis by admitting that 'it is difficult to relate absurdities without seeming to perceive them'. He would, however, have preferred the abstracts to have been written 'more in the manner of an old chronicler than of a modern'. Southey's own practice generally adheres to this precept, and he does not attempt to burlesque the original in his own translation from the Vulgate *Merlin*, but some ironic colouring does, nevertheless, steal into his account of Merlin's narration to his master Blaise, 'who seems to have been his confessor as well as historiographer', or into his interpolated commentary on the Vulgate: 'the writer very properly remarks upon Merlin, for having taught his mistress so much, *quil en fut depuis, et est encore tenu pour fol*'.[58] His ironic faculty is, in fact, the subject of praise in *Monthly Review*'s notice of the edition:

> Mr. Southey may deservedly be ranked with those most entertaining writers Tressan and Ellis, in the art of briefly telling a long story. We believe that he could make, even out of Cassandra and the Grand Cyrus, books not merely readable but very amusing.[59]

That Ellis's elegant wit did, despite the reservations of the reviewers, earn a wider popularity for the romances is suggested by Mrs Scott's finding the volume engrossing; by the later acknowledgments of his work by, for example, Milman, Moir and Porden; and by the fact that the *Specimens* went into a

---

[56] Review of Ellis and Ritson in *Edinburgh Review*, 7 (January 1806), 387 – 413.
[57] *Annual Review*, 4 (1806), 536 – 44. *Monthly Review*, 5 (1806), 281 – 87.
[58] *The Byrth, Lyf, and Actes of King Arthur. With an introduction and notes by Robert Southey*, 2 vols (1817), I, xliii – xlvi.
[59] *MR*, 87 (December 1818), 370 – 82.

second edition in 1811.[60] Ellis's influence may also be seen in John Dunlop's *History of Fiction*, which purposely provides only 'a meagre outline' of the *Book of Merlin* since it had previously been 'analysed by Mr. Ellis . . . and of course is already known to the English reader in a form more agreeable' than Dunlop himself 'could pretend to exhibit it'.[61] In summarising many of the prose romances of chivalry, Dunlop's tone is usually staider than Ellis's, but he can occasionally quicken his narrative with an adroitly arch ironic idiom:

> At length this renowned magician [= Merlin] disappeared entirely from England. His voice alone was heard in a forest, where he was enclosed in a bush of hawthorn; he had been entrapped in this awkward residence by means of a charm he had communicated to his mistress Viviane, who, not believing in the spell, had tried it on her lover. The lady was sorry for the accident, but there was no extracting her admirer from his thorny coverture.   (I, p.72)

To critics who had accused him of not treating the romances of chivalry 'in a manner sufficiently serious', Dunlop replied that he 'did not think it necessary to contemplate the exploits of chivalry with the gravity of Ysaie le Triste'. Like Ellis, he adopts a role of ironic and superior aloofness from the medieval work; and thus his modern rationalist outlook counterpoints the earlier period's naivety, mysticism or hyperbole.

As for Scott, whereas his edition of *Sir Tristrem* maintains a firm neutrality appropriate to the presentation of a scholarly text, when summarising other chivalric romances he occasionally betrays a wry wit, echoing Ellis's. *A propos* of *Amadis of Gaul*, for example, he remarks:

> Oriana, during the absence of her lover, is secretly delivered of a son, named Esplandian; but as the heroines of the author are all mothers before they are wives, so they are never trusted with the education of their own children. The little Esplandian is carried off by a lioness.[62]

Similar traces of ironic amusement recur also in *The Bridal of Triermain*, on the occasion of Gyneth's appearance at Arthur's court. That Guenever is 'unruffled' by the fact that Arthur has an illegitimate daughter, and betrays a signal of acknowledged complicity with Lancelot, or that the latter and Tristrem are unwilling to contend for Gyneth's hand ('There were two who loved their neighbours' wives', II. xviii), arouses in Scott a smilingly tolerant delight in the foibles of his imagined world.

The past was, of course, a foreign country. With regard to contemporary

---

[60] Mrs Scott's approval is cited in Johnston, *Enchanted Ground*, 172. See Milman, *Samor*, II. l.397n; Moir in *Forget Me Not* (1827), 327n; Porden, *Coeur de Lion*, XIII. l.95n.
[61] Dunlop, *History of Fiction* (1845), I, 4.
[62] 'Essay on Amadis de Gaul'; in *Essay on Chivalry, Romance and the Drama* (1888), 128.

terrain, in a directly comparable manner to that of Ellis and Dunlop, the urbane wit of such travellers as Richard Warner commented, with amused detachment, on the superstitious beliefs and customs that were encountered in the remoter parts of Wales and Cornwall (see Chapter 2).

Irony: Prose Romance

The later eighteenth century had produced one novel in which a Cervantean concern with knight errantry was evident: Tobias Smollett's *Sir Launcelot Greaves* (1760 – 1762). Smollett, who had translated *Don Quixote* in 1755, makes no specifically Arthurian allusion beyond that of his hero's Christian name, but his novel presents a broadly sympathetic account of a modern man's attempt to achieve a chivalrous conduct of life, although the author's controlling irony admits that the accomplishments of his knight are dashed 'with a mixture of extravagance and insanity'.[63]

Three works of early nineteenth century prose romance far exceed Smollett in their preoccupation with an imagined Arthurian world, but all maintain a distinctly ironic affinity, which links them also with the contemporary scholarship of Ellis and Dunlop. Of these three prose romances, Peacock's *The Misfortunes of Elphin*, which has previously been discussed, is evidently far superior in the rich complexity of its created world, but it need not be treated as an isolated idiosyncratic and unrepresentative work, for it has many links with two very neglected short stories by contemporaries: Henry Davies's 'The Enchanted Shield' and John Oxenford's 'Sir Wigolais of the Wheel' (1849). As Peacock is much better known, I have selected my examples from the two other works, but these instances might easily be paralleled by instances of Peacock's wit.

All three select or adapt plots from medieval literature, but present their narratives from a consciously modern vantage point. Their dominant tone is ironic in its perception of the contrasts between common sense and the marvellous, the present and the past, fact and fancy. The adoption of a deliberately modern style achieves a deflation of the ludicrously high-flown:

> 'Let me go and inquire the cause of grief so great, in form so fair?' said
> Sir Wigolais, to his companion, carefully rounding his period. /
> 'You may go to the —,' began the sullen damsel, hastily.[64]

Moreover, a matter-of-fact naturalism consistently punctures manifestations of human frailty, hypocrisy or affectation, particularly that of the ecclesiastical genus:

---

[63] Tobias Smollett, *The Adventures of Sir Launcelot Greaves* (1905), chapter 13.
[64] John Oxenford, 'Sir Wigolais of the Wheel', *New Monthly Magazine*, 2nd Series 85 (March 1849), 316 – 17.

They, however, stayed not long behind, but, / leaving the good abbot of St Mary's (who not being, like themselves, armed in proof, was fearful of plunging into unknown dangers) at the entrance of the cavern, to pray for their safety and mutter his Ave Marias, . . . fearlessly committed themselves to the perils of an untried element.[65]

The effect of determinedly plain-speaking may point to the underlying continuity of human nature; it may also strip 'heroic' deeds of their meretricious glamour, and reveal a previously hidden ugliness and brutality:

Finding that his conversational powers were of no avail, Sir Wigolais did a smart thing or two on the road, in the hope of gaining some degree of favour. A strong castle by the roadside gave him the first opportunity of coming out . . . Sir Wigolais complied so well with the conditions of the establishment, that he not only came off victor, but left the old gentleman a corpse before his own gate. (p. 316)

In the prose romances, a tension is held between the coolly ironic narrative style and its exotically marvellous subject matter. The content of Arthurian romance — its dragons, damsels in distress, and enchantresses — may be lightly mocked, but the narrator's lightness of tone does not suggest a severe rebuttal of the mode. Conversely, in the swingeingly vituperative critical onsets of the early nineteenth century, the Arthurian subject could be made the target or the vehicle for satiric attack.

Parody

A propensity for humorous parody is manifest throughout the nineteenth century, and probably derives from the period's stylistic eclecticism, which in turn stems from the intense awareness of varying historical styles, and from a preoccupation with style as forming a necessary and identifying quality of human achievement. Parody flourished, particularly in the period from 1810 to 1830 when long critical engagements were fought over the arrival of the differing, and frequently rival, septs of romanticism, and when, in numerous works like Horace and James Smith's *Rejected Addresses* (1812), parody greeted the new poetic idioms of Wordsworth, Coleridge, Scott and Byron.

Whilst 'walking with a friend' in the early years of the century, Reginald Heber had composed impromptu 'the happiest imitation of the George-Ellis-

---

[65] Davies, 'Enchanted Shield', 198 – 99.

specimens' which his anonymous friend had ever seen.[66] The result — a parody of Middle English verse romance — was written down the following day, and later published as *The Boke of the Purple Faucon*. But whereas Heber's parody was affectionate, William Jerdan's review of Tennyson's 'The Lady of Shalott' was derisive. Regarding it as 'a strange ballad without perceptible object', he imitated Tennyson's predilection for feminine rhymes, portmanteau adjectives with their final syllables archaically stressed, and the 'ludicrous associations' of Shalott:

> On either side the dishes lie
> Brave plates of beefsteaks, beefsteak pie,
> That stuff the wame and feast the eye;
> And 'bout the table beer runs by
>   To many a thirsty throat.
> The yellowleavèd piccalilly,
> The greensheathèd pepper-chilli,
> Tremble (pen me aught more silly!)
>   Round about Shallot!![67]

William Aytoun, who wrote a series of parodies for *Tait's Edinburgh Magazine* which were later collected in book form under the title of the *Bon Gaultier Ballads*, included Tennyson's 'Morte d'Arthur' as one of the butts. Aytoun could have perceived in Tennyson's Arthur a type of the swooning humourless hero, pictured in a crisis of lonely agony, whom he would later castigate in his onslaughts on the Spasmodic School. The parody 'La Mort d'Arthur. Not by Tennyson' describes how the wounded king creeps down to the lake and swoons there:

> No man yet knows how long he lay in swound;
> But long enough it was to let the rust
> Lick half the surface of his polish'd shield;
> For it was made by far inferior hands,
> Than forged his helm, his breastplate, and his greaves,
> Whereon no canker lighted . . .[68]

Aytoun's parody is also directed at the Arthurian romance world *per se*. As introduction to the poem when it first appeared in *Tait's*, he mockingly describes those people who

are fond of excursions into the realms of old romance, with their

[66] Amelia Heber, *Life of Heber*, I, 341. Heber also wrote a humorous verse tale set in medieval Wales, *A Ballad* (Chester, ?1830).
[67] 'Poems by Alfred Tennyson', *Literary Gazette*, 8 December 1832, 772–74.
[68] Lines 10–15; in 'Puffs and Poetry by Bon Gaultier', *Tait's Edinburgh Magazine*, NS 10 (October 1843), 651–52.

Launcelots and Guenevers, their enchanted castles, their bearded wizards, and such odd branches of learning. There needs a winged griffin, at the very least, to carry them out of the every-day six-and-eightpenny world, or the whizz of an *Excalibur* to startle their drowsy imaginations into life.   (p. 649)

Seeming initially to defend the use of the 'poetical topics of the world around us', Aytoun then subtly undermines the demand for these topics, by suggesting that a suitable one would be 'newspaper advertising', especially 'toilette advertisement'. An instance he cites of such modern fame concerns the Leadenhall Street barber named Mechi, a veritable 'Wizard of the Hone'. It is to his practical accomplishments that 'La Mort d'Arthur' bathetically leads:

> . . . his helm, his breastplate and his greaves,
> Whereon no canker lighted, for they bore
> The magic stamp of MECHI'S SILVER STEEL.   (14 – 16)

Aytoun's rich parody employs an Arthurian subject to fulfil a double function: to parody Tennyson's handling of the material, and also, by means of this parody, to mock the language of contemporary commercial advertising. An Arthurian subject thus serves as both the object and the vehicle of satire.

Political Satire: High Burlesque

If the previous sections have provided many examples of low burlesque (whereby a lofty subject is given a humbler treatment), then satire also took the form of high burlesque, and ridiculed its targets by describing them in a loftier style.

Political satire on the Duke of Wellington often assumed this form. The link between King Arthur and Arthur Wellesley was frequently made in the years that marked the termination of Bonaparte's empire (see Chapter 1), but in the 1830s Wellington was, as leader of the Tories, often made the target of opprobrious comparison. When Bulwer Lytton subtitled his poem 'The Rats and the Mice' as 'A Fable of the Days of King Arthur. Addressed to His Grace the Duke of Wellington', he implied much more than the stock time-setting 'in the days of King Arthur', for, in this attack on the Duke's conservative attitude to parliamentary reform, Lytton is alluding to Wellington's Christian name, and ludicrously comparing him with the earlier hero.[69] A far ampler analogy is worked out in the 'Lines written after reading the Romance of

---

[69] In Edward Bulwer Lytton, *The Siamese Twins, A Satirical Tale of the Times, with other Poems* (1831).

Arthur's Round Table', which opens with a paean of 'past times' when 'England's chiefs' who sat around Arthur's table concerned themselves primarily with domestic provision for a 'well-fed people', instead of seeking distractions in international affairs:

> They never glow'd with love for all mankind;
> Ne'er left their countrymen in want and pain,
> To soothe the woes of Portugal or Spain,
> Ne'er shed one tear o'er Moslem or Hindoo,
> Or cared a single curse for Timbuctoo.[70]

Wellington, the modern Arthur, is clearly marked for censure. A further criticism is that the earlier knights had displayed the virtues of loyalty and yet maintained a fearless independence, whereas 'around Arthur's table now' the sitters are cravenly submissive to Wellington's autocratically 'supreme behest'. A comparable set of allusions recurs in William Maginn's article 'The Fraserians', whose members meet at 'a round table', although they had not 'thought of the supremacy of Arthur' at the time the table was chosen.[71] By 'Arthur', the poem represents the political career of Wellington, whose ministry had fallen in 1830, but whose return to power was again thought to be imminent:

> And down, for that and weightier reasons,
> Sunk Wellington for certain seasons.
> But even then some Merlin said,
>   Arthur is only gone a while —
> Again he'll raise his hook-nosed head; . . .
>   I prophesy,
>   With certain eye,
>   That four years will not quite go by
> Ere the Duke Arthur we again shall meet,
> Just as of old, the Lord in Downing Street.

The special promise of Arthur's Messianic return had thus become the very grounds of despair.

Evidence that this Wellingtonian association lasted into the 1840s is provided by a political cartoon of 1843. In ridiculing the competitions to select the paintings that would decorate the newly rebuilt Houses of Parliament, the *Punch* artist H. G. Hine drew a *King Arthur's Court*, which represented Wellington as the legendary monarch, with Henry Brougham as a clown, and Lord Lyndhurst and Robert Peel in attendance. Alluding to the Callcott glee

---

[70] 'An Oxonian', 'Lines written after reading the Romance of Arthur's Round Table', ll. 8 – 12; in *Blackwood's*, 30 (May 1830), 705.
[71] 'The Fraserians; or, The commencement of the year thirty-five. A Fragment', *Fraser's*, 11 (January 1835), 1 – 27.

of 'When Arthur first in court began', *Punch* then invited its readers to determine which of the present public celebrities could best be described as those 'serving men', all of whom were 'thieves'.[72]

The Italian Medley Poem

A pervasive influence on English poetry in this period was exerted by earlier Italian poets, and particularly by Ariosto, Harington's Elizabethan translation of whom having been followed by a later cluster: the work of William Huggins (1757), John Hoole (1783), Henry Boyd (1784), and William Stewart Rose (1823). Ariosto's critical reputation and widespread popularity were frequently celebrated; and what especially appealed were his masterly control of an exuberantly fantastic plot, and his combination of a vivacious irony with a humane sensibility. Moreover, what made Ariosto's influence specially relevant for the Arthurian Revival was that *Orlando Furioso* had included several references to the Arthurian legends and to the enduring role of Merlin. In particular, Bradamante's visit to Merlin's tomb (Canto 3) was a subject that continued to attract the attention of painters and illustrators in England.[73] Attribution of the Italian's influence appears in the preface to Richard Hole's *Arthur; or, the Northern Enchantment*, whose heroes are said to be 'rather those of Ariosto than of Homer', whilst a *Blackwood's* article in 1819 corroborates the view that it is 'a poem from the School of Ariosto'.[74] For Scott, the Italian poet was the 'divine Ariosto', and evidence of an interlocking Ariostan plot may be detected in *The Bridal of Triermain*, whose gentle irony may also be associated with the same source, as in the playful description of the antics of Guendolen's maidens with Arthur's armour:

> Two, laughing at their lack of strength,
> Dragg'd Caliburn in cumbrous length;
> One, while she aped a martial stride,

---

[72] *Punch*, 5 (July 1843), 38 – 39. King Arthur is dressed in eighteenth century costume, and wears a full-bottomed wig. His appearance thus recalls that of King Arthur in O'Hara's *Tom Thumb*, as illustrated by Cruikshank in 1830.

[73] The scene was treated by Thomas Coxon in his plates for Harington's translation (1591); by Jean Michel Moreau for the Baskerville edition (1773); by Conrad Martin Metz (RA 1783, cat. 424); and by Joseph M. Gandy (RA 1815, cat. 799).

[74] Richard Hole, *Arthur; or, the Northern Enchantment* (1789), iv. Memoir of the late Richard Hole', *Blackwood's*, 5 (April 1819), 68. Acknowledgement of Ariostan precedent occurs also in another poem not mentioned by Merriman: Hugh Downman's 'Ode, On reading Mr Hole's "Arthur" '; in *Poems*, second edition (Exeter, 1790). For reviews of this, see *Critical Review*, NS 1 (February 1791), 173 – 76; and *Gentleman's Magazine*, 61 (March 1791), 254 – 55.

> Placed on her brows the helmet's pride;
> Then scream'd, 'twixt laughter and surprise,
> To feel its depth o'erwhelm her eyes.   (I. xvii)

Scott was himself termed the 'Ariosto of the North' by Byron; Milman alludes to an Ariostan incident in *Samor* (VII. 859 – 62); Heber writes warmly of 'the richness and various delight' of Ariosto's 'enchanted and enchanting wilderness'; Peacock commends Ariosto's 'free range of the whole field of imagination and memory'; and Lytton repeats the encomium, seeing in Ariosto 'the final concentration of chivalric romance.'[75] Such an ambience pervades the early work of Praed. Not only does he refer in 'Gog' to Hoole's translation of *Orlando Furioso* (which 'is but so-so'), but he evidently derives from Ariosto Linda's suicidal ruse for evading her attacker:

> The latter part of Linda's history
> In Ariosto's work is an ingredient;
> I can't imagine how my monks and he
> Happened to hit upon the same expedient.   (335n)

That medieval romance should be regarded humorously was Byron's view in 1822, noting that a 'great defect' of Boiardo was 'his treating too seriously the narratives of chivalry'.[76] Byron approved, instead, of the 'gaiety of Pulci', whom he saw not only as the precursor of Berni and Ariosto, but also as 'the founder of a new style of poetry very lately sprung up in England. I allude to that of the ingenious Mr. Whistlecraft.' Although William Tennant had published a medley poem in ottava rima as early as 1812 (*Anster Fair*), John Hookham Frere, the author of Whistlecraft's *Prospectus and Specimens of an Intended National Work* (1817 – 1818, later known as *The Monks and the Giants*), claimed that his inspiration came directly from reading some extracts from Pulci quoted in Ginguené's *Histoire Litéraire de l'Italie*.[77] Accepting Ginguené's opinion of Pulci's intention, Frere declared that his own aim was identical: a 'burlesque of rude and uninstructed common sense'. Consequently, he presents as ostensible narrators the plebeian Whistlecraft brothers, harness and collar-makers of Stowmarket in Suffolk. From their vulgarly prosaic yet well-meaning viewpoint, the Arthurian legends require practical resuscitation:

> It grieves me much, that Names that were respected
> In former ages, Persons of such mark,

---

[75] Heber's review of J. H. Hunt's translation of Tasso, *Quarterly Review*, 25 (July 1821), 436. Thomas Love Peacock, *The Four Ages of Poetry* (Oxford, 1947), 12. Lytton, *Poetical and Dramatic Works*, II, 269.
[76] *The Works of Lord Byron*, edited by Ernest Hartley Coleridge, 7 vols (New York, 1966), IV, 283.
[77] Frere, *Monks and Giants*, 6. R. D. Waller points out that this was a misreading of Pulci's intention.

And countrymen of ours, should lie neglected,
Just like old portraits lumbering in the dark: . . .
I'll air them all, and rub down the Round Table,
And wash the Canvas clean, and scour the Frames,
And put a coat of varnish on the Fable,
And try to puzzle out the Dates and Names.   (Proem. x – xi)

From Pulci, Frere adopted the ottava rima stanza and, like his model, employed it to establish a tone of conversational intimacy, freely alluding to contemporary persons and events, digressing copiously in defiance of conventional structure, achieving additional verbal surprise by startling or imperfect rhymes, and continually moving from seriousness to jest.

What is distinctive in Frere's version is that, by inventing an ignorant narrator, this precludes the poet's adopting a narrative role *in propria persona*. As a result, the Whistlecraft device proves an irksome constraint for although the fiction is well-maintained throughout the opening sections (see, for example, the gourmandizing menu in I. iv) the poem tends to shift towards a delicate irony and a scholarly allusiveness, both of which accord ill with the Whistlecraft *weltanschaung*. Moreover, the potential for humorous digression is cramped by Frere's being obliged to remain within a narrow framework. Paradoxically, there is no real vulgarity, either, in the Whistlecraft idiom, which remains comparatively elevated in tone. Frere's burlesque is, in effect, mild and without rancour or specific personal target. Despite a persistent suspicion that his previous career as satirical anti-Jacobin in collaboration with George Ellis and George Canning would have encouraged Frere to intend a private allegory, perhaps based on his first-hand experience of the Peninsular War, contemporary critics could not discover any tangible allusions, and the poem's blandness was considered essentially 'frivolous' or 'whimsical'. Among the reasons given by Frere for not having completed the work was that

> most people would imagine it was some political satire and went on hunting for a political meaning, so I thought it was no use offering my jokes to people who wouldn't understand them.[78]

A notable lack of the amorous interest required for commercial success was discerned by Samuel Parr and Ugo Foscolo but, in spite of the poem's being considered by its contemporary critics as unlikely to gain widespread popularity, its influence on Byron has since been widely acknowledged.[79] The latter's *Beppo* (1818), which adopts the same verse form, excels, however, in the three areas where Frere is weakest: Byron provides a dominant lovers' plot, and tells the story in his own voice, whilst satirising incisively. If *Beppo*

---

[78] *The Works of the Right Honourable John Hookham Frere in Verse and Prose*, edited by W. E. Frere, second edition, 3 vols (1847), I, 166.
[79] See Samuel Parr, 'Note on Odoherty and his Imitators', *Blackwood's*, 3 (August 1818), 533. Ugo Foscolo, 'Narrative Poetry of the Italians', *Quarterly Review*, 21 (April 1819), 486 – 556.

and *Don Juan* (1819 – 1824) were to remain tales of modern life, Byron was also to attempt a burlesque treatment of a medieval narrative in his ottava rima translation of Pulci's *Morgante Maggiore* (1823), but, through constraining himself to work too closely within the confines of another writer's period and language, Byron's translation lacks verve, spontaneity and verbal inventiveness, and was abandoned after completion of one unsuccessful canto. The wit and fluency of *Don Juan*, however, had stimulated the composition of a number of other ottava rima poems, in which the ostensible subject was sometimes modern (for example, Leigh Hunt's 'The Dogs', 1822), or was taken from the past, whether classical (Barry Cornwall's 'Gyges', 1820) or medieval (as in John Moultrie's 'Godiva', 1820, and Praed's 'Lidian's Love', 1826).

One such poem in which its first reviewers correctly perceived a 'borrowing from Byron' or an example at 'second-best' of the 'Whistlecraft school' was John Moultrie's *La Belle Tryamour*.[80] Although Frere's work has continued to receive some critical attention, Moultrie's Arthurian poem has not been made the subject of any extended criticism since its first appearance. It may, therefore, now be accorded a more protracted examination.

As acknowledged source, Joseph Ritson's edition of Thomas Chestre's *Sir Launfal* provides Moultrie with a loose narrative thread, but Moultrie treats the original with great and comic irreverence. The heroic past is burlesqued by the presentation of Arthurian characters as all-too-human, and their failings are rendered in a pronouncedly nineteenth century idiom. King Arthur is fashionably 'sick of the blue devils' or suffering from Maria Edgeworth's 'Ennui'. His psychological problem is referred to Merlin since the latter is a compendium of modern lore:

> He knew as much as ever mortal knew;
> And, for a judge of poetry, might vie
> With any in the Quarterly Review;
> Was master of the art of pharmacy
> In all its branches, and could mend a shoe,
> Or breathe a vein, or give a horse a ball,
> With any modern farrier of them all.   (I. xlviii)

As his diagnosis is that Arthur is 'dying of a quiet life' (lxv), he prescribes marriage to provide the necessary 'noise or strife'. By means of a magic glass, Arthur is then shown Guenever bathing with her attendants in Dublin, where their conversation is callowly Hibernian:

> 'Oh, how delicious is this cooling stream!' —
> 'I'll thank you, Miss MacTwolter, not to splash!' —

[80] See *Ward's Miscellany*, 1 (1837), 822 – 24; *Athenaeum*, 22 April 1837, 278 – 79.

'Biddy O'Blarney! — why how cold you seem!'
'Well! I declare I've got a water rash!'   (I. xciii)

As was briefly indicated in Chapter 2, Arthur's Irish venture forms an
ironic parallel with George IV's state visit to Dublin in 1821. In particular, an
ambience of marital infidelity pervades both occasions. Queen Caroline,
whom George had unsuccessfully attempted to divorce on the grounds of
adultery, had died just before the Dublin visit: Arthur's Queen was to fall
under a similar suspicion:

> All the world knows Anne Boleyn was a martyr —
> So was the late Queen Caroline, I've heard;
> So might have been the spotless wife of Arthur,
> Had similar impeachments been preferr'd.   (II. iv)

Subsequently, Arthur's royal marriage runs its expected course: 'Soon, from
this Virgo, Gemini were born, / And then she made King Arthur Capricorn'
(II. ii). Whereas the broadly humorous strokes in the delineation of these
scenes recall the tone of Fielding's *Tragedy of Tragedies*, when Moultrie
eventually reaches the central section of his main plot the treatment of Launfal
and his fairy bride is only gently ironic: for here Moultrie notes with
deflationary realism that the half-starved Launfal does not ignore the
opportunity offered by the marriage feast:

> over his repast so long he tarried
> That Tryamour scarce thought he'd ever finish:
> She laugh'd to see the loads his trencher carried,
> The goblets that he quaff'd of mead and Rhenish;
> Playing at once the lover and the glutton,
> And murmuring tenderest raptures o'er his mutton.   (III. clxv)

Moultrie, in effect, consciously exploits the full potential range of the octave
rhyme:

> In which I can be gay, or grave, or 'daft', or
> Pathetic, or sarcastic, or sublime,
> Just as the maggot bites.   (I. xliii)

The conversational suppleness of the verse form allows for such sudden
transitions of mood, and 'the pathetic' is copiously evoked by Moultrie's
sentimentalising treatment of the young girl, Blanch, who dies of an
unrequited love for Launfal. Moreover, by assuming the Byronic role of
masterful narrator, Moultrie endows his poem with greater depth and
complexity, for the loquacious author, studiedly contemporary, presents the
impromptu narration almost as if it is an irresistible flow of digressive reverie.
Not only does the mood glide from the 'daft' to the 'sublime' but the poet's

monologue rattles on, away from his notionally medieval plot to a lively awareness of his own contemporary world. Since almost half of the poem consists of 'digression', there exists a balanced antithesis between Moultrie's imagined past world and his actual present. The Arthurian episode of Blanch is, for example, given its modern equivalent in the poet's sentimental autobiographical effusions over one Ione, whilst Moultrie's irony matches burlesque of the medieval with mockery of, for instance, contemporary prudery:

> I own I hate that squeamish affectation
> (Itself the worst indecency) which sees
> In Nature's fairest works abomination,
> Faints at bare necks, and thinks it right to sneeze,
> If painter's art, or bard's imagination,
> Disrobe a Venus higher than the knees.   (I. xcvi)

Moultrie's bowdlerising revisions for the 1837 edition of his poetry would, however, remove the above and similar passages. The revised version also excises what probably appeared to the later Moultrie a dated catalogue of theatrical stars, but by curtailing the once 'modern' digressions he weakens the original poem's youthful dash and satiric vivacity. It is, of course, a bravura piece and extremely light in tone: its range of contemporary references is slight, and mainly limited to Cambridge or to fashionable literature of the day. Significantly, although deriving his style from Byron (whom he pretends to outdo — 'I undoubtedly surpass him / In his own metre', I. lxxiii), Moultrie selects Byron as the butt for his keen attacks on profligacy. As a confessed 'Tory — / At least an Anti-Gallican' (III. l.), Moultrie evidently dislikes what he takes to be Byron's assumed liberalism; in opposition to which, Moultrie announces his own orthodox position:

> And I acknowledge that I've still preferr'd
> The old worn paths — for I can safely trust 'em;
> To love one's country, and to keep one's word,
> Are good old maxims, nor will time e'er rust 'em —
> Our modern creeds are wiser, I dare say,
> But sometimes lead us deucedly astray.   (II. xix)

The poem is intensely 'literary' in that it is packed with allusion to Moultrie's own reading; and because Moultrie adopts the role of omniscient author flicking his wit in every direction, the poem approximates to a burlesque on the poetic genre itself. Any shred of a Coleridgean suspended sense of disbelief is persistently rent. The hypothetical reader is taken closely into Moultrie's confidence, told that the tale is based on Spenser ('entangled . . . / In . . . confounded mazes allegorical', III. lxix) and on an 'old romance' edited by 'that prince of puppies', Joseph Ritson (I. xlii); informed of Moultrie's allusions and additions; and kept abreast of Moultrie's manipulation of the narrative ('I hate all dry details, so I omit / The courtship', I. cvi). The poet admits to the reality of serialised publication, promises the succeeding canto by the 'first of next July' (I. cxxxvi) and frankly confesses to its constraints: 'I wish I could afford a serious stanza / But haven't space' (I. cx). Moultrie goes much further than the age-old device of self-deprecation ('I wish I could describe . . .', I. lxxi), by continually asserting his role as poetic tyro; invoking his Muse to tell him whether he has a 'chance of succeeding' in the 'trade' (I. xxix); and by displaying an apparent candour with regard to his own attitude towards writing the poem; 'I'm sadly weary of this canto' (I. lxvi), for example. Within this context, the catalogue of stage worthies (II. xxxiv-l) is germane to the underlying histrionic imagery of Canto I, wherein Moultrie uses his memories of theatre-going to indicate his later sense of a lost childhood 'enchantment', for the pantomime figures of Harlequin and Columbine at Astley's and Sadler's Wells (II. xlii-xliii) were paradisal visions of reality, and not 'but painted canvas' or 'mere machinery'. True to the conventions of this mode, George IV's Irish visit may be best represented as 'pantomime' (I. cxv), and Moultrie repeatedly deems his own poem to have the properties of stage illusion: he writes, for instance, 'I've not, as yet, produced upon the stage / My hero' (I. cxxii), and, on introducing Merlin into the poem, Moultrie recollects having once seen him upon the boards — in a memorable description of the early nineteenth century theatrical conception of this figure:

> I saw him once, myself, upon the stage,
> And therefore my account may be relied on;
> He was, at that time, of a monstrous age,
> Black-rob'd, white-hair'd, and round his waist was tied on
> A zone inscribed with spells obscure and sage:
> Green was the dragon which he used to ride on:
> And when across the stage his flight he took,
> The pit look'd awe-struck and the galleries shook.   (I. xxxix)[81]

Moultrie's anti-poem ran into three cantos in *Knight's Quarterly Magazine* from June 1823 to January 1824, but the promised final canto did not appear in April 1824, and the publication of five extra stanzas in August evidently marked the abandonment of the work. The immediate cause of this sudden

[81] Moultrie could have seen Merlin in Dryden's *King Arthur* at Covent Garden in 1819, or in the anonymous *Merlin's Cave* at the Royal Amphitheatre in 1814, or in O'Hara's *Tom Thumb* at the Haymarket, Drury Lane and Covent Garden in 1805 – 1807. As he refers to visits to Astley's and Sadler's Wells at the age of six (i.e. in 1805) and as *The Dream of Life* (p. 376) denotes a visit to *Tom Thumb*, this play would seem to have been his most probable source. O'Hara's stage directions do not, however, mention a dragon, although Merlin does 'rise' dramatically to accompanying 'Thunder and Lightning' (II. ii). Dryden's stage directions indicate that Merlin descends 'in a Chariot drawn by Dragons' (II. i).

termination appears to have been a personal dispute between the publisher, Charles Knight, and his two chief verse contributors: Moultrie and Praed.[82] But the fact that the poem was never completed afterwards suggests that Moultrie had lost interest in the subject. His major reason for doing so is indicated by the 'great uneasiness' expressed at the levity of the magazine, by another contributor's father, Zachary Macaulay, with the result that his son, Thomas Babington, briefly withdrew from active participation. As Praed, the prime mover of the magazine, notes in his 'Castle Vernon', Moultrie's *Tryamour* was offending an important section of its readers:

> The great, the gay, the learned and the fair,
> Return at last to prudence and formality;
> And reverence, as their fathers did before 'em,
> Dry bread, dry talk, cold water and decorum.[83]

Although an introductory note to Moultrie's final contribution claimed that he would 'never forget Ariosto and his filthy lessons', Moultrie's decision to give up 'these sportive warblings', followed by his ordination and marriage — not to Ione — in 1825, mark him as an early exponent of a revulsion against Regency wit and 'immoral' values. Moultrie's 1837 revision of the poem is considerably chastened, and an introductory sonnet apologises for the 'unpruned blossoms' of his

> youth's wild fervour, ere [his] heart had yet
> Submissive bow'd to the acknowledged sway
> Of loftier duty.

A heightened awareness of these lofty claims of duty would later be invoked by Bulwer Lytton in his *King Arthur*, but this exalted tone did not wholly preclude the display of a burlesque wit. Lytton had been an admiring acquaintance of Praed at Trinity College, Cambridge and had contributed also to *Knight's Quarterly Magazine*. He had, besides, written a broadly humorous poem on Sir Gawaine (see above), whilst *The New Timon* (1846) exhibited a satirical ferocity directed at aristocratic profligacy. Citing an Ariostan precedent for the introduction of humour into his 'Epic Fable', Lytton does not employ an ottava rima stanza form but his sporadic mockery of contemporary kings, statesmen and ecclesiastics, and his portrayal of Sir Gawaine as an anti-heroic satirist, reveals the continuing Byronic tradition in tone and content:

---

[82] See Sullivan ed. *British Literary Magazines: Romantic Age*, 208 – 15.
[83] 'Castle Vernon', *KQM*, 1 (October 1823), 227 – 35.

Woes that have been are wisdom's lesson-books —
From Abel's death, the men of peace should learn
To add an inch of iron to their crooks
And strike, when struck, a little in return —
Had Abel known his quarterstaff, I wot,
Those Saxon Ap-Cains ne'er had been begot!   (VI. xv)

The persistence of Trinity's association with a comic Arthurianism was
maintained by John Sterling, who was there from 1824 to 1827, and who was
later to provide a further example of the octave style, coupled with Arthurian
allusion, in the 1840s. According to Thomas Carlyle, Sterling's 'Coeur de
Lion' had been 'on hand for some time' before Sterling's Naples trip in 1842,
but on his return it 'rose into shape'.[84] By December 1843, eight cantos existed
in rough draft, two of which were printed posthumously in *Fraser's* in 1849. To
Sterling, the poem was

> becoming a kind of *Odyssey*, with a laughing and Christian Achilles for
> hero. One may manage to wrap in that chivalrous brocade, many things
> belonging to our Time, and capable of interesting it.[85]

The poem takes the form of a burlesque upon the crusading adventures of
King Richard I:

> The lion-hearted was a Christian man,
> And, therefore, loved the Saracens to throttle;
> A boon companion, too, and partisan
> Of all whose watchword was 'Sirloin and Bottle!'   (I. ii)

An Arthurian connection derives from Sterling's following the medieval
legend (see Chapter 1) that Richard owned Arthur's sword 'Caliburn', and
which Sterling interweaves with associations of his own Neapolitan excursus,
for Richard is made here to drop the sword accidentally into the interior of
Mount Etna, from where it is retrieved by a 'fisher'. In Carlyle's opinion, 'if a
man *would* write in metre, this sure enough was the way to try doing it'; whilst
another listener, Barclay Fox, recorded it in his journal as 'a spirited,
chivalrous Ariostic work', giving scope for 'vigorous sketches and flashes of
humour'.[86]

This comic tradition thus remained exhilaratingly rooust until the end of
the 1840s.

---

84 Carlyle, *Life of Sterling*, 299.
85 *Ibid.*, 326.
86 *Ibid.*, 320. *Barclay Fox*, 349.

4

Fairyland Allegory

In contrast to the historico-chronicle tradition which, although stemming from the fabulous accounts by Geoffrey of Monmouth, nonetheless claimed a commitment to historical verisimilitude and entailed a gradual erosion of the marvellously improbable elements of the legend, there also existed a rival tradition of 'romance', which derived from imaginative literature. The attempted separation of the two traditions is evident in the earliest years of the Arthurian Revival, especially in the work of Thomas Warton. His verses 'On the Birth of the Prince of Wales' (1762) suggest that 'elfin charms' had in 'magic night' been responsible for the 'elder fame' of 'Arthur's Board', but that these 'Gothic' values should now yield to 'perfect day', to a modern 'Truth's meridian ray' in which civil would replace military power for the amelioration of mankind.[1]

A similar dichotomy would be voiced and treated more amply in 'The Grave of King Arthur': between 'Truth' and 'Fiction', as represented by a historical Christian Glastonbury versus an otherworld island with a pagan or prelapsarian aura:

> There, renew'd the vital spring,
> Again he reigns a mighty king;
> And many a fair and fragrant clime,
> Blooming in immortal prime,
> By gales of Eden ever fann'd,
> Owns the monarch's high command   (61 – 66)

The Glastonbury claim was, however, officially preferred in Warton's poem, and this was to remain the orthodox location of Avalon for Burges (1801), a

---

[1] *The Poetical Works of Thomas Warton*, edited by Richard Mant, 2 vols (Oxford, 1802).

Heber birthday poem to Charlotte Dod (c. 1820), Porden (1822), Bowles (1825), Hogg (1827), Cookson (1828), Peacock's *The Misfortunes of Elphin* (1829), Parker (1831), Pennie (1832), Alford (1832) and Beresford-Hope (1841 and 1843).[2] Even when Glastonbury is not specified it is probably implied, as in Finlay's *Wallace* (1802) which presents Avalon within the context of a known topography — of Caerleon, the 'Armoric shore' and 'Snowden's summits hoar'. Nevertheless, although Warton's poem was ultimately to dismiss the otherworld island version as a 'fiction', its elaborate presentation within his poem had created a lasting and contrapuntal image, and the concept of a paradisal 'green isle' remained a powerful focus for some later depictions of Avalon. For example, in Anne Bannerman's 'The Prophecy of Merlin' Arthur sails on a long voyage ('How many times he watch'd the sun, / And saw it sink he never knew', 104 – 105) until he reaches a 'yellow beach', the presumed property of the Queen of the Golden Isle, but which receives no more exact name.[3] Nor do Peacock's islands in two early works: *The Round Table* shows Arthur on an unnamed solitary island, whilst the paradisal island in *Calidore* is simply 'Terra Incognita'.[4] In a similar manner, Ord's poem conveys Arthur to nameless fairy 'halls beyond the morn'.[5] During the 1830s it became more frequent to denote this distant isle as Avalon. A prime agent of this change may have been Thomas Keightley's widely read *The Fairy Mythology* which, although noting that writers seem to 'be unanimous in regarding Glastonbury and Avalon as the same place', also narrates the Ogier legend, in which Avalon is the mid-ocean residence of Morgue la faye and Arthur.[6] Moreover, a vignette by William Henry Brooke provides an illustration of this magical castle of lodestone (I, p. 69). It is within an aura heavy with comparative mythology that William Herbert presents his isle of Avalon, 'where still the yearly wound / Of him, who wielded once Excalibar, / Is ever heal'd'; whereas George Darley's 'Merlin's Last Prophecy' portrays an Arthur on the 'far isle of Avalon' with Morgain and Merlin's 'potent daughters'; but this hero is, like Peacock's, keenly abreast of foreign affairs, sufficiently so to hear of Queen Victoria's accession and to make her a present of 'his enchanted sword'.[7]

Besides the influential image of Arthur's green isle that was evoked by Warton's verse, the critical viewpoint that Warton also pioneered had an immense effect on the reception of medieval, and Arthurian, romance literature, for in his *Observations on the Fairy Queen* Warton's sympathetic consideration of Romance argued for a critical judgment that could accommodate a historical awareness of the differing aesthetic criteria that had

---

[2] Heber's poem is printed in Smith, *Heber*, 99 – 100.
[3] Anne Bannerman, *Tales of Superstition and Chivalry* (1802)
[4] Peacock, *Works*, VIII, 312.
[5] Ord, *England*, 93.
[6] Thomas Keightley, *The Fairy Mythology*, 2 vols (1828), I, 74.
[7] William Herbert, *Attila, King of the Huns* (1838), Book XII. ll. 416 – 18.

shaped artefacts: thus, he found it 'absurd to think of judging either Ariosto or Spenser by precepts which they did not attend to'.[8] Since Spenser had adopted the essence of Ariostan romance, which was to 'consist of allegories, enchantments, and romantic expeditions, conducted by knights, giants, magicians, and fictitious beings', Warton acknowledged that *The Faerie Queene* was 'destitute of that arrangement and economy which epic severity requires' (I, p. 16), but he discovered compensating qualities: not only were these romances valuable for their 'historical pictures' of 'ancient usages and customs', but 'above all' for the fact that their 'fictions and fablings' contributed to 'rouse and invigorate' all the powers of imagination. The very quality of fabling might thus contribute to an education of the emotions, for the 'fancy' could be stored with these 'sublime and alarming images', and, although Warton does not claim 'Truth' for these fictions, he recognises (as Wordsworth would later, in Book V of *The Prelude*) that 'fabling' could powerfully engage 'the affections, the feelings of the heart', and that the imaginative sublimity of romance was attributable to its being 'magnificently marvellous' (II, p. 268).

The enduring popularity of Dryden's *King Arthur* indicates a continuing public taste for the marvellous. Regularly performed in the eighteenth century, and enjoying successful London revivals in 1803, 1819 and 1827, a 'rapturous' reception was especially accorded to the 'magic surprises' and 'fairy changes' of the 1842 production, which was 'simply a succession of scenes of enchantment'.[9] The artist who drew a scene from the play for the *Illustrated London News* provides additional testimony to what was adjudged the play's most popular feature by selecting for his subject 'the fairy land of the poem — the enchanted wood — by which Arthur is approaching the bridge, when the two syrens rise before him from the water with the following luring song . . .'[10] The precise nature of the play's enchantment had been previously noted by Walter Scott in the introduction to his edition of the play. According to Scott, Dryden had not availed himself of 'any fragments of Arthur's romantic renown' such as 'Excalibar' or Merlin, 'the fiend-born necromancer'.[11] By so doing, Dryden had, in Scott's view, reduced Arthur and Merlin to the stature of 'the prince and the magician of a beautiful fairy tale, the story of which, abstracted from the poetry, might have been written by Madame D'Aunois'. That Scott wished to augment the role of enchantment is indicated by his speculations as to what Milton might have made of the legends; and Scott dwells with fascination on what appeared to him the essential legendary core, namely the adventure at the Ruinous Chapel, the Perilous Manor, the Forbidden Seat and the Dolorous Wound.

[8] Warton, *Observations on the Fairy Queen*, I, 15.
[9] *Examiner*, 19 November 1842, 742.
[10] *ILN*, 26 November 1842, 461.
[11] *The Works of John Dryden*, edited by Walter Scott, 18 vols (1808), VIII, 109 – 10.

A perception that Arthur's knights belonged within a romance context had been indicated by an early Southey poem, significantly entitled 'Romance'.[12] Southey's own interest in the publication of medieval romances was highly influential, but Scott's selection of these four quintessentially magical motifs provides a notable focus for later concepts of the nature of Malory's work. These dominant motifs recur also in the Introduction to the first canto of *Marmion* where Scott recalls four major Malorian incidents; one of which (Sir Launcelot's defeat of 'proud Tarquin') belongs solely to normal chivalric adventure, but the remaining three are suffused with a heightened sense of enchantment:

> As when the Champion of the Lake
> Enters Morgana's fated house,
> Or in the Chapel Perilous . . .
> Holds converse with the unburied corse; . . .
> He took the Sangreal's holy quest,
> And, slumbering, saw the vision high   (258 – 68)

For a later poet wishing to break a lance in 'the fair fields of old romance', the constituents of such a revival are frequently magical:

> Where long through talisman and spell . . .
> Fay, giant, dragon, squire and dwarf,
> And wizard with his wand of might, . . .
> Around the Genius weave their Spells   (288 – 99)

His later critical essay on medieval romance was to define the genre as a 'fictitious narrative . . . the interest of which turns upon marvellous and uncommon incidents'.[13] If the marvellous forms the staple content of romance, then a corresponding artistic freedom is awarded the author of modern 'Romantic Poetry', which is thereby freed from the Epic's technical and historical rules of probability. In 'a word', the author of Romantic Poetry

---

[12] The 'genius' of Romance views Arthur's Round Table knights with rapture:
> She gives them to the minstrel lore,
> Hands down her Launcelot's peerless name,
> Repays her Tristram's woes with fame;
> Borne on the breath of song,
> To future times descends the memory of the throng.

'Romance', ll. 62 – 66; in *Poems* by Robert Lovell and Robert Southey (Bath, 1795). The poem is not mentioned by Merriman.

[13] 'Essay on Romance'; in *Essays on Chivalry, Romance*, 65.

is 'absolute master of his country and his inhabitants'.[14] Thus, despite Scott's earlier emphasis on traditional Malorian incidents, his later poem *The Bridal of Triermain* bears only tangential relation to the conventional Arthurian corpus on to which Scott has fancifully grafted a variant of the Sleeping Beauty tale. Not only does Scott's narrative encapsulate a triple time-setting from post-Roman through the medieval to the nineteenth century, but the plot turns on two explicitly marvellous events: the charming of Gyneth to sleep by Merlin, and then Roland's eventual spell-breaking reveille. This motif of the enchanted maiden, which is analogous to that of Lewis's 'captive maid' in 'Sir Guy the Seeker', was a dominant romantic image, and was, significantly, chosen as the subject of Thomas Stothard's frontispiece illustration of the poem, in an 1815 design selected for *The Royal Engagement Pocket Atlas*.[15] Here, the accompanying lines from Scott describe the situation immediately prior to Gyneth's awakening: 'Gently, lo! the Warrior kneels, / Soft that lovely hand he steals', III. xxxix). The poem was illustrated again when Henry Selous made two drawings for *Poems and Pictures* (1846).[16] Both of these feature Gyneth, and the second portrays the moment when she has just been charmed to sleep: 'so lovely seem'd she there, / Spell-bound in her ivory chair' (II. xxvii).

Although Malory's *Le Morte Darthur* had, in contrast, generally reduced the supernatural elements which were so profuse in many of his French sources, Scott's association of Malory with the specifically marvellous is echoed by Thomas Uwins's choice of subjects for illustrations to the edition of Malory issued by Walker and Edwards in 1816.[17] All four designs avoid the typically Malorian milieux of tournament and battle. Instead Uwins selects from only the most highly charged romantic incidents: Arthur receiving his sword from the arm in the lake, the Questing Beast drinking from a fountain, Launcelot slaying a dragon that has emerged from a tomb, and Percivale's vision of a lion and a snake. Two of these designs (*The Lady of the Lake* and *The Vision of Sir Percivale*) were exhibited at the Old Watercolour Society in 1816.[18] At the same institution there was hung in 1837 another painting which had also focused on

[14] *The Bridal of Triermain, or The Vale of St. John* (Edinburgh, 1813), xvi.
[15] In addition to the frontispiece, Stothard contributed fifteen vignette illustrations of the Arthurian passages in *The Bridal of Triermain*.
[16] These illustrations are on pp. 165 and 174.
[17] *The History of the renowned Prince Arthur*, 2 vols (1816). This was edited by Alexander Chalmers: see Barry Gaines, 'The Editions of Malory in the Early Nineteenth Century', *Papers of the Bibliographical Society of America*, 68 (Spring 1974), 1 – 17.
[18] See *A Memoir of Thomas Uwins*, by Mrs Uwins, 2 vols (1858), I, 153.

the magical element in Malory: Copley Fielding's *The Fairy Lake, a scene from La Mort d'Arthur*.[19]

The view that such incidents formed the essence of Arthurian story recalls Arthur's agelong association with fairyland, an association which was proclaimed in two Middle English passages that were frequently cited in the early nineteenth century. The first occurred in John Lydgate's *Fall of Princes*, and was a reference that Gray's essay on Lydgate had remarked upon: 'This errour abideth yet among Britons . . . / He [= Arthur] as a king is crowned in faerie'.[20] Secondly, there was Chaucer's *Wife of Bath's Tale*, which had claimed:

> In th'olde dayes of the king Arthour, . . .
> Al was this land fulfild of fayerye.
> The elf-queen, with hir joly companye,
> Daunced ful ofte in many a grene mede.[21]

Such stray allusions had, moreover, been massively elaborated by Spenser, whose *Faerie Queene* had enjoyed a critical revival in the eighteenth century, as is evident from the widespread use of the Spenserian stanza form;[22] by the references to having read him in youth;[23] and by the poetic tributes afforded to Spenser's 'sweet verse' (Southey), 'Spenser's elfin dream' (Scott), 'sweet creations' (Moultrie) and 'fairy themes' (Wordsworth).[24] There is, besides, common reference to, or imitation of, such Spenserian motifs as the magic mirror given to Britomart by Merlin. Furthermore, Spenser had explicitly linked the fortunes of Britain, represented by Prince Arthur, with those of Fairyland, whose latest Elfin ruler was Gloriana; and as Gloriana symbolised Queen Elizabeth I so Fairyland also is sensed to lie not remote from British soil, albeit entry is restricted to those 'taught . . . by the Muse' (*FQ*, VI. introd. ii). Arthur is, for example, bred beside the river Dee, whilst Merlin has a cave near Carmarthen. Despite the 'Promethean' origin of Elfe, and the

[19] See *Athenaeum*, 29 April 1837, 308.

[20] *Lydgate's Fall of Princes*, edited by Henry Bergen, 4 vols (1924), III. ll. 3109 – 3112. 'Some Remarks on the Poems of John Lydgate'; in Gray, *Poems, Letters, Essays*, 367.

[21] *The Tale of the Wif of Bathe*, ll. 3 – 5; in *The Complete Works of Geoffrey Chaucer*, edited by Walter W. Skeat (1912).

[22] The Spenserian stanza form is used in 'Arthurian' poems by Bouchier, Heber, Finlay, Ord, Burges, Hoyle and Woodley.

[23] See, for example, Smith, *Heber*, 13; and Edward Bulwer Lytton, *Miscellaneous Prose Works*, 3 vols (1868), II, 63.

[24] Southey's review of Ritson, in *Annual Review*, 2 (1804), 528. Scott, *Marmion*, Introduction l. 272. Wordsworth, 'Artegal and Elidure', l. 49; in *Poetical Works*.

inclusion of much classical material, Spenser's poem may also be seen as a national epic, setting forth a British mythology of fay and errant knight.

In reaction against an eighteenth century ethos of neo-classical naiad and faun, the later interest in fairies suggests a desire to celebrate a national folklore — 'our land's first legends', according to Lytton (*KA*, I. i). A special concern with such works as La Motte Fouqué's *Undine*, the introduction of fairy-like costumes for ballerinas, and the growth of Fairy Painting mark parallel developments in the arts. On the part of travellers, there was, for instance, a growing interest in discovering and relating evidence of regional folklore (see Chapter 2); and extensive scholarly investigations were pursued in Crofton Croker's *Fairy Legends and Traditions of the South of Ireland* (1826), Thomas Keightley's *Fairy Mythology* (1828) and Anna Bray's *Legends from the Border of the Tamar and Tavey* (1836).

An important aspect of such legend was that it exhibited the residue of a mythopoeic, poetic, pre-rational stage of human culture. Such a condition was commonly represented by means of the concept of 'childhood'; the mental life of a child thus being equated with the cultural standard of 'early' society, for, as Blair had earlier remarked, the 'infancy of societies' was considered especially favourable to the creation of poetry.[25] Accordingly, ancient legends — those relics of the childhood of the race — were thought to form very suitable reading matter for latter-day infants. Indeed, a typical feature of the transmission of the Arthurian legend was that it was told orally to children. 'The Iron Gate', for example, is explicitly based on a story told by the author's 'grandame', whilst Louisa Stuart Costello rhetorically enquires, 'What infant but the name of Arthur knows?'[26] Edward Donovan refers to King Arthur as 'the visionary hero that amused our infant fancy', and 'Legends of Arthur's chivalrous reign' were 'cherish'd' in Cookson's 'boyhood's hour'.[27] In Mary Shelley's *Frankenstein* (1818), stories of Arthur's Round Table had figured among the boyhood reading of Henry Clerval; and Mrs Sherwood's *The Cloak* (1836) describes a mother telling her children stories of King Arthur and the Knights of the Round Table, 'with the wonderful exploits of the enchanter Merlin'.[28] In America, Emerson testifies

[25] Hugh Blair, 'A Critical Dissertation on the Poems of Ossian'; in *The Poems of Ossian, the Son of Fingal*, translated by James Macpherson, new edition (Edinburgh, 1812), 370.
[26] 'A Dream', l. 24; in *The Maid of the Cyprus Isle, and other poems* (1815).
[27] Donovan, *South Wales*, 129. Cookson, *Glastonbury*, ll. 363 – 65.
[28] Mary Shelley, *Frankenstein*, edited by M. K. Joseph (1969), chapter 2. Mrs Sherwood, *Popular Tales* (1860), 336: this allusion has previously been noticed by Humphrey Carpenter and Mari Prichard, *The Oxford Companion to Children's Literature* (Oxford, 1984), 31.

to the continuing popularity of the abridgments of *Le Morte Darthur*.[29] Similarly, Elizabeth Barrett Browning's 'The Fourfold Aspect' (1844) includes amongst childhood reading the story of

> How King Arthur proved his mission,
>   And Sir Roland wound his horn,
> And at Sangreal's moony vision,
>   Swords did bristle round like corn.[30]

Longfellow's 'The Castle Builder', too, describes his 'dreamy boy' as 'an eager listener unto stories told / At the Round Table of the nursery'.[31] The essentially fictional nature of such stories provides a continuous subcurrent that drew upon and fed the fairy tradition.

A Defence of Fairyland

That the oral traditions were acknowledged to be legendary or mythological indicated the accomplished or imminent death of popular belief in them, and Keightley was accordingly aware that local traces would soon be lost were it not for his documentation. This decline of intuitive and traditional belief was, as a number of scholars have noted, attributed to the influence of modern rationalism and utilitarianism, and was regularly deplored.[32] In Thomas Hood's ironic 'A Lament for the Decline of Chivalry', King Arthur and all those 'armadillo' knights are at rest, for their role as heroic champions has been taken over by the modern lawyer. Fairyland was thus associated with that other victim of modern utilitarian scepticism: the chivalric code, the decline of which was constantly mourned by poets who thought, like Beresford-Hope (see Chapter 1), that 'the crude theories' of modern pride in 'a microscopic age' had overturned 'the bright abodes of hallowed poesy'.

Reaction, however, to this envisaged threat to poetry took a number of positive directions. One vigorous rebuff to crabbed philosophy was a deliberate and sportive celebration of the marvellous, whereby the poem revels in its departure from neo-classical rules or the demands of realism. Scott's *Bridal* is defiantly exuberant in its kaleidoscopic assortment of characters and time-schemes, of enchanted goblets and invisible palaces. The past is clearly

---

[29] *The Early Lectures of Ralph Waldo Emerson*, edited by Stephen E. Whicher and Robert E. Spiller, 3 vols (Cambridge, Mass., 1966), I, 257.
[30] Lines 51 – 54; in *The Poetical Works of Elizabeth Barrett Browning* (1904).
[31] Lines 6 – 7; in *The Poetical Works of Henry Wadsworth Longfellow*, 11 vols (1877), V. Although the poem did not appear until 1867, it had been written on 14 December 1848.
[32] See, for example, M. H. Abrams, *The Mirror and the Lamp: Romantic theory and the critical tradition* (New York, 1953).

represented as being vivider and larger than life: Arthur's horse, for example, on feeling a drop of the poisoned draught,

> Screaming with agony and fright,
> He bolted twenty feet upright!
> The peasant still can show the dint
> Where his hoofs landed on the flint.   (II. x)

This heightened colouring of the past, when 'Strength was gigantic, valour high' (I. xix), is consciously set against a trivially mediocre present, of 'Hessian boot and pantaloon'. Such a light-hearted delight in fanciful invention may be associated with the generic influence of Ariosto (see Chapter 3) on account of the lively wit and sprightly pace of Scott's narration, united with a delicate perception of amorous emotion.

The young Praed's three Arthurian poems belong to the same inventive genre. 'Gog', for instance, incorporates the eponymous giant, Sir Paladore, Captain Craven and a monk in a wildly improbable mélange set in the Arthurian era 'When all was wit, and worth and praise, / And planting thrusts, and planting oaks' (20 – 21). *Lillian* was a bravura piece written as playful explanation of a friend's conundrum: 'A dragon's tail is flayed to warm / A headless maiden's heart'.[33] With considerable licence, Praed borrows Sir Eglamour from a Percy ballad and/or Ellis's *Specimens of Early English Metrical Romances* (or possibly from Shakespeare's *Two Gentlemen of Verona*), allocates him a role as a Round Table knight, sites Merlin near Brentford, and achieves the metamorphosis of fairies into dragons. Further transformations are the subject of 'The Legend of the Haunted Tree', wherein the discontended hero, Wilfred, is charmed by a fairy into the Arthurian knight Sir Isumbras, in order to learn that there are drawbacks to worldly 'passion' and 'strife'.

The two prose tales which were discussed in Chapter 3 exemplify a similar fascination with the marvellous. Henry Davies's 'The Enchanted Shield' draws closely on Welsh sources, but, with distinct originality, describes how Arthur and his knights attempt a two-fold quest: to rid Bardsey Island of idolaters, and to acquire the 'renowned Pridwen', a magic shield concealed there by Merlin. After successfully attacking the Druid priests, Sir Galath rescues, with the aid of Tristan's magic incantations, the long-lost daughter of Arthur, whilst Arthur obtains the coveted shield which, ironically, will work his downfall, since envy of the article will incite Modred to rebellion. John Oxenford's 'Sir Wigolais of the Wheel' follows the medieval tale of Gawain's son, a Gareth-like youth who accompanies a sulky damsel from Arthur's court to achieve an adventure in the land of Corotin. The adventures comprise

---

[33] Lady Flora Hastings was later to base her own poem of Border chivalry, 'Sir Osric', upon the same conundrum as had been set for Praed: *Poems* (1841).

much magic, a spell, enchanted weapons, an enchanted stone, giants, a sword-bridge, a monster and a wizard. Moreover, like Praed's, both tales are scholarly, sophisticated and deftly ironic treatments of their exotic subjects.

As few poets would have claimed, like Blake, to have seen a fairy funeral, the marvellous was generally admitted not to possess mundane truth. A poet could, however, as in Coleridge's 'Frost at Midnight', blur the sharp distinction between dream and waking reality, or, by building a 'bridge from Dreamland', unite the rational with the imaginative, the cerebral with the emotional. Lowell's phrase, associating imagination with the dream, is indicative of the widespread recurrence of dreaming within contemporary literature.[34]

Dreams were, in effect, employed in a rich variety of ways.[35] As an alternative non-rational form of knowing, a dream may prefigure a later event. Thus, Roland de Vaux's dream of Gyneth, or Galahad's of the Egyptian Maid, provides the poem with an aura of gradually revealed destiny which the protagonist must discover and resolve; the poem thereby gaining in organic impetus. Moreover, dreaming may carry the resonance of prophetic foreboding, and lend authority to Arthur's projected fears in Emerson's poem, or Geriant's in 'The Enchanted Shield'. A dream setting of his material allows the author to adopt a widely varying attitude to the material presented. It may provide merely a convenient framework for a time-shift (and a character-shift in Praed) or for the creation of a purely imaginary Arthurian kingdom, as in Alexander Macleod's dream of the world of chivalry. The attribution of part, or all, of a poem's action to a dream may induce a reader's willing suspension of disbelief, as when Lytton encloses his epic between the key words of 'Fable-land' (I. i) and 'Dream-land' (XII. ccv). The more supernatural moments in Lytton's poem are often placed within the boundaries of a dream or a vision: thus, Gawaine's encounter with the fairies occurs when he lies beneath the 'fairy's oak', so the incident may be rationally explained as a dream; and Arthur's metaphysical quests tend to be very private visions which are kept separate from the public action.

By recapturing the medieval literary mode of using a dream framework such as had been employed in the *Roman de la Rose*, *Piers Plowman*, and Chaucer's *House of Fame*, an appropriately medieval form was thus adopted to suit the medievalist material; and an intricate texture of realism and fancy may be created when the entire poem is cast as a dream account. Both Louisa

---

[34] *The Vision of Sir Launfal*, l. 4; in *The Poetical Works of James Russell Lowell* (1891).

[35] Dreams are also represented in Arthurian painting and illustration. Prince Arthur's dream of the Faerie Queene was painted by Henry Fuseli (1788) and Henry Lejeune (1843). Thomas Uwins's *Vision of Sir Percivale* (1816) showed Percivale asleep, and Arthur was portrayed thus in Frederick Pickersgill's *Amoret, Aemylia and Prince Arthur in the Cottage of Sclaunder* (1845). Henry Selous's drawing of Gyneth's enchanted sleep has been referred to above; and Samuel Williams drew Rhonabwy asleep on a calfskin in 'The Dream of Rhonabwy', in *The Mabinogion*, translated by Lady Charlotte Guest, 3 vols (1849).

Costello and Beresford-Hope adopt 'A Dream' as title for poems, dreaming providing in each case an entrée into the Arthurian world. Costello's poem assumes the existence of an historical Arthur whose manner of death remains controversial. Her dream therefore attempts to discover the truth of this event, by questioning a 'fairy form'. Part of the answer is revealed, but the 'mystery' of how Arthur left 'for heaven the realms below' remains unexplained, for the dreamer is 'seiz'd by hands unseen', and 'hurl'd'. She then awakes and rises, lamenting that her 'dream was vain' (53 – 55). Not all dreams, however, are granted even this admixture of playful enquiry. The resurrection of Glastonbury's history is achieved by Alford in a series of dreams and visions which yield historically authentic tableaux. His powers do not extend to the successful prediction of the Abbey's future, but (as shown in Chapter 1) the mantic role is apportioned to those whose prophecies of Britain's future are lent an apparent veracity by being narrated with the wisdom of hindsight. But such literal authenticity may be supererogatory when the Arthurian material is treated as a metaphor. Thus, in Beresford-Hope's 'A Dream', the 'beautiful old belief' that Arthur was 'but asleep' and would return to 'free Britain' in 'an hour of peril' becomes a symbol for the writer's faith that the lost age of chivalry may be revived in Victorian Britain.

Allegory

A sceptical attitude towards the historical Arthur sometimes resulted not in his eradication but in his transfer to a mythological plane where he was accorded singular attention. A decline in historical role was thereby often countered by an allegorical reading which offered an alternative means of asserting Arthur's enduring relevance. William Owen-Pughe cautiously described a dual figure in his *Cambrian Biography*: herein Arthur was not only, as the bards and triads revealed, an early sixth century Silurian chieftain, but he was also the mythological character portrayed in the *Mabinogion*. Reaching out into the 'allegorical attributes' of this mythology, Owen-Pughe defines Arthur as 'the Great Bear, as the epithet literally implies', and suggests that this constellation, which describes 'a circle in a small space', had given rise to the concept of Arthur's Round Table; and he notes that Telyn (or Harp) of Arthur is the 'British appellation' for the constellation Lyra.[36] Readily compiling mythological analogies, Owen-Pughe claims that in the story of Culhwch and Olwen he recognised 'adventures, which must have had a common origin with those of Hercules, and with the Argonautic voyage'. He suspects that in Arthur may be detected the attributes of Nimrod, 'the mighty hunter before the Lord', and he supplements this comparative mythological

[36] Owen, *Cambrian Biography*, 13 – 18.

technique with etymological derivations that reduce personal names to allegorical entities: thus, Arthur is the offspring of Uther Bendragon, or 'Wonder the Supreme Leader', and Eigyr, or 'Generating Power'. Such theories were vastly augmented by Edward Davies's *Mythology and Rites of the British Druids* which adopted Jacob Bryant's theory that all ancient mythology was essentially one, and had been divinely related in the early books of the Old Testament, but that a widespread idolatrous variant had relapsed into worship of the sun (Helios) and the moon (often represented as the Ark).[37] Davies's Helio-Arkite interpretation of *Sir Tristrem* was mocked by Southey for suggesting that Mordred was the 'raven sent out from the Ark', or that intercourse with Essyllt alludes to 'the incorporation of the primitive religion of the Britons with the rites of the Phoenician cow'.[38] Similar Helio-Arkite concepts were also advanced in George Stanley Faber's *The Origin of Pagan Idolatry*, wherein Arthur is treated as a manifestation of the recurrent solar hero; Morganna's character is said to have been taken from that of the White Goddess; whilst Merlin's imprisonment within a rock is held to represent a druidical initiation rite.[39] An extensive chapter on 'The Mythological Reign of Arthur' in Algernon Herbert's *Britannia after the Romans* again belittles the historical role of Arthur (see Chapter 1), but by drawing Arthur within a framework of comparative mythology he identifies him with Hercules or the 'terrestrial Apollo', whilst the Round Table represents the Zodiac.[40]

This perception of the analogous relationships between different national mythologies, and the resulting attempt to formulate a universal mythology, provided a powerful influence on the work of William Blake, who had probably engraved plates for Jacob Bryant's seminal work *A New System of Mythology* in 1774 to 1776.[41] Blake, too, knew William Owen-Pughe, and probably relied on him for a knowledge of the 'Welsh Triades' which formed the basis for Blake's *The Ancient Britons*. The *Descriptive Catalogue* which accompanied the exhibition of this painting in 1809, by pitting Arthur versus the Romans (!) in his last battle, reveals Blake's idiosyncratic manipulation of the historical tradition and his adoption of Owen-Pughe's mythological equation of Arthur with the constellation Arcturus. A Galfridean core may be detected in Blake's account of Arthur as a 'Prince of the fifth century, who conquered Europe, and held the Empire of the world in the dark age', but Blake identifies the stories of Arthur with 'the acts of Albion', who was

[37] For Jacob Bryant's theories, see Ruthven Todd, *Tracks in the Snow* (1946), 29 – 56; and W. D. Paden, *Tennyson in Egypt* (New York, 1971), 75 – 88.
[38] Southey ed. *King Arthur*, I, liii.
[39] Faber, *Pagan Idolatry*, III, 321.
[40] Herbert, *Britannia*, I, 94.
[41] See Todd, *Tracks in the Snow*, 29 – 56.

Patriarch of the Atlantic and the Atlas of the Greeks.[42] As for the three heroes
who survived the last battle, in Blake's version they are deprived of their
original Welsh names (Morvran, Sanddo and Glewlwyd) — which were later
to be given in Taliesin Williams's *Cardiff Castle* (1827) — but are represented
instead as the Strongest, the Beautifullest and the Ugliest; and Blake's
catalogue makes clear their allegorical significance: the Strong representing
'the human sublime', the Beautiful 'the human pathetic', and the Ugly 'the
human reason'; all of whom had once formed part of an original fourfold man.
Within his epic poem *Jerusalem, the Emanation of the Giant Albion* (1804 – 1820)
strands of Arthurian legend are enmeshed with Biblical and personal myths:
Gwiniverra is one of the 'beautiful Emanations' of Skofeld, one of the 'Twelve
Sons of Albion' (I. 5); Merlin appears to be man's 'Immortal Imagination'
(II. 36); whereas Arthur, 'the hard cold constrictive Spectre' (III. 54),
becomes Albion's Satanic antagonist, and represents a Druid and a
Philosopher belonging to the empirical tradition of Bacon, Locke and
Newton.[43] Starting with comparatively well-known Arthurian materials,
Blake's ultimate interpretation of them is highly novel; but, although
remaining an extreme case, his work is symptomatic of a widespread tendency
to reduce a historical concern or to place it within very much broader
frameworks of reference.

    Moreover, an inclination to moralise and to admit the legends only for an
ultimate truth they embodied, allied with an assumed freedom to reshape the
legends drastically, led inexorably towards an allegorical treatment. As
massive precedent, there was Spenser's very plastic handling of Arthurian and
fairy themes to fit a moral and political allegory. Contemporary critics, too,
had often viewed Arthurian romance principally in terms of a hidden allegory.
Friedrich Schlegel's *Lectures on the History of Literature* had extended an
extremely sympathetic consideration to medieval Arthurian literature, and
praised the 'poetical clothing of the marvellous' for 'beautifying the fiction'
and 'ennobling the feeling'.[44] Furthermore, and particularly in the Grail
romances, the medieval poets had, he claimed, conducted an allegory on two
planes — a general and a particular — for they endeavoured

> under the form of Arthur and his knights . . . to shadow forth the idea of
> a spiritual knighthood . . . And . . . there is every reason to believe that
> in all these poems the object was not merely to shadow out a spiritual
> and allegorical chivalry, but also to embody the peculiar ideas of . . . the
> chivalry of the religious orders of knighthood, such as the Templars and
> the Knights of St John.   (I, p. 315)

---

[42] *Poetry and Prose of William Blake*, edited by Geoffrey Keynes (1956), 608 – 12.
[43] See S. Foster Damon, *A Blake Dictionary* (1973).
[44] *Lectures on the History of Literature, Ancient and Modern*, translated from the German of Frederick
Schlegel, 2 vols (Edinburgh, 1818), I, 314.

Schlegel's writings are freely quoted by Kenelm Digby's *The Broadstone of Honour* (1822).[45] Saturated in Malory, and convinced of the historical reality of Arthur, Digby's chief concern was the moral regeneration of society by means of chivalry. Aware that it was impossible to revive an archaism, he accepted the need for chivalry ('a philosophy of the heart') to adopt new forms. A corollary of this approach was that he saw 'romantic fictions' as 'often professedly allegorical'; the adventures and scenes recorded were not indeed true, but they represented truths:

> In the *Morte d'Arthur* the beauty of the youthful form, and the brightness of the warrior's aspect, armed, in complete steel, are described as symbolical of goodness and of heavenly purity.[46]

Ralph Waldo Emerson's lecture *The Age of Fable* (1835) would, initially, censure 'Gothic fables' for being mere amusement by means of 'unchosen and miscellaneous prodigies'.[47] Far superior, he claimed, were works that displayed 'a fine allegory conveying a wise and consistent sense'. This adverse criticism is, however, qualified by the admission that

> a fairy tale, a romance, has often (I may say, always) a moral in spite of itself. He who constructs a beautiful fable only with the design of making it symmetrical and pleasing will find that unconsciously he has been writing an allegory. (I, p. 259)

Included among Emerson's journal entries is a prose outline of an ostensible fairy tale in which Arthur wanders in the 'wood of Cornwall' among the 'dauncing fayries' before he follows two white kids, on a Sangreal quest.[48] Because the work remained incomplete, one is unable to ascertain whether Emerson would have, consciously or otherwise, constructed an allegory, but, as his draft of a poem 'King Richard's Death' had originally been entitled 'King Arthur's Death', it would seem that Emerson was principally interested in generalities rather than in the particular, in the death of a monarch *qua* monarch rather than in an individual historical figure.[49] The process is carried further in the two 'Merlin' poems, for the Merlin of these is given no traditional Arthurian location or biography: he is simply a representative of poethood, which is viewed under two aspects: a prophetically inspired individuality, and a contrasting and complementary aspect of Apollonian pattern-making.

---

[45] Digby's quotation from Schlegel is briefly noted in Girouard, *Return to Camelot*, but no recent attention has apparently been paid to Schlegel's Arthurian interest.

[46] Kenelm Henry Digby, *The Broad Stone of Honour: Godefridus* (1829), 158.

[47] Emerson, *Early Lectures*, I, 257.

[48] *The Journals and Miscellaneous Notebooks of Ralph Waldo Emerson*, edited by W. H. Gilman, A. R. Ferguson *et al.*, 16 vols (Cambridge, Mass., 1960), II, 63 – 64.

[49] Emerson, *Journals*, I, 188.

In contrast, Wordsworth's 'The Egyptian Maid' (1835) appears to combine a fully Arthurian narrative with a cogent allegorical framework. J. D. Merriman has advanced an illuminating and credible interpretation of the three main figures in this schema.[50] Merlin herein represents the rational or scientific intellect, opposed to the imagination and hence devoid of moral knowledge. The ship represents art, imagination and instinctive life but, as revealed by the idol on the prow, it is a type of pagan hedonism, and intrinsically heartless; its sinking can only be relieved by Galahad, who represents reinvigoration by Christian moral conduct, and the perfect wedding of spirit and action.[51] A schema of ulterior moral significance also controls R. H. Horne's 'The Three Knights of Camelott', which adopts the Spenserian practice of endowing its personae with names that signify their bearers' attributes. Accordingly, Amorel is a 'lover gay' whilst Sir Leontine has martial courage. The fairy fashion of the knights' apparel, armour and accoutrements is attributed, in Horne's footnote, to a Chaucerian influence from *Sir Thopas*:

> His doublet was of violet hue,
> And glistened with the morning dew;
>   His helm of emerald bright;
> And round his waist a diamond zone,
> Like a far constellation shone,
>   With scintillating light.[52]

However, the manifest prettiness of this armour exemplifies the slightly effeminate, inconstant sensuousness of Sir Amorel, its wearer. By contrast, the armour of Sir Galohault is emblematic of sturdy, practical dependability: 'A suit he wore of iron mail, / Well overlaid with bar and nail' (97 – 98). Fittingly, in a neo-Spenserian plot, whereas Amorel is beguiled by beautiful enchantresses, and Leontine is felled by satyrs, the redoubtable Galohault slays a giant, and releases a company of captive lords and ladies: a virtuous and modest plainness is thus seen to be more efficacious than is an ostentatious beauty. Horne does not, however, drive home an entirely merciless moral

---

[50] Merriman, *Flower of Kings*, 160 – 67.

[51] Galahad's role here is strikingly similar to that of Galath in Henry Davies's 'The Enchanted Shield'. In the latter work, King Arthur had betrothed his 'fair and beauteous daughter Anna' to the 'immaculate' son of Sir Lancelot, but she had been shipwrecked and lost in the current off Bardsey Island. During Arthur's later expedition against Bardsey's idolaters and enchanters, Anna is discovered 'spell-bound' behind a wall of fire, from which a charm created by the 'sage' Tristan rescues her. Sir Galath then claims his affianced, and hastens away with her 'to regain the light of heaven' where he is rewarded with her fair hand. Although Galath is deemed a 'preux' chevalier, he is not here associated with the Grail quest, and like Wordsworth's hero he is married to a princess who had been presumed drowned. Accordingly, Wordsworth's celebration of Galahad's nuptials, and his avoidance of a Grail context, appears a less idiosyncratic and bizarre handling of the legend than has previously been thought.

[52] Lines 37 – 42; in Richard Hengist Horne, *Ballad Romances (1846)*.

message, as Amorel and Leontine are allowed to recover and rejoin the convivial knights at Camelott without pointed ignominy. A more rigorous control, however, is exerted over James Russell Lowell's *Vision of Sir Launfal* (1848). Despite the reference to 'the elfin builders of the frost' who carve in 'fairy masonry', this fairyland remains on the level of playful conceit, without autonomy, and subservient to the dominant Christian allegory, which consists of an attack on the mystical or chimerical or exotic as typified by the traditional Grail quest. Since the mind has its own mountains, there is no requirement to seek out Montsalvat: 'Daily, with souls that cringe and plot, / We Sinais climb and know it not' (Prelude. 11 – 12). The theme of man's obliviousness to a God who is always nearby is illustrated by the story of Sir Launfal — Lowell fancifully appropriates this name — who has sought the Holy Grail throughout the world in vain, only to discover, when at last sharing his food with a leper, that the leper is revealed as Christ; for the Grail is ultimately a symbol of 'whatso we share with another's need' (II. viii). Lowell's castle is ostensibly set in the 'North Countree' (I. ii) but, just as the chronology has been transferred to a post-Arthurian era, Sir Launfal being deprived of his original biography, and the other characters in the poem remaining unnamed, the natural background in the poem is deliberately unlocalised. It is correspondingly generalised and made tightly allegorical in effect by means of the taut contrast between the opposing qualities of winter and summer, warmth and cold, light and darkness — and, by implication, truth and fantasy.

The strength of the contemporary tendency towards allegorical genre may be seen, too, in the approach made to the Arthurian subject by the painter William Dyce. Commissioned in 1847 to paint a series of Arthurian frescoes for the Queen's Robing Room in the Palace of Westminster, Dyce went back to Malory as chief source, but he read *Le Morte Darthur* largely in terms of a Christian allegory — 'a sort of *Pilgrim's Progress* of the Middle Ages' — and he saw in the Grail legend

> a tolerably intelligible religious allegory, strongly tinctured with the monastic ideas of the thirteenth century and seemingly, to some / extent, intended to throw discredit on chivalric greatness.[53]

As a result of these perceptions, Dyce's main action is seen in quasi-Spenserian mode — even though individual character and incident, such as the stories of Tristram and Gawaine, are drawn from medieval romance — because each fresco was intended to illustrate a single category of virtue, namely Religion, Courtesy, Mercy, Generosity, Hospitality, Courage and Fidelity. Had it been adopted by Dyce, Prince Albert's initial suggestion would have created an even more overtly Spenserian work, for it would have

---

[53] Letter to Sir Charles Eastlake, 20 July 1848; quoted in Pointon, *Dyce*, 105 – 06.

included a central compartment in which Arthur would appear as 'mythological type of the whole' — the very function which Prince Arthur was to have
performed in *The Faerie Queene*.

Another extremely ambitious work in this genre was Bulwer Lytton's *King
Arthur* which, although having been treated as an isolated sport by recent
critics, requires an extended treatment on account of its being a major
representative of the contemporary allegorical mode. Lytton claimed to have
attempted an epic fable based on our 'national romance', with a fusion of the
'Probable, the Allegorical and the Marvellous'.[54] A degree of probability is
attained by ascribing Arthur to a defined historical role as leader of the
Silures, 'the patriot Prince of South Wales' who is the preserver of 'Cymrian
Nationality', and by providing copious glosses on the Welsh cultural
background. Lytton thus rejects Geoffrey of Monmouth's fabling as to the
Arthurian conquest of Rome, but a poetic licence is assumed in denoting the
Mercians as Arthur's chief foes. The cultural mix is heightened by the poet's
adoption of the manners of medieval chivalry for his Dark Age characters, and
the inclusion of supernatural machinery derived from 'the Romance of the
North', which takes the specific forms of 'the Fairy, the Genius [and] the
Enchanter'. That the poem has derived from the 'world of Fable-land' (I. i)
and will finally relapse into 'Dream-land' (XII. ccv) allows Lytton his
necessary entry into the imaginary world his narrative demands.

Fairies certainly appear regularly throughout the poem. Their recurrence in
imagery fulfils a mainly decorative role by suggesting an enchanted innocence
and beauty, as in 'Lips with such sweetness in their honied deeps / As fills the
rose in which a fairy sleeps' (XI. cxxxix). Lancelot's fairy upbringing is
narrated from Ellis's summary of traditional French sources, but Lytton also
endows him with a useful crystal ring with which he can successfully prosecute
his quest for Arthur, since the ring houses a 'fairy hand' that points unerringly
in the direction of the King. Mourning a vanished springtime of the world,
when 'what is now called poetry was life' (IV. xxxiv), Lytton elegises over

> Nature, not then the slave of formal law!
> Her each free sport a miracle might be;
> Enchantment clothed the forest with sweet awe;
> Astolfo spoke from out the bleeding tree;
> The fairy wreath'd his dance in moonlit air;
> On golden sands the mermaid sleek'd her hair   (IV. xxxiii)

Moreover, Sir Gawaine is compared to 'a fairy child' in his frank wildness
(I. c); yet Lytton's evocation of the enchanted Ariostan world circumscribes

[54] See Taylor and Brewer; John Hazard Wildman, 'Unsuccessful Return from Avalon', *Victorian
Poetry*, 12 (1974), 291 – 96; and James D. Merriman, 'The Last Days of the Eighteenth Century
Epic: Bulwer Lytton's Arthuriad', *Studies in Medievalism*, 2 (Fall 1983), 15 – 37. The Lytton
quotation is from *Poetical and Dramatic Works*, II, 1.

its autonomy, and subordinates it to a grand abstract strategy. Even the lively fairies who assault Gawaine under their oak have shrunk to diminutive physical stature and are part of Merlin's purgatorial scheme for the moral purification of Gawaine; controlled by the overall plan, they lack the whimsical independence of their counterparts in *The Pilgrims of the Rhine* (1834). Similarly, the Lady of the Lake, whose intents are elusively enigmatic in medieval literature, is integrated within the Merlin-controlled quest for the magic sword, since she leads Arthur to the Meteor Isle where he will find 'the diamond glaive', which he achieves after a series of trials. A flood of personification points to the generalised allegorising ambience as the Lady explains her role: 'Ever I rise before the eyes that weep / When, born from sorrow, Wisdom wakes the will' (VII. xi). The overriding tendency of the poem, at all levels, is towards abstraction, synthesis and allegory. The language consistently moves away from particularisation towards broader categories, as in the following scenic description:

> Dark, to the right, thick forests mantled o'er
> A gradual mountain sloping to the plain;
> Whose gloom but lent to light a charm the more,
> As pleasure pleases most when neighbouring pain;
> And all our human joys most sweet and holy,
> Sport in the shadows cast from Melancholy.   (I. v)

This landscape is conceived in terms of general picturesque effect in the contrast between light and plane (1 – 2). By line 4, attention has veered from the visual to the contrast between pleasure and pain. By line 6, we have reached an abstract personification of Melancholy. Elsewhere, the poem is full of scenery (rivers, vales, mountains, forests, fountains, cataracts, caverns, seas) and of animal life (birds, dogs, horses, wolves, even walrus) but Nature in Lytton is inert dead matter, and each scene or beast has no intrinsic life but is used as an allegorical emblem. The Vale of Carduel where Arthur watches the knights' pastimes represents a superficial existence of sensuous ease; the glow-worm seen by Caradoc is explained by Merlin as a premonition of Caradoc's own funeral torch; and the bitter herb given Arthur to taste is Wisdom.

The transformation of Genevieve into a dove, and Merlin's use of the guiding raven, show Nature metamorphosed into moral categories. Individual characters betray the same tendency. Arthur himself is steadily ennobled into the epitome of chivalry: he gives 'the pure kiss of courteous chivalry' (IV. viii); has a 'fair, serene, undaunted, godlike brow' (V. lxviii); towers 'erect, with empire on his brow' (VII. xli); is 'God's elected Man' (XII. cxlii); and 'Nature's masterpiece, perfected Man' (XII. clxxvii). Lancelot, Merlin and Caradoc all aspire to a state of 'Soul-hood', whilst Genevieve and Genevra both represent 'Beauty sublimed into the type of soul' (XII. ciii). The savage idolater, Faul, becomes the rescuer of Genevieve; Harold the Saxon (a 'type of the strong Saxon soul', XII. cxciv) displays heroic mercy; and pagan Crida, the father of Genevieve, achieves a final reconciliation with Arthur. These individual human actions are steadily linked to an ulterior moral significance within a larger pattern of meaning. The numerous adventures that are recounted — voyages, treks, a descent into the Underworld, and the many battles — are ultimately allegorical struggles on a moral plane: thus, Arthur's hard-won sword represents the victory of those who value 'Honour more than Fame' (VII. xcvii), and the winning of his shield denotes the attainment of 'Freedom' (X. lxxix). Moreover, Lytton is intent on fusing the individual into a moral type, a social class, a nation or, finally, mankind. In his preface to *The Last of the Barons* (1843), he had claimed that he would, unlike Scott, aim at bringing into full display

> the characters of the principal personages of the time . . . and the great social interests which were involved in what, regarded imperfectly, appear but the feuds of rival factions.[55]

In his epic poem, too, he concentrates on the leaders (whether king, prophet, pagan priest or abbess), and there are very few peasants or seamen at work in these great land- or sea-scapes. The conflict between Arthur and his enemies is broadened into a clash between the rival cultures of Cymry and Saxon, who are themselves part of a wider conflict between Christ and Woden; and Christianity is seen in undenominational terms, without the agency of priests. And yet, even this apparent division will be softened, as his preface explains:

> I have endeavoured to distinguish their separate nationality, without enforcing too violent a contrast between the rudeness of the heathen Teutons and the polished Christianity of the Cymrian Knighthood.[56]

Finally, this distinction will be effaced by a union of both races: the ultimate aim is the fusion and amelioration of all mankind. Time is similarly abstracted. Although set ostensibly in the sixth century with the manners of medieval chivalry, the medievalism is only slightly conveyed. Indeed, Lytton is also conducting an allegorical political subplot in that many of the Welsh knights represent parliamentary figures of the 1830s, whilst the Vandal court symbolises the regime of Louis Philippe, and the prelate Henricus stands for Henry Philpotts, the Puseyite Bishop of Exeter (see Chapter 1). The wide-angled view of all British history moves from the Ancient Britons to their heirs, the Tudors, and thence to Queen Victoria's broad dominions ('From the dumb icebergs to the fiery zone', VII. lxxix), and comes full-circle with the prophesied return of 'the soul of Arthur' (VII. lxxxiv).

[55] Edward Bulwer Lytton, *The Last of the Barons*, 2 vols (1896), I, 25.
[56] *Poetical and Dramatic Works*, II, 5.

This idealising principle of Lytton's, so clearly conceived and ably defended, brings its own problems. It does not work effectively as allegory, for allegory requires a vivid foregrounding (as in Spenser, Bunyan or Orwell) of the overt action in order to give life to the consequent analogies. But Lytton reduces the vital particularity of his foreground: the characters have a vapid sameness which obviates dramatic interest; the potentially John Martinesque scene-painting lacks awe or mystery; and the high incidence of dream and vision blurs the waking action. This eagerness to dispense with concreteness throws a massive strain on his own ultimate reality, which he is compelled to delineate openly. Impatient with

> the old familiar train
> That fill the frail Proscenium of our deeds,
> The unquiet actors on that stage, the brain,
> Which, in the spangles of their tinsell'd weeds,
> Mime the true soul's majestic royalties   (XI. cii)

he continually nudges the reader to point out that his backdrops are purely stage effects and his protagonists dummies, but, for 'the true soul's majestic royalties', he can present only some very clichéd anonymity:

> Yea, the hard sense of time was from the mind
> Rased and annihilate; — yea, space to eye
> And soul was presenceless? What rest behind?
> Thought and the Infinite! the eternal I,
> And its true realm the Limitless, whose brink
> Thought ever nears: What bounds us when we think?   (XI. cxi)

A little archaic language, an exclamation mark, repetition, rhetorical question marks and capitalisation are used to mask the emptiness of the shrine.

The Great Enchanters

Within early nineteenth century literature, the magician often assumed a dominant role. Not only did Goethe's *Faust* (1808) embody such a figure, so too did a variety of minor works reflect this type of the romantic outsider, *viz.* Lewis's 'Sir Guy the Seeker', Leyden's 'Lord Soulis', Hemans's 'The Necromancer', Campbell's 'Lochiel's Warning' and Scott's portrayal of the wizard Michael Scott in *The Lay of the Last Minstrel* (1805). For Arthurian literature, there was, of course, an enchanter at hand in Merlin, who had never quite yielded up his popular reputation as a prophet, even during the low tide of Arthuriana in the seventeenth and eighteenth centuries. In the 1790s there is an important cluster of Merlin poems, stressing his vatic powers (as in Blake's 'Merlin's Prophecy', c. 1793; John Penn's 'Mount Merlin'; and John Rose's *Caernarvon Castle*); or his role as enchanter (as in Humphry Davy's unpublished manuscript poem 'The Death of Merlin' of about 1795 – 1796).[57]

Indicative of Merlin's enduring reputation in this period is the constant endeavour of the inventor John Joseph Merlin (1735 – 1803) to capitalise on the fame of his namesake. Opening a mechanical exhibition named Merlin's Museum in about 1783, he later attempted to raise subscriptions for a Merlin's Necromantic Cave, of which a contemporary handbill portrays the attractions:

> Under the entrance to the cave will be a dark subterranean cavern . . . wherein the author will make use of his supposed necromantic power, in imitation of the celebrated Ambrosius Merlin, called the necromancer. A variety of phantoms, red and white dragons . . . will be seen and heard, making the most horrid and mournful shrieks and noise . . .: the goddess of darkness will also appear in a sable habit, wearing bat's wings.[58]

Unhappily, John Joseph Merlin failed to raise the funds necessary for the Cave's construction, but in other respects he succeeded in formulating fresh ways of popularising the Merlin legend, for he commissioned John Milton in 1788 to design a copper medal showing Merlin Ambrosius on the obverse, and

---

[57] John Rose's *Caernarvon Castle, or, the Birth of the Prince of Wales. An opera in two acts* was first performed at the Theatre Royal, Haymarket on 12 August 1793, and was published in the same year. In this work, Merlin prophesies the future glory of the Princes of Wales, especially that of Prince George, the son of King George III. Humphry Davy's poem is in Personal Notebook (13h) in the Library of the Royal Institution. The complete text of the poem is printed in my article 'An Unpublished Poem by Humphry Davy: Merlin in the Late Eighteenth Century', *Notes and Queries*, 233 (June 1988), 195 – 96. Neither Rose nor Davy is mentioned by Merriman.

[58] 'Merlin's Cave', *Chimney Corner Companion*, 10 (1827), 223 – 24. For contemporary literary allusions to this inventor, see James Lawrence's reference to the modern Merlin's Mechanical Tea Table ('What tho' his magic board, with tea-cups crown'd, / Presents the cream, or waves the muffin round') in 'The Bosom Friend' (1791), Book III. ll.4 – 8, in *The Etonian Out of Bounds*, 3 vols (1828), I; 'The Wax-works, Clock-work, all the marvellous craft / Of modern Merlins' (Wordsworth, *Prelude*, VII. ll.685 – 86); Dominie Sampson's 'rolling his eyes and gaping with his mouth like the great wooden head at Merlin's exhibition' (Scott, *Guy Mannering*, chapter 51); and Charles Lamb's 'Sonnet III', which was later revised in order to avoid a reference to 'the wizard wand / Of Merlin', because this was 'likely to suggest a burlesque association with a wizard of that name in Oxford Street': *The Life, Letters and Writings of Charles Lamb*, edited by Percy Fitzgerald, 6 vols (1892), VI, 466. Merlin's Museum was in Princes Street, just off Oxford Street.

then in 1802 he paid eighty guineas to have his chariot painted with scenes from the life of Merlin.[59]

In the early nineteenth century, Merlin is, next to Arthur, the most frequently mentioned character in the Arthurian corpus, his presence in Spenser's *Faerie Queene* helping to ensure his enduring prominence. Although most allusions to him are, in fact, very incidental (as in Keats's reference to Merlin paying his demon 'all his debt' in 'The Eve of St Agnes'), nevertheless, in poems such as Coleridge's 'The Pang More Sharp Than All' a rich allusiveness results.[60] This work, which Coleridge subtitles 'An Allegory', narrates, under the guise of an elegy for a dead infant, the loss of a Love which is presented in terms of a Spenserian persona ('an Elfin Knight') who, having won a tournament, has stolen away: he is also a 'magic Child' whose 'strong art' has implanted his own 'magic image' in the narrator's heart,

> As in that crystal orb — wise Merlin's feat, —
> The wondrous 'World of Glass', wherein inisled
> All long'd for things their beings did repeat.[61]

A footnote supplies the source of Coleridge's allusion (*FQ*, III. ii. 19) but, whereas the mirror of Britomart had revealed only hidden truths that 'appertaynd' to the viewer, Coleridge attributes to it the more personally affective power of reflecting the viewer's desires.

As the previous chapter has shown, Merlin could even more radically transcend his original Arthurian context by figuring as an archetypal wizard in theatre productions throughout the eighteenth century, a tradition that was carried over into nineteenth century pantomimes like Charles Dibdin's *Wizard's Wake*, the anonymous *Merlin's Cave*, Thomas Dibdin's *Merlin's Mount* and Richard Nelson Lee's *Harlequin, Mother Redcap, Merlin and Princess Snowdrop*, or the still more outlandish *Merlin* by Lambert A. Wilmer, which is set in North America (see Chapter 3). Merlin, in fact, grows into one of the richest and most complex figures in Arthurian mythology. One major tradition, which was considerably encouraged by George Ellis's summary of the Lincoln's Inn Library manuscript of Henry Lovelich's *Merlin*, was that Merlin was the son of an incubus, and revealed this diabolical origin 'by a

---

[59] See *John Joseph Merlin, The Ingenious Mechanick* (1985), 111 – 12, 131 – 32.
[60] 'The Eve of St. Agnes', l. 171; in *The Complete Poems of John Keats*, edited by John Barnard, second edition (Harmondsworth, 1977).
[61] Lines 39 – 41; in *The Poems of Samuel Taylor Coleridge*, edited by Ernest Hartley Coleridge (1912).

complete covering of black hair'.[62] As a being whose nature is divided between man and demon, endowed with supernatural powers, and with a capacity for good or evil, his potentiality as a Romantic figure is evident. Allusion to his demoniac birth occurs frequently (in Scott's 'Thomas the Rhymer', Heber, Leigh Hunt and Moultrie), and he is often given an appropriately *fauve* appearance: 'a savage shape' and 'matted beard' in Milman's *Samor* (II. 393 – 96), or a swart visage with 'raven hair' in Heber's *Morte d'Arthur* (III. xxiv). At one extreme, Merlin assumes a predominantly diabolical nature in Heber's *The Masque of Gwendolen*, where he plays a Comus-like role in his attempted seduction of the heroine, before meeting with damnation in his final 'hour of retribution':

> Haste, haste to meet him,
> Ye rulers of the damn'd, and open wide
> Your everlasting gates, to entertain
> The master of the spell!   (175 – 78)

Merlin's traditional role in helping Uther Pendragon displace Gorlois in the bed of Ygraine at Tintagel was generally avoided as a subject, except in John Magor Boyle's *Gorlaye*, in which Merlin acts as the evil agent of a discreditable Uther, and receives an amply detailed description, in terms that derive from Milton's Satan and Byron's hero-villains:

> The leader of that midnight crew;
> Enveloped in a shaggy coat, . . .
> A baldric circled round his waist, . . .
> His rugged beard uncomb'd, unclipt,
> Like bristles of the mountain boar, . . .
> His eye retained its glance of pride,
> And spoke unconquerable will   (pp.102 – 03)

Nor does Merlin's appearance belie his moral nature. Evidently adept in the black art, he summons spirits 'with sign, and malison, and spell' to favour Uther's enterprise (p.105). Less evil than the above but subject to bursts of splenetic malevolence is Worthsworth's Merlin, whose 'freakish will . . . sapped good thoughts, or scared them with defiance'.[63] And in one of the most concentratedly 'faerie' poems of the period — Buchanan's 'Merlin's Tomb' — he is again represented as the possessor of formidable necromantic power but, because he is a 'fool', he becomes so besotted by sexual dalliance with his

---

[62] Ellis, *Specimens of Early English Metrical Romances*, I, 212.
[63] 'The Egyptian Maid', ll. 23 – 24.

'witch-bride' Viviane that he is inveigled into bestowing upon her the 'fatal spell' whereby he is imprisoned beside a hawthorn tree.[64]

But if such debased qualities could be imputed to an expected process of epic degeneration, a contrary development is more prominently evident. The Brentford crowd who appealed to Merlin ('a wizard sage, but comical') for interpretation of a meteorological augury, in Praed's *Lillian* (II. 11), attest to his retained mantic insight; and, in maintaining his prophetic role, Merlin remains a powerful agent for foretelling the rise of political liberalism, as in 'Merlin's Prophecy for the Year 1831', or for presenting national history via a forecast vista, as in Peacock, Milman, Rowland Williams and Lytton.[65] Moreover, Merlin's skills exceed the more passive role of prophecy by assuming the active role of enchanter whose powers may direct the poetic action. Thus, in the legendary record of 'The Iron-Gate', Merlin supervises the sleeping king in the hollow hills, or in Darley's fanciful poem lauds Queen Victoria from his distant island. The scope of his interventions ranges considerably. In Peacock's *The Misfortunes of Elphin* he has a ludicrously minor role, his magical powers evident only in his 'magic hamper'. In Moultrie's *La Belle Tryamour*, Merlin takes a higher profile, curing the King of 'the blue devils' by showing him the lovely Guenever divesting for a bathe. Again, a light-hearted portrayal of him in Thomas Hogg's *The Fabulous History of Cornwall* assigns him powers beyond the grave, for he is able to grant the numerous wishes of an importunate woodcutter before finally retracting his gifts when the suppliant proves ungrateful.

In more serious guise, Merlin is elevated towards a position in which he, as mage, controls the poem. Such a situation is manifest in Anne Bannerman's 'The Prophecy of Merlin' in which an aura of Gothick horror pervades the scene where Merlin, in monk's cowl, summons the 'mighty form of Urien' from the grave, and presents Arthur with 'the hand of blood', thereby signifying the recipient's imminent defeat at the battle of Camlan. But if Merlin is here morally neutral, though awesome, in three later poems he rises to a position of beneficent deus *in* machina. The first of these works is Scott's *The Bridal of Triermain*, which awards him a theatrical entrance:

> rent by sudden throes,
> Yawned in mid lists the quaking earth,
> And from the gulf, tremendous birth!
> The form of Merlin rose.   (II. xxv)

Subsequently, he utters a 'magic doom' which consigns Gyneth to a slumber from which she may be awoken only by a knight 'renown'd / As warrior of the

[64] 'Merlin's Tomb'; in *The Glasgow University Album for 1838*, 1 – 9.
[65] 'Merlin's Prophecy for the Year 1831'; in *Monthly Magazine*, NS 11 (January 1831), 1 – 3; reprinted in *Carmarthen Journal*, 7 January 1831, 4; and *Monmouthshire Merlin*, 8 January 1831, 4.

Table Round' (II. xxvi). So as to prove the mettle of later contenders, Merlin constructs an elaborate allegorical test: Roland de Vaux has, accordingly, to remain unmoved by the African maids in the Hall of Fear, then to reject the 'boasted brilliant toys' of wealth, and to withstand the allurements of Asia's willing nymphs, besides forgoing the offer of the thrones of France, Spain, Germany and England. Once De Vaux has negotiated these hazards, Merlin's 'fiends' are dispersed. Symptomatic of the wizard's benevolence is that, repentant for having condemned Gyneth to so long a slumber, Merlin had 'Her sleep of many a hundred year / With gentle dreams beguiled' (III. xxxvii). He is thereby in clear contrast to the 'Genie of the earth' who sires Guendolen and trains her to guile the 'champions of the Christian name' (II. iii).

An even more pronounced philanthropy is displayed in Wilmer's *Merlin*. Scott's character had been induced to intervene principally in revenge for the death of his kinsman Vanoc but, in Wilmer, Merlin immediately announces his supernatural powers and indicates that he has 'lent a propitious ear' to a 'hapless' maiden with 'grief opprest' because she fears her lover is drowned.[66] Above the human drama, there is fought out a metaphysical combat between Merlin and the Furies of classical mythology. Merlin withstands them, ostensibly by means of gathering a magic herb from Lapland, but his triumphal outcome is never seriously in doubt, and at the end of the drama Merlin remains ever ready in his Maridunum cave to use his power on behalf of innocent mankind:

> If hostile powers
> Oppose their charms malevolent to ours,
> Swiftly their tidings to my cell convey
> And their designs in ruin will I lay.   (III. iv. 82 – 85)

In Lytton's *King Arthur*, the culmination of Merlin's reputation is achieved within the most elaborate allegorical framework. Although Lytton's earlier poem 'The Fairy Bride' had suggested that Merlin was susceptible to a dreamlike entrancement by an unnamed female, the later work sets him

---

William Maginn contributed a 'Prophecy of Plenty for the Year MDCCCXXXIII', which was signed 'MERLIN', to *Fraser's*, 7 (March 1833), 376.

[66] *Merlin: Baltimore, 1827, together with Recollections of E. A. Poe*, by Lambert Wilmer, edited by Thomas Ollive Mabbott (New York, 1941), I. 1. 35 – 41.

within an absolutely different context.[67] As the great controller of the poem's action, he is named prominently in the thematic announcement: 'Our land's first legends, love and knightly deeds, / And wondrous Merlin' (I. i). And at the close of the poem, he attains almost the status of a biblical prophet: 'Fair as in fable stands the Dragon King — / Below the Cross, and by his prophet's side' (III. cciv). Formerly the childhood tutor of Arthur, Lytton's Merlin is presented not as the child of the Devil or as the infatuate of Nimue but as an ancient revered figure, the 'great Master of the spells of power', 'the mighty weaver of dread webs'. He is an enchanter who has won from the midnight 'The hosts that bow'd to starry Solomon' (I. xl) and sits on a 'Druid throne' in his 'lone turret' reached only by a slender swinging drawbridge; but his magic is white, his wizardry dedicated to only the highest ends, and hence Arthur bows the knee to a power 'sublimer than his own' (I. xlix). Merlin's typical emblem is a fountain:

> I have made the life of spirit mine;
> And, on the margin of my mortal grave,
> My soul, already in an air divine
> Ev'n in its terrors, — starlit, seeks to cleave
> Up to the height on which its source must be —
> And falls again, in earthward showers, like thee.   (II. xxii)

His aspiration may be limited by his mortality, but the reader is assured that the mage has not 'soar'd in vain' (xxiv). As the structural pivot of the poem, he despatches Arthur on the threefold quest, sends Lancelot and Gawaine on their separate ventures, launches the dove and the raven, prompts Caradoc to heroic martyrdom, manipulates the rescue of Genevieve, and arranges the tactics for the final defeat of the Saxon siege. The concept of Merlin as Enchanter-Prophet, the hidden centre of a plot which is almost entirely his construct, had been adumbrated in previous works but no writer before Lytton had so extensively awarded him semi-divine powers.

Merlin has a complementary image in the Queen of Fairy, who exhibits a comparable range of character and function.

As Morgue the fay, she appears in one of Way's translations, 'The Vale of False Lovers'. Unlike her Malorian counterpart, she here embodies less an unmotivated malevolence than a spitefulness born of misprized love, which leads her to install an enchanted vale to detain false, and hence most, lovers. Once again, Heber's *Morte* portrays a sinister figure, and one who is, like

---

[67] Lytton's allusion is glancing, in that Elvar addresses the Fairy as a 'Dream — lovelier far than e'er, I ween, / Entranced the glorious Merlin's eyes' (ll. 55 – 56). It is, however, probable that a contemporary reader would have caught the reference. As William Gifford wrote in 1816:
> All the world knows that this redoubtable conjuror was betrayed into a cavern, and shut up
> by the cruel craft of [the Lady of the Lake] . . .
Cited in *The Works of Ben Jonson*, edited by Frances Cunningham, 3 vols (1910 – 1912), III, 65.

Way's, a victim of the heart. It is likely, too, that Heber had drawn on an Ellis note to Way's 'The Mantle Made Amiss' for Morgue's early biography. According to this note, Morgue's hostility to the court arose from her 'being one day in bed with her love Sir Guiomars' when she was surprised by Queen Guenevere, 'who had the indiscretion to make the story publick'.[68] Heber's version refers to her lover's death at the hands of Arthur, after which event she had thrown herself from a cliff, but during her fall had been transformed into a fay. As mother of an illegitimate Modred, she is jealous, on his behalf, of his succession to the throne, a prospect which is threatened by Arthur's marriage to Ganora. Morgue therefore hatches plots, and dresses to fit the part:

> Her wreath was nightshade, and her sable vest
> All spangled o'er with magic imagery,
> In tighter fold her stately form exprest.   (II. iv)

Since Heber's epic remained unfinished, it is impossible to determine the exact development of the plot, but it seems that one major theme would range Morgue against Arthur: she sends Modred to fetch Urgan's Ring of Invisibility, which she will presumably use against Arthur; and by breathing unrest into Ganora's sleep, it is probable that she intends to encourage the Queen's dissatisfaction with her royal marriage. Although Morgue wields a power inferior to that of Merlin and 'his elfin paramour', it is likely that Merlin will be 'beguiled' from effective opposition (this is his fate in Heber's *Masque*) so that Morgue will, by means of Modred and Ganora, succeed in ruining Arthur and his kingdom. Heber's treatment of Morgue prefigures the role allotted to Morgan le Fay in Riethmuller's *Launcelot of the Lake*, a play which is similarly constructed on the basis of the antagonism between Arthur and a Morgan who is here the abandoned mother of his illegitimate child.[69] Here, too, Morgan's witchcraft earns an initial emphasis: she has a magic wand, summons a dragon-drawn chariot, and inhabits a gloomy Welsh cavern, on whose walls 'various cabalistic figures' are 'dimly visible'. Nevertheless, these supernatural adjuncts are later reduced, and Morgan's ultimate vengeance is achieved wholly through the naturalistic means of adroit tale-bearing, machinations, and an instinctive battleground strategy. Less studiously vindictive, but of enigmatic moral intent, is the fairy lady in Anne Bannerman's 'The Prophecy of Merlin'. When Arthur falls at Camlan, his helpers discover that his mortal shape has vanished from its armour. Meanwhile, in a 'death-like sleep' the King is carried to 'the charmed sea, by magic spell, / By the Queen of the Yellow Isle' (87 – 88). Arthur wakes but helplessly drifts to the isle, on the shore of which stands this Queen of Beauty

---

[68] Way, *Fabliaux*, I, 198.
[69] As Heber's *Poetical Works* were reissued in 1841, two years before the publication of *Launcelot*, it is possible that Riethmuller was directly influenced by Heber's *Morte*.

who offers him a cup of 'sparkling pearl' (138). Her eyes 'of softest blue' constrain him with 'their mild reproach' to accept the drink. Like a Tennysonian lotos eater, his acceptance of the gift signifies a relinquishing, albeit involuntary in this instance, of the heroic quest, and having drained the cup he sees 'something like a demon-smile, / Betray'd the smooth disguise!' (155 – 56). Recognising then her baneful 'hand of blood' which he recalls seeing in Merlin's tower, he realises that an indefinite exile must be passed on this island.

Despite these malign aspects, it is, as with representations of Merlin, benevolence which is the dominant characteristic of the Fairy Queen: Darley's Morgain-le-fay watches over Britain's fortunes and is well-disposed towards the House of Hanover; and, even more remarkably, it is Morgan Le Fay whom J. F. Hollings invokes as the 'nymph of undying Song!' whose lamented absence from the inglorious present symbolises our loss of the 'power of Fancy' in the face of an unwelcome 'sterner Truth'.[70] Heber's *Masque of Gwendolen*, which posits a villainous Merlin, fancifully offsets him by a complementary, benevolent female spirit, Titania, who revives the prostrate heroine with 'potent pharmacy'. Similarly, in Wordsworth's 'The Egyptian Maid', it is the Lady of the Lake, Nina ('A gentle Sorceress, and benign', 95), who intervenes on behalf of the distressed maiden by reprimanding Merlin for his initial spleen and useless regrets. She then urges him to carry the maiden to Arthur's court, where a knight may revive her. To this end, the good enchantress had previously selected Sir Galahad as agent of the maiden's awakening by sending him a premonitory dream of the Egyptian. A comparable polarity is evident in such pantomimes as Lee's *Harlequin and Mother Redcap*, which pits a bad Merlin against a good Fairy Snowdrop; whilst a tutelary nature goddess operates also on the sleep of Wilfred in Praed's 'The Legend of the Haunted Tree'. Since the youth longs only for chivalrous knighthood, and rejects the love of a 'gentle maid', the fairy contrives his moral education by granting his wishes: he is transformed into an Arthurian knight, and, after having suffered from 'fortune' and 'traitorous friends', is remetamorphosed into a Wilfred content now to accept his lot, and wed the girl who loves him.[71] An exemplary morality is, again, displayed by the Lady of the Lake in John Thelwall's *Fairy of the Lake*. Thelwall's initial inclination (see Chapter 2) to have portrayed the Lady as an Egeria-like mistress to Arthur was rejected in favour of the Cambrian tradition which regards her as 'a benignant Spirit' and represents her as 'a personification of essential

---

[70] J. F. Hollings, 'To Morgan Le Fay', *Literary Souvenir*', (1831), 133.
[71] Winthrop Mackworth Praed, 'The Legend of the Haunted Tree', *Literary Souvenir* (1831), 1 – 16. A revised version was printed in *Poems*, I, 124 – 43.

purity'.[72] Despite Thelwall's rationalist reservations, he endows his drama with the most grandiose flourishes of supernaturalism. Ranged against the forces of virtue are Hela (Queen of the Infernal Regions), Incubus (a frozen demon) and a variety of giants and demons. Opposing this strong cast from northern mythology is a Lady of the Lake who is given, on her first appearance, the complete magical apparatus of 'a Throne of Spars and Coral, in a car, or water chariot, drawn by Swans'. Responding to Arthur's 'voice of Anguish', she rescues the hero's sword from the 'impious' goblins, and when Guenever and Tristram are about to be burnt alive in a blazing castle, the Fairy saves them by causing the waters of the lake to rise and quench the fire. She then 'waves her silver Trident' and the scene changes to Caerleon for the coronation and nuptials of Arthur and Guenever. These effected, the Lady's chariot ascends to full choral honours from Taliesin and a choir of nymphs.

The general tendency of all these works dominated by a benevolent mage or fairy is to present a world which is essentially good, uncomplicated, harmonious and ruled by a kindly Deity, for, although an ostensibly pagan mythology is adopted, the tenor is implicitly Christian, and few traces remain of the anarchic or erotic fairies of folklore, with the partial exception of one important subcurrent: the folklore motif of the Fairy Bride.

The Launfal Theme

The legend of the Fairy Bride has enjoyed great literary eminence. It had occurred so frequently in medieval romance that Chaucer mockingly ascribes such an adventure to his over-literary Sir Thopas, who would love an elf-queen since in 'this world no womman' was worthy to be his 'make' (79 – 81). Spenser reverts to the tradition when Prince Arthur follows his quest for the Fairy Gloriana, glimpsed in dream. Its incidence, from the end of the eighteenth century, was profuse. An early and important nineteenth century version of this theme occurs in Scott's edition of the traditional ballad of 'Thomas the Rhymer' in a collection that attracted great interest, *The Minstrelsy of the Scottish Border* (1802 – 1803). The traditional account describes how Thomas sees a 'ladye bright / Come riding down by the Eildon-tree'.[73] She is the 'Queen of fair Elfland', and she invites him to kiss her, which he does and is thus obliged to serve her for seven years. Mounting behind her, he is then carried off to fairyland. To this story, Scott added his own continuation, in which Thomas returns after the seven years, and at a feast in Learmont Castle sings of the Arthurian legends which he has learnt in fairyland. During that night, a white hart and hind are seen on Fairnalie, a

---

[72] Thelwall, *Fairy of the Lake*, 207.
[73] 'Thomas the Rhymer', ll. 3 – 4; in *Poetical Works*.

signal to summon Thomas back to fairyland. Accordingly, he departs and is never seen again in 'haunts of living men'.[74]

In the Romantic period this theme would reappear in many guises, most notably in Keats's 'La Belle Dame sans Merci', but within a strictly Arthurian context the focus of attention is the Sir Launfal legend. This had been reintroduced to English readers by Thomas Warton's *History of English Poetry*, which quoted a section from Thomas Chestre's fourteenth century *Sir Launfal*. Thereafter, George Ellis appended the whole of Chestre's thousand-line poem to his edition of Way's *Fabliaux*, and the text received a scholarly editing in Joseph Ritson's *Ancient Engleish Metrical Romanceës*. A resumé of the poem is given in Thomas Keightley's *Fairy Mythology*, where it is made the subject of an illustration by William Henry Brooke — a choice that would appear to indicate the theme's special attraction. There was, besides, a second and more popular influence at work, namely the lays of Marie de France. A number of these were made available in verse and prose translation. In 1786, John Williamson had produced his prose versions of *Norman Tales* derived from Le Grand D'Aussy's *Fabliaux*. Opening the volume — which went into further editions in 1789, 1790 and 1800 — was *Lanval*, a retelling of Marie's lay.[75] G. L. Way had quarried the tales of *Guigemar* and *Lanval* (and an analogous composition *Gruelan* [= *Graelent*]) from Le Grand's collection, and these had then been succeeded by Louisa Stuart Costello's verse translations of *Bisclaveret* and *Chevrefeuil* (1833).[76] In the following year was issued a version (which is now attributed to R. H. Barham) of *Graelent*, which the author entitled 'The Lay of Sir Lionel' and claimed to have derived from the Breton lay, which he attributed to Marie.[77] An analogous 'The Lay of Sir Amys' by Walter Prideaux appeared in 1840, and David Moir's poem 'Sir Eliduc. A Lay of Marie' was published in *Forget Me Not* in 1827 — under an altered title — and again in *Blackwood's* in 1840.[78] A play by William Caldwell Roscoe, *Eliduc* (1846), was also based on Marie's lay, and was followed in 1849 by a translation of La Motte Fouqué's novel, *Eliduc*, derived from the same source. All those lays that had not been translated by Way were given in 'copious abstracts' in George Ellis's *Specimens of Early English Metrical Romances*. For reviving 'Such notes as from the Breton tongue / Marie translated', Ellis

---

[74] The Arthurian aspect of Scott's continuation of 'Thomas' has unaccountably been overlooked by Merriman, Taylor *et al.*

[75] See Geoffrey Wilson, *A Medievalist in the Eighteenth Century: Le Grand D'Aussy and the 'Fabliaux ou Contes'* (The Hague, 1975).

[76] In Costello, *Specimens of the Early Poetry of France*.

[77] 'The Lay of Sir Lionel', *Blackwood's*, 35 (May 1834), 635 – 43. For Barham's authorship, see A. L. Strout, 'Contributors to *Blackwood's Magazine*'. *Notes and Queries*, 194 (1949), 541 – 43.

[78] Walter Prideaux, *Poems of Chivalry, Faery, and the Olden Time* (1840). David Moir, 'Gildeluec Ha Guilladun. An Armorican Legend', *Forget Me Not* (1827), 309 – 27; and 'Eliduc. A Lay of Marie', *Blackwood's*, 47 (June 1840), 786 – 92.

received the poetic homage of Scott and Eleanor Porden.[79] Marie was herself the subject of a poem in four cantos by Matilda Betham, who appended, at Southey's instigation, complete versions of *Gugemar* and *Lanval* (in Way's version), *Le Fraine* and *Chevrefoil* (in Ellis's) and prose summaries of all the other lays.[80] Keightley, too, provided a summary of *Ywenec*. The special attraction of Marie's delicate psychological analysis of love, set in a well-constructed narrative shot through with occasional gleams of faerie, is testified by the number of contemporary versions. Scott, in *The Bridal of Triermain*, includes 'Lanval with the fairy lance' amongst 'the flower of Chivalry' (II. xiii), and the *Essay on Chivalry* (1814) praises 'the beautiful lay of Lanval'. William Howitt, too, in 'A Visit to Tintagel' presents the Launfal/Tryamour love as one of the most vivid of Arthurian legends. Imagined thus as one of the chief Arthurian personae, Launfal is chosen as hero in two notable poems by John Moultrie and Bulwer Lytton.

La Belle Tryamour's Byronic modern-day digressions have been dealt with in the previous chapter, but the thematic core of Moultrie's poem now requires further attention.

In his main plot, which is explicitly based on Ritson's edition of Chestre, Moultrie adheres closely to the basic structure of the medieval narrative, and often follows Chestre when the latter is most idiosyncratic: in, for example, Launfal's visit to the mayor, or the naming of Ryence as father of Guenever, and Olyroun as the father of Tryamour. Smaller details are similarly carried over: for instance, the names of most Round Table knights, and the serving of Rhenish wine in the fairy pavilion. However, Moultrie's faithful adherence to his source renders his occasional divergences significantly deliberate in intent. One major difference between Chestre and Moultrie is that the latter is flagrantly 'modern' in tone, extremely aware of his own times and their difference from the medieval. The psychology of his characters is, for example, given an early nineteenth century colouring, for the plot is consistently and naturalistically motivated in accord with the expectations of a later age. Thus, Chestre states baldly that

> Marlyn was Artour's counsalere.
> He radde hym for to wende
> To king Ryon of Irlond ryght,
> And fette him ther a lady bryght,
> Gwennere hys doughtyr hende.
> So he dede, and home her broughte.[81]

---

[79] Scott, *Marmion*, Introduction to Canto V. ll. 145 – 46. Porden, *Coeur de Lion*, XII. l.95 and n.
[80] Matilda Betham, *The Lay of Marie* (1816).
[81] Lines 38 – 43; in Ritson, *Metrical Romanceës*, I.

In contrast, Moultrie examines at length Arthur's feeling 'sick of the blue devils', the court's consequent alarm, and then Merlin's diagnosis that the King requires a wife. Again, there is in Moultrie a marked increase in the attention devoted to love affairs: he introduces from *Graelent* the story of how the host's daughter pitied Launfal, but accompanies it with lengthy and sentimental effusions; and there is a radical difference between Chestre and Moultrie in their handling of Launfal's first meeting with Tryamour. The lady in Chestre makes a direct bid for the hero's affections by swiftly offering him a series of specified rich presents if he will agree to love her. In Moultrie she behaves with no such forwardness: instead, she is initially coy and, most importantly, celebrates an official fairy wedding with Launfal before going to bed with him. No such sanction had been necessary in Chestre's version. Moreover, Moultrie's Tryamour displays feelings of general philanthropy: 'She loved mankind, and all mankind loved her' (III. cvi).

Despite this evidently modern, intellectual, emotional and ethical ambience, Moultrie consistently heightens the role of the faerie within his poem. Chestre and his source, Marie de France, refer only sparingly to the Lady's fairy nature. Chestre makes just two allusions to this: her father, we are told, is 'kyng of fayry' (280); and, at the end of the poem, Launfal is taken by her 'to the fayrye' (1035). Moultrie's insistence upon the fairy elements presents a differing complex approach to their role. Firstly, the adjective 'fairy' may operate as a key term, evocative of an exquisitely mysterious beauty, as when Moultrie creates a painterly description of Ryence's grounds, which include

> fairy grottos, fashion'd curiously
> With shells and glittering spars, and odorous bowers
> Bright with all mingled hues of faintly breathing flowers.   (I. lxxv)

Just as this does not necessarily imply that there were fairies at the bottom of his garden, so too with the 'bewitching' beauty of Christine (III. lv), who is a French Protestant emigrée: her 'eloquent witchery' is primarily caused by her 'slight foreign accent' (III. lvi). More frequently, though, Moultrie's imagination is operating at an intenser level. One result of his concern with a deeper characterisation and with an ampler motivation of the plot is that Chestre's incidental references become fully expanded. Merlin is, in the earlier poem, merely a 'counsalere', whereas Moultrie provides a potted biography, from diabolic conception to a final captivity by the Lady of the Lake. Moultrie is, moreover, an intensely 'literary' poet, profuse in allusion to contemporary and previous literature: even his hero is made the author of 'Memoirs of King Arthur's Court and Times' (II. xcvii). Although disregarding 'the confounded allegory' of Spenser, Moultrie draws heavily on the Elizabethan poet for an elaboration of the fairy themes. Besides borrowing Spenser's story of the beguiling of Merlin, Moultrie also takes over the magic

mirror in which Britomart had first seen Artegall. In *Tryamour*, Merlin is once
again the provider of this adjunct, which is then employed to arouse Arthur's
passion. From Spenser, too, is adopted most of the account of Tryamour's
family descent from the original Promethean creation of Elfe. Such allusions
therefore place the fairy material within the tradition of an accepted literary
usage.

Moultrie also confronts the problem, in a rationalist age, of a belief in the
supernatural. It has been argued, writes Moultrie, that

> the whole Fairy race has long since perish'd,
> Extirpated by its relentless foes,
> Philosophy, and Science, who've so flourish'd
> Of late . . . (III. lxxx)

Wondering when 'Philosophy will stop' eroding the 'lawful property' of
poetry, he suggests that poets should react spiritedly against 'the analytical /
Muddlings of science, natural or political' (III. lxxxi). Moultrie's tone is
generally playfully ironic, but he appears to be largely in earnest when
suggesting that poetry needs 'fantasy', and can create its own magic world:

> Know that, beneath the Muse's jurisdiction,
> Such Faery regions every where abound;
> Yea, e'en in crowded cities, or in gaols —
> Surpassing all the beauty of North Wales.   (III. cxl)

Without assigning to Moultrie the full significance of the Wordsworthian
allusion to the power of recollected emotion, or of a Keatsian sense of the
Imagination's ability to create Truth, it would still appear that, for Moultrie,
a 'fiction' can intimate an intuitive truth which may be hidden from the
analytical brain. This intuitive truth may, for example, be perceived in dream
(III. xcii); and, appropriately, when Tryamour falls in love with Launfal, she
contrives to haunt his dreams (III. cxvi), which 'hung a spell around his
heart'. What succeeds in maintaining a reader's belief in Moultrie's fairy is
that she is not an etherial gossamery diminutive, but a creature who is very
human: for neither

> Are Fairies immaterial — shadowy things
> Invested with an unsubstantial glory,
> Trick'd out in sunshine robes and rainbow-wings . . .
> But bright realities of flesh and blood   (III. lxxxix)

He admits that they have the power on occasion to 'throw off their fleshly
dross', but the Tryamour whom we are shown is very much a terrestrial being
when she lies, in 'perfect symmetry', feigning sleep on the first approach of
Launfal:

> And o'er her delicate cheek a flush was gleaming,
> And, with quick tumult, did that bosom swell —
> Whether of some strange raptures she was dreaming
> I know not   (III. clvi)

Finally, Moultrie's world of faery suggests that, when sophisticated pleasantries are over, it remains ultimately a metaphor for romantic love, an experience and a value which continually asserts itself in spite of a sceptical utilitarianism. Amid the serpentine digressions of Moultrie's wit, the theme of romantic love constantly resurfaces, and is embodied in the idiom of fairyland. The lost Ione, for example, who rejected him is 'My dream, my star, my radiant Fairy Queen' (I. xxi). Similarly, of the emigrée Christine, 'Nature meant her for the Fairy Queen / Of mirth' (III. lvii). More amply expressed is

> the hope that I had found
> In thee the embodied phantasy, whose gleams
> Kindled my sleep for years, and pour'd around
> My path the brightness of a poet's dreams   (II. Introduction. x)

Elsewhere, an ideal love that he pictures is 'fresh from the mint of glowing phantasy' (I. lviii), and a 'vision'd form' (I. lix). Within the same enchanted aura is Launfal's unconscious 'bewitching' of the unfortunate Blanch, on account of his 'cursed magic' (II. cxx).

In its widest extension, however, this fairy world often connotes the world of imagination. The region near Windermere is thought enchanted ground because the 'Enchanter' (= Wordsworth) lives nearby. Poetry has, thus, a power which may be described as magical, for the creator has total command over his created world, and whatever he wishes to bring into existence can, however extraordinary, be effected:

> I know I'm lord of all that I survey, —
> Maker, and sole proprietor; I made
> The sun that cheers me with his winter ray, . . .
> Oh! for some bright and delicate creation,
> Fresh from the mint of glowing phantasy . . .
> Away with sad realities — I'll make
> A being from whose love I'll ne'er awake.   (I. lvii – lviii)

In reaction then to a sad reality, the fairy world may offer a rich association of dream, romantic love, imagination and artistic creation.

Bulwer Lytton's 'The Fairy Bride' was published in 1842, but as Lytton's own footnote to the poem in the 1852 collected edition contrasts it with 'his maturer poem' (i.e. *King Arthur* of 1848), and as a footnote in an 1865 selection of his poems speaks of it as 'written in very early youth', a date of composition

very much earlier than 1842 may be assumed.[82] For biographical reasons
which will appear later, it probably belongs to the early 1820s.

'The subject of this tale', Lytton notes, 'is suggested by one of the
Fabliaux'. For this, Way's version, which was widely known, was Lytton's
most likely source. That Lytton knew Way's work at least as early as 1832 is
proved by his use of a quotation in *Eugene Aram* from 'The Knight and the
Sword' in Way's translation, although Lytton does not credit the translator.[83]

Lytton discards the name Launfal in favour of one of his own coining:
Elvar. His handling of the legend displays a comparable freedom of
imagination. In Way, Lanval is, for unspecified reasons, out of favour with an
Arthur who manifests an irrational neglect of him:

> There did the sovereign's copious hand dispense
> Large boons to all with free magnificence,
> To all but one; . . .
> Long had the king, by partial temper sway'd,
> His loyal zeal with cold neglect repaid   (5 – 10)

In Lytton, by contrast, Elvar's poverty is not the result of Arthur's neglect or
the outcome of any individual's action, but rather an indication that there is a
sharp social division between the life of the court and the condition of being
needy:

> Nor peerless deeds, nor stainless line,
> Can lift to Fame the Poor! . . .
> High thoughts ill suit the russet vest   (5 – 10)

Way's Queen attempts to seduce Lanval but, on his repelling her, she
proceeds to Arthur and tells him 'how a saucy knight his queen abus'd / With
prayer of proffer'd love, with scorn refus'd' (193 – 94). Arthur reacts angrily
by summarily imprisoning Lanval, a deed which induces Lanval to plead his
innocence by revealing his love for the fairy. Lytton, however, greatly reduces
the guilt of Arthur and Gwynver. His Queen is moved only by jealousy of
Elvar's lady and curiosity as to her identity. It is Launcelot's challenge in the
lists on behalf of the Queen's beauty that elicits Elvar's response. But, by
stopping short of actually naming his lady, he obliges Arthur to follow
orthodox chivalric ritual and to order that the lady be produced within three
days. Elvar is not, however, committed to prison. On the appearance of the
Fairy Bride at court, Gwynver handsomely concedes defeat:

---

[82] Edward Bulwer Lytton, *Poems*, new edition, revised (1865), 279n. For text of 'The Fairy
Bride', I have used that in *Eva* (1842).
[83] *Eugene Aram*, Book IV. chapter 9; in *Novels*.

> Here spake the Queen, 'The strife is past,'
> And in the lists her glove she cast,
> 'And I myself will crown thy brow,
> Thou love-defended Knight!'   (333 – 36)

Even so, Lytton finds it necessary to explain in his later footnote that he

> has represented Arthur and Guenever, according to the view of their
> characters taken in those French Romances — which he hopes he need
> scarcely say is very different from that taken in his maturer Poem upon
> the adventures and ordeal of the Dragon-King.

Despite these protestations, Lytton does subtly subvert the legend in order to
assert the moral purity of Arthur and his Queen. The latter may admit the
homage of Sir Launcelot (whose shield bears a sunflower for device —
'Where'er thou shinest turns my look') but the exact nature of this homage is
not elaborated upon. Arthur's own character displays no great fault: his wrath
against Elvar can be justified as a natural loyalty to his wife. The monarch
represents, on the other hand, a court which to Lytton appeared too worldly
and superficial, occupied only with the pomp of idle games, not with the
making of a realm or the upholding of a right.

Lytton departs from previous practice by reducing the amount of visual
description. Way's fairy pavilion, banquet and wedding are all concretely and
minutely presented, and the description lingers over the dress, features and
appurtenances of his fairy:

> And now, with costliest silk superbly dight,
> A gay pavilion greets the warrior's sight;
> Its taper spire a cowering eagle crown'd,
> In substance gold, of workmanship renown'd.
> Within, recumbent on a couch, was laid
> A form more perfect than e'er man survey'd . . .
> And o'er her shoulders flow'd with graceful pride,
> Though for the heat some little cast aside,
> A crimson pall of Alexandria's dye,
> With snowy ermine lin'd, befitting royalty   (39 – 52)

But Lytton's Fairy is evoked as 'a gleam', 'a shape', 'a vision', 'a light', and
her wraithlike essence is carefully separated from human attributes. Way's
Lady appears subject to langour and the heat, her human qualities are clearly
stressed: we are not told until fairly late in the meeting that she is indeed a
fairy, and in Bewick's woodcut vignette, as in Brooke's also, the two attendant
ladies are indistinguishable from twelfth century dames. In Lytton, however,
she makes her first appearance by rising through the waters of a fountain, is
evidently more sylphlike and less human. Her solitariness reinforces this

uniqueness. In Way, Lanval first meets beside the brook two 'damsels' who invite him to meet their mistress; they later attend on Lanval at the banquet; and two pairs of damsels precede the Lady's final appearance at Carduel. They supply a naturalistic depth to the Lady's existence, and function as a dramatic prelude introducing the Lady's appearances by gradual crescendo. For Lytton, by contrast, their presence is severely curtailed, being mentioned only once, in an aside, at the Fairy's visit to Arthur's court. The effect is to isolate the Fairy from all other personae in the poem: each appearance she makes is abrupt and unexpected; and she is sharply distinguished from normal earthly life, values and relationships.

Most surprisingly, Lytton breaks with the legend in the manner of its conclusion. Taking into account Lytton's propensity for supplying a happy ending, and his persuasion of Dickens to provide one for *Great Expectations*, it is the more remarkable that Lytton deliberately eschews this kind of conclusion for 'The Fairy Bride'.[84] But, once the Fairy has unveiled herself to the court and thereby rescued Elvar from an unjust accusation, she punishes him for having publicly alluded to her:

> She lower'd the veil, she turn'd the rein,
> And ere his lips replied, was gone . . .
> He seeks the wood, he gains the spot —
> The Tree is there, the Fountain not: —
> Dried up:— its mirthful play is o'er.
> Ah, where the Fairy-bride? . . .
> The Fountain vanished from the glen,
> The Fairy from the earth!   (349 – 66)

Elvar is thus left desolate at the grim conclusion, at which no sign of consolation is offered.

There were two major controlling pressures which seem to have heavily influenced Lytton's treatment of this theme. From Lytton's own recollections, it is revealed that in 1820 at the age of seventeen he fell in love with a young girl he met near the river Brent at Ealing.[85] This idyllic romance was soon broken off by the girl's father, who removed her and forced her into an unwelcome marriage. Three years later she died. Lytton's son would later write:

The impression left on my father by this early 'phantom of delight' was indelible, and coloured the whole of his life. He believed that, far beyond all other influences, it shaped his character, and it never ceased to haunt

---

[84] See introduction by Frederick Page to *Great Expectations* by Charles Dickens (Oxford, 1953), ix.
[85] *The Life, Letters and Literary Remains of Edward Bulwer, Lord Lytton*, by His Son [Edward Robert Bulwer Lytton], 2 vols (1883), I, 159 – 67.

his memory. Allusions to it are constantly recurring in his published works.

This 'phantom' love recurs, for example, in 'To the Lost':

> O my young earth's lost Immortal
> Naiad vanished from the streams!
> Eve, torn from me at the portal
> Of my Paradise of Dreams!   (21 – 24)

Again, in 'A Lament':

> Here we stood, ere we parted, so close side by side;
> Two lives that once part, are as ships that divide,
> When, moment on moment, there rushes between
>   The one and the other, a sea; —
> Ah, never can fall from the years that have been
>   A gleam on the years that shall be!   (9 – 14)

'The Fairy Bride' fits this biographical pattern closely. Encountered unexpectedly by a fountain, the Fairy is the partner in a brief romance, but then vanishes for ever. When viewed in the light of his biography, Lytton's reshaping of the original tale gains added significance at various points. Lytton lost his father early, so was brought up by his mother. His Elvar seems younger than Lanval, and only one parent is named. The poem opens with Elvar's mother giving advice to the 'youth', her experience contrasting with his innocence. Later, when he triumphs in the lists, it is his mother who is at hand to sob 'forth — ''My gallant son!'' ' (144).

To have eliminated the introductory encounter with the two damsels beside the brook has two main effects: the Fairy's appearance becomes unexpected, unprecedented, removed from all social introduction — and therefore like the scene beside the Brent; moreover, the meeting with the Fairy can then be transposed from the overtly erotic couch in the pavilion to the more subtly emotive Fount, a locale that was charged with personal emotion for Lytton. In Marie's analogous lay of *Gruelan*, the fairy had been discovered in the fountain: she had been naked, and evidently was fearful of being raped by the intruder. Not only had this scene been preserved in Way's translation of the tale, but the accompanying illustration by Bewick had depicted the barebreasted lady bathing in the stream. In another poetic version, R. H. Barham evaded the blatant sexuality of this scene by placing his fairy beside the well, where she presumably sits fully dressed. Although Lytton's Fairy rises from the water, no physical detail is given of her, apart from the noting of her blue eyes. In the original versions, it is clear that a physical marriage is consummated in the pavilion. But here Lytton is extremely non-committal:

Ask not the Bard to lift the veil
  That hides the Fairy's bridal bower;
If thou art young, go seek the glade,
And win thyself some fairy maid;
And rosy lips shall tell the tale
  In some enchanted hour.   (67 – 72)

The poem is entitled 'The Fairy *Bride*', but this chaste bridal recalls Lytton's shadowy description of his own adolescent love:

> The sort of love we felt for each other I cannot describe. It was so unlike the love of grown-up people; so pure that not one wrong thought crossed it; and yet so passionate that never again have I felt, nor ever again can I feel, any emotion comparable to the intensity of its tumultuous tenderness.

The Fairy's injunction not to reveal her name was, of course, standard practice among medieval courtly lovers, but it also takes an added colouring from the young Lytton's awareness that his love had to be kept a secret: 'I never breathed her name to a human being. How thankful I am now for my silence!' Nor did he later release her name in his autobiographical account:

> Sweet saint, your name, at least, shall never be exposed to the deliberate malignity, the low ribaldry that have so relentlessly assailed my own.

Most important of his adaptations is the tragic ending, which once again parallels his own devastating experience: 'My voice came back to me without an answer, and we never met again. Never, never.'

That the poem may be read as an allegory of the destructiveness of Time, and the consequent loss of youth, is suggested by Lytton's perception of such a meaning in Schiller's 'To the Ideal', a poem Lytton himself translated in the early 1840s, and compared to Gray's 'Ode on a Distant Prospect of Eton College'; and the latter, like Lytton's autobiographical fragment, recalls a fearful joy snatched on the banks of a Home Counties river.[86] There are comparable connotations, too, in another poem by Lytton, 'The Boatman', where a 'beautiful fairy' that is seen to rise from the buds of an almond bough is a fairy only to the eyes of youth. Ineluctably, these develop into older eyes that see merely an 'insect' for they are unable to recapture the magical vision of childhood. Additionally, 'The Fairy Bride' may be interpreted as an allegory of the loss of inspiration, since imaginative power may be inevitably weakened by the act of communication. A later essay by Lytton on 'The Distinction between Active Thought and Reverie' (1862) employs an analogous conceptual framework. Here, Lytton describes his initial reveries

---

[86] *Schiller's Poems and Ballads*, translated by Edward Lord Lytton (1887), 81.

where 'ideas float before us, rapid, magical, vague, half-formed' but also
'vivid' and 'lifelike'.[87] Yet the rich profusion of these reveries or dreams can
never be recaptured by the process of writing:

> We may, indeed, give the general purport of a meditated argument the
> outlines of a narrative plot, artistically planned, or of a narrative of
> which we have painted on the retina of the mind the elementary colours
> and the skeleton outlines. But where the boundless opulence of idea and
> fancy which had enriched the subject before we were called upon to
> contract its expenditure into sober bounds? How much of the fairy gold
> turns, as we handle it, into dry leaves![88]

This 'want of exact fidelity between thought while yet in the mind, and its
form when stamped on a page' is another indication of Lytton's theoretical
preoccupation with the philosophy of Idealism. Interlocking here with his
experience of emotional loss is his belief in an essential division between the
world of pure forms and the world of created material things. Accompanying
this perception that 'There is a world beyond the visual scope' ('To the Ideal')
is a constant attempt to evoke that world through his own symbols. These
symbols of the unseen are usually feminine and associated with water:

> Like the sweet Naiad of the Grecian's dreams, . . .
> She — the Ideal, in the Wells of Truth — . . .
> *Man* is not there, yet ever may'st thou mark
> The River-Maid her amber tresses sleeking; . . .
> Thou, the wild Armida of the Soul.[89]

As types of an evanescent gleam of the absolute, he invokes Naiad, Egeria,
Angel or Fairy, not as decorative figures from an outworn mythology, nor as a
pretty pantheism, but for their symbolic reality. A passage from *The Pilgrims of
the Rhine* is apposite:

> Is there not a truth also in our fictions of the Unseen World? Are there
> not yet bright lingerers by the forest and the stream? . . . Are the fairies,
> and the invisible hosts, but the children of our dreams; and not their
> inspiration? Is that all a delusion which speaks from the golden page?
> And is the world only given to harsh and anxious travailers, that walk to
> and fro in pursuit of no gentle shadows? Are the chimeras of the passions
> the sole spirits of the universe? No! while my remembrance treasures, in

---

[87] *Miscellaneous Prose Works*, III, 145. See also Jack Lindsay, 'Clairvoyance of the Normal: The
Aesthetic Theory of Bulwer-Lytton', *Nineteenth Century and After*, 145 (1949), 29 – 38; and Michael
Lloyd, 'Bulwer-Lytton and the Idealising Principle', *English Miscellany*, 7 (1956), 25 – 39.
[88] *Miscellaneous Prose Works*, III, 146.
[89] 'To the Ideal', sections i, iii, and viii. It was placed as a prefatory poem to *The Pilgrims of the
Rhine* (1834).

its deepest cell, the image of one no more — one who was 'not of the
earth earthy' — one in whom love was the essence of thoughts divine —
one whose shape and mould, whose heart and genius, would, had Poesy
never before dreamt it, have called forth the first notion of spirits
resembling mortals, but not of them; no, Gertrude, while I remember
you, the faith, — the trust in brighter / shapes and fairer natures than
the world knows of, comes clinging to my heart; and still will I think that
Fairies might have watched over your sleep, and Spirits have ministered
to your dreams![90]

The Fairy Bride is such another emblem of the Ideal, clearly marked as
distinct from, and superior to, the domain of material beings: her dower is a
'love more true than minstrel sings, / A wealth that mocks the pomp of kings'
(45 – 46). Her lover can only be one who has never been allured by 'human
charms', for her love 'may but bless the Pure'. Elvar is eligible because, whilst
never enjoying the love of any 'living shape', he has always 'pined for love'
and followed a quest for the Ideal form. The Fairy's unveiling at the court, to
secure the release of Elvar, therefore necessitates her ultimate disappearance:
the Ideal must remain out of reach lest it lose its essential quality of
remoteness.

The lack of visual detail in Lytton's description of the Fairy is thus quite
deliberate. He has forestalled any potential objection to this approach, by
defending his own use of 'Imagined as opposed to Experienced Character' in
Essays Written in Youth, where his own literary values are formulated:

Superficial critics have often considered the humorous and coarse
characters of a novelist . . . as his very best — forgetful that the very
indistinctness of his ideal characters is not only inseparable from the
nature of purely imaginary creations, but a proof of the exaltation and
intenseness of the imaginative power. The most shadowy and mistlike of
all Scott's heroes is the Master of Ravenswood, and yet it is perhaps the
highest of his characters in execution as well as conception . . . / To such
critics, Undine is not a true creation of genius, because they never saw
anything like her when they angled for dace in the Thames.[91]

Even if one were to accept Lytton's view of 'ideal' characterisation and
concede that the Fairy is more successfully evoked for being 'shadowy and
mistlike', difficulties obtrude in Lytton's poetic realisation, for his theme
requires a sharp distinction between the Material and the Ideal. He partially
achieves this separation by isolating the Fairy from her traditional attendants,
by adopting a four-part division of the plot, and by using a buoyant ballad-like

---

[90] Lytton, *The Pilgrims of the Rhine*, new edition (1840), 14 – 15.
[91] *Miscellaneous Prose Works*, II, 10 – 11.

stanza form which, in comparison with the smooth fluency of Way's heroic couplets, sharpens the abrupt transitions between scenes (maternal advice/ forest/return to the world/tournament/Elvar's downfall). There is, too, some indication that Carduel is overworldly: Elvar's mother refers to economic injustice; Arthur's kingdom is capable of jealousy and pride; its 'thousands' are 'changeful', its 'beauty' faithless; its tournaments cheapen an ideal love; and finally the court has to concede its inferiority to the beauty of the Fairy Bride. But Lytton's idealising tendency works on all he touches: as a result, his purification of the characters of Arthur and Gwynver, his severe reduction of the Launcelot-Gwynver theme, his avoidance of all specific detail of physical description (except for Launcelot's sunflower device) make even his Material personages appear 'shadowy and mistlike'. The poem, for example, opens with the mother's incisive attack on the power of riches: 'On chains of gold and cloth of pile, / The looks of high-born Beauty smile' (3 – 4). This arouses the expectation that Carduel is to be no Ideal court but one contaminated by Mammon, yet by Part III the court offers rather more opportunity to the career of talent:

> Light question in those elder days
> The heralds made of birth and name.
> Enough to wear the spurs of gold,
> To share the pastime of the bold.   (127 – 30)

The final result of Lytton's vaguely uniform idealisation is to reduce the poem to an overall sentimentality, and thus to flaw an initial conception that had much force and freshness.

5

Tennyson and the
Arthurian Revival

Tennyson's relationship with the dominant aspects of the Arthurian Revival may be viewed most tellingly by means of a preliminary survey of the various drafts which he made in the early 1830s but did not publish. These materials consist of notes made from Collinson's *History of Somersetshire*; a sketch in prose ('On the latest limit of the West'); a memorandum later presented to James Knowles ('K.A. Religious Faith'); a five-act scenario; an outline of the character groupings in the early books of Malory's *Le Morte Darthur*; and a projected 'Ballad of Sir Launcelot'.[1]

According to Hallam Tennyson, his father had 'from his earliest years . . . written out in prose various histories of Arthur'.[2] These could have been taken from the books in Dr Tennyson's library, which contained the histories by Hume, Gibbon, Fuller, Lyttelton and Rapin-Thoyras.[3] A concern with historical fact is evident in the notes which Tennyson copied, virtually verbatim, from Collinson — a book which his father's library does not seem to have contained — and a historical residue is carried over into the sketch of 'On the latest limit', which portrays Arthur in retirement after his twelve victories against the Saxons, whilst another draft ('K.A. Religious Faith') specifically mentions the battle of Camlan, and adopts a distinctively Welsh Merlin Emrys.

Topographically, there is a slender thread of reference. Collinson's Glastonbury does not find its way into later drafts, but the 'sacred Mount of

---

[1] The notes from Collinson are reproduced in David Staines, *Tennyson's Camelot* (Waterloo, Ontario, 1982), 175 – 76. The Malory outline (from Harvard Notebook 16) appears in John Pfordresher ed. *A Variorum Edition of Tennyson's 'Idylls of the King'* (New York, 1973), 65 – 66. The prose sketch, memorandum and scenario are printed in Hallam Tennyson, *Alfred Lord Tennyson: A Memoir*, 2 vols (1897), II, 122 – 25. Fragments of 'The Ballad of Sir Launcelot' are printed in *The Poems of Tennyson*, edited by Christopher Ricks, second edition, 3 vols (1987), I, 547 – 48. All Tennyson quotations will be taken from this edition.

[2] Hallam Tennyson, *Memoir*, II, 121.

[3] See Nancie Campbell, *Tennyson in Lincoln*, 2 vols (Lincoln, 1971).

Camelot' is set in Lyonnesse, 'where, save the rocky Isles of Scilly, all is now wild sea'. From Malory are derived the stray allusions to Albyn and the Orkneys, and from the same source spring the romance settings for Joyeuse Garde and Avilion in 'The Ballad of Sir Launcelot', although, if Kemble's summary is to be trusted, Tennyson fancifully makes Avilion the venue for Merlin's downfall.[4]

This ballad would also have included a humorous description of Merlin's physical appearance: as

> one that rode alone,
> Astride upon a lob-eared roan,
> Wherefrom stood out the staring bone,
>   The wizard Merlin wise and gray.
> His legs were thin as legs of pies   (1 – 5)

The comedy is reinforced by the heavy sarcasm with which Merlin berates Launcelot on account of the latter's affair with Guinevere:

> God's death, Sir Knight,
> Your fame will flourish pure and bright.
> You spare no pains. 'Tis your delight
> To seek the Sangraal day and night;
>   It is no fable, by my troth;
> We know you are the cream and pride
> Of knighthood blazoned far and wide,
> The talk of the whole countryside.
>   Good morrow to you both.   (18 – 26)

As this excerpt would have been integrated with the published 'Sir Launcelot and Queen Guinevere' and the unpublished 'Life of the Life within my blood', it appears that Tennyson was compiling a medley poem of grave and gay, albeit not in ottava rima. The humour of this draft had been relished by J. M. Kemble, and aptly recaptured in his letter to W. B. Donne, and so it seems that such a poem would have been given a warm reception among his friends, and that, had Tennyson continued to write in this vein, he would have been viewed as the lineal descendant of Frere, Byron, Praed and Moultrie. That he knew the work of Frere is shown by the early poem withdrawn from the 1827 edition, in which he humorously suggests that critics will accuse him of plagiarism:

> E'en now my conscience pulls me by the button
> And bids me cease to prate of imitation.

---

[4] Kemble's letter is printed in Ricks ed. *Tennyson*, I, 545, 549.

What countless ills a minor bard environ —
'You're imitating Whistlecraft and Byron'.[5]

That he read Ariosto is suggested by the presence of two editions (one with
Alfred's name on the flyleaf) in his father's library at Somersby, and another
copy (Venice, 1577) inscribed by Alfred in 1833. No John Moultrie edition
earlier than 1838 is catalogued in the Somersby library, but Moultrie's
'Godiva' had been quoted in the *Quarterly Review* in 1821, a copy of which was
at Somersby, and Tennyson seems to have derived an image from this for his
later poem of the same title.[6] It is possible that he had heard of Moultrie's
poems when at Trinity, especially as the father, George Moultrie, had been a
friend of Tennyson's father, and a copy of his play *False and true* (1798) was in
the library at Somersby. Nor was a satiric content confined to Tennyson's
Arthurian verse, for in these early years, when stung by criticism from J. W.
Croker and Bulwer Lytton, he flashed into bitter riposte in his poems 'To
Christopher North' (1832) and 'The New Timon, and the Poets' (1846).

Even more evident in these drafts is Tennyson's interest in the wider
interpretations of his material, the selection of an emblem for his Malorian
summary being highly significant. Malory's mention of the finding of 'ye
braunche of an holy herbe that was ye signe of the Sancgraill & no knight
found such tokens but he were a good lyver' (IV. v) is obscure, and was
applied in the *Morte* to the infrequently mentioned Sir Bagdemagus. What is
particularly noteworthy is Tennyson's evident interest in the emblematic
quality of the 'herbe', and the motif's appropriateness for Tennyson's own
conception of a good liver: his Sir Galahad. From this viewpoint, only the
good livers (those whose hearts are pure) prove the successful finders: moral
stature may thus enhance a visionary capacity.

The first prose draft ('On the latest limit') indicates a comparable concern
with moral allegory. In this, Tennyson was projecting a primarily static
description of Arthur's Hall and landscape environs, without a pronounced
narrative content. It could have owed much to the first section of Coleridge's
'Kubla Khan', in its fusion of beauty and fear, and its opposition between
mount and abyss: both works celebrate monarchs and their man-made
paradises beneath whose green hills there pulses a 'ceaseless turmoil', and

---

[5] 'I dare not write an Ode for fear Pimplaea', ll.33 – 36.
[6] William Sidney Walker, 'The Etonian', *QR*, 25 (April 1821), 95 – 112, quotes from Moultrie:
   And let the traces of her raven hair
   Flow down in wavy lightness to the ground,
   Till half they veiled her limbs and bosom fair,
   As clouds in the still firmament of June,
   Shade the pale splendours of the midnight.
Tennyson's 'Godiva' (published 1842) contains the following:
   She lingered, looking like a summer moon
   Half-dipt in cloud: anon she shook her head,

where 'ancestral' voices prophesy war. 'The Palace of Art' provides an analogous situation. Not only does this include an Arthurian verbal vignette ('in the valley of Avilion'), but also the greatest part of the poem consists of a description of an artefact, a 'lordly pleasure-house', built on a 'huge crag-platform', wherein the narrator resides in 'God-like isolation', 'a quiet king'. Carousing in the Palace of Art is matched by feasting on the Mount of Camelot, but the narrator is doomed to fall, the 'abysmal deeps' of her personality laid 'bare' to God and plagued with 'sore despair'. If 'The Palace' is 'a sort of allegory', then the draft, too, would appear to possess the latent potency of, at least, a moral/didactic treatment, commenting on the hollowness of beauty, and the folly of a sensuous *fainéant* king, for surely there is intended a dramatic irony in the Bards' paean of royal glory whilst the Saxons 'ravaged the land, and ever came nearer and nearer', and a Tennysonian parallel with 'The Lotos-Eaters', where the Choric Song lulls other former heroes into inaction.

The second prose draft is far more explicitly allegorical, *viz.*:

K.A. Religious Faith . . .
Two Guineveres. ye first prim, Christianity. 2^d Roman Catholicism . . .
Modred, the sceptical understanding . . .
Merlin Emrys, the enchanter. Science. Marries his daughter to Modred.
Excalibur, war.
The sea, the people.   }   the Saxons are a sea-people
The Saxons, the people. }   and it is theirs and a type of them.
The Round Table: liberal institutions . . .

Tennyson is here densely allegorical: not only does he indicate a typology (the sea and the Saxons), but he clearly indicates a quasi-Spenserian religious schema in which the first and second Guineveres have assumed the role of Spenser's Una and Duessa in representing a true English church and a false Roman one. Whether Tennyson intended the strict numerical parallel between the first Guinevere and Una, and the second and Duessa, is a moot point, but the analogy appears viable. As the draft has been assigned to the early 1830s, it is endowed with considerable contemporary reference to social events. The passing of a parliamentary bill for Catholic Emancipation in 1829, and the rise of Tractarianism, would provide a controversial background for what seems to be an attack on the historical role and current practice of the Roman Catholic Church. The political allusions are also clear-cut, with the presentation of the Saxons as the people pressing against the British state, and thereby suggesting the clamour for electoral reform that

---

And showered the rippled ringlets to her knee   (45 – 47).
Ricks quotes the Moultrie passage but does not decode Moultrie's pseudonym of 'G.M.'.

finally obtained a measure of success in 1832; a process which is indicated by
the adoption of the Round Table as a model for liberal institutions, namely the
newly reformed franchise for the House of Commons. As Chapter 1 has
shown, a similar association of the Arthurian age with the expected freedom
promised by a reformed House had been seen in Henry Sewell Stokes's *The
Song of Albion*, whilst Lytton's Carduel councils would later present a particular
allegory of Westminster politicians. And, like Wordsworth in 'The Egyptian
Maid', who views Merlin as a 'Mechanist' of destructive propensities,
Tennyson's draft, in a fanciful manipulation for which there appears no
literary precedent, contracts a marriage between Merlin's daughter and
Modred ('the sceptical understanding'), thereby suggesting the development
of modern rationalist and anti-supernatural scepticism. Moreover, Modred's
pulling Arthur's 'latest wife' from 'the throne' signals an onslaught upon
received and orthodox religion, and counterpoints the divergence between
'truth' and 'glamour', or the search for true religion, and its palliation in
'enchantment'.

A parallel conception underlies some aspects of the plot drafted in the
scenario for a musical masque. That Mordred here scoffs at the Ladies of the
Lake and doubts whether they really are 'supernatural beings' is indicative
that Tennyson was dramatising a conflict between scepticism and the
supernatural. Merlin's prophecy that Arthur 'shall bear rule again, but that
the Ladies of the Lake can return no more' would certainly bear the allegorical
construction that Heroism (or Religious Faith or Monarchy) will survive by
means of adapting itself to future change, but that the Old Mythology of
fairyland will necessarily perish, its wings clipped by rationalist philosophy.

Additional evidence of Tennyson's employment of allegorical frameworks is
provided by J. M. Kemble's letter regarding the projected 'Ballad of Sir
Launcelot'. Kemble's summary of the poem treats it in such terms:

> Merlin, who tropically is Worldly Prudence, is of course miserably
> floored. So are the representatives of Worldly Force, who in the shape of
> three knights, . . . run against Sir L . . . [whose] own son [is] Sir
> Galahad (the type of Chastity).

Kemble's friendship with Tennyson, and the fidelity of the letter's account to
Tennyson's draft poem, suggests that the interpretation accorded with
Tennyson's own. To these three examples of prosopopeia, there could also be
added the identification of Guinevere with Earthly Beauty, and her
relationship with Launcelot as emblematic of Romantic/Illicit Love.

If these first intentions of Tennyson continually betray a close comparability
with the achievements of his contemporaries, his actual poetic realisations in
his four early Arthurian pieces are, by contrast, far more tenuously linked
with contemporary practice.

Ladies of Shalott

Written by about May 1832, the initial version of 'The Lady of Shalott' is Tennyson's first poem to be wholly engaged with Arthurian material. Comparison of the poem with medieval treatments of the Elaine legend reveals that in Malory's *Le Morte Darthur*, in the Stanzaic *Le Morte Arthur* and in the Italian novella that was Tennyson's most probable source, there is no introduction of a supernatural element: Elaine's misery and death are attributed solely to her unrequited human love.[7] However, the early nineteenth century preoccupation with faerie is evident in the two analogues which derive from the same novella source as does Tennyson's poem. Although these two analogues have been almost wholly overlooked by twentieth century critics, the poems provide a valuable basis for a comparison both between Tennyson's source and his completed poem, and between Tennyson's verse and that of two of his contemporaries.

In the first of these, Louisa Stuart Costello's 'The Funeral Boat', two such fairy allusions are of only slight import.[8] The damsel's 'lonely bark' (40) is fairy-like: 'Frail as the shell whose fairy sail / Sinks before the summer gale' (48 – 49); and Lancelot later vows to make her a grave where 'fairies paint their nightly rings' (183). Both references, however, indicate not only a conventionally rendered prettiness, but also the suggestion that the heroine's physical and emotional feminine delicacy is associated with the sheltering ambience of faerie, in retreat from a harsh everyday world. Much more significant, though, is the song that preludes the bark's arrival among the knights and ladies of the Arthurian court. Here the actual source of the song is left deliberately mysterious —

> Was it the moan of waves . . .
> Was it the sea-bird's mournful cry . . .
> Where is the minstrel . . .? (120 – 27)

However, despite its indeterminate origin, the song's message is unambiguously directed in reproof of Lancelot's flirtatious song to the 'lovely bands' of ladies (96):

> Ah! hush that lute's persuasive tone,
>   By thee too sweetly taught to feign:
> Its melody is sound alone,

---

[7] Thomas Roscoe, whose travel books on Wales were mentioned in Chapter 2, included a translation of the relevant tale from *Cento Novelle Antiche* in his *The Italian Novelists*, 4 vols (1825), I, 45 – 46.

[8] 'The Funeral Boat. A Legend', *Forget Me Not* (1829), 185 – 92. See also my article 'Costello's "The Funeral Boat": An Analogue of Tennyson's "The Lady of Shalott" ', *Tennyson Research Bulletin*, vol. 4, no. 3 (November 1984), 129 – 33.

And truth avoids the fatal strain.
One who has known thy scorn too well,
    Thy lays of falsehood would reprove;
Even from the grave she comes to tell
    How harsh a foe thou art to Love!   (130 – 37)

Thus, Lancelot is morally castigated for being a 'worthless traitor' (178) to the damsel who had died for him; and the supernatural song is employed by Costello as a means whereby moral obloquy is apportioned and publicly announced with greater authority than if spoken by the narrator. The novella had described the contents of an explanatory letter borne by the damsel: this 'scroll' is adopted by Costello, and its message amplified to include the damsel's request to Lancelot for 'One only boon . . . a grave' (174). But whereas the novella concludes upon the last line of the damsel's letter ('fallen a victim only for loving too true'), Costello's narrative continues with an admission by Lancelot of his responsibility for the death, and his promise of twelve months' penance spent away from the court and the camp. Costello's characters are wholly human, the narrative is described in terms of a psychologically naturalistic development, and the faerie is largely confined to inessential décor or to the device of a choric song for the full expression of the poem's unambiguous moral attitudes.

A second analogue to Tennyson's poem is Letitia Elizabeth Landon's 'A Legend of Tintagel Castle', which appeared in October 1832, a month before 'The Lady of Shalott'.[9] Here, once more, the concept of faerie is used as a routine simile for an attractively crowded scene: 'There was many a fair dame, and many a knight, / Made the banks of the river like fairy-land bright' (41 – 42). Nevertheless, in contrast with Costello's naturalistically human heroine, Landon's is a 'wood-nymph' who retires with Lancelot to an 'odorous cave, / Where the emerald spars shone like stars on the wave, / And the green moss and violets crowded beneath' (25 – 27). The poem's imagery associates her with the 'flowers of the forest' which are 'crushed at each step' by the 'proud' feet of Lancelot's courser (5 – 6). That Lancelot first catches sight of her by means of her reflection in a stream suggests her role as nature-spirit; and, appropriately for this context, her funeral bark which sets sail for Tintagel is towed by two white swans. However, despite her occupancy of a similar elfin grot, she has not the same eerie and destructive potency as Keats's La Belle Dame sans Merci. Rather, she shares the common misfortune of generously imprudent womanhood: she 'was left as aye woman will be, / Who trusts her whole being, oh false love to thee' (35 – 36). Furthermore, Landon's sentimental moralising represents the 'lady' as a conventionally pathetic heroine whose disaster is typical of the human condition:

---

[9] 'A Legend of Tintagel Castle', *Fisher's Drawing Room Scrapbook* (1833), 8 – 9.

And these are love's records; a vow and a dream,
And the sweet shadow passes away from life's stream:
Too late we awake to regret — but what tears
Can bring back the waste to our hearts and our years!   (57 – 60)

Like Landon, Tennyson presents an inversion of the Fairy Bride legend: for, in this altered form, the fairy is destroyed by the human. But in Tennyson's poem the role of faerie has far greater obliquity. As for the Lady's nature, it is on the whisper of a reaper that she is described as 'the *fairy* / Lady of Shalott' (35 – 36). The attribution of her fairy nature is thereby credibly contextualised within the countryman's belief in fairies. Moreover, the 'curse' is similarly internalised and presented only from the Lady's own viewpoint: she has heard 'a whisper' say, and she says it herself when she first looks down to Camelot (116). This Tennysonian distancing of himself from an explicit avowal may also be seen at the end of the poem where the knights 'crossed themselves for fear' (166): an action which hints at their terror of a sinister fairy presence, but does not actually assert either that the Lady was a fairy or that their fears were justified. Again, being compared to a 'bold seër in a trance' (128) endows her with a quasi-prophetic role, but the device of comparison ('Like') renders the assertion merely tentative. What might have been treated as purely magical properties — the mirror, the web and the boat — are all given a mundane plausibility. The boat, for instance, is found convincingly moored beneath a willow, and, to embark, the Lady has first to loosen a 'chain': moreover, earlier references to the river ('willow-veiled' with its barges and shallops) have prepared us for the appearance of the Lady's vessel. Tennyson's addition of a mirror to the Lady's bower brings with it some of the enchantment which had originally surrounded one of its main sources — the mirror in which Britomart had first espied Sir Artegall (*FQ*, III. ii. 18 – 26). This wondrous 'myrrhour', constructed by Merlin in the shape of a 'glassie globe', had enjoyed a revived celebrity in the Romantic period. Besides Moultrie's introduction of it into *La Belle Tryamour*, and Coleridge's image in 'The Pang More Sharp Than All' (see Chapter 4), Thomas Pringle had used a relevant quotation from Spenser to preface an extensive series of historical scenes viewed in a magical elfin mirror in 'A Dream of Fairy-Land'.[10] Tennyson, however, does not invest his mirror with extravagantly magical properties: it has, in fact, a workaday practicality, as Waugh first showed, by being a necessary instrument for the weaver to see the back of the tapestry.[11] The 'magic' of its 'sights' may be interpreted as the colourful and emotional pull of the exterior world, and if these sights are woven into the web, what wonder that the web itself be magic? (38). Yet, these naturalistically presented aspects are balanced by a contrasting fairy quality, less in minor

---

[10] 'A Dream of Fairy-Land', fytte iii, in *Friendship's Offering* (1832), 18 – 44.
[11] Arthur Waugh, *Alfred, Lord Tennyson*, fifth edition (1902), 78.

detail than in overall effect. The reflection of Landon's wood-nymph in the stream may be deemed as 'bright as a *vision*, and fair as a *dream*' (17) but the event remains on the level of sober diurnal occurrence, whereas in Tennyson the image of Lancelot flashing into the 'crystal mirror' has an unexpected and compelling effect, creating a magical and dramatic response from the Lady and the mirror. Much of Tennyson's effect here is achieved through a reduction of an orthodox story line. In both other contemporary versions, the Lady's death is directly attributable to her unreturned love for Lancelot, and her final voyage is made with the express aim of confronting him with her corpse. Tennyson's poem lacks such explicit outline: mystery hangs over the web, the mirror, the curse, her death, her voyage, or even Lancelot's awareness of his own role in what has befallen. Moreover, in Malory, Camelot is explicitly stated to be Winchester, and his unlocated romance venues of Carbonek and Lonazep jostle with a recognisable London, Dover, Humber and Salisbury. By contrast, there is in Tennyson a systematic reduction in topographical reference, for whereas Malory's 'Astolat, that is Gylford' (= Guildford, XVIII. ix), lies on Lancelot's direct route from Winchester to London, and the Lady is later carried 'in a charyot unto the next place where Temse (= Thames) is' before being placed in a barge that floats her to Westminster (XVIII. xix), Tennyson chose to follow the *Cento Novelle Antiche* version, which mentions only an unlocated Camelot. His modification of the novella's place-name 'Scalott' to his own 'Shalott' was made, he claimed, for reasons of euphony; an additional clue to the fact that a naturalistic topography lay outside Tennyson's concern. His deliberate suppression of narrative thread presents the action in a staccato series of tableaux: the Lady at her loom, the arrival of Lancelot, the cracking of the mirror, her setting sail, then arrival in Camelot. And Tennyson's 1842 version decreases the exoteric by depriving the Lady even of her parchment which had 'puzzled more than all the rest' by its gnomic terseness:

> 'The web was woven curiously,
> The charm is broken utterly,
> Draw near and fear not — this is I,
>   The Lady of Shalott.'   (1832 version)

If 'The Funeral Boat' and 'A Legend of Tintagel Castle' may be regarded as sentimental and didactic narrative, the absence of outwardly cogent narrative in 'The Lady of Shalott' has considerably broadened the poem's scope and application. That the poem has a secondary significance has been widely canvassed: the exact nature of that significance, however, remains the subject of acute disagreement. The claims of allegory have been strongly advanced, and have divided claimants into three main camps. The first of these has read the poem as illustrating a tragic failure to pursue the lofty demands of Art, through the Artist's succumbing to the attractions of Love and the World. A much larger party has made an exactly opposite interpretation. This sees the poem as heroic rather than tragic, in that it is believed to illustrate the duty of the Artist, *qua* human being, to love and thereby to enter life fully. Neither viewpoint may easily be maintained. As for the former, it runs clean counter to Tennyson's later recorded dictum that:

> The new-born love for something, for some one in the wide world from which she has been so long secluded, takes her out of the region of shadows into that of realities.[12]

There is here no indication that she suffers a moral or aesthetic decline on entry into the world. It is difficult to refute this dictum by invoking the intentionalist fallacy, because the poem itself speaks of the 'shadows of the world' (48) that appear in her mirror, and of these shadows the Lady is 'half sick' (71). The cracking of the mirror suggests an end to mirror- or shadow-gazing, and thus impels a direct confrontation with reality rather than its avoidance through an over-isolated art. On the other hand, those who claim that the Lady makes a wholly justifiable decision and that she achieves a moral victory in choosing love and the wide world do not give due weight to the pathos with which her death is represented, in which there is a greater sense of loss and waste than of positive achievement. Additionally, as the Lady is compared to a seer who can foresee his own 'mischance', the mischance would seem to apply also to her own fate, which she has twice previously described as a 'curse'. Nor can Edgar F. Shannon's claim be supported that her aesthetic triumph is signified by the term 'carolled':

> Although mixed with sadness, befitting a lament for imminent death, it is a carol, a hymn of joy and praise, which is traditionally associated with the birth of Christ — the representation of hope and eternal life.[13]

But, in Tennyson's poem, the context is that the listeners

> Heard a carol, mournful, holy,
> Chanted loudly, chanted lowly,
> Till her blood was frozen slowly,
> And her eyes were darkened wholly   (145 – 48)

The immediate proximity of the adjective 'mournful' does not suggest 'hope and eternal life', and the subsequent description is that of decline rather than rebirth. 'Carol' is used here without its Christian connotations but with a neutral sense of 'song'. Such a suggestion may be justified by an appeal to a

---

[12] Hallam Tennyson, *Memoir*, I, 117.
[13] Edgar F. Shannon, Jr, 'Poetry as Vision: Sight and Insight in "The Lady of Shalott" ', *Victorian Poetry*, 19 (1981), 207 – 23.

very similar use of the term occurring in 'Mariana in the South', another
poem in the 1832 collection:

> 'Ave Mary', made she moan,
> And 'Ave Mary', night and morn,
> And 'Ah', she sang, 'to be all alone,
> To live forgotten and love forlorn'.
> She, as her *carol* sadder grew . . . (9 – 13)

The difficulty involved in maintaining the two above-mentioned allegorical
interpretations has encouraged the widespread adoption of a third: that the
poem contrasts the claims of Life and Art, a conflict the resolution of which is
held in abeyance: as human being in need of human interests and affection,
the artist is impelled to abandon isolation, but ironically the 'world' brings loss
of love, tragedy and death. Critics who relate literature closely to biographical
origins have accepted this third interpretation as an allegorical account of
Tennyson's life in the early 1830s, and have contended that the poem reveals
both Tennyson's desire to develop a broader human concern in his verse, and
his fear that he might spoil his art in so doing. However, whilst this third
ironic viewpoint is considerably more defensible than the two previous, it
should not be awarded the canonical accolade, because the poem ultimately
resists interpretation at an allegorical level. In the light of the fact that most
early critics found the poem difficult or warned against the needless
unravelling of a message, one ought to be intensely wary of a completely
codified explication. This is not to imply that poetry necessarily defies
analysis, merely that analysis of this poem rests uneasily on continually
shifting bases. At even the most superficial level, the poem is not as clear as it
might seem. The crowd, for example, read her 'name' round the 'prow', but
it is not her name that they see, only her title — the Lady of Shalott. Again,
there is rich ambiguity in a crucial statement: she is merely '*half* sick of
shadows'. The elliptical narrative induces mystery, and there is tension
between the narrative lacunae and the clarity of the visually apprehended
surface, a tension which achieves a distinctively dream-like effect. Just as the
Lady cannot be definitively categorised as human or fairy, so the action falls
midway between psychological drama and fairytale. The complex interweav-
ing of imagery (the funeral has 'plumes', as does the sun-like Lancelot); the
'conclusion' of the poem upon an inconclusive note of prayerful adjuration;
and the taut balance between song and silence, between the refrain of Camelot
and Shalott, unite to form a richly allusive work. To select, as an instance, one
bright image from the poem — the shield of Lancelot in which a 'red-cross
knight for ever kneeled / To a lady' (78 – 79) — is to encounter an essential
ambivalence: does the lady represent Guenevere (and therefore Courtly Love
or Adulterous Liaison?) or is she the Virgin Mary, whose image Arthur had
traditionally borne? Or does the image foreshadow Lancelot's final homage to

the dead Lady of Shalott ('God in His mercy lend her grace')? Does it have any relevance to the human actors in the poem? The rich labyrinthine mystery at the heart of the work invites speculative interpretation, and the poem has never lacked for self-appointed guides, but the allusiveness which ripples out from the poem cannot be confined within a strict allegorical schema, as can Lytton's 'The Fairy Bride'. Tennyson's defence of his poetry against 'Dark-brow'd sophist[s]' who would impose such a schema may be seen in another early poem, 'The Poet's Mind' (1830), which treats of the sophist's attempts at understanding as merely a murderous frost that blights poetic growth. Although some later critics have spoken correctly of 'a kind of allegory', 'allegorical pointers' and 'parabolic drift', the claims for widely conflicting, and mutually exclusive, allegorical reductions would indicate that the poem lacks such a clearly enunciated schema and cannot therefore be defined as allegory. In its ability to suggest multiple meanings, none of which can finally and adequately epitomise the poem, it should more accurately be regarded as symbolist, as a precursor of a mode later distinguished from allegory by Yeats, who contrasted allegory, which 'said things which could be said as well, or better, in another way, and needed a right knowledge for its understanding', with symbolism, which 'said things which could not be said so perfectly in any other way, and needed but a right instinct for its understanding'.[14]

The Queen and Her Knight

The fragment of 'Sir Launcelot and Queen Guinevere' was the only portion published by Tennyson of his projected 'The Ballad of Sir Launcelot', which had had many allegorical overtones. In this schema, Galahad (the type of Chastity), Merlin (Worldly Prudence) and three knights (Worldly Force) are ranged against the lovers. That the knights should be physically, and allegorically, defeated is unremarkable in that their vanquisher (Launcelot) is traditionally of martial prowess, but it is noteworthy that Merlin should be 'miserably floored' by Launcelot's verbal ripostes since Tennyson had no literary precedent for such a confrontation between the two, and his own later portrait of Merlin in *Idylls of the King* treats him more sympathetically. Tennyson's invention of a meeting between Sir Galahad and the lovers indicates that a dramatic conflict was intended between such differing types; and, despite the omission of Galahad and Merlin from the published fragment, an inherent polarity remains at many levels within the poem. Natural scenery is, for example, presented in its most contrasting aspects, as in 'a sun-lit fall of rain' (4) or 'sun and shade' (37). The birds are either innocently melodious songbirds ('the linnet piped his song', 'the throstle

---

[14] 'Symbolism in Painting', 146 – 47; in William Butler Yeats, *Essays and Introductions* (1961).

whistled strong'. 10 – 11) or, like the sparhawk, are the predatory cause of the ominous hush that stills the groves. The verse is redolent of other comparisons ('*Like* souls that . . . with full*er* sound . . . the *perfect* fan . . . and fleet*er* now') that create a tautly strained tissue of contraries, which is reinforced by the tensions of the rhyme scheme, which demands three or four successively rhyming line ends. Again, Guinevere paradoxically 'swayed / The rein with dainty finger-tips' (40 – 41); and the 'maiden Spring' (3) is matched by 'the boyhood of the year' (19). The perspective strains into the distance: 'far, in forest-deeps' (7) to the 'topmost' elm-tree (8). The visual delineation is sometimes very precise: for example,

> Now on some twisted ivy-net,
> Now by some tinkling rivulet,
> In mosses mixt with violet
> Her cream-white mule his pastern set   (28 – 31)

Despite this there is an opposite tendency towards the general and idealised. Thus, the poem opens with a simile hovering on the verge of personification ('Like souls that balance joy and pain') and it closes with a general statement ('A man had given all other bliss'). Emotions within the poem are heightened and intense, whether 'tears', 'fear', 'smiles', 'laughed', 'blissful', 'bliss', 'happy' or 'joyous'. These oppositions are complemented by the tension between movement and restraint: as in the birdsong hushed by fear, the rein swayed with finger-tips, or the ringlet blown from the braid.

Clyde de L. Ryals has shown that the imagery has a role far greater than inessential adjunct in that 'it tells in miniature the entire story of the two lovers', with the images of fecundity ('teeming ground', 'chestnut-buds') counterpointing the sexual love of the two protagonists.[15] However, Ryals drives his original and valuable insight too far by attempting to press almost every word of the poem into an explicit schema. This entails some over-ingenious Freudian readings: he claims, for example, that 'treble' (in 'With blissful treble ringing clear', 22) suggests 'three, the masculine number', and that it thus indicates the 'impossible' triple relationship linking Launcelot, Guinevere and Arthur. Moreover, too fixed an insistence on the subordination of every phrase to an Arthurian, and presumably Malorian, framework, limits the relevance of Tennyson's work, in which the purely Arthurian element in the plot had been reduced by the author. In 1842 the poem was, in fact, grouped not with other Arthurian poems but was preceded and followed by a number of love poems ('Lady Clare', 'The Lord of Burleigh', and 'The Beggar Maid'), all of which share a celebration of the power and value of love, and which are all structured by a dramatisation of the social constraints that impede, but may be transcended by, lovers.

---

[15] Clyde de L. Ryals, *Theme and Symbol in Tennyson's Poems to 1850* (Philadelphia, 1964), 134.

What marks the language of 'Sir Launcelot and Queen Guinevere' is the extent to which it draws on Malorian elements.[16] In, for example, Malory's account of Launcelot's love for the Queen (XVIII. i,ii) there occur the words 'perfectyon', 'draughtes', 'maydens', 'joye', and 'payne', all of which become a cluster of key terms in Tennyson's poem. Other words in the poem, such as 'gown', 'waste', and 'bliss' are also distinctively Malorian, whose own lovers ride through woods and meadows in the month of May, all 'clothed in grene outher in sylke outher in clothe' until all are 'bedasshed with herbys, mosses and floures' (XIX. i,ii). But Tennyson avoids producing a servilely limp imitation, by combining an idiom which remains close to Malory with that of language which is evidently of later date, such as the adjectival precision of 'twisted ivy-net' or the details of early nineteenth century fashionable coiffure: 'Blowing the ringlet from the braid' (39), such ringlets forming the subject of frequent attention in other early Tennyson poems based both on legendary and contemporary subjects. Moreover, despite taking up a few verbal cues from Malory, Tennyson removes the 'fragment' from the original narrative and allegorical setting of his draft, and omits all specific reference to placenames, or to a commencement and conclusion of the lovers' ride. Rhythmically, the insistent onward impetus transforms the ride into a quintessential lovers' journey; the movement is without commencement or terminus, and thus assumes the quality of an arrested stasis. Nor is characterisation within the poem accommodated solely to a Malorian canon. When Guinevere is compared to her

> whose elfin prancer springs
> By night to eery warblings,
> When all the glimmering moorland rings
> With jingling bridle-reins   (33 – 36)

the Queen acquires by proximity affinities with the Fairy Bride. Indeed, Scott's edition of the ballad of 'Thomas the Rhymer' is a probable major source for this passage. His 'Queen of fair Elfland' wore a 'shirt' of 'grass-green silk', whilst on her horse's mane hung 'fifty siller bells and nine' so that the bridle rang. She rode a 'milk-white steed' which flew faster than the wind, and when the Rhymer kissed her lips and rode off with her, he surrendered himself totally to her power, and left this world. In Tennyson, Guinevere rides

---

[16] Tennyson knew all three of the early nineteenth century editions of Malory. He had 'first lighted upon' Malory when 'little more than a boy' in what was probably the three volume edition issued by Wilks (and edited by Joseph Haslewood): see Hallam Tennyson, *Memoir*, II, 128. In 1835 he received from Leigh Hunt the two volume Walker and Edwards edition. Tennyson's prose 'outline' which summarised the early books of *Le Morte Darthur* must have been based on Southey's edition for it not only includes the Caxton divisions that were used by Southey (and not by the other two editions) but also retains the archaic spelling of the Southey edition. I have therefore taken all Malory quotations from this edition. Lytton's notes to his 1853 collection reveal that he, too, used Southey's edition.

'a cream-white mule' and wears a 'gown of grass-green silk'. Green being the fairies' colour, she also wears a 'light-green tuft of plumes', thereby reinforcing these elfin allusions, besides associating her with the 'green' of the topmost elm-tree' and the 'grassy capes', just as the lovers' 'blissful treble ringing clear' echoes the song of linnet and throstle; whilst Guinevere's 'golden clasps' recall the 'yellowing' river, or the 'perfect fan' of the chestnut preludes her labial excellence. Seeming 'a part of joyous Spring', she, in turn embodies the beauty, youthfulness and vigour of the landscape. The presentation of the Queen thus gains in rich allusiveness. It also endows her with the amorality of a nature goddess, rather than with the immorality of the sinful queen.

A major result of Tennyson's freeing his fragment from the projected 'Ballad of Sir Launcelot' was that he evaded the implications that a longer poem would have induced him to confront, namely the relationship between Launcelot and the Queen, and the manner in which this relationship was regarded by other personae (for example, Merlin and Galahad) within the poem. As jokingly expressed by Kemble's letter, the theme was potentially risqué:

> I can only offer you Sir L.'s song, though for the sake of my future clerical views and Aelfred's and Sir L.'s character, I must request that it be kept as quiet as possible.

The poetical treatment of an avowed adultery could have deeply offended contemporary moral sensibility, particularly as the draft gives the impression that Tennyson was portraying the lovers sympathetically, Wordly Prudence being floored, and Galahad made to look sheepish. To a limited extent, Tennyson could escape the stricter moral categories by presenting the material as mythic. Certainly, greater moral latitude was accorded Olympian deities or romance enchantresses than would have been tolerated in a modern setting. But, even so, many aspects of the mythical or historical past were felt to require sanitising. The *Morte*'s reputation still suffered for being, in Roger Ascham's phrase, an account of 'open manslaughter and plain bawdry'. This was a charge to which much of Arthurian romance was subject. In a review of Scott's edition of *Sir Tristrem*, William Taylor of Norwich ventured a prophecy on 'this favourite story of our ancestors':

> It will not recover its ancient popularity: our correcter notions of the importance and duty of conjugal fidelity will prevent Essylt . . . from ever becoming a favourite heroine.[17]

---

[17] *Critical Review*, 3rd Series, 3 (September 1804), 51. Scott had himself noted the 'vulgar and obscene language' which was used in medieval tales, and had deplored that the *fabliaux* published by Barbazan and Le Grand were 'revolting, from their naked grossness': *Essays on Chivalry,*

Great uneasiness was later expressed by William Dyce when undertaking research in 1848 for his frescoes in the Palace of Westminster, for 'the chief part' of *Morte Darthur*, he considered,

> turns on incidents which, if they are not undesirable for representation under any circumstances, are at least scarcely appropriate in such an apartment.[18]

Accordingly, had Tennyson chosen to complete and publish his poem as originally drafted, it would have signified a remarkable departure from conventional mores since all other early nineteenth century references to the Launcelot and Guinevere affair were muted, satirical or disapproving. Common to many reworkings of Malory was a constant amelioration of the original characters' immoral sexual behaviour. With Hogg, for example, Launcelot is made the Queen's knight but this homage remains chaste; neither does the drug-induced love of Tristram and Isonde lead to a consummated adultery: Isonde remains a 'faultless queen', her fame 'spotless'. In contrast with Hogg, both Heber and Riethmuller create a slightly darker moral climate: Arthur seems peremptory in both, and in Riethmuller is made the father of an illegitimate Mordred by Morgan le Fay, who is ambiguously described as being close to Arthur in 'birth and blood'. The Launcelot-Gwenever relationship is strictly muted: in both works, Launcelot and Gwenever had met and fallen in love before her arranged marriage to Arthur: they had thus established a mitigating prior claim on each other's affections. Whilst Heber abandoned his poem before the re-introduction of Launcelot and the expected liaison with the Queen, in Riethmuller their reunion is chaste, and it is only Morgan's malevolence which traps Launcelot into visiting the Queen's bower. Thus, neither work

Romance, 22. Even Southey had been instrumental in preventing the publication of de Tressan in England, according to a letter written to Richard Heber in 1802:
> Longman and Rees had thought of translating Tressan's *Romances*. I advised them not to do it — because tho' he was an able man, his books are too modern, and what is worse too French.

The Heber Letters, 1783–1832, edited by R. H. Cholmondeley (1950), 183. Southey was, of course, to edit Malory, but his preface to that work exhibits a similar distaste for one of Malory's chief sources, the Prose *Tristan*:
> I began the perusal of this, as being the most celebrated of all these romances, with great expectations; those expectations were not answered: the story in its progress not only disappointed, but frequently disgusted me. (I, xv)

The Wilks edition of Malory displayed a defensively moral attitude in the preface, claiming that 'for the eye of youth . . . and the fair sex . . . every indecent allusion [had] been carefully expunged' (*La Mort d'Arthur: The Most Ancient History of the Renowned Prince Arthur and the Knights of the Round Table*, 3 vols (1816), I, iv). It noted that the rival edition issued by Walker and Edwards had retained 'the objectionable, and indeed, obscene passages', whereas in Wilks's 'the goatish fancy will seek in vain for the sentence that indelicately describes the feat of the giant'. Moreover, the editor, considering that Malory had made 'too frequent appeals to the name of our great REDEEMER', had also omitted these offending allusions.

[18] Quoted in Pointon, *Dyce*, 105.

represents an actually adulterous liaison: such were the ways in which early nineteenth century writers attempted to accommodate the 'plain bawdry' of much Malorian material.

In comparable fashion, Tennyson removed from an original draft of his poem those lines which probably appeared too overtly sexual:

> Each clasp, a point of brightest light
> Was made, a Lady and a Knight:
> And when the clasp was buckled tight
> The Lady seemed to fold the Knight.

And a slender lyric could, of course, avoid a direct reference to the adultery theme. Tennyson deliberately blurs, by the removal of the poem from its initial context, a distinct moral perspective from which to judge the Launcelot-Guinevere relationship. Accordingly, the fragment includes no biographical detail of Guinevere, but represents the situation obliquely. That she is already married to Arthur is suggested by her title of 'Queen', but Tennyson's poem makes no specific reference to her husband or to the exact nature of the connection between Launcelot and Guinevere. Whilst the story was sufficiently well-known for a reader of the time to have been aware that the pair represented an adulterous love affair, Tennyson concentrates his poem explicitly on the spring-time ride.[19] Although, as Ryals suggests, the imagery may provide an undertow of ominous allusion, a tragic outcome is not allowed to dominate the poem's mood. About succeeding events, the verse is delicately ambiguous:

> A man had given all other bliss,
> And all his wordly worth for this,
> To waste his whole heart in one kiss
> Upon her perfect lips.   (42 – 45)

The suggestiveness is densely organised: 'a man' could mean Launcelot but it also implies 'every man'; and, if every man would do this, it mitigates the heinousness of Launcelot's surrender to passion. Conversely, 'had' has the force of 'would have', and this conditional tense implies that the surrender has not yet taken place, perhaps never will. Furthermore, the placing of 'perfect lips' at the end of the poem gives the phrase a climactic quality, and, in

---

[19] A contributory factor in the diffusion of the legend was that Dante had referred to it in his account of Paolo and Francesca. The scene in which Dante's lovers kiss whilst reading the story of Lancelot was frequently treated by artists: see, for example, John Raphael Smith (RA 1803) and Archer James Oliver (RA 1809). Leigh Hunt's poem *The Story of Rimini* (1816) included an ample retelling, and provided a further stimulus.

The Arthurian knight also seems to have lent his name to a celebrated race-horse: see Abraham Cooper, *Launcelot, the winner of the great St Leger 1840. Painted for the Marquis of Westminster* (RA 1841, cat. 147).

comparison with the dimly adumbrated foreshadowings of woe, the poem's realisation of present joy and beauty is so intense that one must, on balance, see the poem as a celebration of the love affair. But, as the polarities within the poem convey, the ultimate significance of the work remains qualified and oblique. The situation has widened in scope beyond the Malorian context, the characters appear to be moving towards the archetypal, but an exact determining of their roles proves elusive, for if one may be certain that Galahad represents Chastity and Moral Purity, Launcelot and Guinevere are not quite so easily reducible: they certainly typify a Romantic Love, but it is not clear whether this is to be regarded favourably, pejoratively or as a mixed blessing. On account of this ambiguity, the poem cannot finally be classified as an allegory.

Grail Knights

Tennyson's poem of 'Sir Galahad' is not ostensibly concerned with the world of faerie, and makes only one seemingly unimportant reference: 'Sometimes on lonely mountain-meres / I find a magic bark' (37 – 38). But this use of the word 'magic' points to profound implications within the poem. The term would not have been derived from Tennyson's main source for the poem, for the word is not found in Malory's Le Morte Darthur. The comparable term favoured by Malory is 'enchauntement', but it is generally applied pejoratively and suggests the unholy arts of Morgain le fay, who 'was put to scole in a nonnery. And ther she lerned so moche that she was a grete Clerke of Nygromancye' (I. ii). The frequent ships that pertain to Malory's Grail questers may be deemed 'merveyllous', but this epithet seems to carry the connotation of a wonderful and visible sign of Providence, whereas in Tennyson 'magic' has anti-rational associations that derive from a culture which perceives an opposition between fact and fancy. To most readers in the 1830s, the entire Grail story itself would have appeared 'magical', highly improbable, imaginary rather than historical. Southey, for example, objected to the 'blasphemous fiction' of certain aspects of the Grail legend, by which he presumably alluded to such incidents as when the 'fygur in lykenes of a chyld . . . smote hym self in to the breed' at Mass, in Malory XVII. xx.[20] Tennyson, too, later testified to his reluctance about writing an idyll on the Grail theme, on the grounds that for a modern the story was incredible, whereas it would have been accepted as truth by the medieval writer.[21]

In the early nineteenth century, the subject had been treated very glancingly by Scott and Heber, and it is only Charles Hoyle's account in The

20 Southey ed. King Arthur, I, xxiv.
21 Hallam Tennyson, Memoir, I, 456 – 57.

Pilgrim of the Hebrides (1830) which is sufficiently ample to allow meaningful comparison with Tennyson's. Analysis of the relevant section in Hoyle's poem does, however, afford an oblique insight into Tennyson's true individuality. Hoyle (who has been briefly discussed in Chapter 2) draws his reader's attention to Malory's treatment of the Grail legend, but he must have based his own version not only on *Le Morte Darthur* but also on the medieval German poem *Der jüngere Titurel*, a work little known in England but one that had received much more attention in Germany and had formed the subject of a critical controversy in 1829 over its authorship.[22] In Hoyle's version, the Grail appears first to Titurel, who then seeks it throughout Europe, and builds a shrine on Montsalvat for its initial reception. Focusing on the first public appearance of the Grail, Hoyle relates:

> how damsels bright,
> King, queen and paladin were feasting in delight.   (xiii)

> When suddenly the harp-string snapt asunder,
> The startled Troubadour broke off his lay,
> Earth trembled, each bold champion gazed in wonder,
> The bevy of dames was tongue-tied with dismay;
> Winds howled along the gallery; peals of thunder
> Shook bower and buttress: o'er meridian day
> The duskiness of night and awe was flung,
> And merriment in doubt and fear suspended hung.   (xiv)

Titurel is then singled out for acceptance of the individual quest. Hoyle describes how

> Still as he journeys onward, left and right
> The sky is darkened, and the tempests frown.
> While full before, in apparition bright,
> The frontispiece and stairs of heaven are shown,
> Whereon the blissful hierarchies of light
> Ascending and descending wave the crown
> Of gold, the vesture white, and branch of palm,
> And round the chalice sing the sacramental psalm.   (xix)

Although the preparation of the temple receives more attention than does Titurel's final achievement of the Grail quest, Hoyle emphasises the tradition that has been created by Titurel, and how a later line of knights, including those of Arthur's court, will be summoned to the quest. Not only is the hero thus placed in a social setting, but the whole interlude is located within a very

---

[22] For Karl Lachmann's review of K. Rosenkranz's *Über den Titurel und Dantes Comödie*, see Wolfram of Eschenbach, *Titurel*, translated by Charles E. Passage (New York, 1984), 35 – 37.

long historico-topographical poem which introduces the Grail quest by way of
a personal reverie on the scenery of the Grampians:

> The land of shadows, where amid the vale
> Of wonder sits imagination shrined;
> And conjures up with ever-restless wand
> To tenant space and time, the sprites of Elfin-Land.   (xi)

Hoyle's adopted perspective, that of third person narration, allows him as
tale-teller to provide such an introduction, to separate fact from fancy,
historical truth from imagination. Similarly, the incident of the Grail quest is
sealed off by the author's reversion to, and advocacy of, the 'imaginations that
of old / Won audience from the warrior and the sage' (xxiv). The excerpt is
located within space at two levels: the external frame of the Grampians, and
the internal reference to Salvatierra, Britain, Gaul and the Pyrenees. As for
specified time, there is the narrator's time, which looks back to the 'ancient
bards' who told the story; at an earlier remove there is the time of the Grail
story itself, and within this narration a further chronology is indicated by the
Old Testament allusions (Belshazzar, the Red Sea, Saul and Aaron) which
lend by association the warranty of biblical truth to the entire narrative.

In contrast, by employing a first person narrative for his poem, Tennyson
bypasses the conventional dichotomy between reality and imagination,
scepticism and faith, or fact and magic. Since the supernatural is presented
solely from the standpoint of an ecstatic visionary, it is internalised and
becomes part of Galahad's mental state: hence a reader gives credence to the
presentation, on the assumption that he is encountering a deeply subjective
vision, whilst being allowed to maintain, if necessary, his own scepticism
outside this moment of shared vision.[23] Compared with Hoyle's Titurel,
Tennyson's Galahad is a figure intensely isolated from other human lives. His
'good blade' establishes him in militant opposition to male adversaries; and,
although fighting to save ladies 'from shame and thrall', he rejects their
maiden hand or 'kiss of love'. For reinforcement of his loneliness, the shrine
he rides by is 'secret', on 'lonely' meres no helmsman steers him, the towns he
passes in the dead of night are empty of footfalls, and their inhabitants
'dreaming'. As we are not told the content of these dreams, their
unknowability makes their dreamers appear wrapt in inwardness. Whereas
Titurel is closely assimilated to a family (he is Titurisone's son) and to an élite
corps of Grail knights, Galahad is represented without reference to parentage,
and has no companion knight or squire for his journeys. Moreover, as these
travels are unlocalised and allotted no defined time or era, and as the poem

---

[23] I am indebted to the critical approach of Robert Langbaum, *The Poetry of Experience* (New York,
1963).

hovers just before the moment of apotheosis, Galahad appears stilled into a posture of endless becoming or of arrested stasis. Paradoxically, the insistent movement within the poem, complemented by a driving rhythm of hammering horse hoofs, achieves an intense regularity which, as it seems without beginning or end, becomes permanently locked into a moment of vigorous action. This is underpinned by the use throughout of the present simple tense, which endows the narrative not only with a vivid immediacy but also contains the suggestion of recurrent action, of the eternal present that is achieved in myth. Other factors in the poem also make for a universalising effect: namely, the generalised description of Galahad's unnamed opponents (the 'horse and rider reel', 8); the starkly catalogued buildings of man ('hostel, hall and grange; / By bridge and ford, by park and pale', 81 – 82); the bare stylised landscapes that are reduced to a few essential and conventional features ('waste fens', 'windy fields', 'the plain', 'the height'); or the imagery evoking traditional religious emblems ('My spirit beats her mortal bars', 'This mortal armour that I wear', 46, 70).

The poem unquestionably had its primary literary source in Malory, and Tennyson's diction reveals close verbal parallels with *Le Morte Darthur*. Not only does he include the near-archaic terms of 'shrilleth' and 'chaunts', but he adopts a number of distinctively Malorian terms (all-armed, thrall, shame, carved, blessed, goodly), and the influence of Malorian motifs is pervasive. In brief, Malory's Galahad is a 'mayd' and 'surmounted alle other knyghtes'; Tennyson's 'maiden knight' has the 'strength of ten' because his 'heart is pure'. Malory's 'clothe of clene sylke' and 'fayr aulter' evokes Tennyson's 'fair gleams the snowy altar-cloth'; and Malory's 'crakynge and cryenge of thonder' and 'tempest' are fused by Tennyson to produce 'the tempest crackles on the leads'. Again, Malory's 'the floure of the lely' suggests Tennyson's 'pure lilies of eternal peace'. Nevertheless Tennyson does not become completely dependent: just as he used 'magic' instead of 'enchaunte-ment', he uses 'lance' in place of Malory's 'spere', and 'casque' instead of 'helme'. Most notably of all, Tennyson uses the term 'the holy Grail', and possibly follows Spenser's phrase 'holy grayle' (*FQ,* II. x. 53) whereas Malory had alternated between 'holy grayle' and 'Sancgreal'. Tennyson's poem has become so well-known that its novelty in adopting the anglicised form, Grail, has now been overlooked, but Sangraal or Sangreal had previously been the dominant forms, used by Scott, Milman, Darley, Emerson, Pennie, Riethmuller, Elizabeth Barrett Browning, Beresford-Hope, and even Tennyson himself in the manuscript draft of 'The Ballad of Sir Launcelot'. Only Heber's 'Grayle' had preceded Tennyson's use of the term amongst Arthurian Revivalists. Hoyle had gone further in anglicising and modernising by referring to the object as 'the Sacred Chalice'. Tennyson, however, avoids such a colourless expression, whilst declining, on the other hand, to assert the fully medieval connotations of Sangreal. His own Grail is Tennysonian therefore in combining the Catholic and medievalist associations of the 'shrill bell', 'the censer' and 'solemn chaunts' that surround the mystery of the 'blood of God', whilst widening the significance of the quest by portraying Galahad as a universal type of moral virtue.

Galahad has a distinct poetic voice, and his role is realised by Tennyson with superb economy of narrative and precision of auditory or visual effect ('The tempest crackles on the leads', 'The silver vessels sparkle clean') but, conversely, the person of Galahad may be viewed as a Spenserian allegorical type, representing Moral Purity or Virginity; and just as Spenser's knights have Elizabethan as well as medieval affinities, Tennyson's knightly persona may be regarded as having more than local reference to his original Malorian context, from which Tennyson has partially detached him. Signified, too, by its combination of traditional ballad form with a modern personal idiom, the poem develops Galahad into the universal role of quester or moral luminary. Consonant with Tennyson's portrayal of the knight as a type of Chastity (as suggested in Kemble's letter about 'The Ballad of Sir Launcelot') is Tennyson's own statement that the poem was 'something of a male counterpart to St Agnes', who was herself a type of female chastity.[24] Moreover, in the order of poems in the 1842 edition — a matter to which Tennyson paid close attention — 'Sir Galahad' is not placed alongside any of the other Arthurian poems, all of which are located separately. This positioning seems to indicate that Tennyson was less concerned, at this stage, with a specifically inter-related Arthurian grouping of legends than with wider ethical themes that transcend their initial contexts. Thus, not only is 'Sir Galahad' a 'pendant' to 'St Agnes' Eve', it also forms one of a group of three ballads narrated in the first person. The first poem in this group is 'Amphion', which was written in about 1837 – 1838 but is placed in this series on account of its being a directly comparable realisation of another ideal type:

> And I must work through months of toil,
>   And years of cultivation,
> Upon my proper patch of soil
>   To grow my own plantation.
> I'll take the showers as they fall,
>   I will not vex my bosom:
> Enough if at the end of all
>   A little garden blossom.   (97 – 104)

The type here is the modern poet, whose 'Genius must not', in the words of Emily Tennyson, 'deem itself exempt from work'; and whose aspirations, though cast in a lower key than those of Galahad, nevertheless echo the knight's quest and its eventual triumph.[25]

---

[24] Hallam Tennyson, *Memoir*, I, 142.
[25] Emily Tennyson is quoted in Ricks ed. *Tennyson*.

The Death of Arthur

By adopting the death of Arthur for theme, Tennyson selected a topic that lay within the field of the more commonly treated Arthurian subjects. An opportunity is therefore provided for further comparison between Tennyson's work and that of his contemporaries.

In the course of their lengthy Arthurian works, Hogg and Pennie had included accounts of the hero's end that are naturalistically presented, and which emphasise his battlefield defeat and final journey to Glastonbury. But whereas these works are written within a historical convention, Tennyson denies his poem any specific historical setting or mapped topography. There were, of course, other poems which also stemmed from romance sources and endowed the circumstances of the death with a magical aura. Among these poets, William Stewart Rose is a significant, but recently disregarded, figure on account of his introduction of Malorian scenes into his free translation of Le Grand's version of the non-Arthurian Peninsular romance *Partenopex de Blois*. Within this tale, Rose inserts his own heroic couplet description of a palace mural decoration that portrays a number of biblical and literary scenes. Amongst them, three incidents are drawn from Arthurian romance; the last of these consisting of a twelve-line summary of the collapse of Arthur's kingdom, and the departure of the king:

> The sword into the river cast; the hand
> Thrust from the waves to catch the charmed brand;
> The ominous barge, slow parting from the shore,
> Yfraught with doleful damsels weeping sore.[26]

In addition, Malory's account had been summarised and transmitted by the well-known Percy ballad 'The Death of King Arthur'. The 1840s presented a cluster of works on this theme. Not only was there the inclusion of this Percy ballad in the two ballad collections edited in 1842 by Samuel Carter Hall and by Richard John King, but Malory's narrative provided the basis for William

---

[26] William Stewart Rose, *Partenopex de Blois, A Romance in four cantos, freely translated from the French of M. Le Grand* (1807), Canto I. ll. 144 – 47. It has not been recognised by later critics that it was most appropriate, in view of these Malorian additions, for Scott to have dedicated the opening canto of *Marmion* (1808) to his friend Rose for being one who 'has wove / Partenopex's mystic love' (Introduction. ll.324 – 25) and who

        canst fitly tell,
    (For few have read romance so well,)
    How still the legendary lay
    O'er poet's bosom holds its sway; . . .
    And how our hearts at doughty deeds,
    By warriors wrought in steely weeds,
    Still throb for fear and pity's sake   (249 – 57).

The two other Arthurian scenes summarised by Rose are the drinking of the love potion by Tristram and Yseult, and the rescue of Guenevere from the stake.

Bell Scott's Royal Academy painting *King Arthur carried to the land of enchantment* (1847); and, besides forming the subject of Tennyson's 1842 poem, the death of Arthur was the subject of Robert Buchanan's poem 'Arthur's Weird' (1840), and figured also in Riethmuller's *Launcelot of the Lake*. A brief analysis of Buchanan and Riethmuller will conveniently serve not only to resurrect their almost completely neglected work but will also highlight the nature of Tennyson's distinctive contribution.

On account of its wholesale adoption of the spelling, rhythms, tone and narrative style of a traditional ballad, 'Arthur's Weird' is, in effect, a thorough-going re-creation of an earlier mode: as in, for example:

> 'Thou false traitoure! thy compt is come;
>   Receive thy treason's due;'
> And Rone, his spear, a full fadome,
>   He thrust Sir Mordred through.[27]

This deliberate archaism provides a uniformity of tone which strictly controls the poem's tautly limited theme: that man's life is governed by an ineluctable 'weird' or fate. The simplicity of this central concept is matched by the vigorous and direct assertion of motive and event, and by the starkly presented oppositions between Arthur and his 'false nevewe' (1). 'So fierce a fight', one is told, had 'ne'er befel' (49); and there is, similarly, no doubt that Arthur will sail to 'fairy Avalon' (148). Riethmuller's play is correspondingly overt; and, like the poems by Costello and Landon that have been discussed above, it embodies a moral drama that is presented in terms of clear-cut categories of virtue and vice, whilst the action is played out by protagonists who personify such elemental feelings as revenge, ambition, love, courage or heroic constancy.

In contrast, the complexity of Tennyson's 'Morte' constantly eludes a narrow and definite categorisation. By opening the poem with a sentence construction that demonstrates a result ('So all day long') but omits a causative factor, and by avoiding the to-be-expected explanations of why the battle occurred and against whom Arthur was fighting — matters about which, in contrast, Buchanan had provided an explanatory prose introduction — Tennyson removes his 'Morte' from the domain of strict and explicit motivation.

Some indication of Tennyson's independent approach is evinced by his relationship with his main source, Malory's *Le Morte Darthur*. Tennyson's own 'Morte' is, of course, full of Malorian verbal echoes, of diction, formulaic utterance and sentence rhythm, but Tennyson nevertheless maintains a greater distance from his source than Buchanan does. The latter had, for example, evidently used Malory's phrase 'the waters wappe and wawes

---

[27] 'Arthur's Weird', ll.69 – 72; in *Glasgow University Album for 1840*, 46 – 52.

wanne' (XXI. v) in order to form his own lines: ' "What sawest thou?" "Nought save the lake / Did *wap* with wind and wave!" ' (107 – 08). Tennyson, too, had used the phrase in his first draft, when he wrote: 'I heard the water *wapping* on the crag, / And the long ripple washing in the reeds' (116 – 17). But this obsolete term was modified to 'lapping' before publication in 1842; and Tennyson never lets his poem slip into wholesale dependence on Malory, as does Riethmuller in his account of Arthur's death. Since this latter passage has not yet been cited by any previous critic, it deserves quotation at length;

> BEDIVERE: I alone
> Bore from that purple field my wounded king,
> Unto a little chapel near the sea,
> Where we found refuge. Then, with dying hand,
> He gave to me the sword Excalibur,
> And charged me, on my life, straightway to fling it
> Into the dark, deep water. I, much wondering,
> Twice disobeyed; but the third time, he urged me
> With such great instance, that my heart refused
> To anger him by any further doubt:
> So I went down, close to the water's edge,
> And bound the girdle round about the hilt,
> And flung it from me . . .
> Just ere it touched the wave,
> An arm rose from the water, clad in white,
> Grasped the rich-jewelled haft, brandished the steel,
> And then sank with it. Long amazed I stood;
> When, as I turned to where King Arthur lay,
> I saw a little barge draw near the land,
> With ladies all in sable hoods, who wept
> As at a funeral, and did make sore wail;
> And took the king, and placed him in the barge,
> And so departed. Then I called after him
> With bitter cry, to leave me not alone.
> But he replied: 'Comfort thyself, dear friend!
> I go unto the valley of Avilion,
> To heal me of my wound, if it may be.
> Should I ne'er come again, pray for my soul!'
> And therewith, in the distance, all grew dim.
> Alas! I never shall behold him more!   (V. ii. 157 – 87)

In this passage, which is not typical of Riethmuller's usual sub-Elizabethan style of dramatic declamation ('Peace, thou jackanapes! . . . What bloody sight is here? Can it be Launcelot?' etc., etc.), the brevity of Malory's laconic style is re-created, with its rapid exchange of dialogue, interspersed with past tense narration. As Riethmuller makes no reference to having read Tennyson's 'Morte' before composing his own work, the passage's apparent similarity to Tennyson's may depend merely on their both having derived from an identical source. But despite the poem's close affinity certain distinctive features separate Tennyson from Riethmuller. The latter's compression underplays, for example, the supernatural aura of the scene: but Tennyson not only incorporates from an earlier episode in Malory (I. xx) the precise visual detail of the arm 'clothed in whyte samyte' that first proffered Excalibur, but he also expressively charges the occasion by employing the magical intensity of 'mystic, wonderful' (31, 144, 159), and thereby stresses the extreme abnormality of the act by means of a conscious heightening of the epithet. A similarly detailed inclusion, contributing not only an ampler explanation but also an evocation of supernatural ambience, is the description of the forging of the sword by the maiden of the lake: 'Nine years she wrought it, sitting in the deeps / Upon the hidden bases of the hills' (105 – 06). Again, Tennyson evades any historical or Malorian suggestion that Arthur's earthly destination is Glastonbury: instead, Malory's brief allusion to the 'vale of avylion' is expanded by Tennyson into a fully realised evocation of an otherworld isle of the blest. But, notwithstanding these suggestive expansions of fairy attributes, Tennyson paradoxically delimits them by insinuating contrary implications, for, unlike those of Warton or Ord, Tennyson's evocation lacks too overt a faerie connotation: it is, in fact, closer in spirit to the classical elysium of Homer and Lucretius, both of whom were acknowledged by Tennyson as sources for his Avilion.[28] Rather than denoting Avilion as a 'fairy' land, as Buchanan does in his 'Arthur's Weird', which conveys a fate-haunted supernatural atmosphere throughout, Tennyson's poem describes paradise increasingly in landscape terms: it lies 'Deep-meadowed, happy, fair with orchard-lawns / And bowery hollows crowned with summer sea' (262 – 63). Moreover, this landscape, though idealised, incorporates features which recur regularly in other Tennyson poems: orchards and lawns. And although there may be a suggestion here of the apple-trees which were often assumed to have given Avilion its name (an etymology noted by Collinson), there is also the evident fact that here, as in other Tennyson poems, 'orchard' and 'lawn' are distinctively known and English in connotation. Consequently, significant suggestions of faerie are balanced by implicitly contrary tendencies. What appears initially to be exotic and paranormal is often subtly modulated by means of Tennyson's obliquity.

Because we know so much more about Tennyson's life than we do about Buchanan's or Riethmuller's, we can readily detect the pressures of a personal concern. Written during the winter after the death of Arthur Hallam, the

---

[28] See Paden, *Tennyson in Egypt*, 157.

'Morte' displays a clearly typological framework, wherein the wounded King is both a type of the dead Arthur Hallam and of the crucified Christ. Moreover, internal references within the poem frequently reveal a marked tendency towards the apothegmatic, and a generalising sententiousness ('Seeing obedience is the bond of rule . . . Authority forgets a dying king, 94, 121): whilst the Round Table is pictured as 'an image of the mighty world' (235). That the 'Morte' has multiple levels of significance does not, however, mean that the poem is wholly and allegorically explicable. Pertinent to this is Tennyson's reply to the Bishop of Ripon, who had asked whether the three queens on the barge represented Faith, Hope and Charity. To this Tennyson answered:

> They mean that and they do not. They are three of the noblest of women. They are also those three Graces, but they are much more. I hate to be tied down to say, '*This* means *that*' because the thought within the image is much more than any one interpretation.[29]

This quality is greatly enhanced by the indirect methods of narration: thus, Arthur's Avilion quest rests on the assertion of the protagonist alone — from another angle, the watching Bedivere descries only a vanishing speck upon the horizon. Riethmuller, too, distances his Excalibur incident by placing it off-stage, and having it later recounted by Bedivere to the Hermit of Glastonbury. Tennyson's indirection is even greater, for the description of Excalibur's rising from the lake is related initially by Arthur, and the story is then resumed by Bedivere, who imagines an old man telling it 'in the aftertime' (107). Narration is thus delivered at several removes: if the framing 'Epic' is included, then there are four layers: firstly the authorial narrator, then Everard Hall's epic reading, thirdly Bedivere's account and, finally, the old man's imagined story. The successive filtering of such narration through separate sensibilities successfully accommodates the inclusion of apparently fanciful incident, which is relativised by means of being attributed to a private sensibility or which earns credibility through being presented from differing personal viewpoints, and because of the very process of iteration, as if on the Bellman's principle that what is told us three times is true. On the third occasion of its mention, therefore, the poet is enabled to narrate the 'mystic, wonderful' adjectives *in propria persona* as author, before the concluding reference is allocated to Bedivere. An increasingly complex reaction to the poem's mythic material is revealed by the qualification that accompanies assertion ('*if* indeed I go', 257), and the tentative attribution to a third person

---

[29] Hallam Tennyson, *Memoir*, II, 127.

of prophetic utterance: 'Though Merlin sware that I should come again / To rule once more — but let what will be, be' (23 – 24). And all assertions are softened and rendered ambiguous by the frequent references to dreaming which finally create a context in which the actual and the imagined, death, life, the past and the future meld in a twilit zone between sleep and waking. Arthur's slain knights are said to '*sleep*' (16); when carried the wounded Arthur pants 'Like one that feels a *nightmare* on his bed' (177); the stately forms on the barge are 'like a *dream*' (197); and, according to Arthur, more things 'are wrought by prayer / Than this world *dreams of*', 247 – 48).

Complementary to the dreaming faculty, which bestrides the actual and the imaginary, is Tennyson's persistent use of simile. Unlike Riethmuller's language, which is generally sparing in its use of the device, Tennyson's simile is a distinctive stylistic feature. Employed in epic fashion (139 – 41, 266 – 69), the extension lends a classical dignity to the Homeric echoes of the fragment; and the briefer analogies continually point outwards to an exterior reality beyond the present action ('*Like* one who feels a nightmare'), and therefore into a wider relevance not limited to the Arthurian chronology. Moreover, even within an Arthurian time-span, there is continual movement to and fro: the wounded Arthur is 'Not *like* that Arthur who, with lance in rest, . . . / Shot through the lists at Camelot' (222 – 24), and in the concluding frame Arthur reappears '*like* a modern gentleman' (294). These comparisons endow the central character with refracted images of himself which extend and develop his typological significance. Not only is the visual detail continually and precisely conveyed but the entire action is momentarily transferred into the sister art of painting at the moment when the dying Arthur looked 'wistfully with wide blue eyes / *As* in a picture' (169 – 70). This iridescent sheen betokens a rich semantic complexity that poises the poem's events in an ambiguous indeterminacy, for the simile conveys a more lingering tentativeness of analogy than does a metaphor: the 'Black-stoled, black-hooded' forms that crowd the barge are '*Like* a dream'; and after taking his sword Arthur wears it '*like* a king' — but the suggestive ambiguities are never resolved, the pervasive ambiguity remains. The mythic material which Tennyson is celebrating seems to have its own dynamism, it yields to numerous interpretations but its core, while clearly of import, defies absolute clarification, and its surface distinctness belies its opaque depth: the triadic grouping of events intimates a ritual significance which does not appear arbitrary but whose meaning just eludes us; and what are indubitably allegorical leanings do not gell into a fixed allegory.

In great contrast, there is a distinctively different tendency in 'The Epic'. Probably written in 1837 – 1838, this framing poem was, according to Edward Fitzgerald, devised in order to 'anticipate or excuse' the faint Homeric echoes, and 'to give a reason' for telling an 'old-world' fairy tale. Markedly contemporary, it replaced the subtleties of the original 'Morte' with a franker, bolder pointedness in its contemporary relevance, which allowed it to be

placed in 1842 at the head of the English Idyls. Here, Tennyson comes closest
to a comic use of Arthurian material in his published verse.

Significantly, the time of 'The Epic' is set at Christmas, references to which
are placed at two key moments: the opening line ('At Francis Allen's on the
Christmas-eve') was the product of a Tennysonian second thought — and thus
apparently planned — for an earlier draft had not mentioned Christmas until
the fifth line; and the final words are that 'churchbells ring in the Christmas-
morn'. Everard Hall's reading of the Arthurian extract is typified thus as a
specifically Christmas rite, like the games and forfeits that led up to it: it
functions as a traditional and mysterious tale for a winter's night. H. A.
Mason has ably adduced the parallels, at verbal and situational levels,
between Tennyson's setting and Charles Dickens's description of the
Christmas celebrations at Dingley Dell which had appeared in *Pickwick Papers*
in January 1837: namely, the games, mistletoe, forfeits, skating, wassail bowl,
old stories, the name of Allen, and the ironic reference to these 'degenerate
times'.[30] As there is no indication that Tennyson had read these *Pickwick*
chapters before composing his poem, no assertion of a direct influence upon
him may be made. But well before Dickens, the revival of traditional
Christmas festivities had already formed part of the programme of medieval
revivalists. Of these, Scott had in *Marmion* provided a set-piece description of
'Old Christmas', from the Mass sung on Christmas Eve, through the games,
the fare, and the entry of the masquers; whilst Washington Irving's *Sketchbook*
(1820) had contained an extensive account of a contemporary squire's
determination to maintain a traditionally authentic Yuletide. Such a medieval
ambience proved especially conducive to Arthurian association, for medieval
literature had often featured the Christmas feast as an essential motif in
Arthurian story; and there was a recurrent reminder in the oft-quoted Percy
ballad of 'The Marriage of Sir Gawaine', which says that 'The king a royalle
Christmasse kept, / With mirth and princelye cheare' (9 – 10), whilst Percy's
own emendation of 'The Boy and the Mantle' had altered the original
version's setting from 'the third day of May' to Christmas. Furthermore, as
the previous section on the theatre has demonstrated, there was already a
strong bonding between a Christmas entertainment, and a humorous
treatment of the Arthurian legend: so that, whilst Tennyson's introductory
poem cannot be classified as vigorous burlesque, its mood is frequently
humorous. Not only is there the physical fun of the games and the forfeits, but
the narrator's tone is colloquially urbane as he ranges from self-deprecatory
recollection of his own farcical performance as a skater ('three times slipping

---

[30] H. A. Mason, 'The First Setting of Tennyson's "Morte d'Arthur" ', *Essays and Studies*, NS 31
(1978), 98 – 114.

from the outer edge, / I bumped the ice into three several stars' (10 – 11); to a genial banter among the youthful friends. The parson's plaint that there 'was no anchor, none / To hold by' (20 – 21) is met by Francis's 'laughing', and then by Everard's jocular attachment to the wassail bowl. A lambent irony pervades the narrator's self-conscious use of archaism: 'the sacred bush', 'the wassail-bowl'; and there is a playfully punning allusion to medievalism in the parson's 'harping' and 'hawking'. At other points, the idiom has a pithy and genial colloquialism: the epic fragment has been hoarded 'as a sugar-plum for Holmes', despite Everard's having 'God knows . . . a mint of reasons' for not publishing it; and the promise of Hall's reading stirs the narrator 'Like a horse / That hears the corn-bin open' (44 – 45). There is a slily ironic observation of the fact that Hall needed little urging but made 'some prelude of disparagement'; and a broader note is struck when the parson having slept through the performance woke to the silence and 'grunted "Good!" ' The bland overall tone of the events that surround the reading is, however, transcended by the dream passage that follows, for Tennyson having ironically forestalled potential objections to the truth and relevance of the central tale or the dream vision, is thereby empowered to displace a comic and a mundane world.

This dream vision, however, has considerable contemporary relevance, for the framing poem's topicality has been exemplified by the parson's resentment of the dangers he considers are threatening the church, namely the reformist tendencies of the Ecclesiastical Commission, the development of schism within the church, and the attacks from without by the promulgators of the new geology. The 'old honour' which had gone from Christmas, and the 'general decay of faith' are counterparts on a religious level to the modern aesthetic difficulty of recreating the style of the ancient past, 'those heroic times'. But Everard Hall's 'Homeric echoes' have 'modern touches', and the prevalent death imagery of the 'Morte' gives place to signs of new life: the cock crows, the sun rises, and bells ring in Christ's birth. Within the mood of optimistic renewal, the age of Arthur no longer appears to have vanished with the mastodon. On the contrary, it may be reborn in a modern idiom. When the narrator dreams of the second coming of Arthur, it is to imagine him as a 'modern gentleman'; but, although he may have been transformed into 'the fashion of the day', he retains an essential continuity with the traditional Arthurian virtues as represented in the work of Milman, Pennie and Lytton. Returning on Christmas morning, he epitomises the Christian birth in an age of general decay of faith; though 'modern', he is a 'gentleman' and a 'King'. On his return to the waiting crowd, he is 'thrice as fair'; he receives popular acclaim, and he inaugurates pacific benefits: he has 'Come with all good things, and war shall be no more'. He thus manifests the qualities of royalty, religious faith and social amelioration: a triple concept deriving from those heroic times but with, as Young England would reveal, continuing contemporary application.

Arthurian Subject

As preceding chapters have indicated, the Arthurian legend was adopted as a literary subject much more frequently than has been assumed by recent literary historians concerned with the early nineteenth century. This resurgence of interest in Arthur is notable not only for its plenitude but also for its diversity, because the Arthurian Revival derived from richly complex sources, which we are now in a position to summarise.

Of prime importance in this Revival was the recovery of a hero who would, like Alfred or Richard I, impart a historical grandeur to the national pantheon. As putative hero, Arthur enjoyed considerable advantages, for his legend is characterised by its special power of attracting originally discrete elements. This essential adaptability is demonstrated by his dual function in war, wherein he may act as an imperial Continental conqueror, or take the role of partisan leader against a Germanic invader. Yet, contrasting with these feats of arms is his pacific role as a just and benevolent ruler in a golden age: and the nature of his rule appeals both to royalist sentiment and also, by means of the distinctive institution of the Round Table, achieves a measure of egalitarian fraternity, whereby the ancient code of chivalry is upheld against a materialist and selfishly anarchic utilitarianism. In contrast, the cult of Robin Hood, though potent in this period, could never match the range and rich dualisms of Arthur's role. Although retaining his power to symbolise Welsh patriotism, Arthur might represent not only this minority culture but also a Great Britain which saw itself as a harmonious union of Celt and Saxon. Most importantly — and this was a major reason for his supplanting other comparable national heroes — his mythological aura endows him with the Messianic attribute of a promised return: he therefore remains imminent, and of perpetual modern relevance; and his second coming — itself an apt metaphor for the Medieval Revival or Celtic Renaissance — may be constantly reinterpreted to adapt to new meliorist prescriptions. Although he has a slenderly outlined historical career, its indeterminacy provides great scope for controversial theory or for imaginative invention. Moreover, his mythological base is neither too abstract nor confined to one precise geographical area, since local legend clung to widely ranging loci: from major sites in the Eildon Hills, Penrith, Caerleon, Glastonbury, Tintagel and Winchester, to the innumerable other spots where a slender association persisted. A powerful adjunct, too, in the legend's ability to assimilate other material is that the concept of a Round Table brotherhood of knights continually encourages the enlistment of additional heroes, such as Lancelot, Tristram, Galahad, Launfal and later men, whose *gestes* are then inter-related with the core legend, and their love affairs and religious quests then provide a varied texture of human concern. Arthurian literature could thus accommodate a wide variety of type and interest, and was able to engraft most kinds of event. Given, moreover, that the period was especially concerned with supernatural agency, together with a perception of the imaginative and irrational aspects of man, these concerns found a convenient focus in the deeply ambivalent nature of Merlin, a figure who was already the most prominent amongst the personae associated with Arthur. Another contributory factor in the Revival was that contemporary literature was not required to construct a mythology totally afresh, for the gradual recovery of medieval texts revealed a vast international literature on the Matter of Britain, providing an inexhaustible source of theme, character and adventure; and the massive Arthurian context of medieval literature almost entirely eclipsed the potential rivalry of any other potential British hero. Finally, the resilience of the Arthurian myth is shown by the fact that even derisive detraction of it was integrated with the persistent comic elements within the literature to form a vigorous English burlesque tradition, and therefore, paradoxically, helped to ensure the survival of a residue of the original myth.

Because the revival of Arthurian literature was early derived from many differing sources, by the 1830s the diffusion of material was widespread. This situation needs, however, an ampler exemplification at this point in order to re-examine the claim made by Hugh Wilson that the young Tennyson was an 'unscholarly Arthurian' and, not being deeply read in Arthurian literature, had derived his knowledge from more popular sources.[31] As a result, Wilson claims that Tennyson could not have written his Arthurian drafts until 1838 at the earliest, on account of obtaining his knowledge of certain Arthurian incidents from work which first appeared in 1838. Although Wilson was almost certainly correct in his major assumption as to the young Tennyson's lack of advanced Arthurian scholarship, Wilson based his revised dating on a false premise, which was to place too great an emphasis on the role of Lady Charlotte Guest's *Mabinogion* as a source for later Arthurian knowledge. In doing so, Wilson ignored the widespread currency that the legends had achieved by the early 1830s. Since Wilson's theory has not yet been adequately assessed, and because its partial fallacy is pertinent to the dating of the drafts and the diffusion of the legend, his claim should now receive a closer attention.

Three drafts for Arthurian poems are quoted in Hallam's biography, and tentative dates assigned.[32] Of these drafts, the 'earliest fragment of an epic' ('On the latest limit') was 'probably written about 1833'. A second 'memorandum' ('K.A. Religious Faith'), which was presented by the poet to James Knowles in October 1869, was then said to be 'between thirty and forty years old'. Finally, the 'rough draft of a scenario' for a 'musical masque' was found in 'one of his 1833 – 1840 MS books'.

Most later critics have followed Hallam and assumed a dating of around 1833 – 1834 for all three drafts, but Hugh Wilson has argued that the second

---

[31] Hugh H. Wilson, 'Tennyson: Unscholarly Arthurian', *Victorian Newsletter*, 32 (1967), 5 – 11.
[32] Hallam Tennyson, *Memoir*, II, 122 – 25.

draft ('K.A. Religious Faith') cannot have been written before 1838, whilst Henry Kozicki has suggested that it was written in the late 1840s.[33] Wilson's case rests upon his contention that Tennyson had derived certain key phrases in his draft from Lady Charlotte Guest's notes to her translation of *The Mabinogion*:

> The sketch refers to 'Merlin Emrys the enchanter', the 'Battle of Camlan', and 'Modred . . . [who] pulls Guinevere, Arthur's latest wife, from the Throne'. In Lady Charlotte's notes, 'the three wives of Arthur, who all bore the name of Gwenhwyvar', are mentioned immediately following a description of 'the battle of Camlann'; Merlin is not called Emrys in Malory but is so titled by Nennius in a passage paraphrased by Lady Charlotte who referred to the wizard as 'the enchanter Merlin'. And in a note to the battle of Camlann, she described how Modred (spelt 'Mordred' by Malory) 'dragged the queen Gwenhwyvar from her throne'.

Wilson's analysis is, however, unreliable on most points. In her notes to *The Lady of the Fountain* (1838) — the first section that she published of *The Mabinogion* — Guest mentions Modred, Camlan and, a few *pages* further on, the three wives of Arthur, but the incident of Gwenhwyvar's being dragged from the throne occurs only in *The Dream of Rhonabwy*, which was not published until 1844, a date well outside the years of composition suggested by Tennyson. Moreover, the paraphrase of Nennius, which refers to 'Merlin Ambrosius . . . after whom the spot was called Dinas Emrys', did not appear until her translation of *Lludd and Llevelys* in 1849. In attempting to overturn Tom Peete Cross's extravagant claim that the young Tennyson had known the specialist Celtic studies by Edward Davies and William Owen-Pughe, Wilson appears unaware of the many other possible sources of such information, which — with the exception of the pulling from the throne — were far from uncommon.[34] Even this phrase, however, had occurred in a translation into English of the relevant Welsh triad, in the *Cambro-Briton* in 1822.[35] Moreover, this translation used 'pulled', like Tennyson, not the 'dragged' of Lady Charlotte. Reference to Camlan was frequent, and Tennyson could have encountered it in Scott's *Bridal of Triermain*: it figured also in the undated notes he made from Collinson's *Somerset*. Besides appearing in a *Cambro-Briton* translation of Arthurian triads, the three Guineveres had been referred to in Ellis's notes to Way's widely read *Fabliaux*,

---

[33] Henry Kozicki, *Tennyson and Clio* (1979), 114.

[34] Tom Peete Cross, 'Alfred Tennyson as a Celticist', *Modern Philology*, 18 (1921), 149–56.

[35] 'The Triads. No XXII. Triads of the Isle of Britain: (Relating to Arthur)', *Cambro-Briton*, 3 (May 1822), 387–94.

in Faber's *Origin of Pagan Idolatry*, and in Tennyson's most available source: the history of England by Rapin-Thoyras, which was included in his father's library at Somersby. Warner's *Walk Through Wales* had alluded to 'Merlin, or Merddin Emries'; and Mrs Hemans's *Welsh Melodies* included a note on 'Merddin Emrys', deriving from Owen's *Cambrian Biography*.[36] 'Modred' is a spelling given by Geoffrey of Monmouth, John Lydgate, Ellis, Bannerman and Heber. 'Enchanter' was a stock epithet for Merlin: Spenser calls him 'Enchaunter'; Dryden, Malory, Southey, Wordsworth and Heber term him 'Enchanter'; whilst the identical phrase, 'enchanter Merlin', is found in Keightley's *Fairy Mythology*, Anne Plumptre, Dunlop, Ellis, Wordsworth's 'Artegal and Elidure', Hogg, and the *Critical Review* article on Scott's *Triermain*.[37] As Wilson's arguments against an early 1830s dating appear baseless, there seems no reason to dispute the dating of about 1833 given by Hallam Tennyson. What has been indicated, however, is the existence of many more possible sources for this material, which should no longer be assumed to have been so arcane as to be confined to a solitary source.

Having taken account of the large amount of Arthurian scholarship and literary creation within the early nineteenth century, we may no longer regard Tennyson as a pioneer of the subject. On the contrary, he often appears quite distinct from many contemporary Arthurian currents. In subject, the early published verse of Tennyson avoided certain Arthurian areas that had already attracted the attention of many of his contemporaries. Working outside the traditional concern with a historical Arthur, Tennyson displays no interest in any of the topographical sites commonly associated with Arthur's birth (e.g. Tintagel) or his tomb (e.g. Glastonbury) or the location of his court (e.g. Carlisle or Winchester). Nor does he describe Arthur's role as a sixth century *dux bellorum* achieving twelve victories over foreign invaders. Neither is Arthur presented as a Celtic or, more particularly, as a Welsh figure. Tennyson thus appears very clearly separate from scholarly historians, topographers or participants in the Welsh Revival. What is more, besides moving away from burlesque, Tennyson rejects also some favoured areas of the romance literary tradition, such as Launfal, Morgan le Fay and the Loathly Lady. The fairy elements are thus curtailed, and the opportunity for bawdy burlesque removed. One may indicate the extent of comparative isolation from received tradition, by noting that Tennyson moves sharply away, too, from the post-Renaissance convention of fancifully free adaptation of legendary material.

---

[36] Warner, *Walk Through Wales*, 124.
[37] *Critical Review*, 4th Series, 3 (May 1813), 473–82.

It is evident that, far from pioneering the Arthurian subject, Tennyson in fact declined to use much of the Arthurian material that was, as I have already shown, widely available in his time. Moreover, it needs emphasising that this material was richly varied in source. Apart from the medieval chronicle tradition, vestiges of which lingered on as the central corpus to be analysed by historians from the sixteenth to the nineteenth century, there were the records in Giraldus and Camden of the Glastonbury excavations, whilst Selden's theory on the location of Camelot foreshadows the later wanderings of a Warner and a Roscoe. Local legend had been reported from the Pentland Hills to St Michael's Mount, and thence to Brittany. Arthurian texts, whether in medieval manuscripts or in early printed books, had been collected, edited and regularly re-issued, whilst the Welsh triads relating to Arthur had been translated in the *Cambro-Briton*.[38] Furthermore, a considerable amount of foreign literature had been recovered from markedly diverse origins. The French *fabliaux* and *lais* exerted a strong influence through Way's versions; Costello made verse translations of two Tristan poems from the French, and Lewis added another: Costello turned into English Villemarqué's French version of a Breton original; and an episode from the Vulgate *Merlin* (available in Southey's introduction to Malory, and in Dunlop) provided the source for a Buchanan poem.[39] De Tressan's retelling of the Tristan legend had been Englished by William Taylor of Norwich, who had also produced versions of *Libeaus Desconus* and *Bliomberis*.[40] Although German literature played a smaller role than did French in influencing the English Arthurian Revival, Taylor also provided translations of Charles Stolberg's ballad 'Sir Egerwene' (1810), whilst lengthy extracts translated from Hartmann von Aue's *Iwein* and from Wieland's *Geron der Adelige* were included in *Historic Survey of German Poetry* (1828).[41] George Soane had translated Benedikte Naubert's *Der kurze Mantel* in 1826; translations of Friedrich Halm's play *Griseldis* (the first act of which is set in Arthur's court) appeared in 1840 and 1844, and the play was staged at

[38] The library of the redoubtable bibliophile Richard Heber (1773 – 1833), half-brother of Reginald, included a *Tristan* and a *Prince de Leonnois* (both published in Paris, 1586), a *Lancelot du Lac* (Paris, 1494), and illuminated manuscripts of the *San Graal*, *Merlin*, *Lancelot de Lac*, *Meliadus* and *Giron le Courtois*. See *Bibliotheca Heberiana*, 13 parts (1834 – 1837), part 4, 236; part 9, 177; part 11, 154 – 55.

[39] David Lewis's translation of 'Avec Yseult et les amours' appeared in *Cambrian Quarterly Magazine*, 1 (1829), 104 – 05.

[40] 'Trystan and Essylda' is retold in William Taylor, *Tales of Yore*, 3 vols (1810), I, 1 – 33; 'Bliomberis' and 'Sir Libeo' in II, 107 – 80, 214 – 74.

[41] 'Sir Egerwene' (= Sir Agravain) appeared in *Monthly Magazine*, 29 (1810), 356 – 57. Taylor's translations of Wieland had first appeared in *MM*, 54 (1822), 310 – 13; 57 (1824), 406 – 09, 508 – 12. Taylor's pioneering work in this field seems to have been totally overlooked by recent Arthurian critics.

Edinburgh in 1841.[42] In 1848 Platt translated Uhland's poem 'Merlin of the
Wood'; and other writers had dug even deeper: Charles Hoyle must have
derived his Titurel scenes from an original source in German, and John
Oxenford's 'Sir Wigolais of the Wheel' acknowledged its derivation from a
Volksbuch.[43]

Tennyson's only raid on such material had been to make use of the 'Dama
di Scalotta' story from the Cento Novelle Antiche, but in doing this, of course, he
was not alone, as the analogous poems by Costello and Landon testify. Yet,
apart from his distinctively individual accretions to the Italian story,
Tennyson's poetic development led him away from the powerful literary
conventions of fancifully free adaptations of Arthurian legend — and in doing
so, Tennyson distanced his work from that of Spenser, Dryden, Blackmore or
Richard Hole — and returned, instead, to what had once been regarded as a
quasi-canonical romance summary of Arthurian legend: Malory's Le Morte
Darthur. That Tennyson was well apprised of rival handlings of the material is
shown by the existence, in the Trinity MS, of 'The Ballad of Sir Launcelot',
and by the prose drafts of the early 1830s which include many non-Malorian
concepts, such as the Sacred Mount of Camelot; the three Guineveres; Merlin
Emrys, who marries his daughter to Modred; Merlin's oak tomb; and
Guinevere's throwing the presented diamonds into the river. Tennyson's
progression away from the above, and towards the use of Malory as his major
source, is an important development in the course of the Arthurian Revival.
As has been shown, Tennyson added almost as much as he derived from
Malory; nonetheless, he was largely instrumental in altering popular attitudes
towards Malory, and the focal centre of Arthurian study would thereby be
shifted from Geoffrey of Monmouth, Spenser, Drayton or Warton; and the
resonances of this adjustment are to be heard plainly throughout the Pre-
Raphaelite movement. This shift towards Malory was latently important in
that it would bring into central prominence the 'guilty love' of Launcelot and
Guinevere, the quest of the Sangraal, and the incestuous descent of Mordred.
In many respects, a more tragic doom-laden atmosphere would prevail; but
these later developments were not yet apparent in the 1840s. At that point, the
contribution wrought by Tennyson was less evident. He had certainly
neglected much material that was commonly treated, although in 'The Lady
of Shalott' he had taken a story that was popularly current. If he had given a
novel prominence to the role of Galahad as Grail hero, had lent an unusual

---

[42] Sir R. A. Anstruther's translation of Halm's Griselda was performed at Edinburgh on 26
January 1841, and published in 1840 and 1844: see Literary Gazette, 25 July 1840, 485. Q.E.D.'s
translation, Griselda, was published in 1844: see Athenaeum, 17 February 1844, 153 – 54. For a
review of Halm's play, see Athenaeum, 25 February 1843, 175 – 76.
[43] The Poems of Ludwig Uhland, translated by Alexander Platt (Leipzig, 1848), 364 – 68. John
Oxenford may have found his source in Volksbücher (Leipzig and London) which included 'the
Romance of Tristan and Isoude' and 'the Romance of Wigolais'. Its recent publication was
mentioned in The Archaeologist, and Journal of Antiquarian Science, 2 (March 1842), 28 – 29.

glamour to the morally ambivalent love of Launcelot and Guinevere, and had
established an unlocated Camelot as the Arthurian capital, he had remained
more orthodox in his moral idealisation of Arthur, and in the promulgation of
the political myth of the need for the chivalrous hero's return in modern guise.
The Arthurian world of Tennyson, although often differing in emphases from
those of his contemporaries, was not so significantly unapproachable in
subject matter that it met with total critical hostility. That it did meet with
some is, of course, undeniable, hence it now remains to examine critical
reactions to the attributes of Arthurian literature within the period.

Critical Reception of Arthurian Literature

It is evident from analysis of critical reviews in the early nineteenth century
that there was only minimal critical hostility to an Arthurian subject. Of the
more than eighty reviews I have read which cover all types of Arthurian
subject — with the exception of Tennyson's — from Thelwall's *Fairy of the Lake*
(1801) to Lytton's *King Arthur* (1848), there are only three which deprecate the
subject itself. Two of these criticisms are levelled at one work: Milman's epic
Samor; and both found the historical events 'obscure':

> The struggles of our ancestors, the ancient Britons, against the Saxons,
> that obscure period of our history . . . can hardly be very attractive to
> the imagination.[44]

> an obscure and uninteresting portion of our Anglo-Saxon history would
> bear down and tame high poetical powers: but this is the subject Mr
> Milman has chosen.[45]

In extenuation it should be stated that in this poem Arthur had been allotted a
very minor role, and that the chief protagonists were Vortigern and Rowena,
or the much lesser known Samor, Caswallon and Argantyr. Similarly,
although Arthur played a dominant role in Pennie's historical drama *The
Dragon King*, *Gentleman's Magazine* felt, despite its own pronouncedly
antiquarian leanings, that Pennie's work through 'illustrating, by the
historical drama of Britain, her early peculiarities in customs and manners',
would have little chance of finding 'fit audience in times like these'. This
reviewer, however, dissociated his own critical judgement from that of

---

[44] *Theatrical Inquisitor*, 13 (August 1818), 41 – 51.
[45] *New Annual Register*, 39 (1818), 185 – 92.

popular taste, and affirmed that he seconded Bowles's verdict in placing Pennie 'high among the living poets of Great Britain'.[46]

To be set against these assertions of the lack of public knowledge of, or interest in, Arthurian history, there are a number of contrary claims. For example, *Cambrian Quarterly Magazine* writes of John Parker's 'The Celtic Annals':

> The title is a vast and glorious one, and embraces events and ages of an extent and importance which are worthy of the proudest efforts of the British muse.[47]

Wordsworth's 'The Egyptian Maid' elicited praise from the *Examiner* for being a 'subject from the times of romance' and 'animated with the very spirit of the Old Romance'.[48] In addition, at least six reviews of Lytton's *King Arthur* welcomed the choice of subject. Although Lytton was later to complain of the lack of critical understanding of his poem, it met with, in general, a favourable response.[49] For *New Monthly Magazine*, the name of Arthur was one 'round which an imperishable affection clings'.[50] William Spalding in *Edinburgh Review* dwelt at length on the attraction felt by 'the highest poetic minds' since the Renaissance for the 'romantic beauty of the Tales of the Round Table'; and, whilst *Eclectic* and *Morning Post* wrote of the great 'national' topic of King Arthur, *Sharpe's London Journal* asseverated that 'the authentic history of England can furnish no better hero for an English epic than our traditionary Arthur', and the *Sun* applauded the 'superb' subject for being 'patriotic!' and 'worthy of imparting inspiration to a Briton!'.[51]

Notwithstanding the fact that these expressions of approval balance those of deprecation, it would be erroneous to suppose that contemporary criticism was itself so neatly polarised, for the overwhelming majority of reviews were less prescriptively concerned with the poet's adoption of certain historical periods — whether classical, medieval or modern — than with the manner in which a chosen topic was treated. Most early nineteenth century critics were,

---

[46] *Gentleman's Magazine*, 103 (January 1833), 60. Bowles's encomium occurred in the preface to his poem *St. John in Patmos* (1832), and was quoted in J. A. Heraud's review: 'Historical Drama', *Fraser's*, 5 (July 1832), 670 – 82. See also Leitch Ritchie's praise in *The Wye and its Associations* (1841), 106n.

[47] *CQM*, 4 (1832), 100 – 06.

[48] *Examiner*, 26 April 1835, 259 – 60: a review by Forster.

[49] *Life of Lytton*, by his grandson, II, 470 – 71.

[50] *NMM*, 2nd Series, 85 (March 1849), 307 – 14.

[51] *ER*, 90 (July 1849), 173 – 212. *Ecl*, NS 26 (1849), 449 – 60. *MP*, 22 March 1848, 3; *SLJ*, 10 (1849), 373 – 79; *Sun*, 20 March 1848, 3.

in fact, significantly pragmatic in their reaction to artistic selection of historical period: a rigorously prescriptive, even doggedly perverse approach, was more often confined to a work's formal qualities. And in their evaluation of these, early nineteenth century reviewers were often much closer verbal critics than has generally been assumed. Thus, in addition to *Samor*'s being charged with 'obscurity', it encountered far greater critical hostility on the grounds of its language and versification. Even sympathetic readers like Southey found that the verse was too 'full' of power and beauty, with the result that the narrative was clogged: 'With less poetry, *Samor* would have been a better poem'.[52] Reginald Heber concurred, feeling that the poem was 'so overloaded with beauties, that the attention was lost and wearied'.[53] Elsewhere, it was considered to be 'laboured' (*British Critic*), 'clogged' (*Monthly Review*), obscure and often absurd (*New Monthly Magazine*), 'tedious' (*Theatrical Inquisitor*) and 'bombastic' (*North American Review*).[54] Such criticisms attach themselves, also, to Pennie's *Dragon King*, which *Cambrian Quarterly Magazine* recommended for its 'great romantic interest' but found some fault with Pennie's 'occasionally giving to the world, what he conceives to be poetry, when, in fact, he is perpetrating downright prose'.[55] The same work appeared to Heraud 'ludicrously grandiloquent'.[56] Again, amongst 'many well-expressed thoughts' and 'an unusual command of language', Ord's *England* was tasked with its 'downright flatness of expression' when 'occasionally his muse is languid or slovenly, and occasionally ungraceful'.[57] Lytton's *King Arthur*, too, received a significant proportion of adverse comment. It seemed to the *Athenaeum* reviewer that the poem made a parade of antique learning, but contained few 'fresh images', was careless and lacked design, whilst *New Monthly Magazine* also noted its verbal flaws.[58]

A common, and important, factor in many of these hostile critiques is that they are often implicitly related to an attack on the poet's adopted genre. Comments on *Samor* and *King Arthur* suggest that Milman and Lytton were considered too ambitious in their attempt at epic poetry, whilst Francis Jeffrey

---

[52] See letters to Walter Scott and to C. H. Townsend, in *Life and Correspondence of Robert Southey*, edited by Charles Cuthbert Southey, 6 vols (1849 – 1850), IV, 30 – 32, 338.
[53] Heber's review of Milman's *The Fall of Jerusalem*, in *Quarterly Review*, 23 (May 1820), 198 – 225.
[54] *BC*, NS 10 (July 1818), 52 – 59. *MR*, 87 (December 1818), 337 – 56. *NMM*, 10 (October 1818), 247 – 49. *TI*, 13 (August 1818), 41 – 51. *NAR*, 9 (1819), 26 – 35.
[55] *CQM*, 4 (1832), 254 – 59.
[56] *Fraser's*, 5 (July 1832), 670 – 82.
[57] *Gentleman's Magazine*, NS 4 (August 1835), 163 – 64.
[58] *Ath*, 11 March 1848, 262 – 63; and 27 January 1849, 87 – 89. *NMM*, 2nd Series, 85 (March 1849), 307 – 14.

mocks Thelwall's 'pretensions to epic and dramatic fame'.[59] An intense awareness of the appropriateness, or lack, of correct genre is marked throughout the period, and is both a legacy from eighteenth century neo-classical criticism (with its hierarchy of genres) and also a sign of the nineteenth century's search for appropriate new forms. Such criticism of Arthurian works is common. Milman, himself, considered Heber's *Morte d'Arthur* to lack 'the stirring qualities' of romance, disapproved of the poem's psychological closet-drama, and found *The Masque of Gwendolen* deficient in the 'ease and lightness' which were presumably thought necessary for a masque.[60] Ord's *England* was held to show a radical defect of lack of structure, comparable to 'Harding the Chronicler, or Robert of Gloucester'.[61] Parker's hexameters were considered unsuitable for an ancient British story (*Cambrian Quarterly Magazine*), and Moultrie's use of ottava rima in *La Belle Tryamour* was thought by the *Athenaeum* ill-advised for any but a modern subject.[62] The same journal believed that the material of Riethmuller's *Launcelot of the Lake* was 'better suited for opera or melodrama than tragedy, and calling for lyric interludes'.[63] *Sharpe's London Journal* suggested that Lytton's *King Arthur* should be judged not as epic but as a 'metrical romance', and *Examiner* thought Horne's 'The Three Knights of Camelott' a fairy tale, 'but not of Mr Horne's right fairy kind'.[64]

The early critical reception of Tennyson's poetry was governed by the same concerns as have been outlined above. Of the fourteen reviews and articles, published between 1832 and 1849, which commented on 'The Lady of Shalott', only five were distinctly inimical, the others being broadly favourable. Among the hostile, it was not, however, the Arthurian connotations of the poem that earned reproof. J. W. Croker, it is true, adds a satirical footnote identifying Tennyson's Camelot with

the same Camelot, in Somersetshire, we presume which is alluded to by Kent in *King Lear* —
    'Goose! if I had thee upon Sarum plain,

---

[59] *Edinburgh Review*, 2 (April 1803), 197 – 202.
[60] *Quarterly*, 43 (October 1830), 386.
[61] *Gentleman's Magazine*, NS 4 (August 1835), 163 – 64.
[62] *CQM*, 4 (1832), 100 – 06. *Ath*, 22 April 1837, 278 – 79.
[63] *Ath*, 13 January 1844, 31.
[64] *SLJ*, 10 (1849), 373 – 79. *Exam*, 6 June 1846, 355. Elizabeth Barrett admired Horne's 'Three Knights' for possessing 'more definite and distinct images than he is apt to show'; whilst Robert Browning's praise was profuse: 'the Camelott adventure' was 'sylvan "to the height" — perfect!': *The Letters of Robert Browning and Elizabeth Barrett Barrett 1845 – 1846*, 2 vols (Cambridge, Mass., 1969), I, 358 – 59; William Kingsland. 'Robert Browning as a Letter-Writer: Extracts from Rare Letters', *Poet-Lore*, 8 (1896), 79.

I'd drive thee cackling home to Camelot.'[65]

But Croker's facetiousness is apparent. Any supposition that he was really unaware of Camelot's Arthurian association should be discounted by reference to his strictures on Leigh Hunt's *The Story of Rimini*. In his *Quarterly* article, Croker had correctly detected that Leigh Hunt's account of the *enfances* of Launcelot was heavily derived from Ellis's *Specimens of Early English Metrical Romances*, and that Hunt's lament for the death of Paulo was very closely modelled on Sir Ector's lament for Sir Launcelot in Malory. Quoting with approval the Malorian passage, Croker observes that 'To us the old romance has far more of poetry, of sentiment and of nature'.[66] Croker cannot therefore be enrolled among the intrinsic enemies of Arthurian subject matter. What Croker does dislike in 'The Lady of Shalott' is what he considers to be its verbal inanity and imprecision, and the false rhyming of 'river' with 'lirra'. In this opinion he is echoed by Bulwer Lytton's review in *New Monthly Magazine* but, once more, Lytton cannot, as the author of three Arthurian poems, be considered essentially hostile to the subject.[67] Neither can William Jerdan, whose slashing review in *Literary Gazette* ridiculed the 'ludicrous associations' of the name of Shalott as 'an onion which could make nobody shed tears', and then parodied the metrical pattern and diction of Tennyson's poem (as Chapter 3 has shown): 'On either side the dishes lie / Brave plates of beefsteaks, beefsteak pie . . .' Yet Jerdan does not object to the Arthurian legend itself, nor reasonably could he, since he had two months previously admiringly quoted an entire poem by his close literary associate, Letitia Landon's 'A Legend of Tintagel Castle', which was an analogue of Tennyson's poem, and in which the Arthurian matter was well to the fore. Landon's was 'a touching legend', he wrote.[68] Moreover, a previous analogue, Louisa Costello's 'The Funeral Boat', had been recommended by *Literary Gazette* as 'pretty', although 'not new', and its Arthurian subject had occasioned no remark.[69]

Further verbal flaws were detected by Heath, who objected to the inaccuracy of the term 'cloud-white'; by Fanny Kemble Butler who ridiculed the use of 'dusk' as a verb; and by a *Times* article, attributed to Manley Hopkins, which appeared to relish Jerdan's pun by alluding to the fact that Shalott 'calls to mind recollections of beefsteaks, rather piquant than

---

[65] *Quarterly* 49 (April 1833), 81 – 96; reprinted in John D. Jump ed. *Tennyson: The Critical Heritage* (1967).
[66] *QR*, 14 (January 1816), 473 – 81. The derivation was also noted in *Blackwood's*, 2 (November 1817), 194 – 201.
[67] *NMM*, 2nd Series, 37 (1833), 69 – 74.
[68] *Literary Gazette*, 6 October 1832, 625 – 26.
[69] *Lit Gaz*, 11 October 1828, 642 – 43.

odorous'.[70] Nevertheless, the verse was not universally condemned: *The Times* wrote admiringly of its 'sweet wild music', the *Christian Examiner* discovered 'exquisite beauty of imagery', and the *Church of England Quarterly Review* article by Leigh Hunt commended it as 'a series of long-drawn musical iterations'.[71] Of Tennyson's later Arthurian poems, John Sterling disliked the harsh 'r' sounds in 'Sir Launcelot and Queen Guinevere', and he did not consider the 'Morte d'Arthur' was 'costly jewel-work'.[72] These strictures are, however, in a minority, for the *Morning Post* judged 'Sir Galahad' to be 'perfect in its execution'; James Russell Lowell described it as 'one of the most exquisite of Tennyson's poems'; and the 'Morte' was lauded for its 'power of expression' (Forster in *Examiner*), its 'richness of language' (Gilfillan in *Tait's*), for being 'rich and overflowing in all the charms of thought and language' (*Morning Post*), having 'that grand melancholy music of blank verse' (Horne), and for producing 'that effect which only a [true] poem does' (Poe in *Democratic*).[73] What is especially notable is that two reviews commented on the subject matter. John Forster admired the 'rich colouring of old romance' that pervaded the 'epic fragment on the good old English subject of King Arthur', and of this the *Morning Post* declared, 'The subject is of course familiar to our readers'.

This evidence of the availability of the subject of the 'Morte', and its generally favourable critical reception, is not necessarily weakened by the well-publicised, and often adverse, criticisms which have been assumed to provide proof of the novelty of Tennyson's Arthurian subject. The nature of these adverse criticisms is, however, much more closely related to questions of genre than to subject *per se*, and they should be judged within the context of the early nineteenth century concern with appropriate genre, which has been indicated above. Again, Tennyson's preoccupation with appropriate genre provides an essential connection between his draft poems and his published work, on one hand, while accounting also for certain critical hostilities which his published verse aroused.

In the early drafts for Arthurian poetry there is, as in all his verse, a constant concern with, and experiment in, varying poetic forms. The allegorical categorisation, which was directly comparable with much of the work by his contemporaries, was, however, with the exception of 'Sir Galahad', evaded in Tennyson's published work. Nevertheless, critical

---

[70] Hallam Tennyson, *Memoir*, I, 90. Tennyson's revisions of 1842 were attacked by Fanny Kemble Butler in *United States Magazine and Democratic Review*, 14 (January 1844), 62 – 77. *The Times*, 12 October 1848, 3.

[71] *Chr Exam*, 23 (January 1838), 305 – 27. *CEQR*, 12 (September 1842), 361 – 76; reprinted in Jump ed. *Tennyson*.

[72] *Quarterly*, 70 (September 1842), 385 – 416; reprinted in Jump ed. *Tennyson*.

[73] *Morning Post*, 9 August 1842, 6. Lowell, *Poetical Works*, 146. *Examiner*, 28 May 1842, 340 – 41. *Tait's* NS 9 (August 1842), 502 – 08. R. H. Horne ed. *A New Spirit of the Age* (1844), reprinted in Jump ed. *Tennyson*. *Democratic Review*, 15 (December 1844), 580.

reaction to his poetry sometimes revealed a ready disposition to assert and explain an allegorical content. An extreme instance is offered by Henry Sutton, whose essay entitled 'The Poet's Mission' constructs an elaborate framework for 'The Lady of Shalott', which he interprets as the need for an artist to eschew wordly fame.[74] Sutton works out this schema down to the finest detail: the early reapers, for example, represent 'those who, though engaged in the business of the world, can yet see clearly in the twilight and the obscure watches of the night' and thus will be likely 'to appreciate the poet's labours'. As for the 'mirror blue', blue is 'Love's colour'; Lancelot epitomises Popularity or Fame; the voyage to Camelot is an attempt to 'puff off' one's own talents; the garments of 'snowy white' signify 'the outward hypocritic garb of honesty'; and by the knights of Camelot, one should understand 'the reviewers'. This interpretation sufficiently impressed Coventry Patmore that he wrote to ask Sutton's permission to make use of his 'discovery' of the 'sense of "The Lady of Shalott" ' in an article on Tennyson's *The Princess* that Patmore was preparing.[75] Four years earlier than Sutton, R. H. Horne had also descried an allegory in Tennyson's 'Morte d'Arthur':

> The idea of the death, or fading away of Fairy-land, allegorically conveyed . . ., is apparently the main basis of the design, and probably original.[76]

Horne is here adumbrating a kind of poem very similar to his own practice, for 'The Three Knights of Camelott' is, as Chapter 4 has shown, a strongly allegorical fairy poem. What is of especial note is that Horne discovers in the 'Morte' the very allegory of which John Sterling's celebrated *Quarterly* review bemoaned the lack. Although Sterling was dismissive of those poems in the 1842 collection which he regarded as 'Allegories, Moralities, didactic poems' (such as 'The Palace of Art' and 'The Two Voices'), on the grounds of their 'speculations' having the 'commonplaceness, vagueness and emptiness of dreams, though the dreams of genius', he paradoxically professed to regret the absence of an allegory in the 'Morte':

> The poet might perhaps have made the loss of the magic sword, the death of Arthur, and dissolution of the Round Table, a symbol of the departure from earth of the whole old Gothic world, with its half-pagan, all-poetic faith, and rude yet mystic blazonries.

---

[74] Henry Sutton, 'The Poet's Mission', *Howitt's Journal*, 3 (15 January 1848), 39–42.
[75] Letter of 3 January 1848, in *Memoirs and Correspondence of Coventry Patmore*, edited by Basil Champneys, 2 vols (1900), I, 158–59. Patmore's review appeared in *North British Review*, 9 (May 1848), 43–72.
[76] Horne ed. *New Spirit*, in Jump ed. *Tennyson*, 156.

Sterling's implication is that, had Tennyson imparted this ulterior level of interpretation, the poem might have achieved a 'stronger human interest'. In lacking this, the 'miraculous legend of Excalibur does not come very near to us'; and although Sterling claims that this legend 'as reproduced by any modern writer must be a mere ingenious exercise of fancy', he nevertheless conveys the suggestion that the loss of the magic sword would gain modern significance by being made a symbol of the old order. Sterling's observation has been given enormous critical attention, not least through what has been considered to be its influence over Tennyson's later development. Much of this attention has been effected by William Allingham's account of Tennyson's saying in 1867 that he

> was prevented from doing his Arthur Epic, in twelve books, by John Sterling's Review . . . [He] had it all in [his] mind, could have done it without any trouble.[77]

Tennyson was, as Allingham noted, far more susceptible to censure than to praise, and Sterling's review, which was 'meant to be friendly', evidently continued to rankle with Tennyson, whereas Allingham saw it as 'a thin pretentious piece' (p. 315). A dispassionate reading of Sterling does not, however, show him to be essentially inimical to the Arthurian subject in toto. Firstly, although he is primarily intent upon promoting a literature dealing with modern life, and thus rates Tennyson's 'English Idyls' as 'the most valuable part' of his writings, Sterling does not elevate classical myth above the romantic: the theme of 'Ulysses' is, for example, reproved also and considered less deserving than that of the 'great voyages of the modern world, Columbus, Gama, or even Drake'. Besides, a mythological theme could be improved by being given an allegorical import. One suspects that it is the 'legend of Excalibur' — a deliberate Tennysonian selection of the more supernatural elements of the Arthurian story — that provoked Sterling's dismissiveness, and that, had Tennyson concentrated upon the historical attributes of Arthur as a political leader, for example, then Sterling would have found the poem more accessible. Paradoxically, Sterling's own critical vocabulary is underpinned by medievalist idioms, as when he states that 'to the affections of others', and 'the fairest images of the world', legend must play a subservient role, like 'a loyal giant to a fairy mistress'. Similarly, Sterling's critical desideratum, 'the poetical representation of our time', he describes as a 'quest after the poetic Sangreal'. Neither should Sterling's own poetic practice be ignored, for, as Chapters 1 and 3 have shown, another 'legend of Excalibur' figured very prominently in the long poem he himself

[77] William Allingham, A Diary 1824 – 1889, edited by Helen Allingham and D. Radford (Harmondsworth, 1985), 150.

began in the winter of 1842: Sterling therefore appears to have been able to accommodate the Arthurian legend when treated in a burlesque genre.

What was often implicit in these critiques of genre was the question of viability of the modern use of an ancient literary form. When *Literary Gazette*, for example, commended Praed's 'The Legend of the Haunted Tree' for being a 'modern antique', his 'lively' style was praised for its power to resuscitate a past age of chivalry.[78] More commonly, however, the phrase was used disparagingly. In 1812, George Colman's *Poetical Vagaries* had included a parody of Scott, entitled 'The Lady of the Wreck'. This mocks the new fashion, set by Scott, for metrical romances; and Colman's preface therefore announces:

> The author . . . has attempted in this instance to become a maker of the modern antique, a vendor of new coinage begrimed with the ancient aerugo; a constructor of the dear pretty Sublime and / sweet little Grand — a writer of a short epic poem stuffed with Romantic knick-knackeries; and interlarded with songs and ballads à la mode de 'Chevy Chase', 'Edom of Gordon', 'Sir Lancelot du Lake' etc.[79]

A like charge against Scott is resumed by William Hazlitt in his *Lectures on the English Poets* (1818), which accuses Scott's verse of 'betraying a modern air in the midst of the antiquarian research . . . It is history or tradition in masquerade . . . The forms are old and uncouth; but the spirit is effeminate and frivolous'.[80] Hazlitt returns to this theme in *The Spirit of the Age* (1825), wherein Scott is again branded as 'a modern Antique' for unsuccessfully fusing old forms with new feelings.[81] In reviewing Pennie's *The Dragon King*, *Athenaeum* lodged a similar complaint:

> amidst descriptions of scenery, given with antiquarian accuracy, we may feel that the characters themselves are modern; their language, prejudices, and knowledge, the growth of the present century . . . A suit

[78] *Lit Gaz*, 30 October 1830, 697 – 98. The term appears to have been given widespread currency by John O'Keefe's popular play *Modern Antiques; or, The Merry Mourners*, which opened at Covent Garden on 14 March 1791.
[79] George Colman, the Younger, *Poetical Vagaries* (1812), 39 – 40.
[80] William Hazlitt, *Lectures on the English Poets. The Spirit of the Age* (1910), 155.
[81] *Ibid.*, 226.

of splendid armour and a bald head will not present us with a Caesar, or a plumed hat a Henri Quatre.[82]

Such criticisms also attached themselves to 'The Lady of Shalott'. Objecting to the 'imitations of certain antique specimens' which had given rise to Tennyson's 'The Owl', *British Quarterly Reveiw* questioned whether it was 'wise or profitable to be manufacturing modern antiques, whose best recommendation is a very indifferent imitation of rust', and sarcastically adverted to the 'rejuvenescence of our literature' that had been prompted by the 'revived study of the Percy Ballads'.[83] This reviewer's objections to 'The Lady of Shalott' includes what is evidently a dislike of ballad refrain:

> The poem is written . . . in a style of versification which to us is extremely disagreeable . . ., the first part of the stanza ending with 'Camelot', and the second with 'The Lady of Shalott', or 'Island of Shalott' . . . A refrain of this description . . . when persevered in throughout a poem of / some length . . . becomes intolerable. (pp. 63 – 64)

William Henry Smith appeared to concur with this judgement, for although admitting 'the worthy example of old English ballad-makers' he too condemned 'The Lady of Shalott' on account of Tennyson's 'torturing himself to unite old balladry with modern sentiment in his "Lady of Shalott", for ever rhyming with that detested town of Camelot'.[84] Such critical reactions against ballad form were, by the 1840s, distinctly rearguard as not only were traditional ballads, such as those in Percy's collection, continually being reprinted, but modern literary ballads based on historical or legendary material had been widely written in the eighteenth century, and the form had attained considerable importance in Romantic poetry, especially that of Scott, Coleridge and Keats. The use of ballad form for modern Arthurian literature, particularly that based on the romance as opposed to the historical tradition, had been commonplace since Anne Bannerman had composed her 'Prophecy of Merlin' (1802) and Scott had published his continuation of the original ballad of 'Thomas the Rhymer' (1803). But, as none of these ballads, with the exception of Alford's 'The Ballad of Glastonbury', contained a refrain, Tennyson's 'The Lady of Shalott' could, with its reiteration of Camelot and Shalott, be judged therefore as slightly innovatory. The use of refrains, of course, was not confined to Tennyson's Arthurian verse: it was, in fact, a

---

[82] *Ath*, 4 February 1832, 73. For a comparable discussion of later Victorian attitudes to medievalism, see Michael Bright, 'Metaphors of Revivalism', *Victorian Poetry*, 24 (Autumn 1986), 245 – 60.

[83] *BQR*, 2 (August 1845), 66 – 67.

[84] *Blackwood's*, 65 (April 1849), 453 – 67.

favoured device of the young Tennyson, who not only admired folk ballads like 'Helen of Kirkconnell', in which a refrain is found, but he also used refrains himself in a wide variety of poems on contemporary and legendary subjects, ranging from the repetition of a girl's name in the whimsical poems on 'Lilian, 'Adeline' or 'Lisette', to the more subtly orchestrated effects of the two Mariana poems, 'Oriana', 'A Dirge' and 'Recollections of the Arabian Nights'. Where Tennyson had been original was in his use of ballad form with a first person narration in 'Sir Galahad'. Of previous Arthurian poems, only Percy's 'The Legend of King Arthur' had attempted this. Tennyson's novelty here, however, provoked no critical comment.

A further shift in Tennyson's continual quest for an appropriate form involved his toying with the genre of musical masque. As the *Athenaeum* reviewer of Riethmuller had intimated, such a medium would have consorted very well with precedent. Not only had there been post-Renaissance masques rich in Arthurian content by Gascoigne, Jonson and Davenant, but Dryden and Purcell's dramatic opera of *King Arthur* had been guided further in this direction by Garrick's revision of the work, which he re-titled *King Arthur; or, the British Worthy. A Masque*. A congruent tendency was revealed in Kane O'Hara's version of Fielding's *The Tragedy of Tragedies*, for O'Hara steered the original burlesque away from a parody of heroic drama, and, paradoxically, inserted a series of sentimental songs. A number of other references also suggest the suitability of the masque or opera form for the Arthurian legend. Besides two masques that included Arthurian allusions (Garrick's *The Institution of the Garter* and Colman's *The Fairy Prince*), there had been John Seally's unperformed burlesque opera (*The Marriage of Gawaine*) and Rose's musical drama *Caernarvon Castle*. Scott's *Bridal of Triermain* was converted into an opera by Ellerton (1831), and into a 'grand chivalric entertainment', which incorporated songs, by Pocock in 1834. Thelwall's *The Fairy of the Lake*, subtitled 'A Dramatic Romance', came close to masque form in its profusion of choruses, and its spectacular scenic transformations, as when Caer-Leon is conjured up, 'splendidly illuminated, and decorated with martial trophies, banners, wreaths, and braids of flowers' (III. vi). In Leigh Hunt's masque *The Descent of Liberty* (1815) Arthur and his Knights of the Round Table are represented in a 'vision' raised by the fairy wand of Poetry, in homage to Liberty, and to celebrate the downfall of a wicked Enchanter (= Napoleon). For the Christmas of 1816, Reginald Heber wrote *The Masque of Gwendolen* for private performance; and a germane allusion to such a mode occurs in Peacock's *Melincourt* (1818), when Mr Derrydown outlines a series of his wishes:

I will be a knight of the round table. I will be Sir Lancelot, or Sir Gawaine, or Sir Tristram. No: I will be a troubadour — a love-lorn minstrel. I will write the most irresistible ballads in praise of the beautiful Anthelia. She shall be my lady of the lake. We will sail about

Ullswater in our pinnace, and sing duets about Merlin, and King
Arthur, and Fairyland.[85]

In greater, although analogous, detail are the welcoming festivities for Queen
Elizabeth, which Scott derived from the masque of *The Princely Pleasures* (1575)
and described in *Kenilworth* (1821). Upon the castle battlements were placed
'gigantic warders . . . designed to represent the soldiers of King Arthur'.[86] In
the pageant, a 'stranger, in a well-penned speech, announced herself as that
famous Lady of the Lake, . . . who had nursed the youth of the redoubted Sir
Lancelot, and whose beauty had proved too powerful for the wisdom and the
spells of the mighty Merlin' (chap. 30). After the performance of a masque
including Britons and Druids, there appeared the 'fiend-born Merlin', whose
speech then celebrates Elizabeth as the heir and custodian of British unity
(chap 37). Moreover, Peacock's *The Misfortunes of Elphin* incorporates so many
songs which are functionally relevant to the thematic structure that the novel
tends towards an operatic form, with its hero as the bard Taliesin, and its
finale as a bardic congress at Caerleon.[87]

These Arthurian-related works formed part of a wider revival of a lyrical
poetic drama, of which a notable example, Shelley's *Prometheus Unbound*
(1820), was certainly known to Tennyson, and clearly influenced his
abandoned lyric for 'The Ballad of Sir Launcelot' — 'Life of the Life within
my blood'. Besides, there was latent within Tennyson's work a pronounced
affinity with musical form, revealed by his solicitude for vocalic and
consonantal values, by the number of poems that are entitled 'Song', and by
the thematic and structural importance of the concept of musicality in his
verse, in such a poem as 'The Lotos-Eaters'. Arthur Hallam had early
recognised the 'variety' of Tennyson's 'lyrical measures', but it was not until
the 1840s that generous praise was given to this aspect of his poetry. Leigh
Hunt viewed 'The Lady of Shalott' as essentially a work of music, 'a series of
long-drawn musical iterations' which he 'did not well understand'; and
Emerson, too judged that in Tennyson 'the musical expression is first, the
thought second'.[88] Milnes, Forster, Horne and *The Times* united in admiration
of 'the harmonies', 'the grand cadence', 'that grand melancholy music' and 'a
sweet wild music'. Knowing that Tennyson had contemplated the use of a
masque form, one may thus note the appositeness of such a form for him. The
earliest prose draft ('On the latest limit'), so static in conception, had
culminated not in martial action but in the bards' singing of the King's
glories. In choosing a ballad form for other poems, Tennyson exploited the
potentialities of the form's assured propinquity with music. In 'The Lady of

85 *Melincourt*, chapter 8; in *Works*, II.
86 *Kenilworth*, chapter 26; in *Novels*.
87 See Butler, *Peacock Displayed*.
88 *Dial*, 3 (October 1842), 273 – 76.

Shalott', the refrain has already been noted, but other musical associations also provide the poem with a richly antiphonal structure that contrasts music with spoken language. The Lady's voice first reaches us as a 'song that echoes cheerly' (30) and contrasts with the reaper's whisper (35). Conversely, the funeral which proceeds with 'plumes and lights / And music' (67 – 68) stimulates her spoken regret: ' "I am half sick of shadows", said / The Lady' (71 – 72). Lancelot's meteor-like presence flashing upon the scene is accompanied by his song of 'Tirra lirra' (107) which prompts the Lady's cry, 'The curse is come upon me' (116). As she floats down to Camelot, she is chiefly evoked — particularly after Tennyson's revisions for the 1842 version — in musical terms: 'singing her last song' (143) and 'singing in her song she died' (152), after which all song is silenced, and Lancelot's adjuration is couched in normal speech ('he said', 169). Music has thus contributed to the poem in two main ways: it enriches the image of the Lady as an artist/ musician, and, by means of its contrasted oppositions to spoken discourse, it conveys thereby the taut contrarieties of the poem's subject. Whilst none of the other Arthurian lyrics can match this poem's major musical intensity, they do contain correspondingly minor connotations. For example, after the birdsong (piping linnet and whistling throstle) of the second stanza, Launcelot and Guinevere ride into sight and sound 'With blissful treble ringing clear' (22); and the additional fragment quoted by J. M. Kemble consisted of Launcelot's 'song'. And, as the promised goal nears for Sir Galahad, the heightened tension is conveyed against a background musical crescendo and diminuendo: 'A rolling organ-harmony / Swells up, and shakes and falls' (75 – 76). The 'Morte', too, displays affinities with a musical mode. Not only is the poem enclosed within two auditory images (opening with the noise of the battle, and closing with the wailing that dies on the mere), but there are also the minor motifs of the sound of the sea-wind singing over the bones of ancient men (47 – 48), and Arthur's prophecy that he will be 'sung of' (34). And the ending, so entirely suitable for the medium of masque, indicates a Tennysonian break with the Malorian tradition of continuing the story after Arthur's death and up to the less spectacular departures from life of Launcelot and Guinevere. Although Everard Hall's epic had presumably employed this material in his twelfth and final book, Tennyson's presentation of only the eleventh enables him to terminate the poem on the same plane as he had originally envisaged for his musical masque, which proposed: 'Fifth Act. The battle. Chorus of the Ladies of the Lake. The throwing away of Excalibur and departure of Arthur'. Finally, one may cite Tennyson's decision to surround the fragmentary 'Morte' with the two enclosing sections of 'The Epic'. The result is partly to enhance the theatrical qualities of the 'Morte', which, instead of being encountered privately as a work of printed literature, is delivered to its hearers as a public oral performance. The poem's musical qualities are manifestly highlighted by the performer-poet who 'Read, mouthing out his hollow oes and aes, / Deep-chested music' (50 – 51); and the influence of 'the tone with which he read' (277) is suggested as a contributory factor in the poem's successful reception. Later, as the narrator dreams of a neo-Arthurian hero, the hailed return is marked by a hundred bells that begin to peal, a prelude to his awakening to hear the 'clear church-bells ring in the Christmas-morn' (303). Moreover, the fact that the poem is read aloud at Christmas tends to place the reading within the context of the traditional Christmas entertainments, of which Chapter 3 has given an account. Placed within this setting, the event (and the poem it frames) are given the formal qualities of a seasonal musical rite.

Tennyson was to make a further generic experiment by beginning to write an epic. Once again, his decision to do so is unremarkable, for, in spite of the displacement of epic from the dominant role it had enjoyed in neo-classical criticism, the early nineteenth century witnessed, as Byron complained ('Another epic! Who inflicts again / More books of blank upon the sons of men?'), an explosion in the numbers of epics written.[89] In contrast with the five written between 1670 and 1770, there were eighteen between 1800 and 1812.[90] What had declined was the readily acknowledged pre-eminence of Homer and Virgil, for there was a willingness to widen the definition of epic in order to include the work of 'Ossian', and to accommodate the Italian romantic epics, of which a steady flow of translations appeared.[91] This did not result in a complete abandonment of classical form or a dearth of allusion to classical mythology: although new epic narrative tended to avoid an opening *in medias res*, the narrator still retained his opening thematic announcement, divided his work into books, and maintained the decorum of a lofty Miltonic style. A classical form was thus often employed to accommodate a non-classical subject, such as Milman's *Samor*. Homer remained a powerful symbol of the energy and grandeur of poetic creation, and there was ample authority for Tennyson's later incorporation of 'Homeric echoes' into his poem on Arthur. What did, however, mark the decline of orthodox classicism was the absence of any epic, except Keats's *Fall of Hyperion* (1820), taking Graeco-Roman mythology as its subject, whilst only one (Charles Peers's *The Siege of Jerusalem*, 1823) selected a subject from classical history — and even so, this impinged on the Judaeo-Christian. In notable contrast, a favourite subject for nineteenth century epic was British history, particularly that concerned with recent successes in the French wars. Additionally, a patriotic enthusiasm was felt for very much earlier history, whether early British or Anglo-Saxon (and featuring Alfred, especially). In the background, of course, there was always a consciousness of Milton's precedent in abandoning his projected Arthurian

---

[89] Byron, *English Bards and Scotch Reviewers*, ll.383 – 84; in *Works*.
[90] See Chapter 1. note 126.
[91] See Donald M. Foerster, 'The Critical Attack upon the Epic in the English Romantic Period', *Publications of the Modern Language Association*, 69 (1954), 432 – 47; and 'Critical Approval of Epic Poetry in the Age of Wordsworth', *PMLA*, 70 (1955), 682 – 705.

epic, but this very well-publicised rejection of the subject paradoxically contrived to retain it among the range of possibilities for a future epic poet. The merits of Arthur as a viable epic hero were, for example, considered by Southey in 1804, and rejected:

> if we take the Arthur of romance, he is eclipsed by his own knights, — of the historical Arthur, his actions are of no consequential importance.[92]

Moreover, in Coleridge's opinion an Arthurian epic was prevented by an apparent lack of modern relevance:

> In my judgment, an epic poem must either be national or mundane. As to Arthur, you could not by any means make a poem on him national to Englishmen. What have *we* to do with him?[93]

These views have been frequently cited as indicative of the unpopularity of an Arthurian subject. However, in the excerpt from Coleridge's *Table Talk*, Arthur is merely being dismissed as an epic hero, not necessarily totally rejected as a subject for poetry; and, despite Coleridge's sense of the gulf that separated him as a modern Anglo-Saxon from Arthur as a defeated minor British chieftain, there remains the persistent query as to which of Coleridge's table companions may have raised the possibility of Arthur as epic hero, or whether (and why) Coleridge chose Arthur as his instance: in either case, it seems that an Arthurian subject remained a latent possibility sounded at that time, even though, as in the case of Wordsworth, it may have been eventually rejected.[94] The question of an Arthurian epic had, in fact, been debated by John Thelwall in his *The Peripatetic* as long ago as 1793; and the author's mouthpiece, Sylvanus, defends the suitability of Arthur for the role of hero:

> The traditions and records of this prince furnish as noble a theme as the epic muse could wish to dwell upon; the successes which frequently attended his arms were amply sufficient to entitle him to the honours of heroic poetry: nor can I see that the final issue of the struggle between the Saxons and the Britons throws the least shade upon his triumphs. Add to this, that the fabulous age in which he lived, gives to the

[92] Letter to C. W. W. Wynn, 30 December 1804; in *Selected Letters*, I, 295.
[93] 'Table Talk', 4 September 1833; in *Coleridge's Miscellaneous Criticism*, edited by Thomas Middleton Rayor (1936), 429.
[94] See *The Prelude*, I, ll.166 – 85; in *Poetical Works*.

imagination of the poet that latitude for daring exertion, which no later period of history can properly afford.[95]

Despite Southey's and Coleridge's reservations, there does appear in the early nineteenth century a strong affinity between Arthurian subject and epic poetry. Many of the poets who wrote of Arthur, indeed, wrote separate epics on non-Arthurian themes (Thelwall 1801, Bowles 1804, Hoyle 1807, Sotheby 1809, Pennie 1817 and 1823, and Atherstone 1830); and, since references to Arthur frequently recurred within a Welsh or English medieval setting, early nineteenth century epics consistently maintained a steady flow of Arthurian allusions (Burges 1801, Southey 1805, Cottle 1808, Merivale 1814, Meredith 1818, Porden 1822, Collingwood 1836, Herbert 1838). There is, too, a minute Arthurian role within Blake's quasi-epic poem on British history, *Jerusalem* (1804 – 1820). On a larger scale, Arthur had figured as a minor protagonist in Milman's epic *Samor* (1818), and as tragic hero in Heber's 'sort of epic' *Morte d'Arthur* (pub. 1830). Given that Tennyson's 'Morte' was followed by Lytton's *King Arthur*, the association of Arthur with an epic context appears a consistent development within literary tradition.

Critical reactions to the epic form were extremely diverse. In analysing *Samor*, the *Theatrical Inquisitor* ranked epic as the 'highest and most meritorious class' of poem, yet the reviewer was unaware of any modern attempt except Milman's.[96] Leigh Hunt, who also rated epic as the 'supreme species of poetry', had discovered a successful modern work in Keats's *The Fall of Hyperion*: 'The *Hyperion* is a fragment — a gigantic one, like a ruin in the desert, or the bones of the mastodon'.[97] The terms of this commendation may even have supplied Tennyson's 'The Epic' with an image: 'Why take the style of those heroic times? / For nature brings not back the Mastodon' (35 – 36). A further clue to the enduring epic tradition is afforded by a review of the revival of Dryden and Purcell's *King Arthur* in 1842, which followed Thelwall, and Scott's *Marmion*, in regretting Dryden's failure to complete his projected epic on the subject.[98] To be set against these favourable recommendations, however, is a persistent complaint that the 'general public' is neglectful of epic. As was expressed by W. J. Fox in his review of Tennyson's 1830 volume:

---

[95] John Thelwall, *The Peripatetic: or, Sketches of the Heart, of Nature and Society*, 3 vols (New York, 1978), II, 49.
[96] *TI*, 13 (July 1818), 41 – 42.
[97] 'Imagination and Fancy', *Indicator*, 2 and 9 August 1820; quoted in Theodore Redpath, *The Young Romantics and Critical Opinion 1807 – 1824* (1973), 497 – 99.
[98] *Illustrated London News*, 19 November 1842, 446.

The old epics will probably never be surpassed, any more than the old coats of mail; and for the same reason; nobody wants the article.[99]

With regard to Pennie, it was claimed by *Gentleman's Magazine* that the epic was currently the most unpopular of literary undertakings, whilst the *Literary Gazette* echoed this sentiment in its review of Lytton's *King Arthur*.[100] Three main reasons for this neglect were frequently cited. First came the charge of want of relevance to the modern age. On these grounds, Jeffrey attacked Keats's *Hyperion*:

> There is a fragment of a projected Epic, . . . of which we cannot advise the completion. For though there are passages of some force and grandeur, it is sufficiently obvious, from the specimen before us, that the subject is too far removed from all the sources of human interest, to be successfully treated by any modern author.[101]

The very phrasing here adumbrates John Sterling's later assault on Tennyson's use of the Excalibur legend; and Monckton Milnes was similarly coolly dismissive of the 'Morte' as revealing 'the archaeological character which must belong to all really epical poetry'.[102] Secondly, the elevated style in which epics were written was often held to be too imitative of previous epic poets, especially of Milton (see *Theatrical Inquisitor* on *Samor*), and the conventions of epic form were considered to act as deleterious constraints upon poetic freedom of expression (see Jeffrey on Barlow's *Columbiad*).[103] Finally, the sheer physical length of the epic was not thought to be conducive to being read by a large modern audience. Heber noted that an age 'which has rioted so much in the richness of original productions' looked with 'something more than weariness on the long and irregular narratives' which the previous century had taken pleasure in.[104] Moreover, an emphasis on intensity of emotional experience, and/or a densely metaphorical style in which every rift was loaded with ore, tended to favour the creation of shorter, very concentrated pieces. Such was Tennyson's frequent practice. He quarried subjects from Homeric epic ('The Lotos-Eaters', 'Ulysses') but through concentration on one character's emotional mood during a crucial period, presented a brilliantly vivid vignette. Of the projected 'Ballad of Sir Launcelot' only a 'Fragment' was published, and, of Everard Hall's epic only one book. The writing of 'fragments' had, since Coleridge, formed part of romantic tradition, and one adopted early by Tennyson in his juvenile poem

[99] *Westminster Review*, 14 (January 1831); reprinted in Jump ed. *Tennyson*, 23.
[100] *GM*, 103 (January 1833), 60. *Lit Gaz*, 3 February 1849, 75 – 76.
[101] *Edinburgh Review*, 34 (August 1820); reprinted in Redpath, *Young Romantics*, 497.
[102] *Westminster Review*, 38 (October 1842), 373.
[103] *Edinburgh Review*, 15 (October 1809), 24 – 40.
[104] *Quarterly*, 25 (July 1821), 428.

'The Coach of Death: A Fragment'. This construction of fragments is analogous to the building of Gothick ruins, and suggests an imitation of the incomplete relics of medieval poetry that had been recovered by literary scholarship. The incompleteness of the fragment, besides betraying a romantic fascination with the fragmentary relics of catastrophic change, also serves as a token of the modern romantic poem's reliance on an imaginative momentary inspiration, the passing of which leaves the poet unable to complete the poem through mere craftsmanship (see Coleridge's 'Kubla Khan'). Moreover, its apparent spontaneity and irregularity align it with early 'Spasmodic' verse (cf. Philip Bailey's Festus, 1839), which was usually inordinately long but whose digressiveness and internal psychological crises are essentially opposed to epic form. In his publication of an epic fragment, Tennyson — like Thelwall, Heber, Atherstone and others who published similarly entitled verse — could effect a compromise between the long narrative and the short, between an architectonically constructed heroic plot and a microcosmic examination of particularity. This decision to avoid a full-scale work was welcomed:

> We are not sorry that Mr. Tennyson has not given us a new edition of the Round Table [i.e. a work like that of Blackmore or the projected works by Dryden and Milton]. We like his fragments — if they are such — better than we fancy we should have liked the complete and canto-divided poem. There is a vigour in these efforts, which, perhaps, would have flagged under continuance.[105]

Tennyson later claimed that such was his purpose: he realised that if he 'meant to make any mark at all, it must be by shortness'.[106]

Intensely aware of the possibilities latent in various forms, as well as being hypersensitive to the least suspicion of adverse criticism, Tennyson did not wholly abandon his epic form, but fitted it within a contemporary frame. It is difficult therefore to accept the accuracy of Tennyson's later statement to Allingham that the plan for an Arthurian epic was abandoned on account of Sterling's review, since the frame was written long before this, in 1837 – 1838, and the frame itself signifies a break, whether temporary or final, in the writing of the epic. It is to style rather than content that 'The Epic' addresses itself. Assuming that the epic contains 'a truth', the colloquial introductory passages suggest that 'the fashion of the day' may be the necessary medium for communication. Of the 'heroic times', it is the style, 'the faint Homeric echoes', for which apology is made; and the accentuation of the verse's tonal qualities enhances the preoccupation with form: the 'hollow oes and aes' and 'the tone with which he read'. But form is ultimately transient; as the 'old

---

105 Christian Teacher, NS 4 (October 1842), 415.
106 Hallam Tennyson, Memoir, I, 166.

order changeth, yielding place to new', a new form is provided for Arthur ('like a modern gentleman / Of stateliest port'), a form which is 'thrice as fair', but which nevertheless embodies a continuity of inner truth: it is Arthur, and not another, who is come again — 'he cannot die'. The provision of such a framing device was, of course, not confined to Arthurian poetry: Tennyson employs a similar technique for the fairytale story in 'The Day Dream', also in about 1837 – 1838, whilst the medieval legend of 'Godiva' is prefaced by four lines recounting the author's genesis of the poem in Coventry. There had been, too, a significant precedent in Scott's construction of *The Lay of the Last Minstrel* and *The Bridal of Triermain*, where the device had met with divergent critical responses. The *Critical Review* had welcomed this 'mode of introducing romantic and fabulous narratives':

> It attaches a degree of dramatic interest to the work, and at the same time softens / the absurdity of a Gothic legend by throwing it to a greater distance from the relation and auditor, by representing it, not as a train of facts which actually took place, but as a mere fable either adopted by the credulity of former times, or invented for the purposes of amusement and the exercise of the imagination. [107]

In contrast, the *Eclectic Review*, although praising the Arthurian section, thought that the 'introductory poems' were 'too long and not in harmony with the tale: nor have they intrinsic merit sufficient to recompense for their intrusion'. [108]

Tennyson must have hoped that his frame would palliate possible hostility towards the 'Morte'; and Monckton Milnes certainly accepted 'The Epic' in this spirit: it 'succeeds in gracefully linking on the old English story to present English domestic life'. [109] So, too, did George Gilfillan, who disclosed how 'the feelings of a bygone age' (as evinced by Arthur's death) had a meaning 'deeply significant to us', and that the closing incidents in 'The Epic' asserted the link between past and present, and 'spread a rich mellowness of tint over the whole'. [110] Notwithstanding these appreciations, Henry Chorley considered the frame to be merely one of the new 'crotchets' which had vitiated the contents of the 1842 volumes. [111] Leigh Hunt, too, condemned what he took to be 'the studious airs of indifference' with which the poem was introduced. Hunt's review is, once again, *au fond* a disparagement of Tennyson's genre, for Hunt's complaint is that the 'Morte'

---

[107] *CR*, 4th Series, 3 (May 1813), 474 – 75.
[108] *Eclectic*, 10 (October 1813), 377.
[109] *Westminster*, 38 (October 1842), 373.
[110] *Tait's*, NS 9 (August 1842), 505.
[111] *Athenaeum*, 6 August 1842, 700 – 02.

treats the modes and feelings of one generation in the style of another, always a thing fatal, unless it be reconciled with something of self-banter in the course of the poem itself, or the mixture of light with grave, as in Pulci and others. The impossibility of a thorough earnestness must, somehow or other, be self-acknowledged.[112]

Although Tennyson's critics have not hitherto done so, Hunt's critique must be evaluated within the context of the burlesque traditions described in Chapter 3. It is true that Hunt's earlier *The Story of Rimini* (1816) had not been narrated with deliberate irony, but he had evidently altered his approach by 1832 when he published 'A Gentle Armour', which was based on Way's translation of the fabliau *Three Knights and a Smock*, for, in contrast to Way, Hunt introduces a wrily mock-heroic tone:

> Arms and a vest I sing, which meant in blame,
> His glorious hauberk to a knight became,
> And in the field such dire belabouring bore,
> As gentle linen never stood before   (1 – 4)

His strictures against Tennyson, requiring that the latter should write an ironic or a medley poem — such as Moultrie's *La Belle Tryamour* — is evidence of the strength of the comic conventions so often governing the use of Arthurian material in the early nineteenth century — which had shaped Tennyson's early draft for 'The Ballad of Sir Launcelot', and which, though absent from the four published Arthurian poems, had been introduced into 'The Epic' frame, albeit unnoticed by Hunt.[113]

In fine, critical reception was generally much more concerned with genre than with the question of an Arthurian subject. A similar concern for genre is evident in Tennyson's continual experiment with the various possible forms his Arthurian poetry would take. There is, clearly, considerable overlap between Tennyson's practice — especially in his drafts — and that of his immediate predecessors and contemporaries, and in critical reaction to the work of all. Tennyson's poetry was often reviewed very favourably: but when it was not, the reason for this may often be attributed to the fact that his abandonment of projected allegorical and burlesque poems laid him open to attack by critics whose perception of the manner in which an Arthurian story

---

[112] Quoted in Jump ed. *Tennyson*, 132.
[113] The expectation that a modern work would treat its Arthurian subject humorously is evident in the *Illustrated London News* review of Lytton's *King Arthur*. *ILN* indicates that readers who were aware of the 'vigorous satire' in Lytton's previous poem, *The New Timon*,

> may, probably, have been misled by the first announcement of the present work . . . in which they may have expected the hero of farcical renown, rather than him of fairy legend and knightly song.

ILN, 25 March 1848, 200.

should be told was largely governed by the standard contemporary procedures from which Tennyson had diverged.

That Tennyson's poetry was initially thought to be idiosyncratic is attested by much critical comment from his contemporaries. That the nature of his achievement was often apparent even to his detractors may also be seen in contemporary reviews. His failure to provide an allegory for John Sterling or an Italian medley poem for Leigh Hunt has already been noted. Even keener was the critical perception that Tennyson's poetry, in not being 'reflective', did not supply sufficient authorial comment. There is, for instance, the discarding by Tennyson, on Arthur Hallam's advice, of the footnotes that had been planned to accompany the 1832 volume.[114] Tennyson's 1827 collection had, as was common practice, provided notes and epigraphs in abundance to reveal scholarly sources and analogues. Their removal allows the Tennyson poem greater autonomy, by not being explicitly linked to precedents and parallel incidents. Separated thus from an exterior corpus of knowledge, which might be needed for its interpretation, the poem is required to furnish its own meaning. The resulting complaint of Tennyson's 'obscurity' (particularly in 'The Lady of Shalott') was voiced by, amongst others, Croker in the Quarterly and Jerdan in the Literary Gazette whilst the Spectator disliked his 'puzzling' allegory and Blackwood's his 'intolerable vagueness'.[115] British Quarterly Review, after complaining that 'The Lady of Shalott' was 'so obscurely told' that the reviewer 'would on no account' take upon himself 'the responsibility of giving the briefest summary of it', assessed the kindred quality of 'Mariana' with considerable acuity:

> In this there are, without doubt, very graphic touches, but we feel ourselves abruptly plunged amongst details, which we have to put together for ourselves in the best manner we are able. An effect is produced as if the several objects had been cut out of a picture, and the brilliant fragments were thrown at hap-hazard before us.[116]

The absence of a foregrounded narrator was thus felt to be disorienting in a manner comparable to encountering a lack of perspective or conventional composition in a painting. This identical quality, however, whereby orthodox methods of comprehension were powerless to interpret the poem, appealed to some of the poem's advocates. J. S. Mill, for example, acknowledged that the 'precise nature of the enchantment' remained a 'mystery', but one 'which no-one would press to explain', and Edgar Allan Poe discovered in Tennyson an admirable proponent of his own aesthetic theories:

---

[114] 'You may put a note or two if you will, yet Milton did not to Paradise Lost': Hallam Tennyson, Memoir, I, 90.
[115] Spectator, 4 June 1842, 544. Blackwood's, 65 (April 1849), 458.
[116] BQR, 2 (August 1845), 62.

There are some passages in his works which rivet a conviction I had long
entertained, that the indefinite is an element in the true *poiesis*. Why do
some persons fatigue themselves in endeavours to unravel such phantasy
pieces as 'The Lady of Shalott'? As well unweave the *ventum textilem*.[117]

The same view was advanced by Manley Hopkins: 'The Lady of Shalott', he
claims,

is pure sensuous poetry. We forbear to ask too closely what hidden
meanings dwell in its misty dreaminess. We would not for the world
break our toy to discover its concealed music.[118]

In 1850, Charles Kingsley recalled how, fifteen years previously, 'The Lady of
Shalott' had come as a 'revelation', and he detected Tennyson's contribution
to a restoration of the qualities originally found in traditional balladry:

We are never jarred in them as we are in all the attempts at ballad
writing and ballad-restoring before Mr Tennyson's time, by discordant
touches of the reflective in thought, the picturesque in nature, or the
theatric in action . . . While the new poetaster informs you of the
abstract notion, the ancient poet gives you the concrete fact; as Mr
Tennyson has done with wonderful art in his exquisite 'St Agnes', where
the saint's subjective mysticism appears only as embodied in objective
pictures.[119]

The Tennyson poem was thus seen by contemporary critics as belonging to a
poetry of enactment rather than of comment, the poet retracting his role but
casting 'his own spirit into any living thing, real or imaginary' (Fox, 1831),
and 'embodying himself' in 'moods of character' (Hallam, 1831), with the
'faculty of self-absorption in the identity of other idiosyncracies' (Horne,
1844). This perceived difference from conventional authorial strategies by
which the poetic action is 'related' (in the sense of 'narrated' and 'connected')
to the reader is not accompanied by a transposition into a dramatic mode
whereby the created characters talk solely to each other, or to the reader in
dramatic soliloquy. In Tennyson, the situation concurs more readily with J. S.

[117] John Stuart Mill, 'Poems Chiefly Lyrical', *London Review*, I, (July 1835); reprinted in Jump
ed. *Tennyson*, 88. Edgar Allan Poe, 'Marginalia', *United States Magazine and Democratic Review*, 15
(December 1844), 580.
[118] *The Times*, 12 October 1848, 3.
[119] *Fraser's*, 42 (September 1850); reprinted in Jump ed, *Tennyson*, 174.

Mill's definition of poetry as opposed to eloquence, in that the latter is 'heard', whereas poetry is 'overheard'.[120]

If there is much evidence of Tennyson's apparent apartness from much contemporary practice, there is a corresponding tendency to see Tennyson's poetry as completely hermetic, rarefied, highly polished and introvert. Such accusations were made: John Sterling detected a lack of human interest, and Francis Garden claimed that Tennyson 'seldom penetrates to the heart' because he, like Keats, separates 'the world' from 'the actings of the imagination'.[121] H. M. McCluhan's more recent focus on the perspicuity of Arthur Hallam's critique has been followed by a critical realignment that has stressed Tennyson's affinities with the symbolists: D. J. Palmer has emphasised Tennyson's ambivalence and his technique of 'suspending in symbolic form the tensions and divisions of his mind'; John Dixon Hunt has written on Tennyson's iconic distancing; William E. Buckler on the 'symbolist aesthetic' in 'Morte d'Arthur'; and the present book has given additional support to these readings. But, although Tennyson's techniques have been well-described as 'pre-symbolist', one cannot convincingly make a complete Mallarmé of him.[122] Though Tennyson discarded what were often assumed to be relating devices, he established his own procedure for efficient communication. In his poetry the pictorial image is generally crucial, and its attractiveness was frequently admired. Forster's *True Sun* review noted the 'scenic picturing' in 'The Lady of Shalott', Mill the power of 'scene-painting' therein, and Forster again 'the picturesque truth' of the language of the 'Morte'.[123] But, whilst Tennyson selects his placenames from romance and does not specify, say, a Cornish or Somerset location, the landscape he evoked nevertheless belonged, as Mill said, 'to the actual world', or, as more precisely expressed by Kingsley, to the scenery 'which he can see in every parish in England', whether the long fields of barley or the pale yellow woods waning in

---

[120] 'Thoughts on Poetry and Its Varieties' (1833, revised 1859); reprinted in *English Critical Essays; Nineteenth Century*, edited by Edmund D. Jones (1947), 347.

[121] Francis Garden (?), 'Poems', *Christian Remembrancer*, 1 (July 1842); reprinted in Jump ed. *Tennyson*, 102.

[122] H. M. McCluhan, 'Tennyson and Picturesque Poetry' (1951); reprinted in *Critical Essays on the Poetry of Tennyson*, edited by John Killham (1960), 67 – 85. D. J. Palmer, 'Tennyson's Romantic History'; in *Tennyson*, edited by D. J. Palmer (1973), 23 – 51. John Dixon Hunt, 'The Poetry of Distance: Tennyson's *Idylls of the King*'; in *Victorian Poetry*, edited by Malcolm Bradbury and David Palmer (1972), 89 – 121. William E. Buckler, *The Victorian Imagination* (Brighton, 1980), 177.

[123] *True Sun*, 19 January 1833, 3; quoted in Edgar Finley Shannon, Jr, *Tennyson and the Reviewers* (Cambridge, Mass., 1952), 18. Mill in *London Review*. Forster in *Examiner*.

the stormy east wind.[124] As has often been noted, this scenery pictured with such fresh precision and supported by rich auditory effects is not a purely decorative phenomenon, for these landscapes are also landscapes of the spirit, embodying the feelings aroused in the poem, reflecting back the emotions projected by the situation within the poem. The external simulacrum provides an immediate credibility and a relevance to normal life, as it is commonly experienced; mentally and internally, the 'scenery' is, in Mill's phrase, 'in keeping with some state of human feeling'; or, in Horne's, it shows 'the loveliness of the truth seen through the medium of such emotion as belongs to the subject he has in hand'. Because recent critics have given little attention to the concept of feeling in Tennyson's poetry, the importance of this quality for his earlier critics requires recognition. The emphasis here laid on feeling by Mill and Horne may be supported, too, by Tennyson's high valuation of the faculty: 'true feeling', he wrote in 1833, 'is all that is really valuable on the windy side of the grave'.[125]

It is noteworthy that for each of his four Arthurian poems Tennyson chose a personal name, or names, as title, and thereby broke with the frequent practice of giving an impersonal title like 'The Funeral Boat', 'The Fairy Bride' or 'A Legend of Tintagel Castle'. This marked interest in human character (and other poems had dealt with a wide range of personalities, from St Simeon Stylites to the Gardener's Daughter) focuses less on character as revealed in public action than on the private world of feeling, intensified and crystallised at a pre-climactic moment. And just as no effective climax and practical outcome is achieved, so neither is this concentration on feeling directed, as in Wordsworth, at moral or epistemological rewards for the emotional sensibility. There is less speech than soliloquy, and Tennyson's characters move in an essential solitariness: there is, for example, the Tennysonian originality of declaring that Excalibur was wrought by the 'lonely' maiden of the Lake. Malory's Sir Bedivere could be dismayed by the practical consideration that he was being left alone among his 'enemyes': in practice, he joins a society of monks. But Tennyson's knight contemplates not physical danger but a spiritual alienation — 'companionless, . . . / Among new men, strange faces, other minds'. There was early critical recognition, too, of Tennyson's perspicuity in portraying feminine characters, and this faculty was especially apt, for the role of women was often seen as essentially circumscribed and private. Each poem, then, commandingly communicates a 'private' emotion — which is nonetheless universal — in particular, a frustrated sense of longing or of regret, romantic passionate love, religious aspiration or a mood of heroic melancholy. There is intensity in the very human concern, the cry

---

[124] *Fraser's*, 42 (September 1850), 245 – 55; reprinted in Jump ed. *Tennyson*.
[125] Hallam Tennyson, *Memoir*, I, 101.

> that shivered to the tingling stars,
> And, as it were one voice, an agony
> Of lamentation, like a wind, that shrills
> All night in a waste land, where no one comes,
> Or hath come, since the making of the world.   (199 – 203)

And the human feeling thus evoked, over the old order yielding place to new, bridges the gap between past, and/or mythic, time and Tennyson's own period. As was testified by Kingsley:

> We can trust him with the Past, for he has discovered the great historic secret of finding the Present in the Past, and embodying in outwardly obsolete legends eternal truths which shall stand good to the end of time.[126]

Kingsley's article shows him, too, to have discovered the secret. Others required longer.

The Influence of Tennyson's Early Arthurian Poems

The essential privacy of Tennyson's poetic expression had as concomitant his avoidance of any formulation of his general literary theory or a close explication of his own poetry. Some measure of Tennyson's isolation from current cultural fashions may also be gauged by his lack of impact on other Arthurian poetry within the period.

   To determine proof of his direct influence is difficult. Henry Alford, one of Tennyson's associates at Cambridge, would have known the lines in 'The Palace of Art' (written between October 1831 and April 1832) which refer to Pendragon's deepwounded child's dozing on 'sloping greens' in the valley of Avilion. These lines may have encouraged Alford's own Arthurian interests (see Chapter 2), and led to his description of Arthur's charmed slumber in 'the westward-sloping vale of Avalon' in *The School of the Heart* (written between 1831 and 1835). But since Alford had family connections in the Glastonbury area, and because his poem is ultimately very different from Tennyson's, no direct influence can be proved. Both poems could have arisen from a common source, perhaps known and discussed by other members of their Cambridge circle. As Tennyson's poems were circulated in manuscript at Cambridge, even after his departure, it is possible that a Young England figure like Beresford-Hope, who was at Trinity from 1837 to 1841, could have known of them, and that this might have influenced his own adoption of Arthur as

---

[126] 'Recent Poetry and Recent Verse', *Fraser's*, 39 (May 1849), 570.

chivalrous Messiah. Moreover, the insertion of Arthurian legends into the second edition of his poem 'Prester John' in 1843 may be attributed to the publication of Tennyson's work in 1842, for the first edition in 1841 had lacked these references. However, Beresford-Hope also drew on the ballad and topographical traditions so confirmation of Tennyson's influence is not available. Again, it is likely that Horne owed his title of 'The Three Knights of Camelott' to Tennyson's use of that placename in 'The Lady of Shalott' and 'Morte d'Arthur'; and it is certain that this latter was the subject of Aytoun's parody in October 1843. A note of Lowell's draws on Malory for illustration of the Grail legend, but as he also reveals that 'Tennyson has made Sir Galahad the subject of one of the most exquisite of his poems' it is very probable that Tennyson's choice of hero influenced Lowell's choice of subject, and that the nineteenth century aspects of Tennyson's knight had affected his treatment of Launfal. On the other hand, Emerson, who reviewed Tennyson sympathetically in 1842, owed nothing to Tennyson in his 'Merlin' poems; and Bulwer Lytton, a hostile reviewer of Tennyson in 1832, and the instigator of a public quarrel with him in 1845, denied any indebtedness to Tennyson over the *King Arthur*. 'I have', Lytton wrote, 'filled no pitcher' from his 'fountains'.[127] Nor was Tennyson mentioned in Dyce's plans for Arthurian frescoes in the House of Lords in the late 1840s.

Further corroboration of Tennyson's dearth of immediate influence is also afforded by the treatment of Arthurian themes in painting and book illustration. Of the relevant twenty-six graphic works, seven were based on medieval literature, six on theatrical performances, seven on contemporary poetry (three on Scott's *Bridal*, and one each on Bannerman, Leigh, Peacock's *Round Table*, and the anonymous 'Merlin and the Knight'), two on Malory, and four others on miscellaneous sources, but none on Tennyson.[128] Of the twenty-two paintings associated with such themes, only two works certainly derive from a Tennysonian source. Five probably had their source in Malory; three in Spenser; two in Chaucer; one each in Ariosto, Dryden, Lytton, the Welsh triads, and the French Tristan legends; whilst two more were based on the historical tradition and three others

---

[127] Lytton, *King Arthur* (1870), vi. Lytton's unpublished draft (Hertford County Record Office, ref. D/EK W21) for the 1870 preface had elaborated upon the differences between his own poetry and Tennyson's. These differences centre upon Lytton's preoccupation with writing a 'National Poem' which incorporates a 'Saxon element'; and his claim that, unlike his own work, Tennyson's is 'uniformly grave and stately. He admits none of the playfulness to be found in the Fabliasts'.

[128] See Appendix E.

derived from topography.[129] The two that were inspired by Tennyson were both American, and both took 'The Lady of Shalott' as subject. Sophia Peabody, later the wife of Nathaniel Hawthorne, made her 'sketch' in about 1839, and Christopher Pearse Cranch his 'scene' in 1844.[130] That it should have been America that first provided these works of art suggests that the weakness of inherited literary traditions there allowed Tennyson's poetry to find a readier welcome. Additionally, since America had no Arthurian topographical sites, no local Arthurian folklore, no chronicle tradition, and lacked — if not disliked — the British interest in Arthur as a national hero (see the *North American Review* criticism of *Samor*), American literature was consequently drawn towards the literary romance rather than the historico-topographical, and the fame of Tennyson benefited from this orientation.

Although a study of Tennyson's influence after 1850 lies outside the strict scope of this book, a brief survey may usefully indicate both how Tennyson's Arthurian poems were to be taken up by other writers, and also how Tennyson's own treatment of Arthurian themes would significantly alter. During the 1840s in England, Tennyson's Arthurian work was still marginal to the main development but, by the mid-1850s, his influence is apparent on a number of major figures in poetry, painting and graphic design. In 1850 Holman Hunt made his first sketch of *The Lady of Shalott*; 1852 saw the exhibition of Robert Scott Lauder's *The Lady of Shalott* at the Royal Scottish Academy, and the first set of book illustrations — a set of twelve by an amateur 'Lady' of Nottingham.[131] In 1853 James Smetham's *The Lady of Shalott* was submitted, albeit unsuccessfully, to the Royal Academy, and in the following year John Everett Millais made his drawing on the same theme.[132] Mrs Craik's prose tale 'Avillion' placed a quotation from the 'Morte' as epigraph to the opening chapter; and in the same year Edward Burne-Jones (then twenty) was writing to his friend Cormell Price, 'Learn "Sir Galahad"

---

[129] See Appendix D.

[130] See letters from Elizabeth Peabody to William J. Rolfe, and from George William Curtis to John S. Dwight, in John Colin Eidson, *Tennyson in America* (Athens, Georgia, 1943), 40, 212n, 220n.

[131] *William Holman Hunt: Catalogue of the Walker Art Gallery Exhibition* (Liverpool, 1969), 69 – 70. Cat. no. of Lauder was 405: cf. also *Art Journal* (1854), 106. *The Lady of Shalott*, illustrated by A Lady (Nottingham, 1852).

[132] *Letters of James Smetham*, edited by Sarah Smetham and William Davies (1891), 49. *Millais: An Exhibition organised by the Walker Art Gallery and the Royal Academy of Arts, London* (1967), cat. no. 347, pl. 20. Eidson (112, 239n) claims that Tennyson's 'Morte' was the model for Henry B. Hirst's 'Lancelot of the Lake', *Sartain's Union Magazine*, 10 (January 1852), 6 – 7; but the intense aura of enchantment and time-travelling in the latter poem indicates a closer affinity with the conventional poems described in Chapter 4 than with Tennyson. The poem is not listed by Northup *et al.*

by heart. He is to be the patron of our Order'.[133] A characteristically Tennysonian colouring may be discerned in the blank verse poems of Owen Meredith (1853); and, in the same year, Ford Madox Brown and Dante Gabriel Rossetti were discussing the possibility of illustrating the 'Morte'.[134]

An important aspect of Tennyson's achievement was that his adoption of Malorian material would encourage the Pre-Raphaelite writers and artists to employ the stories in *Le Morte Darthur* as an indirect means of expressing a range of powerful personal and emotional complexities. Yet, although Tennyson was to prove a major influence upon Pre-Raphaelitism (particularly through his minutely detailed scenery charged with human emotion, and its hypnotic fixity pregnant with symbolic inference), he would himself develop and modify the direction of his own poetry, which would move considerably towards a more conventional approach. The 'Epic' frame had signalled a very explicit contemporary relevance and had approached an authorial attribution (via Everard Hall). In other Tennyson verse of the later 1830s, he was displaying a greater interest in fixing his poetry upon a particular and actual location, as in 'The Golden Year', written at Llanberis in 1839, which includes mention of a climb in Snowdonia, and the sound of blasting in the local slate quarries. A revived interest in writing his major Arthurian poem led him, like others in the antiquarian tradition, to Cornwall in order to visit Tintagel at first hand, and to search for King Arthur's Stone at Camelford in the summer of 1848. On this expedition he met the local poet Henry Sewell Stokes, and paid a visit to R. S. Hawker at Morwenstow, whence he departed 'carrying a pile of books and manuscripts', amongst them R. J. King's *The*

---

[133] Mrs Clark (= Dinah Maria Mulock), 'Avillion; or, The Happy Isles', chapter 1; in *Romantic Tales* (1853). Georgiana Burne-Jones, *Memorials of Edward Burne-Jones*, 2 vols (1904), I, 77.

[134] Of four Arthurian poems by Owen Meredith (= Edward Robert Bulwer Lytton, the son of the author of *King Arthur* and 'The Fairy Bride'), one treats of Guenevere as beauty ('Queen Guenevere'), another describes a king's death-voyage to Avalon ('King Hermandiaz'), another is a version of the Elaine of Astolat story ('Elayne le Blanc'), whilst the remaining one ('The Parting of Launcelot and Guenevere') shows evidence of a Tennysonian idiom: for example, in the sub-title 'A Fragment' and in style:

> So he stood
> Long in his mind divided: with himself
> At strife . . .
> When all the estates were met, and noble judges,
> Arm'd clean with shields, set round to keep the right,
> Before you sitting throned with Galahault
> In great array, on fair green quilts of samyte,
> Rich, ancient, fringed with gold, seven summer days,
> And all before the Earls of Northgalies,
> Such service then with this old sword was wrought   (124 – 58)

Owen Meredith, *Poems*, 2 vols (Boston, Mass., 1875), II. *The Diary of Ford Madox Brown*, edited by Virginia Surtees (New Haven, 1981), 130.

Fairy Mythology of Tintagel.[135] A journal that he was keeping at the time reveals that on the excursion he was reading William Penaluna's *An Historical Survey of the County of Cornwall* (1838), a very unremarkable historical survey, with scant Arthurian reference, but which indicates that he was consulting topographical sources.[136] An unpublished poem of about 1856, probably written on a visit to Wales, establishes the Welshness of Arthur in a way that was new to Tennyson, who had hitherto seemed very remote from the Welsh Revival: 'Land of stream and mountain peak, / Land of Arthur and Taliessin'.[137] Prefacing *Idylls of the King* in manuscript was a historical note on Arthur as a sixth century hero, and, in the composition of the note, Tennyson had drawn on the antiquarian tradition, just as he read works such as Edward Davies's *Mythology of the British Druids*, a copy of which he was given in 1846. The *Idylls* would employ a number of conventional strategies that the earlier Tennyson had forgone, such as the use of a real geography (see Almesbury, Bude and Bos in *Guinevere*, 1859) and a chronological time-scheme (see 'When the Roman left us' in *Guinevere*) and there was again a drift towards moral allegory evinced by the provisional subtitle: *the True and the False.*

This later career of Tennyson indicates that much of his early idiosyncracy, which separated him from the work of many of his contemporaries, appears correspondingly more individual in the light of his later development. The achievement of his early Arthurian poems thus marks a moment in, and not a permanent condition of, the Arthurian Revival.

---

[135] See Tennyson's journal entry:
    June 30th . . . Called on Mr Stokes.
    July 3rd. Went with candles into great cave, round the rock thro' surf. Mr S bore me on his back thro' surf.
Hallam Tennyson, *Materials for a Life of Alfred Tennyson*, 4 vols (1894 – 1895), I, 354. The passage was not included in the published *Memoir*. Richard John King was a celebrated scholar whose edition of early ballads — including Arthurian ones — appeared in 1842, and has been noted above. I cannot, however, trace his work on Tintagel. The source for this reference is Byles, *Life of Hawker*, 194.
[136] Hallam Tennyson, *Memoir*, I, 276.
[137] 'Harp, harp, the voice of Cymry', ll.6 – 7.

Appendix A

List of Poetry, Drama and Prose Fiction Concerned with the Arthurian Legends

Key

P = Poetry, D = Drama, F = Prose Fiction.
* denotes that the item has not previously been listed by Northup and Parry, Tillotson, Eggers, or Taylor and Brewer.
For information on reviews, I have frequently consulted William S. Ward, *Literary Reviews in British Periodicals 1798 – 1826: A Bibliography*, 3 vols (New York, 1972 – 1977).

Alford, Henry. 'The Ballad of Glastonbury' and *'Sonnet XIV.Glastonbury' (P). In *The School of the Heart and other poems*, 2 vols (London: Longman, and Cambridge: Deighton, 1835). The title poem also includes a *reference (Lesson the sixth. ll. 340 – 42) to Arthur in vale of Avalon. Review: *Monthly Repository*, 10 (1836), 324.

Anonymous. *Merlin's Cave; or, Harlequin's Masquerade* (D). Performed at Royal Amphitheatre, 11 April 1814. Announced in *The Times*, 12 April 1814, 3, as an 'entire new Comic Pantomime'.

——————. *'Bwrdd Arthur; or, the Institution of King Arthur's Round Table. A fragment from the original British' (P). In *Cambro-Briton*, 2 (1821), 181 – 82.

——————. *'Merlin Redivivus' (P). In *Monmouthshire Merlin*, 23 May 1829, 4.

——————. *'Merlin's Prophecy for the Year 1831' (P). In *Monthly Magazine*, NS 11 (January 1831), 1 – 3; reprinted in *Carmarthen Journal*, 7 January 1831, 4; and in *Monmouthshire Merlin*, 8 January 1831, 4.

——————. *'The Legend of Shewin' Shiels' (P). In *Metrical Legends of Northumberland*, edited by James Service (Alnwick: printed and sold by W. Davison, 1834).

——————. * *Ye Seconde Parte of ye Tragycall Hystorie of Thomas Thumbe* (D). Performed at English Opera House, 12 June 1840. British Library Add MS 42955, ff 940 – 974b (March – June 1840). Reviews: *Athenaeum*, 13 June 1840, 483; *Examiner*, 14 June 1840, 371.

——————. * *Harlequin and Good Kynge Arthur, or the Enchanter Merlin and the Queene of Faery Land* (D). Performed at Sadler's Wells, 26 December 1842. Reviews: *Illustrated London News*, 31 December 1842, 539; *Literary Gazette*, 31 December 1842, 910; *The Times*, 27 December 1842, 5.

——————. *'The Ylle Cutt Mantell; A Romaunt of the Tyme of Gud Kynge Arthur. Done into modern English from an authentic version' (P). In *United States Magazine and Democratic Review*, 14 (May 1844), 465 – 76.

——————. *Jack the Giant Killer, or the Knights of the Round Table* (D). Performed at Royal Surrey Theatre, 13 April 1846. BL Add MS 42992, ff 679 – 710 (Feb – April 1846). Nicoll gives 13 February for the first performance, but the play was announced as a new piece for the Easter holiday-makers. Reviews: *Examiner*, 18 April 1846, 246; *Illustrated London News*, 11 April 1846, 243; and 25 April 1846, 274.

——————. *'Merlin and the Knight' (P). In *The Rose; or Affection's Gift for 1848*, 134 – 35. New York.

Aytoun, William Edmonstoune (= 'Bon Gaultier'). *'La Mort d'Arthur. A fragment. Not by Alfred Tennyson' (P). In *Tait's Edinburgh Magazine*, NS 10 (October 1843), 651 – 52. Included in 'Bon Gaultier', *The Book of Ballads*, second edition (1849).

Bannerman, Anne *'The Prophecy of Merlin' (P). In *Tales of Superstition and Chivalry* (London: Vernon and Hood, 1802). Published anonymously. Reviews: *Annual Review*, 1 (1802), 720 – 21; *British Critic*, 21 (January 1803), 78 – 79; *Critical Review*, 2nd Series, 38 (May 1803), 110 – 13; *Monthly Mirror*, 15 (February 1803), 102 – 03; *New Annual Register*, 23 (1802), 318; *Poetical Register*, 2 (1802), 431 – 32.

Beresford-Hope, Alexander James. *'A Dream' (P). There are also Arthurian allusions in *'Prester John' (ll. 53 – 54); *'A Vision of Babylon' (ll. 1 – 7); and *'Winchester' (ll. 1 – 4). In *Poems*, second edition (London: Rivingtons, 1843).

Boyle, John Magor. *Gorlaye, or A Tale of the Olden Tyme* (P). (London: Baldwin and Cradock, 1835).

Bray, Edward Atkyns. *'To Merlin' (P). Included in 'Commemorative Distichs and Other Inscriptions, intended for and partly inscribed on the Rocks of Bairdown, Dartmoor', and dedicated to his father, 18 October 1806. In *Poetical Remains, Social, Sacred and Miscellaneous*, edited by Mrs Bray, 2 vols (London: Longman, 1859), II.

Buchanan, Robert, 'Merlin's Tomb' (P). In *Glasgow University Album for 1838* (Glasgow: Richardson), 1 – 9.

——————. 'Arthur's Weird' (P). In *Glasgow University Album for 1840*, 46 – 52. Both poems were signed 'B'. 'Merlin's Tomb' was later included in Robert Buchanan, *Tragic Dramas from History*, 2 vols (Edinburgh, 1868), and both were included in the anonymous *Fragments of the Table Round* (Glasgow, 1859). Critics have often confused this author (1785 – 1873) with Robert Williams Buchanan (1841 – 1901), and do not note the appearance of the poems before 1859. The 1838 volume also contains *'Sonnet, to a Fountain in a Cave', which has a reference to Merlin (ll. 7 – 8).

C.. *'St. Michael's Mount' (P). In *Fisher's Drawing Room Scrapbook* (1832), 11 – 12. Reprinted in G. N. Wright ed, *People's Gallery of Engravings*, 3 vols (London: Fisher, 1845 – 1846), II, 53 – 54.

Cookson, Christopher. *Glastonbury Abbey: A Poem* (P) (Taunton: Bragg, 1828). Published anonymously. For attribution, see Robert Arnold Aubin, *Topographical Poetry in Eighteenth Century England* (New York, 1936), 363; and my Chapter 1. note 30. Review: *Monthly Review*, 3rd Series, 11 (1829), 119 – 20.

Costello, Louisa Stuart. *'A Dream' (P). In *The Maid of the Cyprus Isle, and other Poems* (London: Sherwood, Neely and Jones, 1815).

——————. *'The Funeral Boat. A Legend' (P). In *Forget Me Not* (1829), 185 – 92. Review: *Literary Gazette*, 11 October 1828, 642 – 43.

——————. *'The Legend' (P). In *A Summer amongst the Bocages and the Vines*, 2 vols (London: Bentley, 1840), I, 297 – 301. Review: *Quarterly*, 68 (June 1841), 57 – 87.

Darley, George. *'Merlin's Last Prophecy' (P). In *Athenaeum*, 14 July 1838, 495 – 96. Signed 'G.D.'. Assigned to Darley by Claude Colleer Abbott, *The Life and Letters of George Darley, poet and critic* (London, 1928), 89.

Davies, Henry. *'The Enchanted Shield. A Round-Table Adventure' (F). In *Stories of Chivalry and Romance* (London: Longman, Rees, Orme, Brown and Green, 1827), 149 – 209. Published anonymously. Author identified in *Carmarthen Journal* review. Reviews: *Cambrian Quarterly Magazine*, 1 (1829), 368 – 78; *Carmarthen Journal*, 31 August 1827, 4; *Literary Gazette*, 3 March 1827, 136; *Literary Magnet*, NS 3 (1827), 196.

De Vere, Aubrey. 'King Henry II at the Tomb of King Arthur' (P). In *The Waldenses or the Fall of Rora: a Lyrical Sketch, with other poems* (Oxford: Parker, 1842). Northup and Parry, Eggers, and Taylor and Brewer list no edition earlier than 1884.

Dibdin, Charles Isaac Mungo. *Wizard's Wake: or, Harlequin and Merlin* (D). Performed at Sadler's Wells, 23 August 1802. *Plot, Songs, Chorusses, & Co. in the comic pantomime called 'Wizards Wake: or, Harlequin and Merlin'* (London: Glendinning, 1803).

Dibdin, Thomas John. *Merlin's Mount; or, Harlequin Cymraeg and the Living Leek* (D). Performed at Sadler's Wells, 26 December 1825. Review: *The Times*, 27 December 1825, 3.

Ellerton, John Lodge. *Triermain* (1831). An operetta which was apparently not performed, Listed by Nicoll, IV, 92n.

Ellylles. 'The Grave of King Arthur' (P). In *Cambrian Quarterly Magazine*, 2 (July 1830), 276 – 77. Northup and Parry incorrectly assign this to John Jenkins (?), and list only its appearance in John Jenkins ed. *The Poetry of Wales* (London, 1873).

Emerson, Ralph Waldo. 'Arthur's Dream' (P). Uncompleted work of (?) 1821 – 1822. In *The Journals and Miscellaneous Notebooks of Ralph Waldo Emerson*, edited by W. H. Gilman *et al*, 16 vols (Cambridge, Mass., 1960), I, 188.

————. 'Merlin I', 'Merlin II' (P). In *Poems* (London: Chapman, Brothers, 1846). Reviews: *Athenaeum*, 6 February 1847, 144 – 46; *Democratic Review*, 20 (May 1847), 396.

Frere, John Hookham. *The Monks and the Giants* (P). First published as *Prospectus and Specimen of an Intended National Work*, by William and Robert Whistlecraft (London: Murray, 1817 – 1818). Reviews: *British Critic*, NS 8 (October 1817), 396 – 99; *Edinburgh Magazine and Literary Miscellany (Scots Magazine)*, NS 3 (August 1818), 162 – 64; *Gentleman's Magazine*, 89 (September 1819), 247 – 48; *Literary Gazette*, 20 June 1817, 35 – 37; and 386 – 88; *Monthly Magazine*, 46 (August 1819), 57; *Monthly Review*, 85 (April 1818), 400 – 06; and 86 (July 1818), 273 – 79; *Quarterly Review*, 21 (April 1819), 486 – 556.

H., J.. *'Lines, supposed to have been written on Saint Michael's Mount, Cornwall' (P). In *European Magazine*, 62 (1812), 450.

Heber, Reginald. *Fragments of the Masque of Gwendolen* (D). Written in 1816 for a Christmas party. Amelia Heber, however, printed only 'some extracts' in *The Life of Reginald Heber*, by his Widow, 2 vols (London: Murray, 1830), I.

————. *Morte d'Arthur: A Fragment* (P). Written c. 1810 – 1819. In *Life*, II. Both works are reviewed in: *Christian Remembrancer*, 13 (March 1831), 134; *Literary Gazette*, 19 June 1830, 398 – 400; *Quarterly Review*, 43 (October 1830), 386.

Hogg, Thomas. *The Fabulous History of the Ancient Kingdom of Cornwall* (P) (London: Longman, Rees, Orme, 1827). Reviews: *Gentleman's Magazine*, 97 (September 1827), 257; *Royal Cornwall Gazette*, 14 July 1827, 4.

Hollings, J. F. (?James Francis). *'To Morgan Le Fay' (P). In *Literary Souvenir* (1831), 133.

Horne, Richard Hengist. 'The Three Knights of Camelott' (P). In *Ballad Romances* (London: Ollier/Smith, 1846). Reviews: *Athenaeum*, 14 February 1846, 168 – 69; *Examiner*, 6 June 1846, 355; *Foreign and Colonial Quarterly Review*, 7 (1846), 497 – 506.

Hoyle, Charles. *The Pilgrim of the Hebrides: a Lay of the North Countrie* (P) (London:

Longman, Rees, Orme, Brown, and Green, 1830). See Canto III. part 3. stanzas xiii – xxiv.

Hunt, Leigh. *The Story of Rimini: a Poem* (P) (London: Murray, 1816). See Canto III. 63 – 64, 535 – 68, 599 – 600. Reviews: *Blackwood's*, 2 (November 1817), 194 – 201; *Quarterly Review*, 14 (January 1816), 473 – 81.

Landon, Letitia Elizabeth. *'A Legend of Tintagel Castle' (P). In *Fisher's Drawing Room Scrapbook* (1833), 8 – 9. Review: *Literary Gazette*, 6 October 1832, 625 – 26.

Lee, Richard Nelson. *Harlequin and Mother Red Cap; or, Merlin and Fairy Snowdrop* (D). Performed at Adelphi Theatre, 26 December 1839. BL Add MS 42953, ff 631 – 649. Reviews: *Athenaeum*, 28 December 1839, 989 – 90; *Examiner*, 29 December 1839, 823; *Literary Gazette*, 28 December 1839, 831; *Morning Chronicle*, 27 December 1839, 2.

Leigh, Percival. *Jack the Giant Killer* (P) (London: Orr, 1843).

Leyden, John *Scenes of Infancy: descriptive of Teviotdale* (P) (Edinburgh: Longman and Rees, 1803). See Part I. ll. 51 – 70; Part II. ll. 505 – 20. Reviews: *Annual Review*, 2 (1803), 563; *British Critic*, 23 (May 1804), 483 – 88; *Imperial Review*, 2 (August 1804), 515 – 21; *Lady's Monthly Museum*, 13 (July 1804), 57 – 58; *Literary Journal*, 2 (16 December 1803), 652 – 53; *Monthly Review*, 45 (September 1804), 62 – 65; *New Annual Register*, 24 (1803), 328; *North British Magazine*, 1 (February 1804), 12 – 24, (March 1804), 169 – 74; *Poetical Register*, 3 (1803), 446.

Lowell, James Russell. *The Vision of Sir Launfal* (P) (Cambridge, Mass.: Nichols, 1848). Reviews: *Brownson's Quarterly Review*, 6 (April 1849), 265 – 74; *North American Review*, 68 (January 1849), 261 – 62.

Lytton, Edward George Earle Lytton Bulwer, *Baron*. 'The Fairy Bride' (P). In *Eva, a True Story of Light and Darkness; The Ill-Omened Marriage, and Other Tales and Poems*, second edition (London: Saunders and Otley, 1842). BL and National Union Catalog also list (Paris: Galignani, 1842) and (Leipzig: Tauchnitz, 1842). Northup and Parry, and Taylor and Brewer incorrectly list first edition as (?) 1849. Review: *Tait's Edinburgh Magazine*, NS 10 (January 1843), 122 – 28.

————. *'The Lady and the Dogs. From the Fabliaux' (P). in *Eva* (1842).

————. *King Arthur* (P). Published anonymously in 3 parts, and then in 2 vols (London: Colburn, 1848 – 1849). Second ed. (1 vol) with author's name in 1849. Reviews: *Athenaeum*, 11 March 1848, 262 – 63; and 27 January 1849, 87 – 89; *Eclectic Review*, NS 26 (1849), 449 – 60). *Edinburgh Review*, 90 (July 1849), 173 – 212; *Examiner*, 4 March 1848, 147 – 48; and 27 January 1849, 52 – 54; *Illustrated London News*, 25 March 1848, 200; *Literary Gazette*, 11 March 1848, 178 – 80; 3 February 1849, 75 – 76; and 4 August 1849, 569; *Morning Post*, 22 March 1848, 3; and 31 January 1849, 3; *New Monthly Magazine*, 2nd Series, 85 (March 1849), 307 – 14; *Sharpe's London Journal*, 10 (1849), 373 – 79; *Sun*, 20 March 1848, 3; 22 January 1849, 3; and 30 January 1849, 3.

Michell, John. *'Tintagel Castle' (P). In *Forget Me Not* (1829), 85 – 88.

Milman, Henry Hart. *Samor, Lord of the Bright City: An Heroic Poem* (P) (London: Murray, 1818). Reviews: *Athenaeum*, 14 March 1840, 211; *British Critic*, NS 10 (July 1818), 52 – 59; *British Lady's Magazine*, 3rd Series, 1 (July-September 1818), 30 – 34; *Literary Chronicle*, 1 (8 June 1818), 161 – 63; and (15 June 1818), 179 – 81; *Literary Gazette*, 25 April 1818, 260 – 61; *Miniature Magazine*, 2 (December 1818), 40 – 41; *Monthly Magazine*, 48 (August 1819), 60; *Monthly Review*, 87 (December 1818), 337 – 56; *New Annual Register*, 39 (1818), 185 – 92; *New Monthly Magazine*, 10 (October 1818), 247 – 49; *North American Review*, 9 (1819), 26 – 35; *Quarterly Review*, 19 (July 1818), 328 – 47; *Theatrical Inquisitor*, 13 (July 1818), 41 – 51: (August 1818), 118 – 22.

Moultrie, John (= 'Gerard Montgomery'). *La Belle Tryamour* (P). In *Knight's Quarterly*

Magazine; Canto I in vol I. no. 1 (June 1823), 145 – 79; Canto II in vol I. no. 2 (October 1823), 378 – 418; Canto III in vol II. no 1 (January 1824), 115 – 57; five additional stanzas in vol III. pt. 1 (August 1824), 224 – 25. Revised as *Sir Launfal*, in *Poems* by John Moultrie (London: Pickering, 1837). Reviews: *Athenaeum*, 22 April 1837, 278 – 79; *Gentleman's Magazine*, NS 8 (July 1837), 51 – 52; *Ward's Miscellany*, 1 (1837), 637 – 40, 822 – 24.

O'Hara, Kane. *Tom Thumb, A Burletta, as it is now performed at the Theatres Royal, Drury Lane, Covent Garden, and Hay-Market* (London: Cawthorn, 1805) (D). First performed in 1780, but not apparently published in its entirety until 1805.

Ord, John Walker. **England: A Historical Poem*, 2 vols (P) (London: Simpkin, Marshall, Baldwin and Cradock, 1834 – 1835). Reviews: *Athenaeum*, 20 June 1835, 472; *Fraser's Magazine*, 10 (September 1834), 344 – 48; *Gentleman's Magazine*, NS 4 (August 1835), 163 – 64; and (November 1835), 528; *Literary Gazette*, 2 February 1839, 71; *Monthly Review*, 2 (June 1834), 273 – 74.

Oxenford, John. *'Sir Wigolais of the Wheel' (F). In *New Monthly Magazine*, 2nd Series, 85 (March 1849), 315 – 24.

Oxonian, An. *'Lines written after reading the Romance of Arthur's Round Table' (P). In *Blackwood's Edinburgh Magazine*, 30 (May 1830), 705.

Parker, John. *'The Celtic Annals' (P). In *The Passengers* (London: Rivington, 1831). Review: *Cambrian Quarterly Magazine*, 4 (1832), 100 – 06; 259 – 61.

Peacock, Thomas Love. *Calidore* (F). Uncompleted. Written in c. 1816. Published in *The Works of Thomas Love Peacock*, edited by H. F. B. Brett-Smith and C. E. Jones, 8 vols (London: Constable, 1924 – 1934), VIII.

————. *The Round Table; or King Arthur's Feast* (P) (London: Arliss, 1817).

————. *The Misfortunes of Elphin* (F) (London: Hookham, 1829). Reviews: *Athenaeum*, 6 May 1829, 276 – 78; *Cambrian Quarterly Magazine*, 1 (1829), 231 – 40; *Literary Gazette*, 7 March 1829, 153 – 55; *Westminster Review*, 10 (April 1829), 428 – 35.

Pennie, John Fitzgerald. **The Dragon-King* (D). In *Britain's Historical Drama; a series of National Tragedies . . . 1st Series* (London: Maunder, 1832). Reviews: *Athenaeum*, 4 February 1832, 73; *Cambrian Quarterly Magazine*, 4 (1832), 254 – 59; *Fraser's Magazine*, 5 (July 1832), 670 – 82; *Gentleman's Magazine*, 103 (January 1833), 60; *Literary Gazette*, 11 February 1832, 83 – 84; *Monthly Magazine*, 13 (February 1832), 240 – 41.

Pocock, Isaac. *King Arthur and the Knights of the Round Table: a new grand chivalric entertainment in three acts* (D). Performed at Theatre Royal, Drury Lane, 26 December 1834. Revived at Royal Astley's, September 1840. BL Add MS 42928, ff 742 – 759b. *Songs, Chorusses . . .* (London: Miller, 1834). Reviews: *Athenaeum*, 3 January 1835, 18; *Examiner*, 4 January 1835, 4; *Gentleman's Magazine*, NS 3 (January 1835), 84; *Mirror*, 3 January 1835, 5 – 6; *New Monthly Magazine*, 2nd Series, 43 (1835), 254 – 55; *The Times*, 27 December 1834, 2.

Polwhele, Richard. **The Fair Isabel* (P) (London, 1815). See Introduction to Canto II. Reviews: *Antijacobin*, 50 (April 1816), 341 – 48; *Augustan*, 3 (September 1816), 255 – 60; *British Critic*, NS6 (July 1816), 90 – 92; *Gentleman's Magazine*, 85 (July 1815), 50 – 53; (October 1815), 330 – 35; *Monthly Review*, 78 (November 1815), 317 – 19; *Quarterly*, 14 (January 1816), 402 – 05.

Praed, Winthrop Mackworth. *'Gog' (P). In *Etonian*, vol. 2. no. 8 (1821) 222 – 34; and no. 9, 327 – 36.

————. **Lillian: a fairy tale* (P) (London: Knight, 1823). Reviews: *British Critic*, NS 20 (1823), 311 – 15; *Literary Chronicle*, 24 May 1823, 326; *Literary Museum*, 56 (1823), 365; *News of Literature and Fashion*, 2 (June 1825), 364; *United States Magazine and Democratic Review*, 14 (June 1844), 660.

──────. *'The Legend of the Haunted Tree' (P). In *Literary Souvenir* (1831), 1 –
16. Review: *Literary Gazette*, 30 October 1830, 697.

Riethmuller, Christopher James. *Launcelot of the Lake, A Tragedy in five acts* (D)
(London: Chapman and Hall, 1843). Review: *Athenaeum*, 13 January 1844, 31.

Roscoe, James. *'The Iron-Gate — A Legend of Alderley' (P). In *Blackwood's
Edinburgh Magazine*, 45 (February 1839), 271 – 74. Published anonymously. Author
identified in J. P. Earwaker, *East Cheshire: Past and Present*, 2 vols (1880), I, 611.

Rose, William Stewart. *Partenopex de Blois; a Romance. Freely translated from the French of
M. Le Grand* (P) (London: Longman, Hurst, Rees and Orme, 1807). See Book I. ll.
109 – 48. Review: *Edinburgh Review*, 13 (January 1809), 413 – 26.

Scott, Sir Walter. *'Thomas the Rhymer. Part III' (P). In *Minstrelsy of the Scottish
Border*, 3 vols (London: Cadell and Davies, 1802 – 1803), III.

──────. *The Bridal of Triermain: or, The Vale of St. John* (P) (Edinburgh: Ballantyne,
1813). Canto I. i – viii had appeared anonymously in *Edinburgh Annual Register for
1809*, 2 (1811), 596 – 99. Reviews: *Critical Review*, 4th Series, 3 (May 1813),
473 – 82; *Drakard's Paper*, 18 December 1813, 398 – 99; *Eclectic Review*, 10 (October
1813), 368 – 78; *Lady's Monthly Museum*, 2nd Series, 17 (December 1814), 340 – 43;
Monthly Magazine, 48 (October 1819), 255 – 56; *Monthly Review*, 73 (March 1814),
237 – 44; *Port Folio*, 3rd Series, 2 (July 1813), 100 – 10; *Quarterly Review*, 9 (July
1813), 480 – 97; *Scots Magazine*, 75 (April 1813), 282 – 86; *Town Talk*, 4 (July 1813),
437 – 39.

Smith, Elizabeth. *'A supposed Translation from a Welsh Poem, lately dug up at
Piercefield, in the same spot where Llewellyn ap Gryffyd was slain, Dec. 10th 1281'
(P) in *Fragments in Prose and Verse* (Dublin: Watson, 1808). Reviews: *British Critic*, 33
(March 1809), 217 – 23; *Critical Review*, 3rd Series, 23 (June 1811), 140 – 50;
Cyclopaedian Magazine, 2 (October 1808), 569 – 71; and (November 1808), 618 – 21;
Eclectic Review, 4 (September 1808), 827 – 32; *Edinburgh Monthly Magazine*, 1
(September 1811), 449 – 58; *Monthly Review*, 64 (January 1811), 67 – 79; *Poetical
Register*, 7 (1808), 553 – 54; *Satirist*, 9 (August 1811), 162 – 63.

Stephens, Frederick George. *'Arthur' (P). Untraced. Mentioned on 26 November
1849 in *The P.R.B. Journal: William Michael Rossetti's Diary of the Pre-Raphaelite
Brotherhood 1849 – 1853*, edited by William E. Fredeman (Oxford, 1975), 9 – 10,
195.

Tennyson, Alfred. 'The Lady of Shalott' (P). In *Poems* (London: Moxon, 1833); and
Arthurian reference in 'The Palace of Art'.

──────. 'Sir Launcelot and Queen Guinevere. A Fragment', 'Sir Galahad', 'The
Epic', 'Morte d'Arthur' and revised forms of 'The Lady of Shalott' and 'The
Palace of Art' (P). In *Poems*, 2 vols (London: Moxon, 1842). Reviews: *American
Review*, NS2 (July 1848), 28 – 39; *Athenaeum*, 6 August 1842, 700 – 02; *Blackwood's
Edinburgh Magazine*, 65 (April 1849), 453 – 67; *British Quarterly Review*, 2 (August
1845), 46 – 71; *Christian Examiner*, 23 (January 1838), 305 – 27; *Christian Teacher*,
NS 4 (October 1842), 414 – 23; *Church of England Quarterly Review*, 12 (October
1842), 361 – 76; *Edinburgh Review*, 77 (April 1843), 373 – 91; *Examiner*, 28 May
1842, 340 – 41; *Howitt's Journal*, 3 (15 January 1848), 39 – 42; *Literary Gazette*, 8
December 1832, 772 – 74; *London Review*, 1 (July 1833), 402 – 24; *Manchester
Examiner*, 8 January 1848, 3; *Morning Post*, 9 August 1842, 6; *New Monthly Magazine*,
2nd Series, 37 (January 1833), 69 – 74; *Quarterly Review*, 49 (April 1833), 81 – 96;
and 70 (September 1842), 385 – 416; *Tait's Edinburgh Magazine*, NS 9 (August
1842), 502 – 08; *The Times*, 12 October 1848, 3; *True Sun*, 19 January 1833, 3;
United States Magazine and Democratic Review, 14 (January 1844), 62 – 77; and 15
(December 1844), 580; *Westminster Review*, 38 (October 1842), 371 – 90.

——————. 'Life of the Life within my blood', and other fragments of 'The Ballad of Sir Launcelot' (P). In Ricks ed. *Poems of Tennyson*, second edition (1987).

Thelwall, John. *The Fairy of the Lake* (D). In *Poems chiefly Written in Retirement* (Hereford: printed by W. H. Parker, 1801). Review: *Edinburgh Review*, 2 (April 1803), 197 – 202.

Whytehead, Thomas. *'Deem not for lack of lance and waving crest' (P). In *Poems* (Cambridge: Rivingtons, 1842). Reprinted as 'An Arthurian Legend' in *Poetical Remains and Letters of the late Rev. Thomas Whytehead* (London, 1877).

Williams, Rowland (= 'Goronva Camlan'). *'The Hall of the Nations' (P). In *Lays from the Cimbric Lyre, with various verses* (London: Pickering, 1846).

Willyams, James Brydges. *'Arthur' (P). Uncompleted work of about 1820. Untraced. See Henry Sewell Stokes, *The Vale of Lanherne, and other poems* (London: Longman, Rees, Orme, Brown, Green, 1836), 101.

Wilmer, Lambert A. *Merlin* (D). In *North American*, 1 (18 and 25 August, 1 September 1827), 110, 118, 126. Reissued immediately in pamphlet form by *North American*.

Woodley, George. *Cornubia: A Poem, in five cantos* (P) (London: Longman, Hurst, Rees, Orme, and Brown, 1819). See Canto III. stanzas xviii – xxx, xxxiii.

Wordsworth, William. 'The Egyptian Maid; or, the Romance of the Water Lily' (P). In *Yarrow Revisited, and other Poems* (London: Longman, Rees, Orme, Brown, Green and Longman, 1835). Reviews: *Athenaeum*, 18 April 1835, 293 – 94; *Examiner*, 26 April 1835, 259 – 60; *Fraser's Magazine*, 11 (June 1835), 689 – 707; *Printing Machine*, 3 (May 1835), 281 – 85; *Quarterly Review*, 54 (July 1835), 181 – 85.

Appendix B

List of Poetry, Drama and Prose Fiction Containing Minor Allusions to the Arthurian Legends

Ainsworth, W. Harrison. *Windsor Castle* (1843) (F). Book III. chapters 1 and 2.

Anonymous. 'The Battle of Vittoria' (P). In *European Magazine*, 64 (August 1813), 146 – 47. Line 53.

──────. 'The Prophecy of Taliesin' (P). In *Cambro-Briton*, 2 (1821), 185 – 88. Lines 59 – 60.

──────. 'Lines written for recital at the late Anniversary of the Cambrian Institution' (P). In *Cambro-Briton*, 2 (1821), 461 – 64. Line 42.

──────. 'Stonehenge' (P). In *Gentleman's Magazine*, 93 (1823), ii. Lines 27 – 28.

──────. 'The Faery President of the Court of Love' (F). In *New European Magazine*, 3 (September 1823), 253 – 64. Pages 254 – 55, 257, 263.

──────. 'Welsh War Song' (P). In *Carmarthen Journal*, 9 March 1827, 4. Line 33.

──────. 'The Knight of the Magic Loom' (P). In *Punch*, 9 (July – December 1845), 189. Lines 10 – 13.

──────. 'Thomas the Rhymer' (P). In *Sharpe's London Magazine*, 22 August 1846, 271 – 72. Lines 61 – 66.

──────. 'Sir Tudor ap Grono' (P). In *Sharpe's London Magazine*, 12 September 1846, 319 – 20. Lines 27, 58, 64.

Anstice, Joseph. *Richard Coeur de Lion* (P). Oxford Prize Poem in 1828. Reprinted in *Oxford Prize Poems* (1839). Lines 59 – 64.

Atherstone, Edwin. *The Sea-Kings in England; an historical romance of the time of Alfred* (F), 3 vols (1830), II. Chapter 8.

Beresford-Hope, Alexander James. 'Kilmallock is a ruined place' (P). In *Poems* (1841). Lines 19 – 24.

Betham, Matilda. *The Lay of Marie* (1816) (P). Canto II. Lines 121 – 30.

Bloomfield, Robert. *The Banks of the Wye* (1811) (P). Book I. Lines 307 – 08, 441 – 48.

Bouchier, Barton. *The Dream of Youth* (1818) (P). Canto I. stanzas lxi – lxiii; and p.66n.

Bowen, Melesina. *Ystradffin* (1839) (P). Part IV. p.107.

Bowles, William Lisle. 'Glastonbury Abbey and Wells Cathedral' (P). In *Gentleman's Magazine*, 95 (July 1825), 70. Reprinted in *Friendship's Offering* (1826), 64. Lines 17 – 18.

──────. 'The Lay of Talbot, the Troubadour' (P). In *Annals and Antiquities of Lacock Abbey* (1835). Part 2. lines 7 – 8.

Browning, Elizabeth Barrett. 'The Fourfold Aspect' (P). In *Poems* (1844). Lines 51 – 54.

Burges, Sir James Bland. *Richard the First*, 2 vols (1801) (P). Volume II, Book XIII. stanzas xxiii – xxxv.

Churton, Edward, 'Margaret Bisset' (P). In *Lays of Faith and Loyalty* (1845). Lines 115 – 16.

Coleridge, Samuel Taylor. 'The Pang More Sharp Than All' (P). In *Poetical Works*, edited by H. N. Coleridge, third edition (1834). Lines 37 – 41.

Collingwood, George Lewes Newnham. *Alfred the Great* (1836) (P). Book II. lines 1085 – 90.

Cornwall, Ebenezer. 'Stonehenge' (P). In *Miscellaneous Poems* (1828). Lines 173 – 85.

Cottle, Joseph. *The Fall of Cambria* (1808) (P). Book IX. lines 374 – 79, 383 – 87, 396 – 406.

Darley, George. *Thomas à Becket* (1840) (D). Act III. i. 9 – 15; V. ii. 83.

Davies, Henry. 'Ode' (P). Recited at the Beaumaris Eisteddfod in August 1832. Printed in *Caernarvon Herald*, 1 September 1832; *North Wales Chronicle*, 4 September 1832; and *Cambrian Quarterly Magazine*, 4 (1832), 544 – 45. Line 96.

Disraeli, Benjamin. *Tancred; or, The New Crusade* (1847) (F). Book II. chapter 15; Book VI. chapter 8.

Emerson, Ralph Waldo. 'The Knights of the Square Table' (1819) (P). Quoted in Taylor and Brewer, 165.

————. 'Politics' (P). In *Essays. Second Series* (1844). Line 5.

Faber, Frederick William. 'A Vision of Bright Seas' (P). In *The Styrian Lake, and Other Poems* (1842). Lines 41 – 45.

Finlay, John. *Wallace, or the Vale of Ellerslie* (1802) (P). Part I. stanza xx.

Giffard, Sir Ambrose Hardinge. 'Roncesvalles' (P). In *Verses* (1824). Line 2.

————. 'St. Michael's Mount' (P). In *Verses* (1824). Lines 17 – 28.

Gladstone, William Ewart. 'An Epilogue in Quindecasyllabics, spoken by David Ap Rice, Esquire' (P). In *Eton Miscellany*, 1 (1827), 191 – 92. Line 15.

H., E.. 'The Witch Ladye' (F). In *New European Magazine*, 2 (1823), 500 – 09. Page 501.

Halleck, Fitz-Greene. 'Alnwick Castle' (P). In *Specimens of American Poetry*, edited by Samuel Kettell, 3 vols (1829); and in *Poetical Works* (1847), Lines 86 – 87.

Haslehurst, George. *Penmaen-Mawr* (1849) (P). 'Song' on pages 77 – 79.

Hawker, Robert Stephen. 'The Silent Tower of Bottreau' (P). In *Records of the Western Shore* (1832); reprinted in *Cornish Guardian and Western Chronicle*, 31 January 1834, 7. Line 11n.

————. 'The Wreck' (P). In *Poems* (1836). Lines 29 – 40.

Hemans, Felicia. *England and Spain* (1808) (P). Lines 129 – 30.

————. 'The Green Isles of Ocean' (P). In *Welsh Melodies*, 2 parts (London, ?1822). Prefatory note.

————. 'Taliesin's Prophecy' (P). In *Welsh Melodies*. Line 11.

Herbert, William. *Attila, King of the Huns* (1838) (P). Book XII. 11. 415 – 18.

Hood, Thomas. *The Plea of the Midsummer Fairies* (1827) (P). Line 141.

————. 'A Lament for the Decline of Chivalry' (P). In *Bijou* (1828), 81 – 85. Lines 13 – 15.

Hoyle, Charles. 'Legend of the Harper' (P). In *Gentleman's Magazine*, 102 (June 1832), 631 – 32. Lines 124 – 26.

————. 'Avebury' (P). In *Gentleman's Magazine*, 102 (May 1832), 432. Line 7.

————. 'Cambria' (P). Unpublished MS in library of Trinity College, Cambridge (R.17.18). Canto II. part 1. stanza xlvi; part 2. stanza xlii and n.

Hunt, Leigh. *The Descent of Liberty* (1815) (D). Stage directions after Scene 3. line 504.

————. 'The Dogs' (P). In *Liberal*, 1 (1822). Lines 293 – 94, 395.

—————. 'Bodryddan' (P). In *Monthly Repository* (October 1837). Lines 106 – 10.

Irving, Washington. *Bracebridge Hall* (1822) (F). Chapters 15, 18, 22, 37.

Jeffreys, M. E. *Hoel the Hostage* (1842) (P). Canto IV. lines 15 – 16.

Johnson, W. R. *The History of England, in easy verse* (1806) (P). Chapter IV. lines 4 – 6.

Jones, of Swansea, *Mr.* 'The Vale of Tywy' (P). In *Cambro-Briton*, 3 (1822), 315. Line 5.

Keats, John. 'To J. H. Reynolds, Esq.' (P). Written 1818. In *Life, Letters and Literary Remains*, edited by R. M. Milnes (1848). Line 34.

—————. 'The Eve of St. Agnes' (P). In *Lamia, Isabella, The Eve of St. Agnes, and Other Poems* (1820). Line 171.

Landon, Letitia Elizabeth. *Romance and Reality*, 3 vols (1831) (F). Vol II. chapter 10.

Landor, Walter Savage. 'An Ode (To Joseph Ablett)' (P). First published in this revised form in *London Journal*, 15 April 1835. Line 3.

Lawrance, Hannah. 'Lady Jane's Merlin: A Tale of Windsor Castle' (F). In *Literary Souvenir* (1826), 219 – 40. Page 231.

Lawrence, James. 'Prologue to The Days of Chivalry' (P). In *The Etonian Out of Bounds*, 3 vols (1828). Vol II. Lines 83 – 84.

Lewis, Matthew Gregory. 'Sir Guy the Seeker' (P). In *Romantic Tales*, 4 vols (1808). Vol I. Lines 217 – 18.

Liddell, Henry. *The Wizard of the North* (1833) (P). Lines 21 – 22.

Lloyd, David. 'British Valour: or; Saint David's Day' (P). In *Characteristics of Men, Manners, and Sentiments* (1812). Stanza ii.

Lloyd, John, 'Drugarn, or, The Druid's Cairn' (P). In *Poems* (1847). Lines 37 – 44.

Llwyd, Richard. *Beaumaris Bay* (1800) (P). Note on pp. 6 – 7.

—————. 'The Castle of Harlech' (P). In *Poems, Tales, Odes, Sonnets, Translations* (1804). Line 1.

—————. 'The Address of the Bard of Snowdon to his Countrymen' (P). In *Poems* (1804). Line 58.

Longfellow, Henry Wadsworth. 'The Castle Builder' (P). Written 14 December 1848. In *Our Young Folks* (January 1867). Line 7.

Lytton, Edward George Earle Lytton Bulwer, *Baron.* 'The Rats and the Mice. A Fable, of the days of King Arthur'. (P). In *The Siamese Twins* (1831).

—————. *Eugene Aram* (1832) (F). Chapter heading to Book IV. chapter 9.

—————. *The Last of the Barons* (1843) (F). Book I. chapters 6 and 8; II. ch. 2; IV. ch. 7; X. ch. 4.

—————. *Harold* (1848) (F). Book III. chapter 3; VII. ch. 5 and 6; X. ch. 6.

—————. *The Caxtons* (1849) (F). Part II. chapter 6; III. ch. 3.

Macleod, Alexander. *The Age of Chivalry* (1839) (P). Stanza xxxi.

Maclise, Daniel (= 'Alfred Croquis'). 'Christmas Revels' (P). In *Fraser's*, 17 (May 1838), 635 – 44. L'Envoy. lines 5 – 6.

Maginn, William, 'The Prophecy of Plenty for the Year MDCCCXXXIII. By Merlin' (P). In *Fraser's*, 7 (March 1833), 376.

—————. 'The Fraserians; or, The commencement of the year thirty-five' (P). In *Fraser's*, 11 (January 1835), 1 – 2. Lines 13 – 14.

Meredith, W. E. *Llewelyn ap Iorwerth* (1818) (P). Canto I. stanzas iv, xxix; V. xl.

Merivale, John Herman. *Orlando in Roncesvalles* (1814) (P). Canto IV. Lines 329 – 32.

—————. 'A Chronicle of the Kings of England' (P). In *Poems Original and Translated*, 2 vols (1838), II. Lines 85 – 98.

—————. 'Paul and Francesca' (P). In *Poems* (1838). Lines 43, 104.

Middleton, Marmaduke. *Poetical Sketches of a Tour in the West of England* (1822) (P). Part III. Lines 444 – 47.

Milman, Henry Hart. *Judicium Regale* (1814) (P). Line 261.

Mitford, John. 'Dedicatory Epistle to the Rev. Alexander Dyce' (P). In *Poetical Works of Thomas Parnell*, edited by Mitford (1832). Lines 693 – 96

Moir, David Macbeth. 'The Tower of Erceldoune' (P). In *Blackwood's Edinburgh Magazine*, 28 (October 1830), 695 – 97. Lines 39 – 44.

Montgomery, James. *Greenland* (1819) (P). Canto IV. Line 149.

Parry, John Humphreys. 'The Heroes of Cymru' (P). In *Cambro-Briton*, 2 (1821), 89. Line 11.

Peacock, Thomas Love. *The Genius of the Thames* (1810) (P). Part I. Lines 108 – 11.

———. *Sir Hornbook: or Childe Launcelot's Expedition, A Grammatico-Allegorical Ballad* (1814) (P).

———. *Headlong Hall* (1816) (F). Chapter 13.

———. *Melincourt* (1818) (F). Chapter 8.

———. *Crotchet Castle* (1831) (F). Conclusion.

Pennie, John Fitzgerald. 'Richard Coeur de Lion's Arrival on the Coast of Palestine' (P). In *Literary Magnet*, NS 2 (1826), 356 – 60. Lines 22 – 24.

Porden, Eleanor Anne. *The Veils; or, The Triumph of Constancy* (1815) (P). Book II. Line 11; Book III. 841 – 42.

———. *Coeur de Lion; or The Third Crusade*, 2 vols (1822) (P). Book VI. Lines 263 – 80; XII. 129 – 32.

———. 'Ode to The King's Most Excellent Majesty' (P). in *Coeur de Lion* (1822). Line 50.

Prichard, Thomas Jeffery Llewelyn. *The Land beneath the Sea* (P). In *Welsh Minstrelsy* (1824). Canto III. Lines 104 – 15.

———. 'The Worthies of Wales' (P). In *Cambrian Wreath* (1828). Lines 9 – 12.

Pringle, Thomas. 'A Dream of Fairy-Land' (P). In *Friendship's Offering* (1832), 18 – 44. Reprinted in *Poetical Works* (1837). Epigraph to Fytte III.

R.. 'English Chronicles' (P). In *Juvenile Forget Me Not* (1830), 156 – 58. Line 9.

Russell, John, *Earl*. 'Francesca da Rimini' (P). In *Literary Souvenir* (1830), 287. Reprinted in *Illustrated London News*, 26 November 1842, 461. Line 56.

Salmon, Thomas Stokes. *Stonehenge* (1823) (P). Reprinted in *Gentleman's Magazine*, 93 (June 1823), 549; in Prichard ed. *Cambrian Wreath* (1828); and in *Oxford Prize Poems* (1839). Lines 29 – 30.

Scott, Sir Walter. *Marmion* (1808) (P). Introduction to Canto I. Lines 258 – 83.

———. 'The Last Words of Cadwallon; or, The Dying Bard' (P). In George Thomson ed. *Select Collection of Original Welsh Airs* (1809), I. Line 19.

———. *The Lady of the Lake* (1810) (P). Canto VI. stanza xxviii n.

———. *The Vision of Don Roderick* (1811) (P). Introduction. stanza iv.

———. *Rokeby* (1813) (P). Canto V. stanza xv n.

———. *Waverley* (1814) (F). Chapters 8 and 9

———. *Guy Mannering* (1815) (F). Chapter 53.

———. *The Antiquary* (1816) (F). Chapters 3 and 6.

———. *Ivanhoe* (1820) (F). Chapters 13, 15 and 34.

———. *The Monastery* (1820) (F). Chapter 16.

———. *The Abbot* (1820) (F). Chapter 27.

———. *Kenilworth* (1821) (F). Chapters 24, 26, 30 and 37.

———. 'Carle, Now the King's Come' (P). Edinburgh broadsheet. Reprinted in *Royal Cornwall Gazette*, 10 August 1822, 4. Lines 67 – 70.

———. *Peveril of the Peak* (1822) (F). Chapter 35.

———. *Quentin Durward* (1823) (F). Chapters 14 and 24.

———. *The Betrothed* (1825) (F). Chapters 17, 20 and 21.

———. *The Talisman* (1825) (F). Chapters 5, 12, 25, 26 and 27.

———. *The Fair Maid of Perth* (1828) (F). Chapters 6, 13, 20 and 22.

————. *Anne of Geierstein* (1829) (F). Chapters 10, 15, 25 and 36.

————. *Castle Dangerous* (1832) (F). Chapters 2, 5, 7, 8 and 11.

Shelley, Mary. *Frankenstein* (1818) (F). Chapter 2.

Shelley, Percy Bysshe. 'Charles the First' (D). Written 1822. Uncompleted. In *Complete Works*, ed. by Roger Ingpen and Walter E. Peck, 10 vols (London, 1965), IV. Scene 2. ll. 368 – 72.

Sherwood, Mary Martha. *The Cloak* (1836) (F). Reprinted in *Popular Tales* (1860), 347 – 67. Page 356.

Sigourney, Lydia Howard Huntley. 'Carlisle' (P). In *Pleasant Memories of Pleasant Lands* (1843). Line 10.

Sotheby, William. *The Cambrian Hero* (?1800) (D). Act V. scene i. Lines 23, 36 – 39; V. iv. 8.

Southey, Robert. *Madoc* (1805) (P). Book III. Line 207; XI. 105 – 06, 142; XVIII. 68.

————. 'At Banavie' (P). In *Anniversary* (1829), 197. Lines 13 – 15.

Sterling, John. 'Coeur de Lion' (P). In *Fraser's Magazine*, 39 (February 1849), 170 – 78; (March 1849), 277 – 82; (April 1849), 405 – 16. See Canto I. stanzas xxxii, xlix, lxiv, lxxvii, lxxviii.

Stokes, Henry Sewell. *The Song of Albion* (1831) (P). Part I. Lines 222 – 42, 274 – 76.

————. 'Dosmerry Pool' (P). In *Cornish Guardian and Western Chronicle*, 3 October 1834, 7. Signed 'Henry'. For attribution to Stokes, see my chapter 2. note 191. Lines 9 – 16.

Sullivan, M. J. 'St. Patrick's Day' (P). In *The Prince of the Lake* (1815). Line 10.

Thomas, William Moy. 'Ogier the Dane' (P). In *Chamber's Edinburgh Journal*, NS 9 (6 May 1848), 304. Line 25.

Trench, Richard Chenevix. Verse fragment in letter to W. B. Donne on 18 October 1829 (P). In *Richard Chenevix Trench, Archbishop: Letters and Memorials*, 2 vols (1888), I, 38. Lines 1 – 3.

Williams, Taliesin. *Cardiff Castle* (1827) (P). Lines 221 – 28.

Wordsworth, William. 'A narrow girdle of rough stones and crags' (P). In *Lyrical Ballads*, 2 vols (1800). Lines 37 – 38.

————. *The Prelude* (1850) (P). See Book VII (written c. 1804). Lines 685 – 86.

————. 'With how sad steps, O Moon, thou climb'st the sky' (P). In *Poems* (1807), 2 vols. Line 9.

————. 'Artegal and Elidure' (P). In *The River Duddon* (1820). Lines 49 – 56.

————. Sonnet X ('Struggle of the Britons against the Barbarians') (P). In *Ecclesiastical Sketches* (1822). Lines 5 – 7.

Yonge, Charlotte Mary. *Abbeychurch* (1844) (F). Chapter 13.

APPENDIX C

Chronological Table of Poetry, Drama and Prose Fiction Primarily Concerned with, or Alluding to, the Arthurian Legends

Column 1 lists those works catalogued in Appendix A.
Column 2 lists those works catalogued in Appendix B.

Date	1	2
1800		Wordsworth, 'A narrow girdle . . .'
		Sotheby, *Cambrian Hero*
		Llwyd, *Beaumaris Bay*
1801	Thelwall, *Fairy of the Lake*	Burges, *Richard the First*
1802	Bannerman, 'Prophecy of Merlin'	Finlay, *Wallace*
	Dibdin, *Wizard's Wake*	
1803	Leyden, *Scenes of Infancy*	
	Scott, 'Thomas the Rhymer'	
1804		Llwyd, *Poems, Tales, Odes*
		Blake, *Jerusalem* (to 1820)
		Wordsworth, *Prelude*
1805	O'Hara, *Tom Thumb*	Southey, *Madoc*
1806	Bray, 'To Merlin'	Johnson, *History of England*
1807	Rose, *Partenopex*	Wordsworth, 'With how sad . . .'
1808	Smith, 'Supposed Translation'	Scott, *Marmion*
		Cottle, *Fall of Cambria*
		Hemans, *England and Spain*
		Lewis, 'Sir Guy the Seeker'
1809		Scott, 'Last Words of Cadwallon'
1810		Scott, *Lady of the Lake*
		Peacock, *Genius of the Thames*
1811		Scott, *Vision of Don Roderick*
		Bloomfield, *Banks of the Wye*
1812	J.H., 'St. Michael's Mt'	Lloyd, 'British Valour'
	Heber, *Morte d'Arthur*	
1813	Scott, *Bridal of Triermain*	Scott, *Rokeby*
		Anon, 'Vittoria'

Date	*1*	*2*
1814	Anon, *Merlin's Cave*	Merivale, *Orlando*
		Peacock, *Sir Hornbook*
		Scott, *Waverley*
		Milman, *Judicium Regale*
1815	Costello, 'A Dream'	Hunt, *Descent of Liberty*
	Polwhele, *Fair Isabel*	Scott, *Guy Mannering*
		Porden, *The Veils*
		Sullivan, 'St. Patrick's Day'
1816	Peacock, *Calidore*	Peacock, *Headlong Hall*
	Heber, *Masque of Gwendolen*	Scott, *Antiquary*
	Hunt, *Rimini*	Betham, *Lay of Marie*
1817	Frere, *Monks & Giants*	
	Peacock, *Round Table*	
1818	Milman, *Samor*	Meredith, *Llewelyn*
		Keats, 'To J. H. Reynolds'
		Peacock, *Melincourt*
		Bouchier, *Dream of Youth*
		M. Shelley, *Frankenstein*
1819	Woodley, *Cornubia*	Emerson, 'Knights of Square Table'
		Montgomery, *Greenland*
1820	Willyams, 'Arthur'	Keats, 'Eve of St Agnes'
		Wordsworth, 'Artegal & Elidure'
		Scott, *Ivanhoe*
		Scott, *Monastery*
		Scott, *Abbot*
1821	Praed, 'Gog'	Anon, 'Lines for recital'
	Anon, 'Bwrdd Arthur'	Scott, *Kenilworth*
	Emerson, 'Arthur's Dream'	Anon, 'Prophecy of Taliesin'
		Parry, 'Heroes of Cymru'
1822	(?) Lytton, 'Fairy Bride'	Wordsworth, *Ecclesiastical Sketches*
		Middleton, *Poetical Sketches*
		Scott, *Peveril of the Peak*
		Jones, 'Vale of Tywy'
		Irving, *Bracebridge Hall*
		Hunt, *The Dogs*
		Shelley, 'Charles I'
		Hemans, *Welsh Melodies*
		Scott, 'Carle, now the . . .'
		Porden, *Coeur de Lion*
1823	Praed, *Lillian*	Scott, *Quentin Durward*
	Moultrie, *La Belle Tryamour*	Salmon, *Stonehenge*
		Anon, 'Faery President'
		E.H., 'Witch Ladye'
		Anon, 'Stonehenge'

Date	*1*	*2*
1824		Prichard, *Welsh Minstrelsy*
		Giffard, 'St Michael's Mt'
1825	Dibdin, *Merlin's Mount*	Scott, *Betrothed*
		Scott, *Talisman*
		Bowles, 'Glastonbury Abbey'
1826		Pennie, 'Richard Coeur de Lion'
		Lawrance, 'Lady Jane's Merlin'
1827	Wilmer, *Merlin*	Hood, *Midsummer Fairies*
	Davies, 'Enchanted Shield'	Anon, 'Welsh War Song'
	Hogg, *Fabulous History*	Williams, *Cardiff Castle*
		Gladstone, 'Epilogue'
1828	Cookson, *Glastonbury*	Anstice, *Richard Coeur de Lion*
		Scott, *Fair Maid of Perth*
		Lawrence, 'Days of Chivalry'
		Cornwall, 'Stonehenge'
		Hood, 'Decline of Chivalry'
		Prichard, ed., *Cambrian Wreath*
1829	Peacock, *Misfortunes of Elphin*	Southey, 'At Banavie'
	Anon, 'Merlin Redivivus'	Trench, 'To W. B. Donne'
	Michell, 'Tintagel Castle'	Scott, *Anne of Geierstein*
	Costello, 'Funeral Boat'	Halleck, 'Alnwick Castle'
1830	Oxonian, 'Lines'	Atherstone, *Sea-Kings*
	Ellylless, 'Grave of King Arthur'	R., 'English Chronicles'
	Hoyle, *Pilgrim of Hebrides*	Russell, 'Francesca da Rimini'
		Moir, 'Tower of Erceldoune'
1831	Praed, 'Haunted Tree'	Peacock, *Crotchet Castle*
	Anon, 'Merlin's Prophecy'	Lytton, 'Rats and Mice'
	C., 'St Michael's Mt'	Stokes, *Song of Albion*
	Hollings, 'To Morgan Le Fay'	Landor, *Romance and Reality*
	Ellerton, *Triermain*	
	Parker, 'Celtic Annals'	
1832	Pennie, *Dragon-King*	Lytton, *Eugene Aram*
		Davies, 'Ode at Eisteddfod'
		Mitford, 'Dedicatory Epistle'
		Hawker, 'Silent Tower'
		Scott, *Castle Dangerous*
		Pringle, 'Dream of Fairy-Land'
		Hoyle, 'Cambria'
1833	Landon, 'Legend of Tintagel'	Liddell, *Wizard of North*
	Tennyson, 'Lady of Shalott'	Maginn, 'Prophecy of Plenty'
1834	Pocock, *King Arthur*	Coleridge, 'Pang More Sharp'
	Ord, *England*	Stokes (?), 'Dosmerry Pool'
	Anon, 'Legend of Shewin' Shiels'	
1835	Wordsworth, 'Egyptian Maid'	Alford, *School of Heart*
	Boyle, *Gorlaye*	Landor, 'To Joseph Ablett'
	Alford, 'Ballad of Glastonbury'	Bowles, 'Lay of Talbot'
	Alford, 'Glastonbury'	Maginn, 'The Fraserians'

Date	1	2
1836		Collingwood, *Alfred the Great*
		Sherwood, *The Cloak*
		Hawker, 'The Wreck'
1837		Hunt, 'Bodryddan'
1838	Darley, 'Merlin's Last Prophecy'	Merivale, 'Chronicle'
	Buchanan, 'Merlin's Tomb'	Maclise, 'Christmas Revels'
		Herbert, *Attila*
		Buchanan, 'Sonnet to Fountain'
1839	Roscoe, 'Iron Gate'	Bowen, *Ystradffin*
	Lee, *Harlequin & Mother Redcap*	Macleod, *Age of Chivalry*
1840	Buchanan, 'Arthur's Weird'	Darley, *Thomas à Becket*
	Costello, 'The Legend'	
	Anon, *Thomas Thumbe Part II*	
1841		Beresford-Hope, 'Kilmallock'
1842	Tennyson, 'Sir Galahad'	Faber, 'Vision of Bright Seas'
	Tennyson, 'Sir Launcelot'	Jeffreys, *Hoel the Hostage*
	Tennyson, 'The Epic'	
	Tennyson, 'Morte d'Arthur'	
	Anon, *Harlequin King Arthur*	
	Whytehead, 'Deem not for'	
	De Vere, 'Henry II at Tomb'	
	Lytton, 'Lady and Dogs'	
1843	Riethmuller, *Launcelot of the Lake*	Lytton, *Last of the Barons*
	Aytoun, 'La Mort d'Arthur'	Ainsworth, *Windsor Castle*
	Leigh, *Jack the Giant Killer*	Sigourney, 'Carlisle'
	Beresford-Hope, 'A Dream'	
1844	Anon, 'Ylle Cutt Mantell'	Yonge, *Abbeychurch*
		E. B. Browning, 'Fourfold Aspect'
		Emerson, 'Politics'
1845		Churton, Margaret Bisset'
		Anon, 'Knight of Magic Loom'
1846	Horne, 'Three Knights of Camelott'	Anon, 'Sir Tudor ap Grono'
	Emerson, 'Merlin I, II'	Anon, 'Thomas the Rhymer'
	Williams, 'Hall of the Nations'	
	Anon, *Jack the Giant Killer*	
1847		Disraeli, *Tancred*
		Lloyd, 'Drugarn'
1848	Lytton, *King Arthur*	Lytton, *Harold*
	Lowell, *Vision of Sir Launfal*	Longfellow, 'Castle Builder'
	Anon, 'Merlin & the Knight'	Thomas, 'Ogier the Dane'
1849	Oxenford, 'Wigolais of the Wheel'	Lytton, *Caxtons*
	Stephens, 'King Arthur'	Haslehurst, *Penmaen-Mawr*
		Sterling, 'Coeur de Lion'

Appendix D

List of Paintings Concerned with the Arthurian Legends

Blake, William. *The Ancient Britons*.
Watercolour.
Exhibited at 28 Broad Street, London in 1809. Number V in Blake's *Descriptive Catalogue*; in *Poetry and Prose of William Blake*, edited by Geoffrey Keynes (1956), 608 – 12. William Michael Rossetti refers to a 'watercolour (or a minor record of it)' in the British Museum; and Seymour Kirkup made a sketch of the painting from memory: see W. M. Rossetti ed. *Rossetti Papers 1862 – 1870* (1903), 170, 172, 178.
Location unknown.
—————. *The Characters in Spenser's 'Faerie Queene'*.
Watercolour and ink on muslin. 45.7 × 135.8 cm. c. 1825.
Prince Arthur is the second horseman from the right: see John E. Grant and Robert E. Brown, 'Blake's Vision of Spenser's *Faerie Queene*: A Report and an Anatomy', *Blake Newsletter*, no. 31, vol. 8 (1974 – 1975), 56 – 85.
Petworth House, West Sussex.
Cattermole, George. *King Henry II Discovering the Relics of King Arthur in Glastonbury Abbey*.
Watercolour.
Exhibited at Royal Academy (234) in 1826.
Location unknown.
Laing Art Gallery has Cattermole's undated watercolour *Interior of Glastonbury Abbey*. According to the *Catalogue of Watercolour Drawings* (1939), this represents 'The discovery of the remains of King Arthur at Glastonbury'. It may therefore be related to Cattermole's RA picture. See my Chapter 1, n. 31.
Collingwood, William. *Tintagel Castle, the Birthplace of Arthur*.
Exhibited at Royal Academy (520) in 1843.
Review: *Art Union* (1843), 173.
Location unknown.
Corbould, George James. *The Knight and the Hag (from the Wife of Bath's Tale)*.
Exhibited at Royal Academy (664) in 1802.
Location unknown.
Cranch, Christopher Pearse. *The Lady of Shalott*.
Painted in 1844. See letter of 27 March 1844, in *Early Letters of George William Curtis to John S. Dwight* (New York, 1898), 162; cited in John Olin Eidson, *Tennyson in America: his reputation and influence from 1827 to 1858* (Athens, Georgia, 1943), 220n.
Location unknown.

Dyce, William. *Religion: the Vision of Sir Galahad and his Company*.
Pen and ink. 22.8 × 30.5 cm.
A design made in 1847 for Dyce's later fresco in the Palace of Westminster.
Reproduced: Marcia Pointon, *William Dyce 1806 – 1864*, plate 156.
Aberdeen Art Gallery.
——————. *Piety: The Departure of the Knights of the Round Table on the Quest for the Holy Grail*.
Watercolour. 23.1 × 44.1 cm.
Exhibited at Royal Academy (889) in 1849.
Reproduced: Pointon, *Dyce*, plate 150.
Aberdeen Art Gallery.
Fielding, Anthony Vandyke Copley. *The Fairy Lake, a scene from La Mort d'Arthur*.
Exhibited at Old Watercolour Society (78) in 1837.
Review: *Athenaeum*, 29 April 1837, 308.
Location unknown.
Fuseli, Henry. *The Knight Finds the Hag Transformed into a Beautiful Young Wife*.
Oil. 80.8 × 68.6 cm. c. 1812.
Reproduced: Gert Schiff and Paola Viotto, *L'Opera completa di Füssli* (Milan, 1977), plate 226.
Petworth House, West Sussex.
Gandy, Joseph Michael. *The Tomb of Merlin*.
Watercolour. 76 × 132 cm.
Exhibited at Royal Academy (799) in 1815.
Reproduced: John Summerson, *Heavenly Mansions* (London, 1949), plate 34.
Royal Institute of British Architects.
Lejeune, Henry. *Prince Arthur's Dream (from Spenser)*.
Exhibited at Royal Academy (107) in 1843.
Review: *Art Union* (1843), 107.
Location unknown.
MacIan, Ronald Robert. *Sir Tristram in the Cave*.
Exhibited at New Watercolour Society in 1839; and Royal Scottish Academy (90) in 1840, where it was titled *King Mark of Cornwall and his Retinue discover Queen Isolt and Sir Tristram in the Cave*.
Review: *Fraser's Magazine*, 19 (June 1839), 743 – 50
Location unknown.
Martin, John. *Arthur and Aegle in the Happy Valley ('Now as night gently deepens round them')*.
Oil. 122.5 × 183.5 cm.
Exhibited at Royal Academy (566) in 1849
Reviews: *Art Journal* (1849), 175; *Athenaeum*, 26 May 1849, 549; *Literary Gazette*, 26 May 1849, 399; *The Times*, 5 May 1849, 5.
Reproduced: Christopher Johnstone, *John Martin* (London, 1974), 93.
Laing Art Gallery, Newcastle.
Montaigne, William John. *Prince Arthur at the battle of Caerbadon. ('He is said to have worsted the Saxons in twelve successive battles')*.
Exhibited at Royal Academy (385) in 1848.
Location unknown.
Palmer, Samuel. *King Arthur's Castle, Tintagel, Cornwall*.
Exhibited at Old Watercolour Society (222) in 1849. See letters to Edward Calvert, 25 July 1848, and to Thomas More Palmer, July 1848, in *The Letters of Samuel Palmer*, edited by Raymond Lister, 2 vols (Oxford, 1974), I, 458, 460.
British Museum has *Tintagel* (1910. 7.16.17) 26 × 36.8 cm. Chalk and watercolour.

Reproduced: Martin Hardie, *Watercolour Painting in Britain*, 3 vols (1966 – 1968), II, plate 153. Ashmolean Museum has *Tintagel Castle; approaching Rain*. Reproduced: David Blayney Brown, *Samuel Palmer 1805 – 1881: A Loan Exhibition* (London, 1982), 60 – 61. Brown also refers to a 'pen scribble' at the Institut Neerlandais, Paris.

Paton, Joseph Noel. *Design for Lancelot, Tristram* and *Galahad* (?).
> In Paton Sketchbook (D4252), c. 1845 – 1847, on pp. 3, 7A, 132D. See Debra N. Mancoff, *The Arthurian Revival in Victorian Painting*, 2 vols. Doctoral Thesis (University Microfilms, 1982), II, 678.
> National Gallery of Scotland.

Peabody, Sophia. *The Lady of Shalott.*
> Sketch made in c. 1839. See letter from Elizabeth Peabody to William J. Rolfe in 1884, quoted in Rolfe's preface to his *Select Poems of Alfred Lord Tennyson* (Boston, Mass., 1885), v – vi; cited in Eidson, 40, 212n.
> Location unknown.

Pickersgill, Frederick Richard. *Amoret, Aemylia and Prince Arthur in the Cottage of Sclaunder (Spenser).*
> 58 × 87 cm.
> Exhibited at Royal Academy (13) in 1845.
> Review: *Art Union* (1845), 180; *Fraser's*, 31 (June 1845), 719.
> Reproduced: from an engraving by G. A. Periam, *Art Journal* (1852), 367 (where it is retitled *Florimel and the Witch*).
> Tate Gallery.

Prout, Samuel. *Arthur's Castle at Tintagel, Cornwall.*
> Exhibited at Royal Academy (560) in 1808.
> Location unknown.

Scott, William Bell. *King Arthur carried to the land of enchantment ('Some men yet say, in many parts of England, that Arthur is not dead; but by the will of our Lord Jesu, carried into another place . . . ' Romance of Arthur).*
> Exhibited at Royal Academy (1184) in 1847; and at Royal Scottish Academy (384) in 1848.
> Review: *Art Union* (1847), 200.
> Reproduced: from an engraving by Linton, in *Illustrated London News*, 8 May 1847, 296; and, from a photograph, in Joanna Banham and Jennifer Harris, *William Morris and the Middle Ages* (Manchester, 1984), 174.
> Location unknown.

Uwins, Thomas. *The Lady of the Lake* and *The Vision of Sir Percivale. From the Romance of Arthur.*
> Exhibited at Old Watercolour Society (43) in 1816.
> Both were used as illustrations for the Walker and Edwards edition of Malory in 1816. See *A Memoir of Thomas Uwins*, by Mrs Uwins, 2 vols (London, 1858), I, 153.
> Location unknown.

Wood, John. *Emmeline.*
> 112 × 99 cm.
> Exhibited at British Institution (424) in 1832.
> Location unknown.

Appendix E

List of Graphic and Other Works Concerned with the Arthurian Legends

Anonymous. John Joseph Merlin's chariot, painted with 'various emblematical figures of Merlin, the ancient British Magician'. 1802. Reproduced, from an engraving by George Perfect Harding, in *Wonderful and Scientific Museum*, 6 vols (London, R.S. Kirby, 1803 – 1820), I, 274.

——————. Illustrations for Thomas Love Peacock, *The Round Table; or, King Arthur's Feast* (Arliss, 1817). Four of these depict Arthur and Merlin prominently: pp. (13), 16, 17, 23.

——————. 'Sweating a Sovereign'. Illustration of the traditional ballad 'When good King Arthur ruled this land'. In *Punch*, 3 (December 1842), 228.

——————. Illustration for 'Merlin and the Knight'. In *Rose, or Affection's Gift* (1844), 134.

——————. Illustration, engraved by C. M. Gorway, for 'Sir Lancelot du Lake'. In J. S. Moore ed. *The Pictorial Book of Ballads, Traditional and Romantic. Second Series* (Washbourne, 1848).

Bewick, Thomas and John. Illustrations for *Fabliaux or Tales, abridged from French manuscripts of the XIIth and XIIIth centuries by M. Le Grand*, selected and translated into English Verse by Gregory Lewis Way, 2 vols. Vol 1 (Bulmer, 1796); vol 1 reissued and vol 2 (Faulder, 1800). Way had made preliminary sketches for these illustrations.
Reviews: *British Critic*, NS 6 (1816), 60 – 65; *Monthly Review*, 23 (1797), 174 – 76; and 36 (1801), 276.

Brooke, William Henry. Illustrations for Thomas Keightley, *The Fairy Mythology*, 2 vols (Ainsworth, 1828). Launfal is depicted in I, 43, and the Island of Avalon in I, 74.
Reviews: *Gentleman's Magazine*, 103 (May 1833), 433 – 36; *Literary Gazette*, 2 February 1828, 73.

Corbould, Edward Henry. Six illustrations, engraved by Smith, for 'Sir Lancelot du Lake'. In Samuel Carter Hall ed. *The Book of British Ballads. First Series* (How, 1842).

Craig, William Marshall. Six illustrations, engraved by S. Noble, R. Rhodes and W. Findon, for [Malory], *La Mort d'Arthur: The most Ancient History of the Renowned Prince Arthur and the Knights of the Round Table*, 3 vols (Wilks, 1816).

'Crowquill, Alfred' (= Alfred Forrester). Illustration of Sadler's Wells production of *Harlequin King Arthur*. In *Illustrated London News*, 31 December 1842, 537.

Cruikshank, George. Five full-page illustrations and two vignettes, engraved by Williams and Bonner, for Kane O'Hara, *Tom Thumb: A Burletta* (Rodd, 1830).
Review: *Literary Gazette*, 8 January 1831, 24.

Franklin, John. Eight illustrations, engraved by Green, T. Williams, Nicholls and T. Armstrong, for 'King Arthur's Death'. In Samuel Carter Hall ed. *The Book of British Ballads. First Series* (How, 1842).

——————. Illustration for 'Sir Launcelot du Lake' (= Way's translation of 'The Vale of False Lovers'). In *Ballads and Metrical Tales* (Burn, 1845).

Hine, Henry George. 'King Arthur's Court'. In *Punch*, 5 (July 1843), 38 – 39.

Leech, John. Illustrations, engraved by H. Vizetelly, for Percival Leigh, *Jack the Giant Killer* (Orr, 1843).

Pocock, Isaac. Designs for Drury Lane production of his *King Arthur and the Knights of the Round Table* (1834). Pencil and watercolour. Theatre Museum, London. Four designs were exhibited at Sunderland: see *The Spectacular Career of Clarkson Stanfield 1793 – 1867* (Tyne and Wear County Council Museums, 1979), 64 – 65. A poster for this production, showing two tilting knights, (which may be by Pocock) is depicted in John Parry's painting *A London Street Scene* (1835). Parry's painting is reproduced in Angus Wilson, *The World of Charles Dickens* (1970), plate facing p. 173.

Rowlandson, Thomas. *The last scene of 'Tom Thumb' at the Scarborough Theatre.* Illustration for William Combe *et at, Poetical Sketches of Scarborough* (Ackerman, 1813). Reproduced in V. C. Clinton-Baddeley, *The Burlesque Tradition in English Theatre after 1660* (Methuen, 1973).

S.,P. Two illustrations, engraved by J.A., of Drury Lane production of Dryden and Purcell's *King Arthur*. In *Illustrated London News*, 19 November 1842, 461.

Selous, Henry. Two illustrations, engraved by C. Gray, for Walter Scott. *The Bridal of Triermain*. In *Poems and Pictures: a Collection of Ballads, Songs and Other Poems* (Burns, 1846).

Review: *Foreign Colonial and Quarterly Review*, 7 (1846), 239.

Stothard, Thomas. Illustrations (sixteen are Arthurian), engraved by Angus Kent, for Walter Scott, *The Bridal of Triermain*. In *The Royal Engagement Pocket Atlas for the Year 1815*.

Thompson. Illustration, engraved by McKenzie, for 'The Prophecy of Merlin'. In Anne Bannerman, *Tales of Superstition and Chivalry* (Vernon and Hood, 1802).

Turner, Joseph Mallord William. Four topographical illustrations, engraved by W. Miller and J. Horsburgh, for *Sir Tristrem* and *The Bridal of Triermain*, in Walter Scott, *Poetical Works* (Cadell, 1834), V, XI. The watercolour design for the 'Mayburgh' plate (incorrectly subtitled 'King Arthur's Round Table', by Turner) in *Bridal* was offered for sale at Phillips's, 15 April 1985: reproduced in *Country Life*, 31 January 1985.

Uwins, Thomas. Four illustrations, engraved by C. Warren, for [Malory], *The History of the Renowned Prince Arthur, King of Britain*, 2 vols (Walker and Edwards, 1816).

Williams, Samuel. Illustration for 'A Day-Dream at Tintagel'. In William Howitt, *Visits to Remarkable Places: Old Halls, Battle Fields, and Scenes Illustrative of striking passages in English History and Poetry* (Longman, Orme, Brown, Green and Longmans, 1840).

——————. Illustrations for *The Mabinogion*, translated by Lady Charlotte Guest, 3 vols (Longman, Brown, Green and Longmans, 1849).

INDEX

(As the Appendices are arranged alphabetically, they are not included in the Index)

A., 'An Ode, on the Birthday of His Royal Highness', 27.
Ablett, Joseph, 85; *Literary Hours*, 85, 86.
Abrams, M. H., 155n.
Adelphi Theatre, 126.
Ainsworth, William Harrison, 59n.
Albert, Prince, 126, 163.
Albrecht von Scharfenberg, *Der jungere Titurel*, 84, 208.
Alderley Edge, 92 – 93.
Alford, Henry, 80 – 82; 'The Ballad of Glastonbury', 20 – 21, 81, 149, 158, 235; *The School of the Heart*, 81, 250; 'Sonnet XIV. Glastonbury', 81.
Alfred, King, 16 – 17, 20, 30, 40, 220, 239.
Allegory, 48, 126, 158 – 67, 169, 172, 179, 193, 194, 198 – 201, 203, 207, 211, 216 – 17, 231, 232, 233, 245 – 46, 254.
Allingham, William, 233, 243.
Allott, Kenneth and Miriam, 88n.
Althorp, John, *Viscount*, 18.
Amadis of Gaul, 122, 133.
Anderson, James, plate 10a.
Aneurin, 20, 105.
Anglesey, Marquess of, 48.
Anglo-Saxon Chronicle, 32.
Annual Review, 89, 114n, 132n, 153n.
Anstice, Joseph, *Richard Coeur de Lion*, 15.
Anstruther, Sir Ralph Abercrombie, 225n.
Anti-Jacobin, 131, 141.
Aran (Raran, Rauran), Mount, 57, 68, 78.
Archaeologia, 68.
Archaeologist, and Journal of Antiquarian Science, 225n.

Ariosto, Ludovico, 139 – 40, 146, 147, 150, 156, 164, 192, 251.
Armorica, 7, 16, 18, 149.
Arne, Thomas, 119.
Arnold, Matthew, 'Tristram and Iseult', 88n.
Arthur: historical figure, 5 – 10; minor role in historical poetry, 10 – 19; and Anglican Church, 19 – 21; in historical Welsh context, 21 – 30; in Milman, Peacock, Pennie and Lytton, 30 – 44, 182 – 83; contemporary relevance, 45 – 49; Messianic role, 49 – 54, 95, 138, 219, 221, 226, 251; in early topography, 55 – 58; antiquarians on, 58 – 65; in guidebooks, 65 – 75; in topographical poetry, 75 – 112; cave legends, 88 – 95; in burlesque, 115 – 30, 137 – 39; ironic treatment, 131 – 35; parody, 135 – 37; and Wellington, 50 – 52, 137 – 39; in Italian medley poem; 139 – 47; in fairyland romance, 148 – 58; 167 – 76; in allegory, 158 – 67; in Tennyson's drafts, 190 – 94; death, 212 – 17; reasons for Revival, 220 – 21; availability of legends, 221 – 26; critical reception, 226 – 29; critical reception of Tennyson, 229 – 50; influence of Tennyson, 250 – 53; in Tennyson's later development, 253 – 54. Plates 2a – 4b, 6b, 8a, 9a – 11b, 14, 15, 16.
Arthur (Longleat MS 55), 60n.
Arthur's Camp, 72.
Arthur's Chair, 68, 69, 76.
Arthur's O'on (Oven), 66, 76 – 77.
Arthur's Stone, 68 – 69, 253.
Arthur's Tomb, 71.
Arthur's tombstone, 70.

Arthur's wassail-cup, 86.
Art Union, 33n.
Ascham, Roger, 204.
Ashmole, Elias, 11.
Astley's (Royal Amphitheatre), 124, 126, 145.
Athenaeum, 19, 36, 52n, 71, 73, 142n, 153n, 225n, 228, 229, 234, 236, 244n.
Atherstone, Edwin, 241, 243.
Aubin, R.A., 12n.
Auray, Castle, 68.
Aurelius Ambrosius, 22, 31, 96.
Avalon (Avilion, Avalonia), 10, 13, 16, 22, 30, 50, 52, 53, 55, 97, 148 – 49, 191, 193, 213, 214, 215, 250, 253n.
Awntyrs of Arthur, The, 97.
Axon, William, 92.
Aytoun, William, 'La Mort d'Arthur', 136 – 37, 251.

Bacon, Francis, 74, 108.
Badon, 8, 10, 11, 12, 31, 55, 58, 60.
Bailey, Philip, *Festus*, 243.
Bairdown, Dartmoor, 96.
Bannerman, Anne, 'The Prophecy of Merlin', 149, 171, 174, 223, 235, 251. Plate 2a.
Baranton, 73.
Barbazan, Etienne, 204n.
Bardsey Island, 63, 102, 156, 162n.
Barham, Richard Harris, 'The Lay of Sir Lionel', 177, 185.
Barlow, Joel, *The Columbiad*, 242.
Bassaleg, 63.
Bath, 61.
'Battle of Vittoria, The', 50.
Beale, Anna, *The Vale of the Towey*, 68.
Beauchamp, Lord, 49.
Beaumaris, 28.
Beckery, 61, 80.
Bede, 19, 20, 43.
Bedivere (Bedwyr), 105, 214, 216, 249.
Benedict of Peterborough, 13.
Beresford-Hope, Alexander James, 149, 155, 210, 250; 'A Dream', 53 – 54, 158; 'Prester John', 251; 'A Vision of Babylon', 53.
Berni, Francesco, 140.
Betham, Matilda, *The Lay of Marie*, 178.

Bewick, John and Thomas, 183, 185. Plates 1a, 1b.
Bijou, 46n.
Bingley, William, *North Wales*, 68, 104.
Bird, Edward, 47.
Blackmore, Sir Richard, 225, 243; *Prince Arthur*, 6; *King Arthur*, 6, 97.
Blackwood's Edinburgh Magazine, 83n, 93, 138n, 139n, 141, 177, 230n, 246.
Blair, Hugh, 154.
Blake, William, *The Ancient Britons*, 159; *Descriptive Catalogue*, 159; *Jerusalem*, 160, 241; 'Merlin's Prophecy', 168.
Bloomfield, Robert, *The Banks of the Wye*, 78 – 79.
Bodryddan, 86, 102.
Boiardo, Matteo Maria, 140.
Book illustration, 52n, 56, 61, 66n, 116, 120, 139, 149, 150, 152, 157n, 159, 177, 183, 185, 251, 252.
Borlase, William, 61.
Bors, 129.
Bourbons, 45.
Bowdler, Henry, 26.
Bowen, Melesina, *Ystradffin*, 86.
Bowles, William Lisle, 79, 86, 227, 241; *Annals and Antiquities of Lacock Abbey*, 79; *Banwell Hill*, 79, 83; 'Glastonbury Abbey and Wells Cathedral', 79 – 80, 149.
'Boy and the Mantle, The', 67, 97, 114 – 16, 218.
Boyd, Henry, 139.
Boyle, John Magor, *Gorlaye*, 112 – 13, 170.
Brangwen (Branguien), 110.
Bray, Anna Eliza, *Legends from the Border of the Tamar and Tavey*, 154; *Letters written during a Tour through Normandy*, 68, 95 – 96.
Bray, Edward Atkyns, 95 – 96; 'To Merlin', 96.
Bright, Michael, 235n.
Brinkley, Roberta Florence, 6n, 121n.
British Critic, 50n, 228.
British Institution, 123n.
British Quarterly Review, 235, 246.
Brittany (Breton), 63, 68, 71, 72, 74, 87, 177, 224.
Britton, John, 60.
Broceliande, 73.
Brompton, John, 14.

Brontë, Charlotte, 52.
Brooke, William Henry, 149, 177, 183.
Brougham, Henry, *Baron*, 18, 48n, 138.
Brown, Ford Madox, 253.
Brown, Iain G., 66n.
Brown, Paul A., 2n.
Browning, Elizabeth Barrett, 229n;
    'The Fourfold Aspect', 155, 210.
Browning, Robert, 229n.
Brut Tysilio, 24, 33.
Bruts, Welsh, 21.
Bryant, Jacob, *A New System of
    Mythology*, 159.
Buchanan, Robert, 'Arthur's Weird',
    213, 215; 'Merlin's Tomb',
    170 – 71, 224.
Buckler, William E., 248.
Burges, Sir James Bland, *Richard the
    First*, 14, 148, 241.
Burke, Edmund, 39, 45.
Burn, Richard, see Nicolson, Joseph.
Burne-Jones, Sir Edward, 252 – 53.
Butler, Fanny Kemble, 230, 231n.
Butler, Marilyn, 44, 47, 237n.
'Bwrdd Arthur', 26n.
Byles, C.E., 254n.
Byron, Lord, 135, 140, 144, 170, 191,
    192, 239; *Beppo*, 141; *Don Juan*, 142.

C., 'St. Michael's Mount', 95, 110.
Cador (Cadwr), 48, 56.
Caerleon (Caerlleon), 7, 29, 31, 44, 55,
    58, 62, 65, 67, 70, 71, 72, 99, 102,
    104, 106, 149, 176, 220, 236, 237.
Caesar, 33, 39, 235.
Callcott, John Wall, 118, 127.
Cambrian Directory, The, 69.
Cambrian Quarterly Magazine, 28n, 36,
    73n, 102n, 103, 224n, 227, 228,
    229n.
Cambridge University, 15, 38, 53, 81,
    83, 99, 108, 144, 250; *Magazine*, 73;
    St John's College, 115; Trinity
    College, 53, 83, 84, 146, 192, 250.
Cambro-Briton, 26n, 27, 28n, 44n, 222,
    224.
Camden, William, 56, 58, 61.
Camel, River, 8, 55, 56, 57, 58, 108.
Camelford, 64, 65, 67, 70, 72, 73, 253.
Camelot, 56, 58, 60, 64, 191, 193, 197,
    198, 200, 217, 224, 225, 229 – 30,
    232, 238, 251.

Camlan (Camlann), 5, 18, 22, 26, 27,
    28, 29, 47, 63, 82, 171, 174, 190,
    222.
Campbell, Nancie, 190n.
Campbell, Thomas, 111; 'Lochiel's
    Warning', 167.
Canning, George, 141.
Caradoc (Cradocke), 26, 115, 165, 173.
Caradoc of Llancarfan, 7, 25.
Carduel, 32, 34, 42, 98, 99, 106, 108,
    165, 184, 189, 194.
Carew, Richard, 56 – 57, 64, 110, 113.
Carlisle, 62, 86, 97, 98, 99, 106, 223.
Carlyle, Susanna Maria, 91.
Carlyle, Thomas, *The Life of John
    Sterling*, 15n, 147.
Carlyon, Clement, 63.
Carmarthen (Caer-Mardin,
    Caermerddhyn, Maridunum), 50,
    55, 57, 58, 65, 68, 69, 70, 71, 99,
    125, 153, 172.
Carmarthen Journal, 28n, 102n, 171n.
Caroline, Queen (consort of George II),
    122; (consort of George IV), 143.
Carpenter, William Boyd (Bishop of
    Ripon), 216.
Carte, Thomas, *A General History of
    England*, 7, 24, 31, 62, 104.
Castel-an-Dinas, 55.
Castle Gunnion, 20.
Castletown, Isle of Man, 88.
Catholic Emancipation of 1829, 21,
    193.
Cattermole, George, 60; *King Henry II
    discovering the relics of King Arthur in
    Glastonbury Abbey*, 13, 60.
Cave Legends, 88 – 95; and see
    Merlin's Cave.
Caxton, William, 59, 203n.
Cento Novelle Antiche, 195n, 198, 225.
Cerdic, 7, 10, 31, 32, 36, 40, 41.
Cervantes, Miguel de, 121, 134.
Chalmers, Alexander, 152n.
Chandler, Alice, 3.
Charles I, 45.
Charles II, 21, 45.
Charles VII, King of France, 16.
Chateaubriand, 37.
Chaucer, Geoffrey, 94, 251; *The House
    of Fame*, 157; *The Squire's Tale*, 83;
    The Tale of Sir Thopas, 131, 162, 176;
    The Wife of Bath's Tale, 116, 153.

Chestre, Thomas, *Sir Launfal*, 73, 99, 142, 177, 178, 179.

Chevalier à l'Epée, Le, 118.

Chimney Corner Companion, 168n.

Chippindale, Christopher, 77n.

Chorley, Henry, 244.

Chrétien de Troyes, *Yvain*, 73.

Christian Examiner, 231.

Christian Teacher, 243n.

Christmas, 98, 105, 116, 123, 125, 126, 127, 128, 129, 218 – 19, 236, 239.

Church, Anglican, 19 – 21, 38n, 193, 218; Broad, 43; Roman Catholic, 21, 43, 45, 193.

Church of England Quarterly Review, 231.

Cilgerran Castle, 12, 22.

Clarke, Adam, 70.

Cobden, Richard, 48.

Cohen, Francis, 117.

'Cokwald's Dance, The', 115.

Coleridge, John, 36.

Coleridge, Samuel Taylor, 98, 135, 235, 242; 'Frost at Midnight', 157; 'Kubla Khan', 192 – 93, 243; 'The Pang More Sharp Than All', 169, 197; *Table Talk*, 240, 241.

Collingwood, George Lewes Newnham, *Alfred the Great*, 16 – 17, 241.

Collingwood, William, *Tintagel, the Birthplace of Arthur*, 66n.

Collinson, John, *The History of Somersetshire*, 60, 61, 190, 215, 222.

Colman, George, the Elder, *The Fairy Prince*, 123, 236.

Colman, George, the Younger, *The Battle of Hexham*, 118; *Poetical Vagaries*, 234.

Conybeare, John, *Richard the First in Palestine*, 15.

Cookson, Christopher, *Glastonbury Abbey*, 12 – 13, 80, 149, 154.

Cooper, Abraham, 206n.

Corbould, Edward Henry, plate 12.

Corbould, George, 116.

Cornish Guardian and Western Chronicle, 111, 112.

Cornwall, 16, 19, 24, 48, 63 – 65, 66n, 72, 74 – 75, 78, 84 – 85, 93 – 95, 96, 107 – 13, 134, 253-54.

Cornwall, Barry, 'Gyges', 142.

Cornwall, Ebenezer, 'Stonehenge', 77.

Cornwall Literary and Philosophical Institution, 108 – 09.

Costello, Louisa Stuart, 'A Dream', 154, 157 – 58; *The Falls, Lakes and Mountains of North Wales*, 75; 'The Funeral Boat', 195 – 96, 198, 213, 225, 230, 249; 'The Legend', 87 – 88; 'Lines written at Bremhill', 86; *Songs of a Stranger*, 86; *Specimens of the Early Poetry of France*, 86n, 177; *A Summer amongst the Bocages and the Vines*, 86 – 88; translates *Chevrefeuil*, 177; 'Laie de mort de Tristan', 224; 'Merlin the Enchanter', 87, 224.

Cottle, Joseph, *The Fall of Cambria*, 25, 241.

Covent Garden, Theatre Royal, 123, 145n, 234n.

Coventry, Walter, 14.

Cowper, William, 'Boudicca', 23.

Coxe, William, *A Historical Tour in Monmouthshire*, 67, 70, 78.

Coxon, Thomas, 139n.

Craig, William Marshall, plates 6a – 8b.

Craig y Dinas, 89 – 90.

Craik, Dinah Maria, 'Avillion', 252.

Cranch, Christopher Pearse, 252.

Creswick, Thomas, 66n.

Critical Review, 139n, 204n, 223, 244.

Crocker, A., 60n.

Croker, John Wilson, 95, 192, 229 – 30, 246.

Croker, Mrs (wife of John Wilson Croker), 95.

Croker, Thomas Crofton, *Fairy Legends and Traditions of the South of Ireland*, 154.

Cross, Tom Peete, 222.

Crouch, Nathaniel, *History of the Nine Worthies*, 6.

Crowquill, Alfred, 127. Plate 11a.

Crozier, Francis Rawdon, 47.

Cruikshank, George, 120, 139n.

D., Q.E., 225n.

Dagonet, 129.

Damon, S. Foster, 160n.

Dane, Joseph A., 131.

Daniel, John, *Ecclesiastical History of the Britons and Saxons*, 8.

Dante, 206n.
Darley, George, 210; 'Merlin's Last
    Prophecy', 52, 149, 171, 175.
Dashwood, Anna Maria, 86.
Davenant, William, *Britannia
    Triumphans*, 121.
Davies, Edward (prebendary of
    Llandaf), *Chepstow*, 76
Davies, Edward (rector of Bishopston),
    24; *Mythology and Rites of the British
    Druids*, 159, 222, 254.
Davies, Henry, 102; 'The Enchanted
    Shield', 102 – 3, 134 – 35; 156, 157,
    162n; 'Ode', 28.
Davy, Sir Humphry, 'The Death of
    Merlin', 168.
'Death of King Arthur, The', 212.
Dee (Deva), River, 57, 68, 78, 83, 153.
Democratic Review, see *United States
    Magazine*.
De Vere, Aubrey, 'King Henry at the
    Tomb of King Arthur', 13.
De Wilde, Samuel, 120.
Dial, 237n.
Dibdin, Charles, 124n.
Dibdin, Charles Isaac Mungo, *Wizard's
    Wake*, 124, 169.
Dibdin, Thomas, *Merlin's Mount*, 125,
    169; *A Metrical History of England*,
    125; *Reminiscences*, 123n; *St. David's
    Day*, 125.
Dickens, Charles, 120; *A Child's History
    of England*, 74n; *Great Expectations*,
    184; *The Pickwick Papers*, 120, 218.
Digby, Kenelm, *The Broadstone of
    Honour*, 161.
Dinas Emrys, 58, 65, 66, 67, 68, 69,
    222.
Dinas Vawr (Dinevowre), 57, 68.
Disraeli, Benjamin, 48.
Dod, Charlotte, 149.
Donne, William Bodham, 191.
Donovan, Edward, *Descriptive Excursions
    through South Wales*, 67, 68, 71, 72,
    104, 154.
Douglas, River, 23, 66.
Downman, Hugh, 'Ode, On Reading
    Mr. Hole's *Arthur*', 139n.
Doyle, Richard, 127n.
Dozmary Pool, 112.
Drayton, Michael, *Polyolbion*, 57 – 58,
    59, 64, 66, 68, 73, 101, 225.

Dreams, 157 – 58, 217, 219.
Drumelzier, 89.
Drury Lane, Theatre Royal, 122, 123,
    125, 127, 130n, 145n.
Dryden, John, 150, 243; *Cymon and
    Iphigenia*, 122; *King Arthur (Arthur and
    Emmeline)*, 6, 33n, 121, 122, 124,
    126n, 127, 145n, 150, 223, 225,
    236, 241, 251. Plates 10a, 10b.
Dubricius, 102.
Dugdale, Sir William, 35.
Dunlop, John Colin, *History of Fiction*,
    53, 133, 134, 223, 224.
Dunstanburgh Castle, 90.
Dunstanville, Francis, Lord de, 56, 64.
Durham, John, Earl of, 48.
Dyce, Alexander, 82.
Dyce, William, 33n, 163, 205, 251.

Earwaker, J.P., 92n.
Eclectic Review, 227, 244.
Ector (Hector), 110, 230.
Eden, River, 62.
Edgeworth, Maria, 142.
Edinburgh Review, 37n, 47, 132n, 227,
    229n, 242n.
Edward I, 25.
Edward III, 11.
Eggers, J. Philip, 2n.
Eidson, John Colin, 252n.
Eildon Hills, 88 – 89, 92, 220.
Elaine, 195, 253n.
Elizabeth I, 49, 153, 237.
Ellerton, John, 236.
Ellis, George, 14, 141, 174, 177, 222,
    223; *Specimens of Early English Metrical
    Romances*, 83, 98, 130 – 31, 132 – 33,
    134, 135 – 36, 156, 169, 177, 178,
    223, 230.
Ellylles, 'The Grave of King Arthur',
    28.
Elphin, 31, 44, 62, 104 – 05, 107.
Emerson, Ralph Waldo, 157, 210, 237;
    The Age of Fable, 161; 'Arthur's
    Dream', 157; 'King Richard's
    Death', 161; 'Merlin, I, II', 161,
    251.
Enderbie, Percy, 61; *Cambria
    Triumphans*, 21.
English Opera House, 121.
Epic, 49, 50, 216, 217 – 19, 228 – 29,
    231, 233, 234, 239 – 45.

Eton College, 35, 85, 120, 168n, 186.
Etonian, 99 – 100, 118n, 192n.
European Magazine, 50n, 76n, 93 – 94, 115.
Evans, Evan, 23, 104; *The Love of Our Country*, 22; *Some Specimens of the Poetry of the Antient Welsh Bards*, 21 – 22.
Evans, John, *Letters written during a tour through South Wales*, 67, 71, 72, 104, 105; *A Tour through part of North Wales*, 104.
Evans, Thomas (bookseller), *Old Ballads*, 104, 117.
Evans, Thomas (topographer), *Cambrian Itinerary (Walks through Wales)*, 68, 103.
Examiner, 41n, 48n, 150n, 227, 229, 231, 248n.
Excalibur (Excalibor, Excalibar, Caliburn, Caliburnus, Kaliburn), 13 – 16, 34, 52, 53, 63, 125, 137, 139, 147, 150, 193, 214, 215, 216, 233, 242, 249.
Eyston, Charles, *Little Monument*, 12.

Faber, George Stanley, *The Origin of Pagan Idolatry*, 84, 159, 223.
Fairy (Faerie, Fay, Fairyland), 16, 19, 22, 32, 71, 72, 89, 91, 94, 100, 101, 121, 123, 125, 126, 127, 128, 143, 148 – 89, 195 – 201, 203 – 04, 215, 217, 229, 232, 233, 236, 237, 244, 245n, 249, 254.
Farington, Joseph, 66n.
Farren, Elizabeth, 33n, 123n.
Faust, 122; Goethe's *Faust*, 167.
Fenton, Richard, *Tours in Wales*, 69.
Fielding, Copley, *The Fairy Lake*, 153.
Fielding, Henry, *The Tragedy of Tragedies*, 119 – 20, 131n, 143, 236.
Finlay, John, *Wallace*, 16, 149.
Fisher's Drawing Room Scrapbook, 95, 196n.
Fitzgerald, Edward, 217.
Foerster, Donald M., 239n.
Forbes, Duncan, 38n.
Forget Me Not, 12n, 111, 133n, 177, 195n.
Forster, John, 41, 47, 227n, 231, 237, 248.
Foscolo, Ugo, 141.

Fouqué, Friedrich, Baron de la Motte, *Eliduc*, 177, *Undine*, 154, 188.
Fox, Barclay, 74n, 147.
Fox, W.J., 241 – 42, 247.
Franklin, John (artist), plate 13.
Franklin, Sir John (explorer), 47.
Fraser's Magazine, 9n, 15n, 19n, 116, 138n, 147, 172n, 227n, 228n, 247n, 249n, 250n.
Frere, John Hookham, *The Monks and the Giants*, 51, 98 – 99, 140 – 41, 191, 192.
Friendship's Offering, 79n, 197n.
Froissart, Jean, 68, 98.
Fuller, Thomas, *The Church History of Britain*, 20, 190.
Fuseli, Henry, 116, 157n.

Gaines, Barry, 152n.
Galahad (Galath), 78, 81n, 102, 156, 157, 162, 175, 194, 201, 204, 207 – 11, 220, 225, 238, 251.
Gandy, Joseph Michael, 139n.
Garden, Francis, 248.
Gareth, 67.
Garrick, David, 236; *Cymon*, 122; *The Institution of the Garter*, 122 – 23, 236.
Gascoigne, George, *The Princely Pleasures*, 121, 237.
Gaskell, Elizabeth, 92 – 93.
Gastineau, Henry, *North Wales Illustrated*, 68.
Gawain (Gawaine, Gawin, Gwalchmai), 34, 49, 78, 107, 114 – 16, 146, 156, 157, 164, 165, 173, 218, 236. Plate 1b.
Gawaine's Chapel, 69.
Gem, 121n.
Genre, 228 – 29, 231 – 46.
Gentleman's Magazine, 9, 19n, 23, 27, 59, 60, 68, 71, 77, 79n, 82, 84, 139n, 226 – 27, 228n, 229n, 242.
Geoffrey of Monmouth (Galfridus), 2, 5, 6, 7, 19, 21, 24, 25, 32, 33, 41, 55, 57, 61, 68, 70, 77, 78 – 79, 102, 109, 110, 112, 148, 159, 164, 223, 225.
George IV, 99, 143, 145.
Geraint (Geriant, Geron), 63, 102 – 03, 157.
Gibbon, Edward, 39, 64; *The Decline and Fall of the Roman Empire*, 10, 190.

Giffard, Sir Ambrose Hardinge,
'Roncesvalles', 50 – 51; 'St.
Michael's Mount', 51, 94 – 95.
Gifford, William, 173n.
Gilbert, Davies, *The Parochial History of
Cornwall*, 64.
Gildas, 6, 33, 58, 104.
Giles, J.A., *History of the Ancient Britons*,
9.
Gilfillan, George, 231, 244.
Ginguené, Pierre Louis, 140.
Giraldus Cambrensis, 9, 13, 23, 25, 30,
55, 56, 58, 60, 61, 64, 66, 70, 104,
224.
Girouard, Mark, 54n, 161n.
Glasgow University Album, 171n, 213n.
Glastonbury, 6, 7, 8, 9, 12, 13, 14, 16,
20, 21, 22, 24, 25, 30, 31, 55, 56,
58, 60 – 61, 65, 67, 79 – 82, 97, 99,
105, 148, 149, 158, 190, 212, 215,
223, 224, 250; Abbot of, 14, 104;
Hermit of, 216; Thorn, 17.
Glein, River, 55.
Goethe, Johann Wolfgang von, *Faust*,
167.
Golagros and Gawain, 97.
Gorlois (Gothlois, Gorlaye), 31, 35, 63,
96, 108, 110, 112 – 13, 170.
Gower, John, 94.
Graelent (Gruelan), 177, 179, 185.
Grail (Sangreal, Sangraal, Grayle), 35,
82, 84, 131, 151, 155, 160, 161,
162n, 163, 191, 192, 207 – 11, 224n,
225, 233, 251.
Gray, Thomas, 23, 253; 'The Bard',
23, 25, 29; 'Ode on a Distant
Prospect of Eton College', 186.
Greenwood, the elder (scene painter at
Drury Lane), 123.
Grey, Charles, 2nd Earl, 18, 90.
Grismond's Castle, 56.
Grose, Francis, *Antiquities*, 60.
Guenevere (Gwenever, Guinevere,
Guinever, Guiniver, Guenever,
Gwynver, Gwiniverra, Gwenyfar,
Gwenyvar, Gwenhwyvar, Ganore,
Geneura), 5, 7, 9, 10, 15, 25, 29,
31, 32, 44, 47, 62, 97, 98, 101, 104,
107, 110, 112, 117, 118 – 19, 127,
129, 133, 137, 142, 143, 160, 171,
174, 176, 178, 182, 183, 189, 191,
193, 194, 200, 201 – 07, 212, 225,
238, 253n, 254; the three
Gueneveres, 6, 7, 9, 21, 222 – 23.
Guest, Lady Charlotte, see *Mabinogion*.
Guizot, Francois, 47.
Gwythno (Gwyddno), 44, 104, 105,
106.

H., J., 'Lines, supposed to have been
written on St. Michael's Mount',
93 – 94.
Hall, Samuel Carter, 212. Plates 12,
13.
Hallam, Arthur, 215 – 16, 237, 246,
247, 248.
Hallam, Henry, *A View of the State of
Europe during the Middle Ages*, 8.
Halm, Friedrich, *Griseldis*, 224 – 25.
Hals, William, 63, 64, 65, 112.
Hamilton, William, 123n.
Hamley, Edward, 'On Revisiting
Cornwall', 78.
Hanes Taliesin, 104.
Hanoverians, 49, 50n, 175.
Harding, James Duffield, 66n.
Hardinge, Sir Henry, 48.
Hardy, J., 'Legends of King Arthur',
92.
Hardyng, John, 5, 59, 229.
Harington, Sir John, 139.
Harlequin, 122, 124, 126, 145.
Harlequin and Good King Arthur, 126 – 27.
Plate 11a.
Harrison, William, 35.
Hartmann von Aue, *Iwein*, 224.
Hartshorne, Charles, *Ancient Metrical
Tales*, 115.
Harvey, A.D., 49n.
Haslehurst, George, *Penmaen-Mawr*, 28.
Haslewood, Joseph, 203n.
Hastings, Lady Flora, 'Sir Osric',
156n.
Hawke, Admiral, 49.
Hawkins, Sir Charles, 109.
Hawthorne, Nathaniel, 252.
Haymarket Theatre, 145n, 168n.
Hazlitt, William, *Lectures on the English
Poets*, 234; *The Spirit of the Age*, 234.
Heath, Charles, *An Excursion down the
Wye*, 78.
Heath, George, 230.
Heber, Amelia, 86, 116; *Life of Heber*,
102.

Heber, Reginald, 82, 98, 102, 140, 149, 228, 242, 243; 'A Ballad', 136n; *The Boke of the Purple Faucon*, 135 – 36; *The Masque of Gwendolen*, 29n, 102, 116 – 17, 128 – 29, 170, 174, 175, 223, 229, 236; *Morte d'Arthur*, 98, 129, 173 – 74, 205 – 06, 207, 210, 223, 229, 241.

Heber, Richard, 205n, 224n.

'Helen of Kirkconnell', 236.

Helio-Arkite theories, 84, 159.

Hemans, Felicia, 100, 102; *England and Spain*, 50; *Juvenile Poems*, 100; 'The Necromancer', 167; 'Taliesin's Prophecy', 27; *Welsh Melodies*, 100, 223.

Hengist, 31.

Henry II, 6, 8, 12, 13, 15, 22, 24, 26, 58.

Henry VIII, 20.

Henry of Huntingdon, 66.

Henry, Robert, *The History of Great Britain*, 7 – 8.

Heraud, J.A., 227n, 228.

Herbert, Algernon, *Britannia After the Romans*, 8, 9n, 159.

Herbert, William, *Attila*, 149, 241.

Hill, Aaron, *Merlin in Love*, 122.

Hilton, William, *Arthur, Monarch of the Britons*, 42.

Hine, Henry George, 138. Plate 11b.

Hingston, Francis, 110.

Hirst, Henry B., 'Launcelot of the Lake', 252n.

Hitchins, Fortescue, *The History of Cornwall*, 64.

Hoare, Sir Richard Colt, 66n, 104.

Hodgson, John, 62; *History of Northumberland*, 91, 92.

Hoel of Brittany, 87.

Hogg, James, 18.

Hogg, Thomas, *The Fabulous History of Cornwall*, 109 – 11, 149, 171, 205, 212, 223; 'On the Death of Her Majesty', 109n.

Hole, Richard, *Arthur*, 139, 225.

Holinshed, Raphael, 5 – 6, 21, 25, 32, 35, 43.

Hollings, J.F., 'To Morgan Le Fay', 175.

Homer, 139, 215, 217, 219, 239, 242, 243.

Hone, William, *Yearbook*, 59.

Hood, Robin, 220.

Hood, Thomas, 'A Lament for the Decline of Chivalry', 45 – 46, 155.

Hoole, John, 139, 140.

Hopkins, Annette B., 65n.

Hopkins, Manley, 230 – 31, 247.

Horne, Richard Hengist, 231, 232, 237, 247, 249; 'The Three Knights of Camelott', 162 – 63, 229, 251.

Housman, John, *A Descriptive Tour*, 62n.

Hoveden, Roger, 14.

Howells, William, *Cambrian Superstitions*, 68, 69.

Howitt, Mary, 92.

Howitt, Samuel, *King Arthur's Castle, Tintagel, Cornwall*, 66n.

Howitt, William, 'A Day-Dream at Tintagel', 71, 73, 178.

Howitt's Journal, 232n.

Hoyle, Charles, 241; 'Avebury', 77; 'Cambria', 84 – 85; *The Pilgrim of the Hebrides*, 83, 207 – 08, 210, 225; 'Stonehenge', 77.

Huggins, William, 139.

Hughes, John, *Horae Britannicae*, 24 – 25, 31, 104.

Hume, David, *The History of England*, 7, 190.

Hunt, Holman, *The Lady of Shalott*, 4, 252.

Hunt, John Dixon, 248.

Hunt, Leigh, 170, 203n, 231, 237, 241, 244 – 45, 246; 'Bodryddan', 86; 'The Descent of Liberty', 236; 'The Dogs', 51, 142; 'A Gentle Armour', 245; 'Llanbedr', 86; *The Story of Rimini*, 206, 230, 245.

Hurd, Richard, 131.

Hutchinson, William, *An Excursion to the Lakes*, 62n; *The History of Cumberland*, 62.

Igraine (Igrene, Igerna), 31, 35, 62, 63, 74, 110, 112, 170.

Illustrated London News, 127, 150, 241n, 245n.

Indicator, 241n.

Ireland, William Henry, *Vortigern*, 39.

'Iron Gates, The', 92.

Irving, Washington, *Sketchbook*, 218.

Iseult (Yseult, Isonde, Isolde, Isoude, Essylt), 35, 83, 87, 90, 110, 127, 159, 204, 205, 212. Plate 7a.

Jack the Giant Killer; or, the Knights of the Round Table, 127 – 28.
James II, 45.
Jameson, J.H., *Juvenile Drama Series*, 120.
Jeffrey, Francis, 228 – 29, 242.
Jeffreys, M.E., *Hoel the Hostage*, 26.
Jerdan, William, 136, 230, 246.
John of Glastonbury, 61, 80.
Johnson, Samuel, 66.
Johnson, W.R., *The History of England*, 17.
Johnston, Arthur, 4n, 11n, 90n.
Johnston, Roger, 123.
Jones, Edward, 100.
Jones, Ernest, 6n.
Jones, Theophilus, *A History of Brecknockshire*, 78.
Jonson, Ben, *The Masque of Oberon*, 123; *Prince Henry's Barriers*, 121.
Joseph of Arimathea, 17, 20, 21, 22, 34, 79, 81.
Joseph of Exeter, 56, 63.
Joyeuse Garde, 73, 191.
Juvenile Forget Me Not, 18.

Keats, John, 235, 248; 'La Belle Dame sans Merci', 177, 196; 'The Eve of St. Agnes', 169; *The Fall of Hyperion*, 239, 241, 242.
Keightley, Thomas, *The Fairy Mythology*, 149, 154, 155, 177, 178, 223.
Kemble, Charles, 33n.
Kemble, John Mitchell, 191, 194, 204, 238.
Kemble, John Philip, 123, 124.
Kempe, Alfred John, 59, 68, 95.
Kenyon, John Philipps, 7n.
'King Arthur's Death', 116.
King, Richard John, 212; *The Fairy Mythology of Tintagel*, 253 – 54.
Kingsland, William, 229n.
Kingsley, Charles, 247, 248 – 49, 250.
Knight, Charles, 146.
Knighton, Henry, 14.
Knight's Quarterly Magazine, 99n, 145 – 46.
Knowles, James, 190, 221.

Kozicki, Henry, 222.

Lachmann, Karl, 208n.
Lady of the Lake (Dame du Lac), 34, 73, 78, 101, 165, 175, 176, 179, 194, 215, 236, 237, 238, 249. Plates 4a, 6b.
Laing, David, 115.
Lamb, Charles, 168n.
Landon, Letitia Elizabeth, 'A Legend of Tintagel Castle', 196 – 97, 198, 213, 225, 230, 249.
Landor, Walter Savage, 'To Joseph Ablett', 85.
Langbaum, Robert, 209n.
Langland, William, *Piers Plowman*, 157.
Lappenberg, J.M., *History of England under the Anglo-Saxon Kings*, 8.
Lauder, Robert Scott, *The Lady of Shalott*, 252.
Launcelot (Lancelot), 10, 16, 35, 41, 51, 53, 61, 78, 98, 102, 107, 110, 117, 129, 133, 137, 151, 152, 162n, 164, 165, 173, 183, 189, 191, 194, 195, 196, 198, 200, 201 – 07, 214, 220, 225, 230, 232, 234, 236, 237, 238, 253n. Plates 5b, 6a, 7b, 12.
Launfal (Lanval), 99, 142, 143, 163, 176 – 89, 220, 223, 251. Plate 1a.
Lawrence, James, 'The Bosom Friend', 168n.
Le Grand d'Aussy, 177, 204n, 212; and see Way.
Lee, Richard Nelson, *Harlequin and Mother Red Cap*, 126, 169, 175.
Leech, John, 52n. Plate 9b.
'Legend of King Arthur, The', 236.
'Legend of Shewin' Shiels, The', 90 – 91.
Leigh, Percival, *Jack the Giant Killer*, 51, 127n, 251. Plate 9b.
Lejeune, Henry, 157n.
Leland, John, 56, 58, 60, 64, 80, 113.
Lewis, David, 224.
Lewis, Matthew Gregory, 92; *The Monk*, 90; 'Sir Guy the Seeker', 90, 152, 167; *Tales of Wonder*, 90.
Leyden, John, 98; 'Lord Soulis', 167; *Scenes of Infancy*, 89.
'Life and Death of Tom Thumb, The', 117.

Life, Death, and Renovation of Tom Thumb, The, 120n.
Lindsay, Jack, 187n.
Lingard, John, *The History of England*, 8.
Liston, John, 120.
Liston, Mrs, 120.
Literary Gazette, 19n, 46, 47, 116, 126n, 136, 225n, 230, 234, 242, 246.
Literary Magnet, 15n.
Literary Souvenir, 84, 175n.
Llanbedr, 86.
Llewarch Hen, 7.
Llewelyn ap Griffith, 25, 26 – 27.
Llewelyn ap Iorwerth (the Great), 22, 26, 28.
Lloyd, David, 'British Valour', 27.
Lloyd, John, 'Drugarn', 76; 'Ode to Princess Victoria', 29.
Lloyd, Michael, 187n.
Llwyd, Richard, *Beaumaris Bay*, 76; 'The Castle of Harlech', 25; 'To his Countrymen', 28.
Loathly Lady, 29n, 114 – 17, 223.
London Journal, 85.
London Review, 247n, 248n.
Long, Brian, 62n.
Longfellow, Henry Wadsworth, 'The Castle Builder', 155.
Lonsdale, Mark, 124.
Loomis, Roger Sherman, 5n, 61n.
Louis Philippe, King of France, 47, 166.
Lovelich, Henry, *Merlin*, 133, 169 – 70; *Saint Graal*, 131.
Lowell, James Russell, *The Vision of Sir Launfal*, 157, 163, 231, 251.
Lowe's Edinburgh Magazine, 74n.
Lucretius, 215.
Lyceum Theatre, 127.
Lydgate, John, 153, 223.
Lyell, Charles, *Principles of Geology*, 39.
Lyndhurst, John, *Baron*, 138.
Lyonesse (Lyonnesse), 57, 191.
Lyttelton, George, *The History of Henry II*, 7, 67, 190.
Lytton, Edward Bulwer, *Baron*, 3, 140, 192, 230; 'The Boatman', 186; 'The Distinction between Active Thought and Reverie', 186 – 87; *Essays Written in Youth*, 188; *Eugene Aram*, 182; 'The Fairy Bride', 106, 172,

181 – 89, 201, 249; *King Arthur*, 29n, 32 – 49, 52, 106 – 07, 118 – 19, 146 – 47, 154, 157, 164 – 67, 171, 172 – 73, 181, 194, 203, 219, 226, 227, 228, 229, 241, 242, 245n, 251; 'A Lament', 185; 'The Lady and the Dogs', 118; *The Last of the Barons*, 166; *The New Timon*, 146, 245n, *The Pilgrims of the Rhine*, 165, 187; 'The Rats and the Mice', 137; tr. Schiller's *Poems and Ballads*, 186; 'To the Lost', 185.
Lytton, Edward Robert Bulwer, *Earl* (Owen Meredith), 184, 253.

M., 'The Cambrian Legend of St. Keyna and Cadoc', 76; 'Description of St. Michael's Mount', 94.
Mabinogion, 34, 105, 158; tr. by Lady Charlotte Guest, 106, 107n, 157n, 221 – 22.
Macaulay, Thomas Babington, 36, 47, 48, 146; *The History of England*, 8.
Macaulay, Zachary, 146.
McCluhan, H.M., 248.
Macleod, Alexander, *The Age of Chivalry*, 97, 157.
Macpherson, James, *Ossian*, 26, 239.
Macready, William, 130n. Plates 10a, 10b.
Madden, Sir Frederick, 86n.
Madocks, William, 105.
Maginn, William, 'The Fraserians', 138; 'A Prophecy of Plenty', 172.
Malkin, Benjamin Heath, 64; *The Scenery, Antiquities and Biography of South Wales*, 69.
Mallet, David, *Northern Antiquities*, 33.
Malory, Sir Thomas, 2, 3, 5, 6, 11, 59, 61, 63, 67, 74, 107, 109, 127, 129, 151, 152, 153, 161, 163, 173, 190, 191, 192, 195, 198, 202, 203, 204, 205, 206, 207, 208, 210, 211, 212, 213, 214, 215, 222, 223, 224, 225, 230, 249, 251, 253; Southey ed., 203n, 205n; Walker and Edwards ed., 152, 203n, 205n; Wilks ed., 203n, 205n.
Manchester Mail, 92.
Mancoff, Debra N., 3n.
Mann, Phyllis G., 100n.

Manners, John Henry, *Journal of Three Years Travels*, 68, 69.
Mantell, Gideon, *Wonders of Geology*, 39.
Marie de France, 87, 177 – 78, 179.
Mark (Marc), 110.
Marlborough, Duke of, 50.
'Marriage of Sir Gawaine, The', 97, 98, 102, 114 – 15, 218.
Mary, the Virgin, 20, 29, 65, 80, 200.
Mason, H.A., 218.
Masque, 121, 122, 123, 194, 221, 236 – 39.
Meiryg, 24.
Melwas (Melvas), 7, 9, 25, 31, 44, 62, 104.
Meredith, Owen, see Lytton, Edward Robert Bulwer.
Meredith, W.E., *Llewelyn ap Iorwerth*, 26, 241.
Merivale, John Herman, 42; 'A Chronicle of England', 9 – 10; *Orlando in Roncesvalles*, 50, 241.
Merlin (Merddin, Marlyn), 10, 14, 18, 20, 26, 27, 28, 31, 40, 45, 49, 52, 55, 58, 63, 64, 66, 67, 68, 69, 70, 73, 74, 75, 76, 78, 83, 84, 85, 87, 88, 89, 90, 92, 93, 99, 100, 102, 103n, 105, 107, 108, 110, 111, 112, 120 – 27, 129, 131, 132, 133, 138, 139, 142, 145, 149, 150, 152, 153, 154, 156, 159, 161, 162, 165, 167 – 73, 178, 179, 190, 191, 193, 194, 201, 204, 217, 221, 222, 223, 224, 225, 237; and Stonehenge, 55, 77, 79. Plates 2b, 6b, 15.
'Merlin and the Knight', 251.
Merlin, John Joseph, 168 – 69.
'Merlin Redivivus', 100.
Merlin, Vulgate, 132, 224.
Merlin's Bridge, 69.
Merlin's Cave: Snowdonia, 27, 75; near Carmarthen, 57, 68, 69, 71, 153; Bairdown, 96; Richmond, 122; London, 168.
Merlin's Cave; or, Harlequin's Masquerade, 124 – 25, 145n, 169.
Merlin's Grove, 71.
Merlin's Hill (Mount), 71 – 72, 78.
Merlin's Museum, 168.
'Merlin's Prophecy for the Year 1831', 171.

Merriman, James Douglas, 2, 11n, 12n, 16n, 49n, 78n, 103n, 115n, 116n, 122n, 123n, 139n, 151n, 162, 164n, 168n, 177n.
Metropolitan Literary Journal, 19.
Metz, Conrad Martin, 39n.
Meyrick, Samuel Rush, *The History of Cardigan*, 62, 104.
Michel, Francisque, 86n, 87.
Michell, John, 'Tintagel Castle', 111.
Michell, Nicholas, 111.
Middleton, Marmaduke, *Poetical Sketches of a Tour in the West of England*, 79.
Mill, John Stuart, 36 – 37, 246, 247 – 48, 249.
Millais, Sir John Everett, 252.
Miller, Thomas, *History of the Anglo-Saxons*, 8 – 9.
Milman, Arthur, 36n.
Milman, Henry Hart, 120, 229; *History of Christianity*, 38n; *Judicium Regale*, 50; *Samor*, 30 – 45, 84, 96 – 97, 107, 132 – 33, 140, 170, 171, 210, 219, 226, 228, 239, 241, 242, 252.
Milner, John, 33; *The History of Winchester*, 8, 59.
Milnes, Richard Monckton, 237, 242, 244.
Milton, John (poet), 67, 73, 82 – 83, 117, 170, 239, 242, 243, 246n.
Milton, John (sculptor), 168 – 69.
Mischler, S.M., 111.
Mitford, John, 'Dedicatory Epistle', 82 – 83.
Moir, David Macbeth, 132 – 33; 'The Decay of Chivalry', 45; 'Sir Eliduc', 177; 'The Tower of Erceldoune', 83.
Monmouthshire Merlin, 100, 171n.
Mont St Michel, 25, 87.
Monthly Magazine, 36, 171n, 224n.
Monthly Repository, 86.
Monthly Review, 19, 132n, 228.
Moore, Thomas, 120.
Mordred (Modred, Medrawd), 5, 7, 8, 25, 29, 31, 47, 55, 58, 67, 97, 98, 108, 129, 156, 159, 174, 193, 194, 205, 213, 222, 223, 225; Modred in Gray and Morgan, 22 – 23.
Moreau, Jean Michel, 139n.
Morgan, Caesar, 'The Shrine of King Arthur', 12, 22 – 23, 24, 25, 42.

Morgan Le Fay (Morgana, Morganna, Morgain, Morgue), 52, 125, 149, 151, 159, 173, 175, 205, 207, 223.

Morning Post, 99, 227, 231.

Morte Arthur, Le, Stanzaic, 195.

Mortimer, John Hamilton, 12, 13.

Moultrie, George, *False and True*, 192.

Moultrie, John, *La Belle Tryamour (Sir Launfal)*, 98, 99 – 100, 142 – 46, 153, 170, 171, 178 – 81, 191, 197, 229, 245; *The Dream of Life*, 120, 145n; 'Godiva', 142, 192, 193n.

Muirhead, Lockhart, 132.

'Myfanwy Vechan', 22, 66 – 67.

Napoleon, 45, 236.

Naubert, Benedikte, *Der kurze Mantel*, 116, 224.

Nelson, Horatio, *Viscount*, 51.

Nennius, 6, 7, 9, 20, 23, 33, 55, 61, 66, 73, 222.

New Annual Register, 226n.

New Monthly Magazine, 36, 48, 59, 134n, 227, 228, 230.

Newell, Robert Hazell, *Letters on the Scenery of Wales*, 69.

Newport, 71, 100.

Nicholls, J.G., 9n.

Nicholson, George, *The Cambrian Traveller's Guide*, 68.

Nicoll, Allardyce, 123n, 127.

Nicolson, Joseph, and Richard Burn, *The History of Westmorland and Cumberland*, 62.

Nightingale, Joseph, *The History of Somersetshire*, 60.

Norden, John, 57.

North American Review, 228, 252.

North British Review, 232n.

Northup, Clark S., and John J. Parry, 1 – 2, 252n.

Ogier the Dane, 149.

O'Hara, Kane, *Tom Thumb*, 119 – 21, 139n, 145n, 236.

O'Keefe, John, *Modern Antiques*, 234n.

Old Watercolour Society, 152.

Oliver, Archer James, 206n.

Opera of Operas, The, 119.

Ord, John Walker, *England*, 18 – 19, 46, 52, 215, 228, 229.

Owen-Pughe, William, 25, 63, 100, 222; *The Cambrian Biography*, 24, 158 – 59, 223; *Myvyrian Archaiology*, 103.

Oxenford, John, 'Sir Wigolais of the Wheel', 134 – 35; 156 – 57, 225.

Oxford University, 15, 50, 77, 82, 85, 123; Trinity College, 79.

Oxonian, An, 'Lines written after reading the Romance of Arthur's Round Table', 137 – 38.

Paden, W.D., 159n, 215n.

Page, Frederick, 184n.

Painting, 3n, 12, 13, 33n, 61, 65 – 66nn, 116, 120, 123n, 125, 139, 152, 154, 157n, 159, 163, 169, 206n, 213, 217, 246, 248, 251 – 52.

Palgrave, Francis, *The Rise and Progress of the English Commonwealth*, 8, 33.

Palmer, D.J., 248.

Palmer, Samuel, *King Arthur's Castle, Tintagel, Cornwall*, 66n.

Palmerston, Henry, *Viscount*, 48.

Pantomime, 122n, 123, 124 – 28, 145.

Paris, Matthew, 14.

Parker, John, 'The Celtic Annals', 29 – 30, 85, 149, 227, 229.

Parody, 135 – 37.

Parr, Samuel, 141.

Parry, Edward, *Cambrian Mirror*, 68.

Parry, John Humphreys, *The Cambrian Plutarch*, 28; 'The Heroes of Cymru', 28.

Passage, Charles E., 208n.

Patmore, Coventry, 232; 'Arthur and his Knights of the Round Table', 74.

Payne, Henry Thomas, 100.

Peabody, Sophia, 252.

Peacock, Thomas Love, 3, 103, 110, 115, 171; *Calidore*, 29n, 149; *Crotchet Castle*, 103; *The Four Ages of Poetry*, 43, 140; *The Genius of the Thames*, 103n; *Melincourt*, 236 – 37; *The Misfortunes of Elphin*, 31 – 47, 103 – 06, 134, 149, 171, 237; *The Round Table*, 18, 42, 123, 149, 251. Plate 2b.

Peardon, Thomas Preston, 33n.

Pedestres, *A Pedestrian Tour*, 69.

Peel, Sir Robert, 138.

Peers, Charles, *The Siege of Jerusalem*, 239.

Penaluna, William, *An Historical Survey of Cornwall*, 254.

Pendragon Castle, 62n.

Peninsular War, 50, 98.

Penn, John, 'Sonnet Written on Mount Merlin', 78, 168.

Pennant, Thomas, *A Tour in Scotland*, 66, 77; *A Tour in Wales*, 66 – 67, 68, 69, 104.

Pennie, John Fitzgerald, 241; *The Dragon-King*, 31 – 44, 97, 149, 210, 212, 219, 226 – 27, 228, 234 – 35, 242; 'Richard Coeur de Lion's Arrival on the Coast of Palestine', 15.

Pentland Hills, 92, 224.

Perceval (Percivale), 35, 152, 157n. Plates 5a, 8b.

Percy, Thomas, 3, 33, 66, 131; *Reliques of Ancient English Poetry*, 10n, 59, 67, 73, 97, 98, 102, 114 – 16, 118, 130, 156, 212, 218, 235, 236.

Pfordresher, John, 190.

Phelps, William, *The History of Somersetshire*, 61.

Phillips, Edward, *The Royal Chace (Harlequin Skeleton)*, 122, 124n.

Philpotts, Henry, 166.

Pickersgill, Frederick R., *Amoret, Aemylia and Prince Arthur in the Cottage of Sclaunder*, 33n, 157n. Plate 14.

Picton, Sir Rowland, 50.

Pinkerton, John, 97, 130.

Planché, James Robinson, 33n.

Platt, Alexander, 225.

Plumptre, Anne, *A Narrative of a Three Years' Residence in France*, 71, 223.

Plynlimmon, Mount, 23, 78, 101, 102.

Pocock, Isaac, *King Arthur and the Knights of the Round Table*, 125 – 26, 129, 236.

Poe, Edgar Allan, 246 – 47.

Poems and Pictures, 152. Plate 15.

Poetical Register, 78n.

Pointon, Marcia, 33n.

Polwhele, Richard, *The Fair Isabel*, 108 – 09; *The History of Cornwall*, 63 – 64, 70, 112; 'Ode written in a Picture Gallery', 63; *Traditions and Recollections*, 95.

Porden, Eleanor Anne, *Coeur de Lion*, 14 – 15, 132 – 33, 149, 178n, 241; 'Ode to the King's Most Excellent Majesty', 51.

Powel, David, *Historie of Cambria*, 25, 66.

Praed, Winthrop Mackworth, 146, 157, 191; 'Castle Vernon', 146; 'Gog', 117 – 18, 140, 156; 'The Legend of the Haunted Tree', 156, 175, 234; 'Lidian's Love', 142; *Lillian*, 156, 171; 'Private Theatricals', 120 – 21.

Pre-Raphaelitism, 1, 2, 4, 225, 253.

Price, Cormell, 252.

Price, Sir John, *The historie of Cambria*, 21.

Price, Thomas, 'A Tour through Brittany', 73.

Prichard, Thomas Jeffery Llewelyn, *The Cambrian Wreath*, 28n, 77, 104; *The Land Beneath the Sea*, 104; 'The Worthies of Wales', 28.

Prideaux, Walter, 'The Lay of Sir Amys', 177.

Prince(s) of Wales, 27, 148, 168n.

Pringle, Thomas, 'A Dream of Fairy-Land', 197.

Proceedings of the Annual Meeting of the Archaeological Institute, 60n.

'Prophecy of Taliesin, The', 27.

Prout, Samuel, *Arthur's Castle at Tintagel*, 66n.

Pugh, Edwin, *Cambria Depicta*, 69, 104.

Pulci, Luigi, 140, 141, 142.

Punch, 138 – 39. Plate 11b.

Purcell, Henry, 236, 241.

Quarterly Review, 36, 87n, 95, 117, 140n, 141n, 142, 192, 228n, 229 – 30, 232 – 34, 242n, 246.

R., 'English Chronicles', 18.

Rapin-Thoyras, Paul de, *The History of England*, 6, 11, 14, 38, 190, 223.

Redding, Cyrus, *An Illustrated Itinerary of Cornwall*, 72, 74 – 75.

Reform Bill of 1832, 18, 46, 193 – 94.

Reid, Hugh, 49n.

Richard I (Coeur de Lion), 13 – 16, 43, 51, 147, 161, 220.

Richardson, Moses Aaron, *The Local Historian's Table Book*, 91n, 92.

Ricks, Christopher, 193n.
Riethmuller, Christopher James, *Early and Late Poems*, 130n; *Launcelot of the Lake*, 129 – 30, 174, 205 – 06, 210, 213 – 15, 217, 229, 236.
Ripon, Bishop of, see Carpenter, William Boyd.
Ritchie, Leitch, 227n.
Ritson, Joseph, 130, 144; *Ancient Engleish Metrical Romanceës*, 99, 177, 178; *The Life of King Arthur*, 9, 31, 104; *Pieces of Ancient Popular Poetry*, 117.
Robert of Gloucester, 5, 229.
Roberts, Peter, 24, 33; *The Cambrian Popular Antiquities*, 63; *Sketch of the Early History of the Cymry*, 24.
Robinson, Henry Crabb, 125 – 26.
Robinson, Richard, 56.
Roby, J., 62.
Rodney, Admiral, 50.
Roland, 50.
Roman de la Rose, 157.
Roscoe, James, 'The Iron-Gate', 93, 154, 171.
Roscoe, Thomas, 224; *The Italian Novelists*, 195n; *Wanderings in North Wales*, 68; *Wanderings in South Wales*, 68, 70.
Roscoe, William Caldwell, *Eliduc*, 177.
Rose, John, *Caernarvon Castle*, 168, 236.
Rose, William Stewart, 139; *Partenopex de Blois*, 212.
Rosenkranz, K., 208n.
Ross, Sir James Clark, 47.
Rossetti, Dante Gabriel, 253.
Round Table, 10, 26n, 28, 29, 35, 46, 61, 62, 70, 125, 127, 131, 138, 141, 149, 151n, 154, 155, 156, 158, 159, 172, 193, 194, 216, 220, 227, 232, 236, 243, 251; in Caerleon, 16, 62, 70, 71; Carmarthenshire, 68; Din Sylwy, 76; Kennel Park, 62; Lansannan, 58; North Wales, 69; Penrith, 58, 62, 66, 67, 76, 97, 220; Stirling Castle, 56, 76; Winchester, 58 – 60, 61; Windsor, 11. Plate 3b.
Rowlandson, Thomas, 120.
Royal Academy, 13, 33n, 116n, 120, 123n, 139n, 206n, 213, 252.
Royal Amphitheatre, see Astley's.
Royal Circus, Theatre, 120n.
Royal Cornwall Gazette, 107 – 09.

Royal Engagement Pocket Atlas, 152. Plates, 3a, 3b.
Royal Scottish Academy, 252.
Royal Society of Painters in Watercolours, 66n.
Royal Surrey Theatre, 127.
Russell, Lord John, 18, 48.
Ryals, Clyde de L., 202, 206.
Ryence, 98, 99, 178, 179.

Sadleir, Michael, 48n.
Sadler's Wells Theatre, 120, 124, 126, 127, 145.
'St. George for England', 10n.
St Germain, 43.
St Julian (Juliot, Ulette), 113.
St Michael's Mount, 51, 55, 93 – 95, 109, 224.
Salmon, Thomas Stokes, *Stonehenge*, 77.
Sartain's Union Magazine, 252n.
Saturday Magazine, 13n, 59.
Schiller, Johann Christoph Friedrich von, 186.
Schlegel, Friedrich, *Lectures on the History of Literature*, 160 – 61.
Scott, Margaret, later Lady, 132.
Scott, Sir Walter, 33, 37, 73, 76, 88, 120, 130, 131, 132, 135, 139, 140, 188, 207, 210, 228n, 235; 'Appendix to the General Preface', 88 – 89; *The Bridal of Triermain*, 76, 97, 125, 133, 139 – 40, 152, 155 – 56, 171 – 72, 178, 222, 223, 236, 244, 251; 'Essay on Amadis de Gaul', 133; 'On Chivalry', 178, 204n; 'On Romance', 151; *Guy Mannering*, 168n; *Ivanhoe*, 115; *Kenilworth*, 237; *The Lady of the Lake*, 76; *The Lay of the Last Minstrel*, 167, 244; *Minstrelsy of the Scottish Border*, 89, 176; *Marmion*, 151, 153n, 178n, 212n, 218, 241; 'Thomas the Rhymer', 170, 176, 203, 235; *The Vision of Don Roderick*, 98; *Waverley*, 76; ed. Dryden's *Works*, 150; ed. *Sir Tristrem*, 63 – 64, 83, 89, 133, 159, 204.
Scott, William Bell, *King Arthur carried to the land of enchantment*, 212 – 13. Plate 16.
Seally, John, 'The Marriage of Sir Gawaine', 115 – 16, 236.

Second Part of the Tragycalle Historie of Thomas Thumbe, The, 121.
Sein, Isle of, 71.
Selden, John, 58, 60, 64.
Selous, Henry, illustrates *Bridal of Triermain*, 152. Plate 15.
Service, James, ed. *Metrical Legends of Northumberland*, 90.
Severn, River, 29, 83, 84, 103n.
Sewingshields, 90 – 92.
Shakespeare, William, 73, 129; *Henry IV, Part 2*, 59; *King John*, 126 – 27; *King Lear*, 229 – 30.
Shannon, Edgar F., Jr, 199, 248n.
Sharpe's London Journal, 227, 229.
Sharpe's London Magazine, 60.
Shelley, Mary, *Frankenstein*, 154.
Shelley, Percy Bysshe, 105; *Prometheus Unbound*, 237.
Sherwood, Mary Martha, *The Cloak*, 154.
Sigourney, Lydia, 'Carlisle', 86.
'Sir Lancelot du Lake', 10n, 59, 116, 118.
Smetham, James, *The Lady of Shalott*, 252.
Smirke, Edward, 60.
Smith, Elizabeth, 'A supposed Translation from a Welsh poem', 26 – 27.
Smith, Horace and James, *Rejected Addresses*, 135.
Smith, John Raphael, 206n.
Smith, William Henry, 235.
Smollett, Tobias, *Sir Launcelot Greaves*, 134.
Snowdon (Snowden), 16, 55, 75, 84, 96, 149, 253.
Soane, George, *Specimens of German Romance*, 116, 224.
Sotheby, William, 241; *The Cambrian Hero*, 88; 'Llangollen', 78.
South Cadbury, 56, 58, 60.
Southey, Robert, 33, 34 – 35, 74n, 89, 98, 114, 132, 153, 159, 178, 205, 228, 240, 241; *Joan of Arc*, 16; *Madoc*, 25 – 26, 90, 241; 'Romance', 151; ed. *The Byrth, Lyf, and Actes of King Arthur* (Malory's *Le Morte Darthur*), 203, 207, 223, 224.
Spalding, William, 227.
Spectator, 246.

Speed, John, *The History of Great Britain*, 12, 13.
Spenser, Edmund, 68, 73; *The Faerie Queene*, 11, 57, 78, 99, 150, 153, 157, 160, 162, 163 – 64, 167, 169, 176, 179 – 80, 193, 197, 210, 211, 223, 225, 251.
Spenserian stanza, 19, 83, 109, 153n.
Staines, David, 1, 190n.
Stanfield, Clarkson, 125.
Stanley, Edward, 14th Earl of Derby, 48.
Stanley, Sir John, 92.
Stanley, Louisa Dorothea, 92.
Steer, Kenneth A., 66n.
Stephen, King, 59.
Stephens, Meic, 50n.
Sterling, John, 231, 232 – 34, 242, 243, 246, 248; 'Coeur de Lion', 15 – 16, 147.
Sterling, Joseph, 'Ode to Plynlymmon Hill', 78.
Stockdale, F.W.L., *Excursions in the County of Cornwall*, 67n.
Stokes, Henry Sewell, 111, 253, 254n; 'Cornubiana', 112; *The Song of Albion*, 18, 111 – 12, 194; *The Vale of Lanherne*, 109.
Stolberg, C.L., 224.
Stonehenge, 39, 55, 77, 122.
'Stonehenge', 77.
Stonehenge. A Poem. 77.
Stothard, Thomas, 116; *Theatrical Portrait of Miss Farren*, 33, 123n; illustrates *Bridal of Triermain*, 152. Plates 3a, 3b.
Stow, John, 58.
Strong, Sir Roy, 33.
Strutt, Joseph, *Sports and Pastimes*, 33.
Stuarts, 6, 21.
Stukeley, William, 66n.
Sullivan, Alvin, 73n.
Sullivan, M.J., 'St. Patrick's Day', 51.
Sun, 48, 227.
Sunderland, John, 12n.
Sutton, Henry, 232.
Sword in the stone, 109. Plate 8a.

Tabart, Benjamin, *Popular Fairy Tales*, 117.
Tacitus, 33.

Tait's Edinburgh Magazine, 136, 231, 244n.

Taliesin (Taliessin), 23, 27, 28, 31, 34, 37, 44, 62, 102, 104 – 06, 176, 237, 254.

Tamworth Castle, 61.

Tancred, King of Sicily, 14, 15.

Tarn Wadling, 98.

Taylor, Beverly, and Elizabeth Brewer, 2n, 116n, 164n, 177n.

Taylor, William, of Norwich, 33, 204; *Historic Survey of German Literature*, 33n; *Tales of Yore*, 224; tr. 'Sir Egerwene', 210.

Tennant, William, *Anster Fair*, 140.

Tennyson, Alfred, *Baron*, 1, 2, 3; parody of, 136 – 37; drafts, 190 – 94, 221 – 23; sources for drafts, 221 – 23; his subject, 224 – 26; critical reception, 229 – 50; genres, 231 – 50; influence, 250 – 53; later development, 253 – 54; 'Adeline', 236; 'Amphion', 211, 'The Ballad of Sir Launcelot', 190, 191, 194, 201, 204, 211, 225, 237, 242, 245; 'The Beggar Maid', 202; 'The Coach of Death', 243; 'The Day-Dream', 244; 'A Dirge', 236; 'The Epic', 217 – 19, 238 – 39, 241, 243 – 45, 253; 'Godiva', 192 – 93nn, 244; 'The Golden Year', 253; 'I dare not write an Ode', 191 – 92; *Idylls of the King*, 1, 201, 254 ('Guinevere', 254); 'Lady Clare', 202; 'The Lady of Shalott', 136, 195, 197 – 201, 229 – 31, 232, 235, 237 – 38, 246 – 47, 248, 251, 252; 'Life of the Life within my blood', 191, 237; 'Lilian', 236; 'Lisette', 236; 'The Lord of Burleigh', 202; 'The Lotos-Eaters', 175, 193, 237, 242; 'Mariana', 236, 246; 'Mariana in the South', 200, 236; 'Morte d'Arthur', 136, 212 – 17, 231, 238, 241, 244 – 45, 248, 249 – 50, 251, 252; 'The New Timon and the Poets', 192; 'Oriana', 236; 'The Owl', 235; 'The Palace of Art', 193, 232, 250; 'The Poet's Mind', 201; *The Princess*, 232; 'Recollections of the Arabian Nights', 236; 'St. Agnes' Eve', 211, 247; 'Sir Galahad', 207 – 11, 231, 236, 238, 251, 252 – 53; 'Sir Launcelot and Queen Guinevere', 201 – 07, 231, 238; 'To Christopher North', 192; 'The Two Voices', 232; 'Ulysses', 233, 242.

Tennyson, Emily, Lady, 211.

Tennyson, George Clayton, 190, 192.

Tennyson, Hallam, *Baron, Materials*, 254n; *Memoir*, 190n, 199n, 203n, 207n, 216n, 221, 231n, 243n, 246n, 249n.

Thackeray, William Makepeace, 109n.

Theatrical Inquisitor, 226n, 228, 241, 242.

Thelwall, John, 102, 229, 241, 243; *The Fairy of the Lake*, 101 – 02, 128, 175 – 76, 226, 236; *The Peripatetic*, 240 – 41.

Theobald, Lewis, *Merlin*, 122.

Thomas d'Angleterre, 87.

Thomas, E., 'Briddyn Jubilee', 50.

Thomas the Rhymer, 83, 88, 89.

Thompson (artist), plate 2a.

Thompson, Aaron, 6.

Thomson, Anthony Todd, 104.

Thomson, James, 42.

Tillotson, Kathleen, 1n.

Times, The, 99, 124, 125, 126, 127, 128n, 129, 230 – 31, 237, 247n.

Tintagel (Tintagil, Tintadgel, Dundagell), 7, 35, 55, 56 – 57, 58, 63 – 64, 65, 67, 70 – 74, 78, 81n, 82, 96, 108, 110 – 13, 170, 196, 220, 223, 253 – 54.

Titurel, 84, 208 – 09, 225.

Todd, Ruthven, 159n.

Tom Thumb, 117, 119 – 21.

Tonkin, Thomas, 56n, 64.

Transactions of the British Archaeological Society, 59n.

Tressan, Comte de, *Corps d'Extraits de Romans de Chivalerie*, 131 – 32, 205n, 224.

Triads, Welsh, 6, 24, 27, 29, 32, 33, 44, 102, 105, 159, 222, 224, 251.

Trinder, Peter W., 27n.

Tristan, Prose, 205n.

Tristram (Tristrem, Tristan, Trystan), 10, 57, 67, 78, 83, 87 – 88, 90, 110, 127, 128, 133, 151n, 156, 159, 1562n, 176, 205, 212, 220, 224, 225n, 236, 251. Plates 7a, 7b.

Trollope, T. Adolphus, *A Summer in Brittany*, 72, 74.
True Sun, 248.
Truro, 107 – 09, 111.
Tudors, 6, 23, 28, 29.
Turgot, Anne Robert Jacques, 47.
Turner, Joseph Mallord William, 66n.
Turner, Sharon, *A History of the Anglo-Saxons*, 9, 17, 20, 24, 25, 32, 33, 67, 73.
Turquin (Tarquin), 61, 62n, 151.
Tyrwhitt, Thomas, 131.

Uhland, Ludwig, 225 .
United States Magazine and Democratic Review, 117n, 231, 247n.
Upton, Nicholas, 65.
Urien, 20, 171.
Usk, River, 29, 100, 106.
Ussher, James, 24.
Uther Pendragon (Uter, Uthyr, Bendragon), 7, 20, 23, 27, 31, 34, 35, 52, 53, 62, 63, 74, 77, 83, 85, 96, 108, 110, 112, 170, 250.
Utilitarianism, 44, 49, 73, 220.
Uwins, Thomas, illustrates Malory, 152, 157n. Plates 4a – 5b.

Vallencey, Charles, 34n.
Vandergucht, Benjamin, *A Portrait in the character of Merlin*, 123n.
Vergil, Polydore, 5, 56, 58.
Verstegen, Richard, 33.
Victoria, Princess, later Queen, 28, 29, 40, 42, 48, 52, 121, 126, 149, 166, 171.
Villemarqué, Theodore Claude Henri Hersart de, 87, 224.
Virgil, 239.
Viviane (Viviana, Vivienne, Nimue), 75, 110, 133, 171, 173.
Volksbücher, 225n.
Volney, Constantin Francois de, *Count*, 39.
Vortigern, 31, 39, 41, 55, 66, 67, 101, 226.

W., T.V., 'A Trip to Tintagel', 74.
Waldron, George, *The History of the Isle of Man*, 88.
Wales (Welsh), 12; minor Welsh references to Arthur, 21 – 30; in topography, 62 – 64; guides, 65 – 72, 75, 134; topographical poetry, 78, 84 – 86, 99, 100 – 03, 180; cave legends, 88 – 90; Peacock, 39, 103 – 06; Lytton, 106 – 07, 164; Tennyson, 253 – 54.
Walker, William Sidney, 192n.
Waller, R.D., 140n.
Walpole, Horace, 37, 49.
Ward's Miscellany, 142n.
Waring, Elijah, 90.
Warner, Richard, 134, 224; *The History of Bath*, 59 – 60; *An History of the Abbey of Glaston*, 12, 60 – 61, 80; *A Second Walk through Wales*, 67, 70; *A Tour through Cornwall*, 67, 72 – 73; *A Tour through the Northern Counties*, 67; *A Walk through some of the Western Counties*, 67; *A Walk through Wales*, 67, 223.
Warrington, William, 25; *The History of Wales*, 8, 21, 26.
Warton, Joseph, 59; 'To HRH the Duke of York', 49 – 50.
Warton, Thomas, 3, 11, 12, 15, 23, 58, 73, 80, 131, 225; 'The Crusade', 14, 80; *A Description of Winchester*, 59; 'The Grave of King Arthur', 11, 13, 15, 21, 22, 60, 61, 67, 73, 148 – 49, 210; *History of English Poetry*, 14, 15, 130, 131, 177; *Observations on the Fairy Queen*, 61n, 149; 'On the Birth of the Prince of Wales', 148; 'On King Arthur's Round Table at Winchester', 59; 'Stonehenge', 77.
Watts, Alaric, 'The Lady and Merlin', 2n.
Waugh, Arthur, 197.
Way, Gregory Lewis, tr. *Fabliaux*, 14, 98, 100, 111, 118, 173, 174, 177, 178, 182, 183, 185, 189, 222, 224, 245.
Webster, Ben, 129.
Wellek, René, 11n.
Wellington, Duke of, 48, 50 – 52, 137 – 39.
'Welsh War Song, A', 28.
West, Gilbert, *Institution of the Order of the Garter*, 10 – 11, 122.
Westall, Richard, 116.
Westminster Review, 46, 242n, 244n.

'When good King Arthur ruled this land', 117.

Whitaker, John, 23; *The History of Manchester*, 7, 9, 33, 61, 63, 64, 67.

Whytehead, Thomas, 'Deem not the lack of lance', 53.

Wieland, Christopher, *Geron der Adelige*, 33, 224.

Wildman, John Hazard, 164n.

Willett, Mark, *A Stranger in Monmouthshire*, 105.

William III and Mary, 42, 45.

William IV, 18.

William of Malmesbury, 69.

William of Newbury, 5.

Williams, David, *The History of Monmouthshire*, 62.

Williams, Edward (Iolo Morgannwg), 27, 89; 'To Ivor the Liberal', 24, 25.

Williams, Richard, 66 – 67.

Williams, Robert, *The History of Aberconwy*, 62 – 63.

Williams, Rowland, 'The Hall of the Nations', 52, 171.

Williams, Samuel, 157n. Plate 9a.

Williams, T.H., 66n.

Williams, Taliesin, *Cardiff Castle*, 27, 160.

Williamson, John, 177.

Willyams, Humphrey, 109.

Willyams, James Brydges, 108 – 09; 'Arthur', 109; *The Influence of Genius*, 108.

Wilmer, Lambert A., *Merlin*, 129, 169, 172.

Wilson, Geoffrey, 177.

Wilson, Hugh, 221 – 23.

Wilson, John, 18.

Winchester, 8, 49, 58, 79, 97, 112, 198, 223; and see Round Table.

Windsor, 11.

Wood, John (architect), *Choir Gaure*, 77n.

Wood, John (artist), *Emmeline*, 123n.

Woodley, George, 107; *Cornubia*, 107 – 08; *Devonia*, 107; *Portugal Delivered*, 107.

Worcester, William, 55 – 56, 110.

Wordsworth, William, 12n, 98, 99, 135, 181, 249; 'Artegal and Elidure', 153n, 223; *Ecclesiastical Sketches*, 20, 45; 'The Egyptian Maid', 162, 170, 175, 194, 223, 227; *The Prelude*, 150, 168n, 240n.

Wright, George Newenham, *Scenes in North Wales*, 68.

Wynn, Charles Watkin Williams, 34.

Wynn, Sir Watkin Williams, 28.

Yeats, William Butler, 201.

'Ylle Cutt Mantell, The', 117.

Young England, 53, 219, 250.

Ysaie le Triste, 53, 133.